# INUYASHA™

**VOL. 25**
Action Edition

Story and Art by
**RUMIKO TAKAHASHI**

English Adaptation by Gerard Jones

Translation/Mari Morimoto
Touch-Up Art & Lettering/Bill Schuch
Cover and Interior Graphic Design/Yuki Ameda
Editor/Urian Brown

Managing Editor/Annette Roman
Director of Production/Noboru Watanabe
Vice President of Publishing/Alvin Lu
Sr. Director of Acquisitions/Rika Inouye
VP of Sales & Marketing/Liza Coppola
Publisher/Hyoe Narita



Printed in Canada.

Published by VIZ Media, LLC
P.O. Box 77010
San Francisco, CA 94107

Action Edition
10 9 8 7 6 5 4 3 2 1
First printing, April 2006

RATED T+ FOR OLDER TEEN

**PARENTAL ADVISORY**
INUYASHA is rated T+ for Older Teen. This book contains violence. It is recommended for ages 16 and up.

www.viz.com

store.viz.com

# INUYASHA

## VOL. 25    Action Edition

## STORY AND ART BY
## RUMIKO TAKAHASHI

# CONTENTS

# THE STORY THUS FAR

Long ago, in the "Warring States" era of Japan's Muromachi period (*Sengoku-jidai*, approximately 1467-1568 CE), a legendary dog-like half-demon called "Inuyasha" attempted to steal the Shikon Jewel—or "Jewel of Four Souls"—from a village, but was stopped by the enchanted arrow of the village priestess, Kikyo. Inuyasha fell into a deep sleep, pinned to a tree by Kikyo's arrow, while the mortally wounded Kikyo took the Shikon Jewel with her into the fires of her funeral pyre. Years passed.

Fast-forward to the present day. Kagome, a Japanese high school girl, is pulled into a well one day by a mysterious centipede monster, and finds herself transported into the past—only to come face to face with the trapped Inuyasha. She frees him, and Inuyasha easily defeats the centipede monster.

The residents of the village, now 50 years older, readily accept Kagome as the reincarnation of their deceased priestess Kikyo, a claim supported by the fact that the Shikon Jewel emerges from a cut on Kagome's body. Unfortunately, the jewel's rediscovery means that the village is soon under attack by a variety of demons in search of this treasure. Then, the jewel is accidentally shattered into many shards, each of which may have the fearsome power of the entire jewel.

Although Inuyasha says he hates Kagome because of her resemblance to Kikyo, the woman who "killed" him, he is forced to team up with her when Kaede, the village leader, binds him to Kagome with a powerful spell. Now the two grudging companions must fight to reclaim and reassemble the shattered shards of the Shikon Jewel before they fall into the wrong hands...

**THIS VOLUME** Inuyasha and friends are in for the fight of their lives—again! This time they square off against the accursed Band of Seven—a group of monsters each with their own special brand of killing techniques. Can Inuyasha and his comrades overcome this bloodthirsty band of killers?

**INU-YASHA**
Half-demon hybrid, son of a human mother and demon father. His necklace is enchanted, allowing Kagome to control him with a word.

**KAGOME**
Modern-day Japanese schoolgirl who can travel back and forth between the past and present through an enchanted well.

**MIROKU**
Lecherous Buddhist priest cursed with a mystical "hellhole" in his hand that's slowly killing him.

**NARAKU**
Enigmatic demon-mastermind behind the miseries of nearly everyone in the story.

**SANGO**
"Demon Exterminator" or slayer from the village where the Shikon Jewel was first born.

**KOHAKU**
Killed by Naraku—but not before first slaying both his own and Sango's father—now he's back again in a newer...if somewhat *slower*...form.

**KOGA**
Leader of the Wolf Clan, Koga is himself a Wolf Demon and, because of several Shikon shards in his legs, possesses super speed. Enamored of Kagome, he quarrels with Inuyasha frequently.

**KAGURA**
A demon created by Naraku from parts of his body, Kagura—the Wind Demon—is Naraku's second incarnation. Unlike others, however, Kagura resents Naraku's control over her and aids him only for her own survival.

# SCROLL ONE

# MUKOTSU

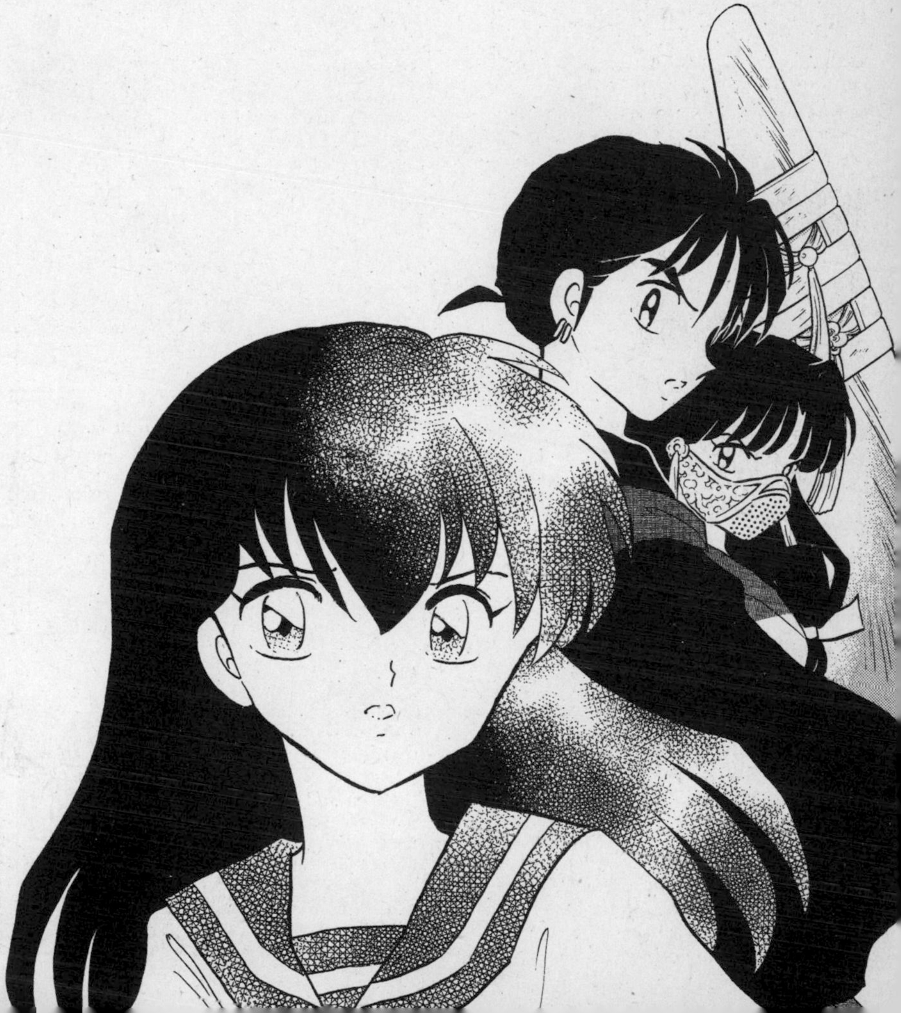

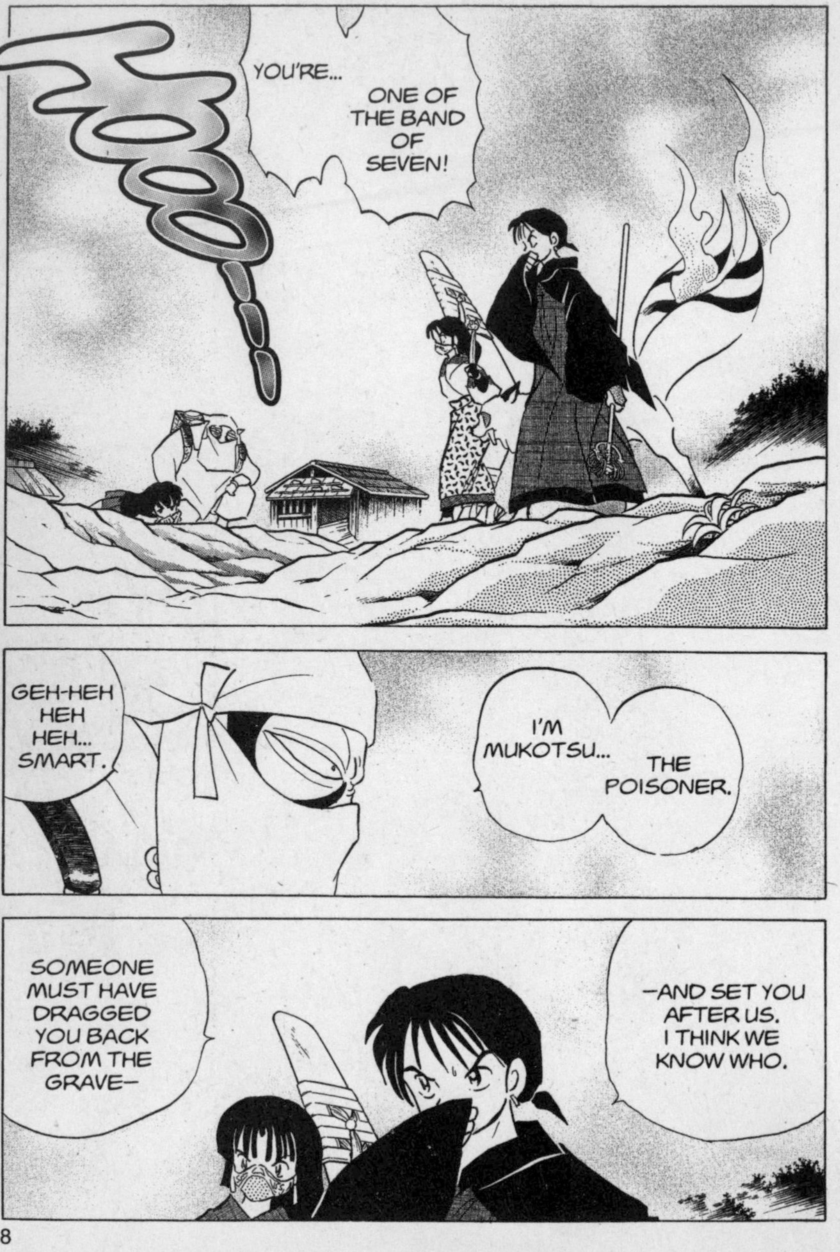
YOU'RE... ONE OF THE BAND OF SEVEN!
GEH-HEH HEH HEH... SMART.
I'M MUKOTSU... THE POISONER.
SOMEONE MUST HAVE DRAGGED YOU BACK FROM THE GRAVE—
—AND SET YOU AFTER US. I THINK WE KNOW WHO.

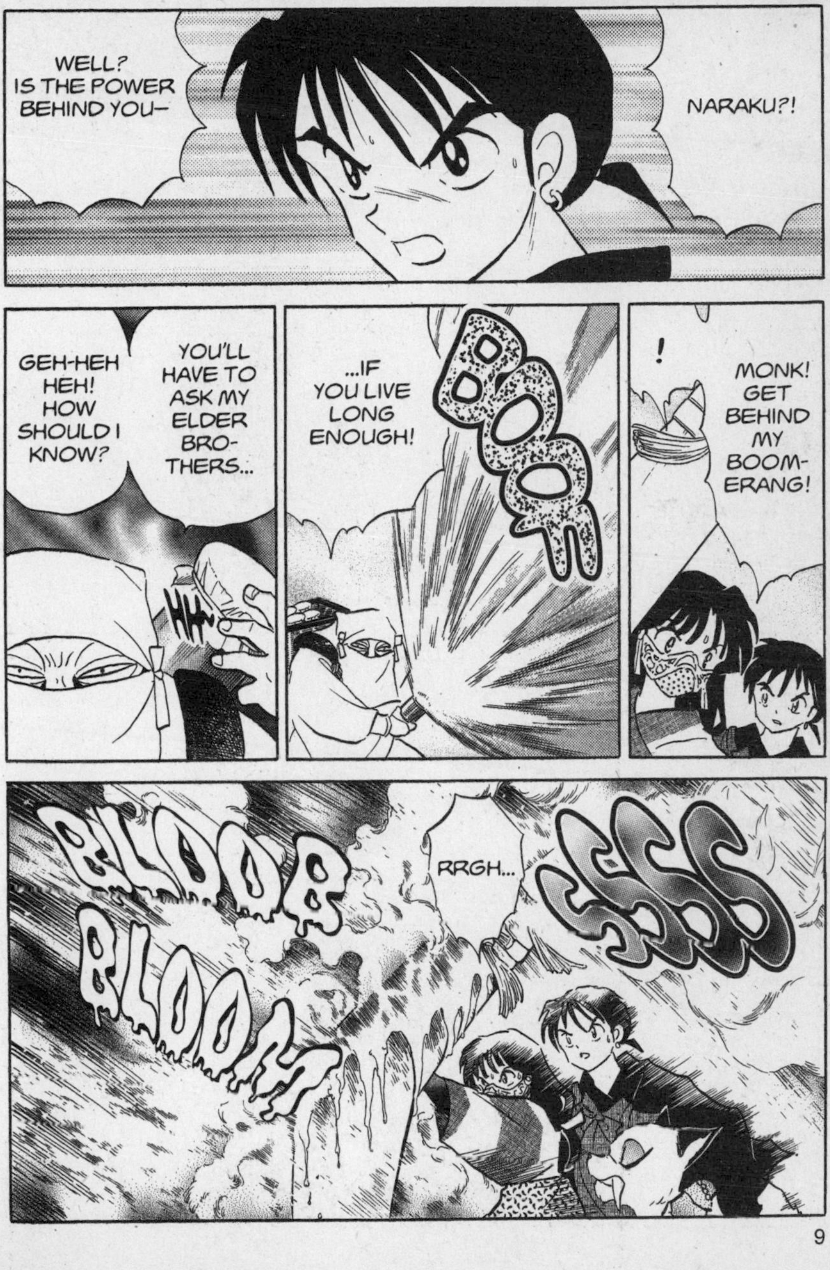
WELL? IS THE POWER BEHIND YOU—
NARAKU?!
GEH-HEH HEH! HOW SHOULD I KNOW?
YOU'LL HAVE TO ASK MY ELDER BROTHERS...
...IF YOU LIVE LONG ENOUGH!
BOOOF
!
MONK! GET BEHIND MY BOOMERANG!
BLOOB
BLOOM
RRGH...
SSSS

GEH-HEH HEH HEH! JUST DIS-SOLVE!

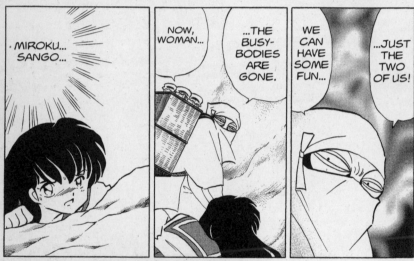

·MIROKU... SANGO...

NOW, WOMAN...

...THE BUSY-BODIES ARE GONE.

WE CAN HAVE SOME FUN...

...JUST THE TWO OF US!

INU-YASHA...

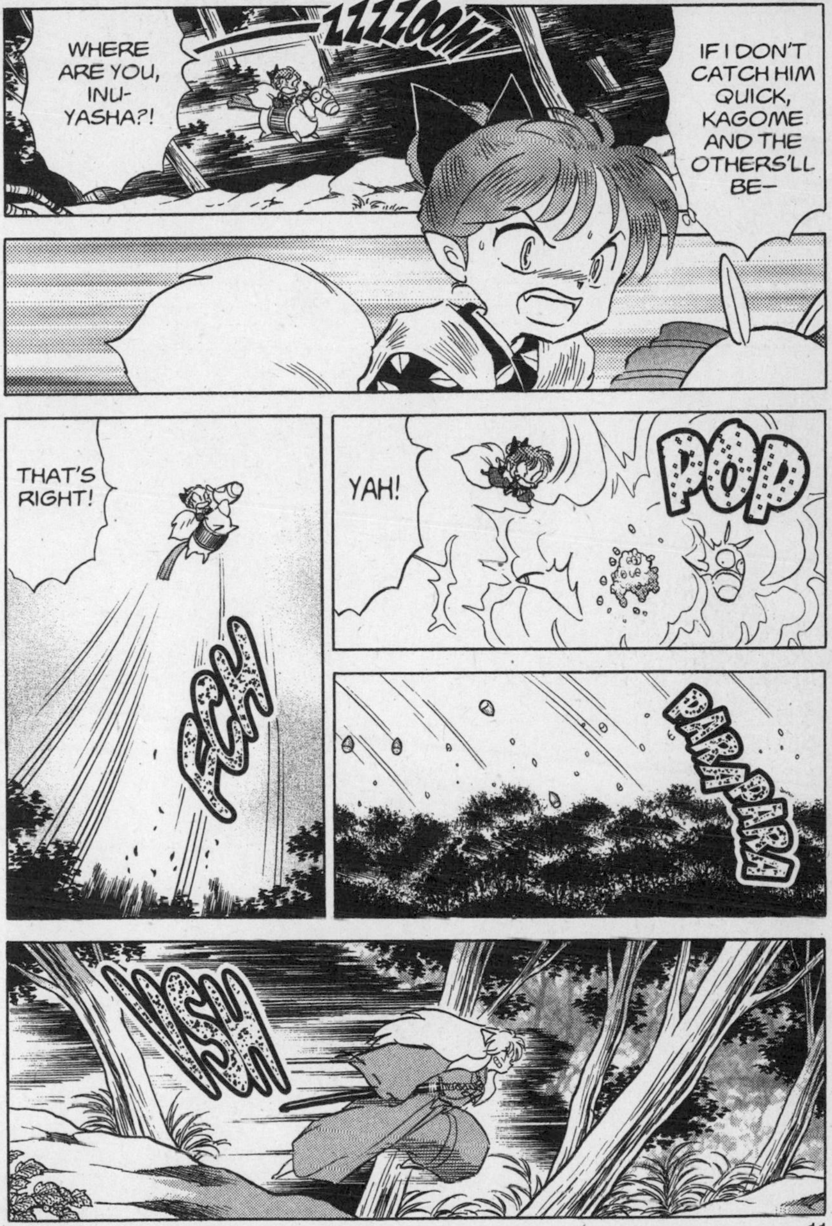
WHERE ARE YOU, INU-YASHA?!
ZZZZOOM
IF I DON'T CATCH HIM QUICK, KAGOME AND THE OTHERS'LL BE—
THAT'S RIGHT!
FZCH
YAH!
POP
PARAPARA
VSSH

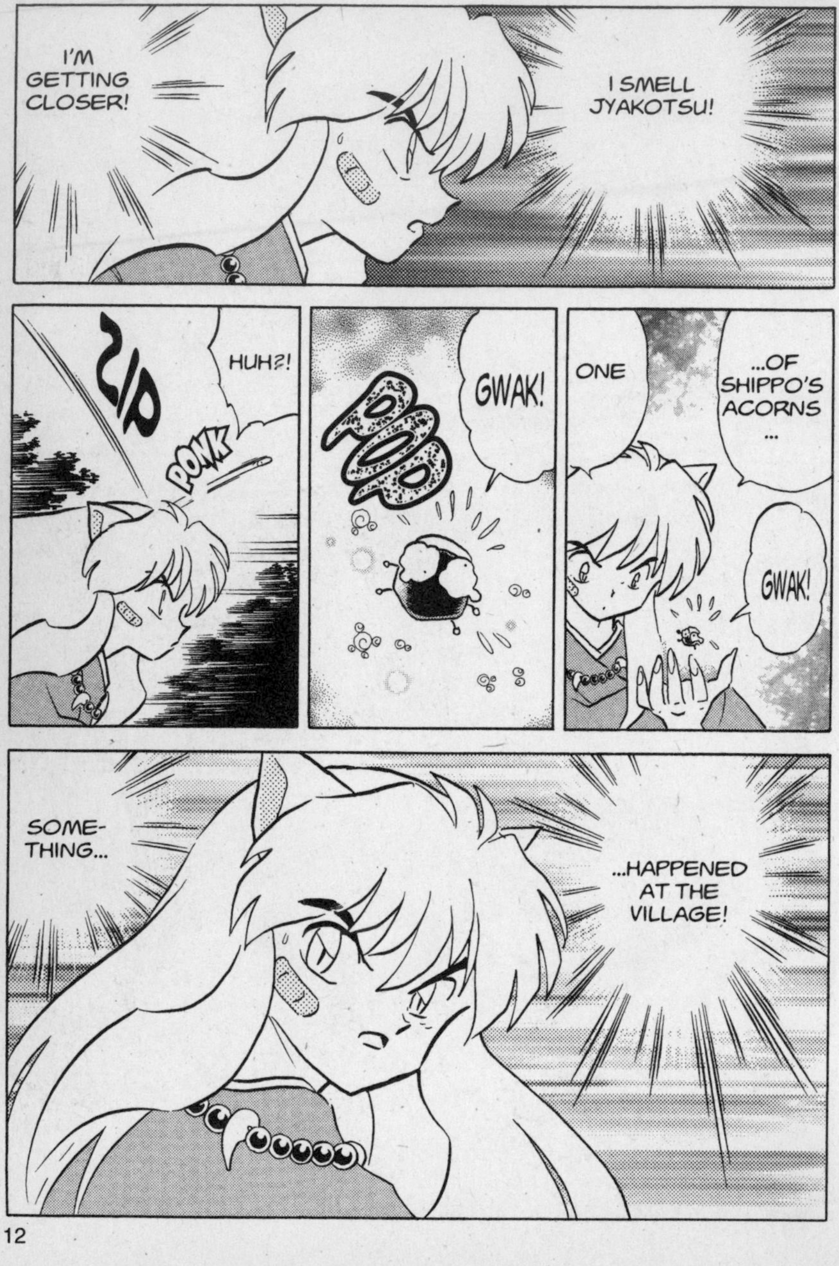
I'M GETTING CLOSER!
I SMELL JYAKOTSU!
ZIP
HUH?!
PONK
POP
GWAK!
ONE
...OF SHIPPO'S ACORNS ...
GWAK!
SOME-THING...
...HAPPENED AT THE VILLAGE!

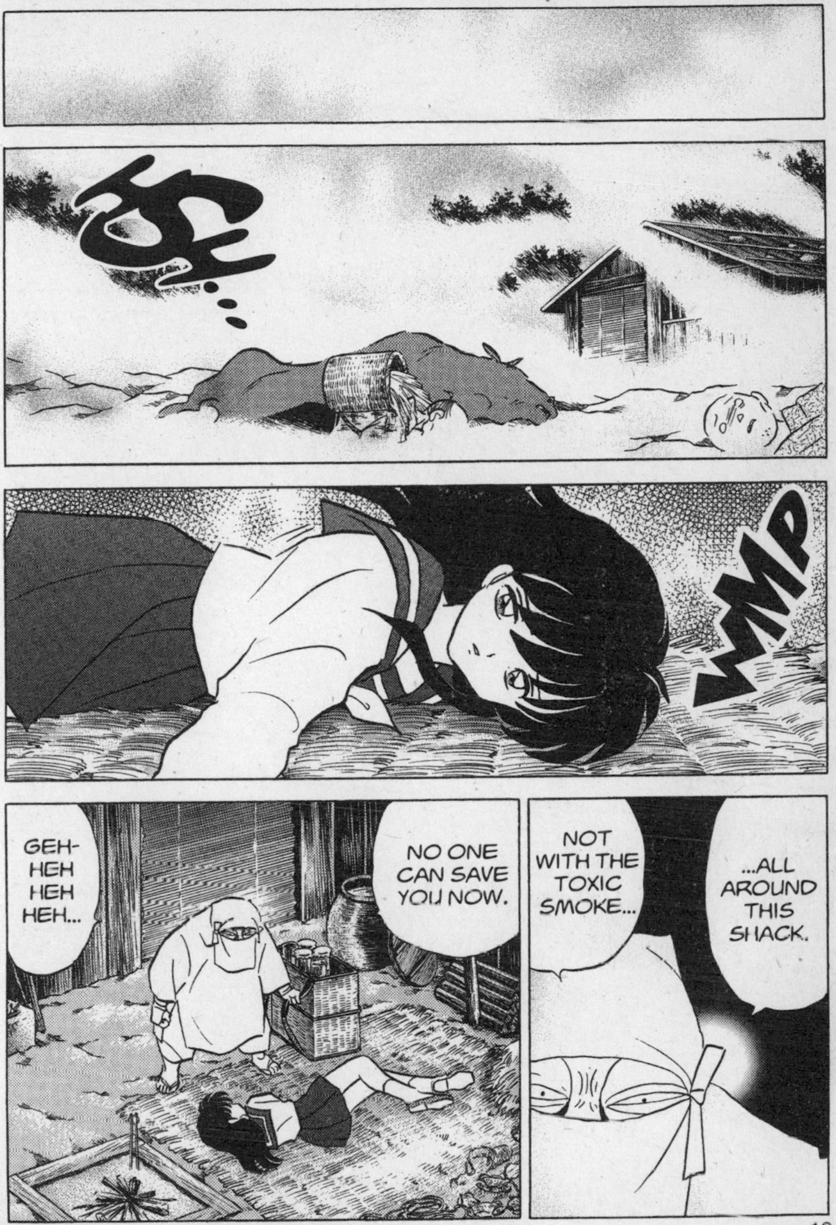

FSH...
WMP
GEH-HEH HEH HEH...
NO ONE CAN SAVE YOU NOW.
NOT WITH THE TOXIC SMOKE...
...ALL AROUND THIS SHACK.

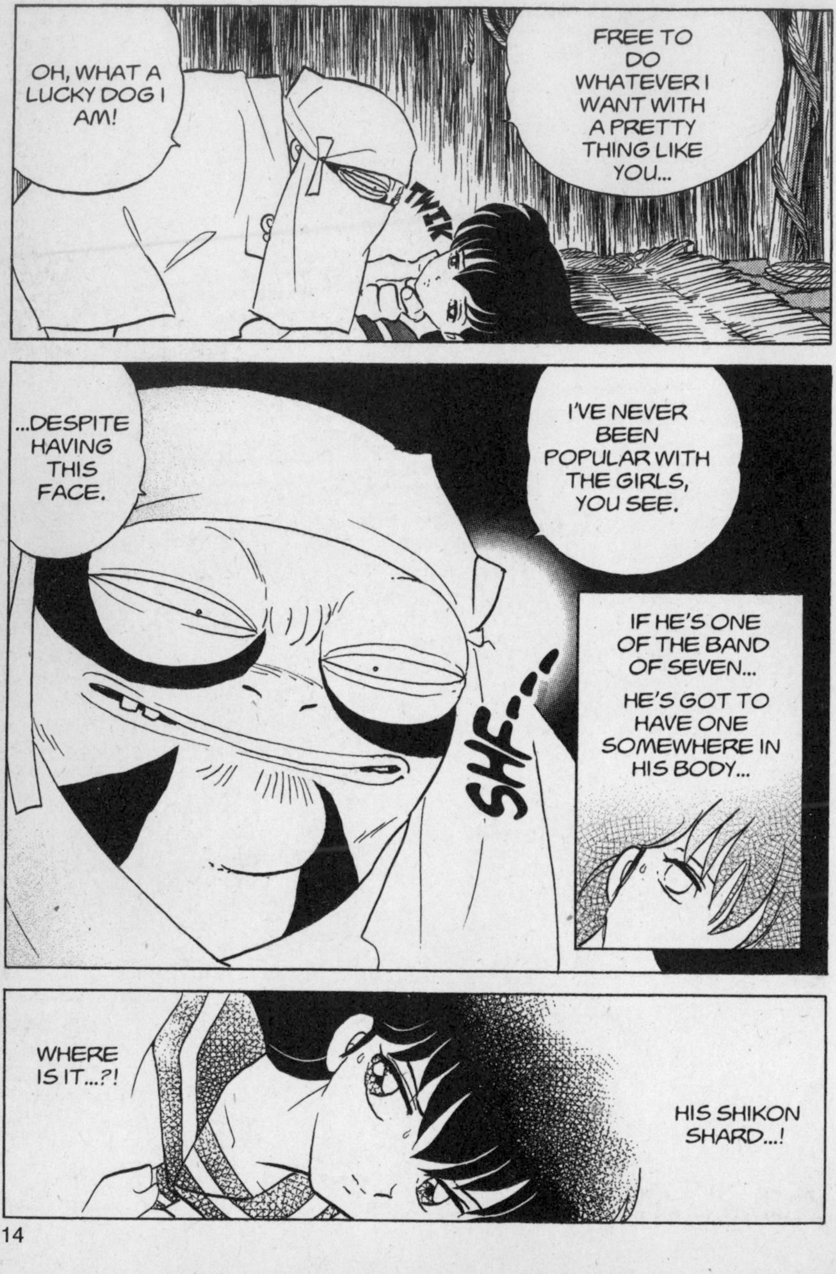
OH, WHAT A LUCKY DOG I AM!
FREE TO DO WHATEVER I WANT WITH A PRETTY THING LIKE YOU...
TWIK
...DESPITE HAVING THIS FACE.
I'VE NEVER BEEN POPULAR WITH THE GIRLS, YOU SEE.
SHF...
IF HE'S ONE OF THE BAND OF SEVEN...
HE'S GOT TO HAVE ONE SOMEWHERE IN HIS BODY...
WHERE IS IT...?!
HIS SHIKON SHARD...!

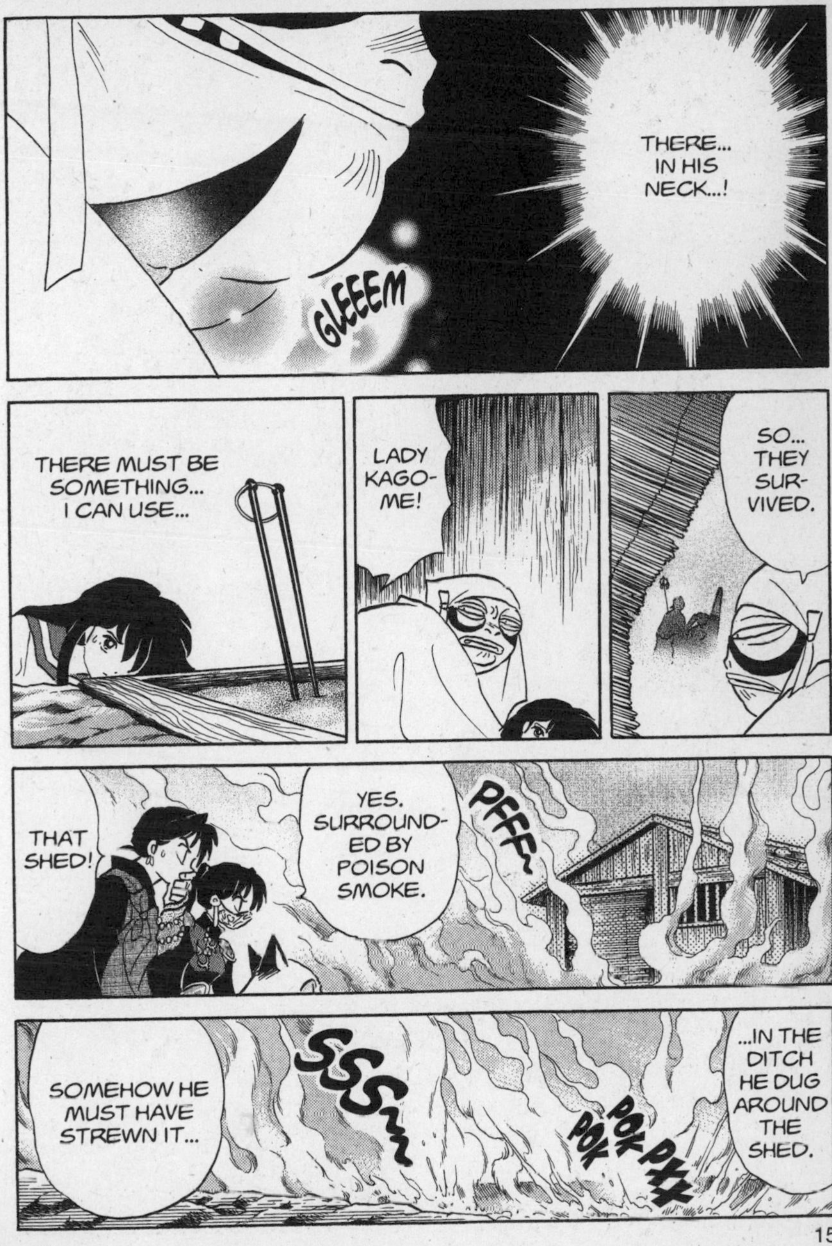
THERE... IN HIS NECK...!
GLEEEM
THERE MUST BE SOMETHING... I CAN USE...
LADY KAGO-ME!
SO... THEY SUR-VIVED.
THAT SHED!
YES. SURROUND-ED BY POISON SMOKE.
PFFF~
SOMEHOW HE MUST HAVE STREWN IT...
SSS~~
POK POK PXXX
...IN THE DITCH HE DUG AROUND THE SHED.

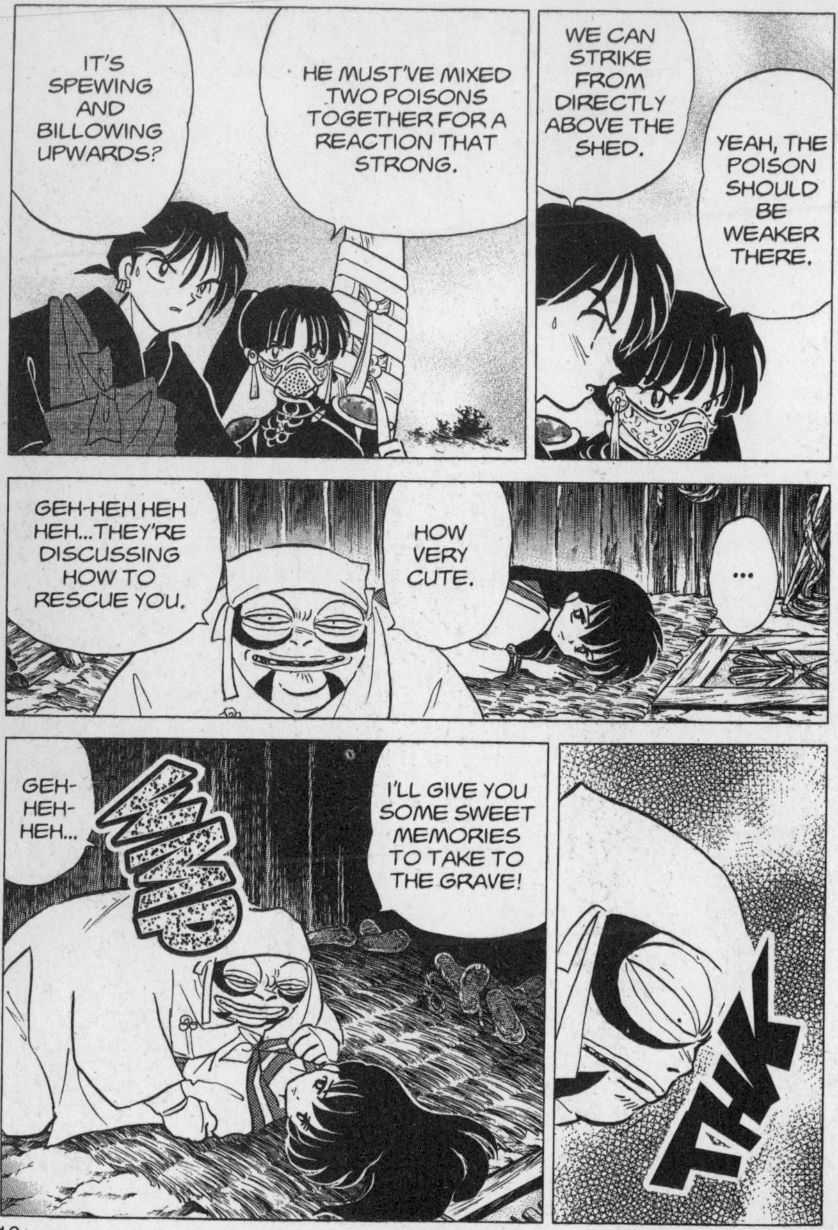
IT'S SPEWING AND BILLOWING UPWARDS?
HE MUST'VE MIXED TWO POISONS TOGETHER FOR A REACTION THAT STRONG.
WE CAN STRIKE FROM DIRECTLY ABOVE THE SHED.
YEAH, THE POISON SHOULD BE WEAKER THERE.
GEH-HEH HEH HEH...THEY'RE DISCUSSING HOW TO RESCUE YOU.
HOW VERY CUTE.
...
GEH-HEH-HEH...
WMMP
I'LL GIVE YOU SOME SWEET MEMORIES TO TAKE TO THE GRAVE!
THK

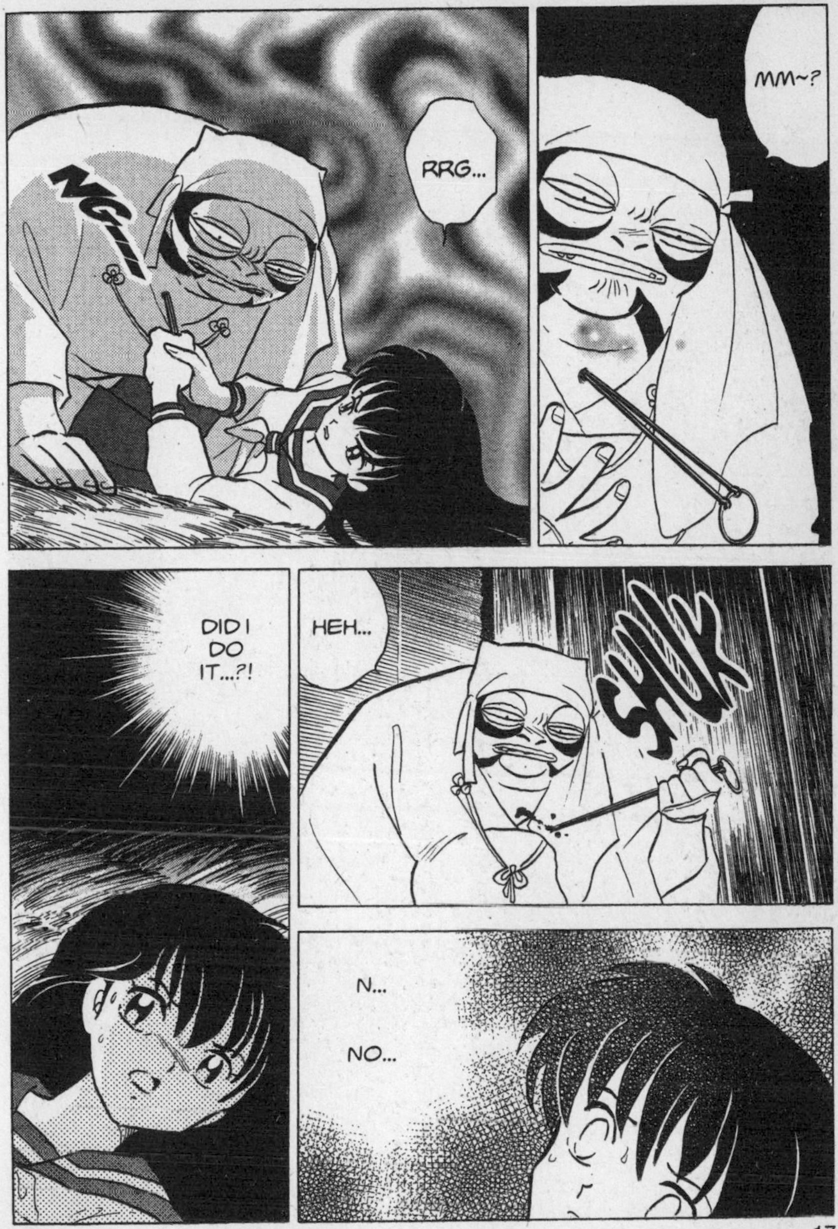
NGIII
RRG...
MM~?
DID I DO IT...?!
HEH...
SHUK
N...
NO...

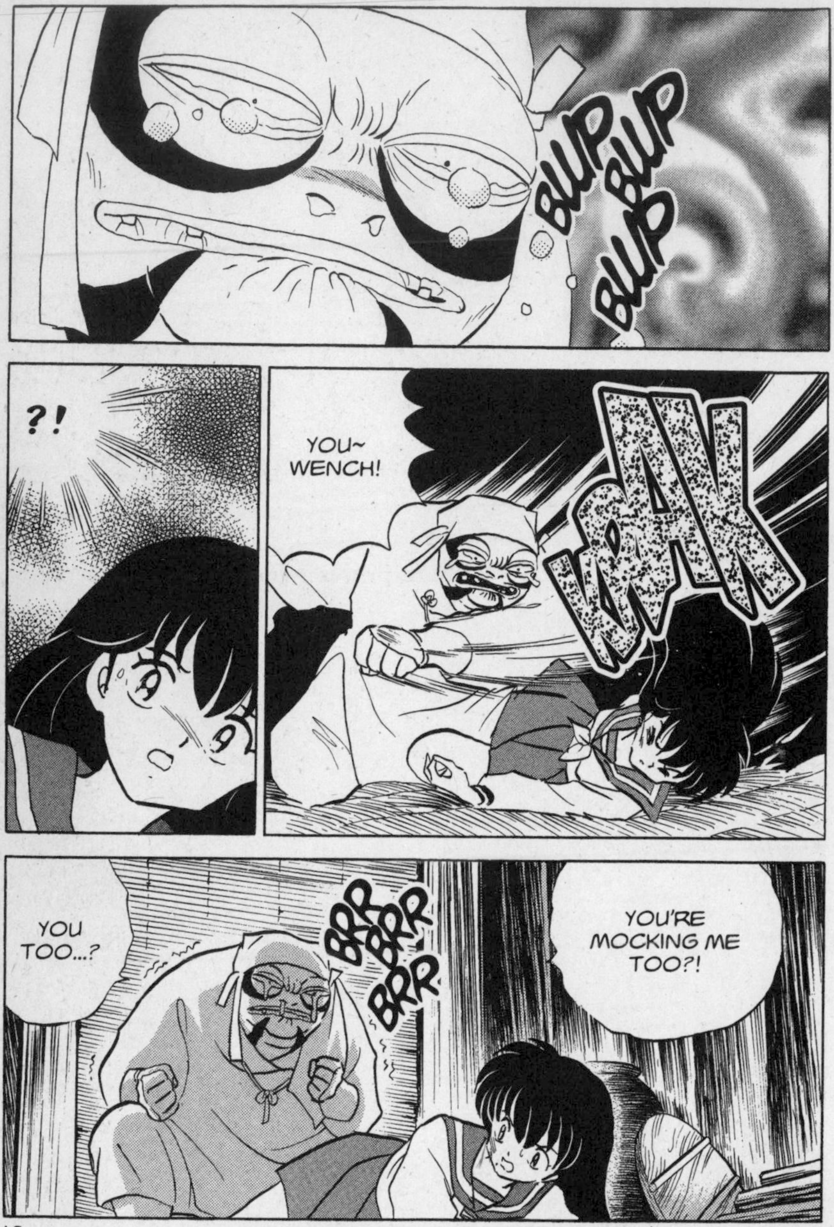
BLUP BLUP BLUP
?!
YOU~ WENCH!
KRAK
YOU TOO...?
BRR BRR BRR
YOU'RE MOCKING ME TOO?!

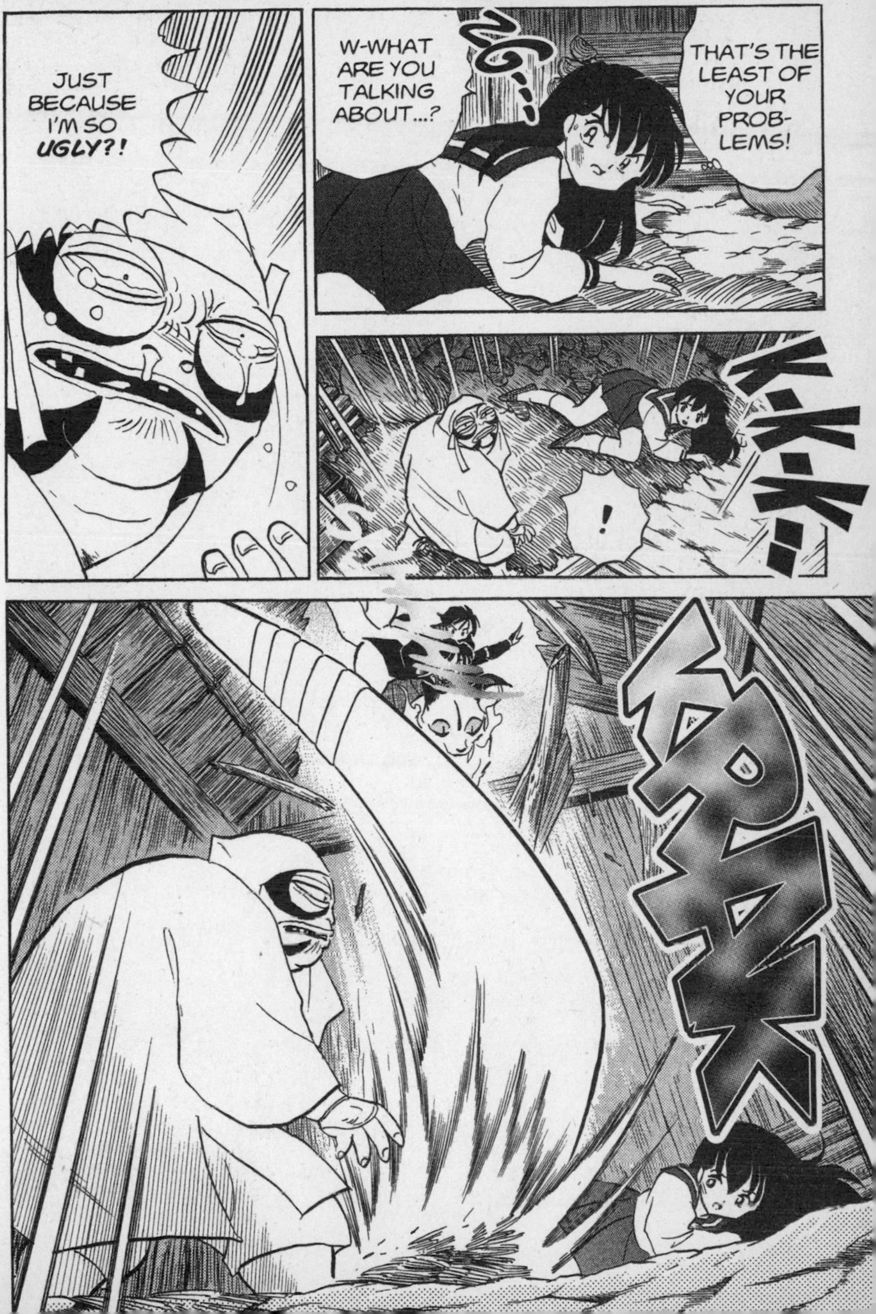
JUST BECAUSE I'M SO *UGLY?!*
ZG...
W-WHAT ARE YOU TALKING ABOUT...?
THAT'S THE LEAST OF YOUR PROB-LEMS!
K-K-K...
!
KRAK

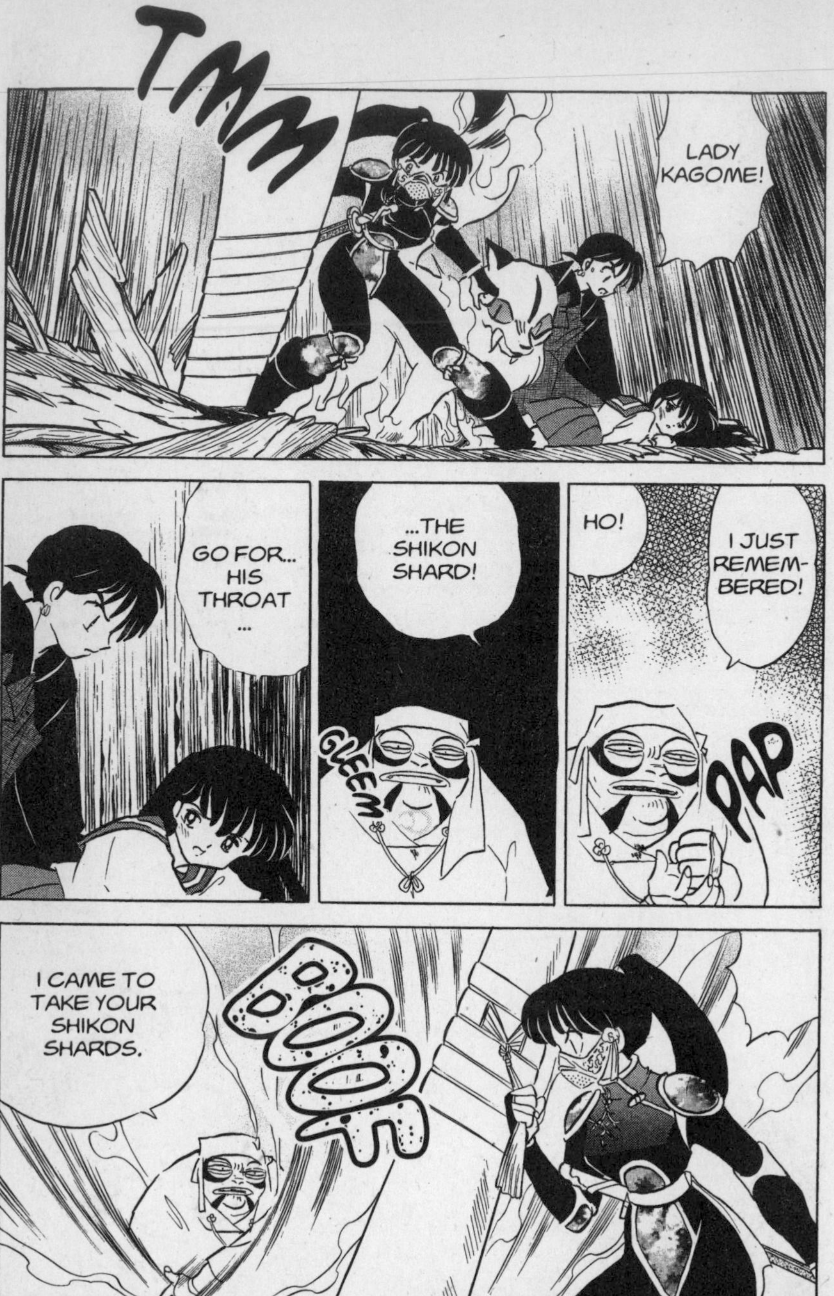
TMM
LADY KAGOME!
GO FOR... HIS THROAT ...
...THE SHIKON SHARD!
GLEEM
HO!
I JUST REMEM-BERED!
PAP
I CAME TO TAKE YOUR SHIKON SHARDS.
BOOOF

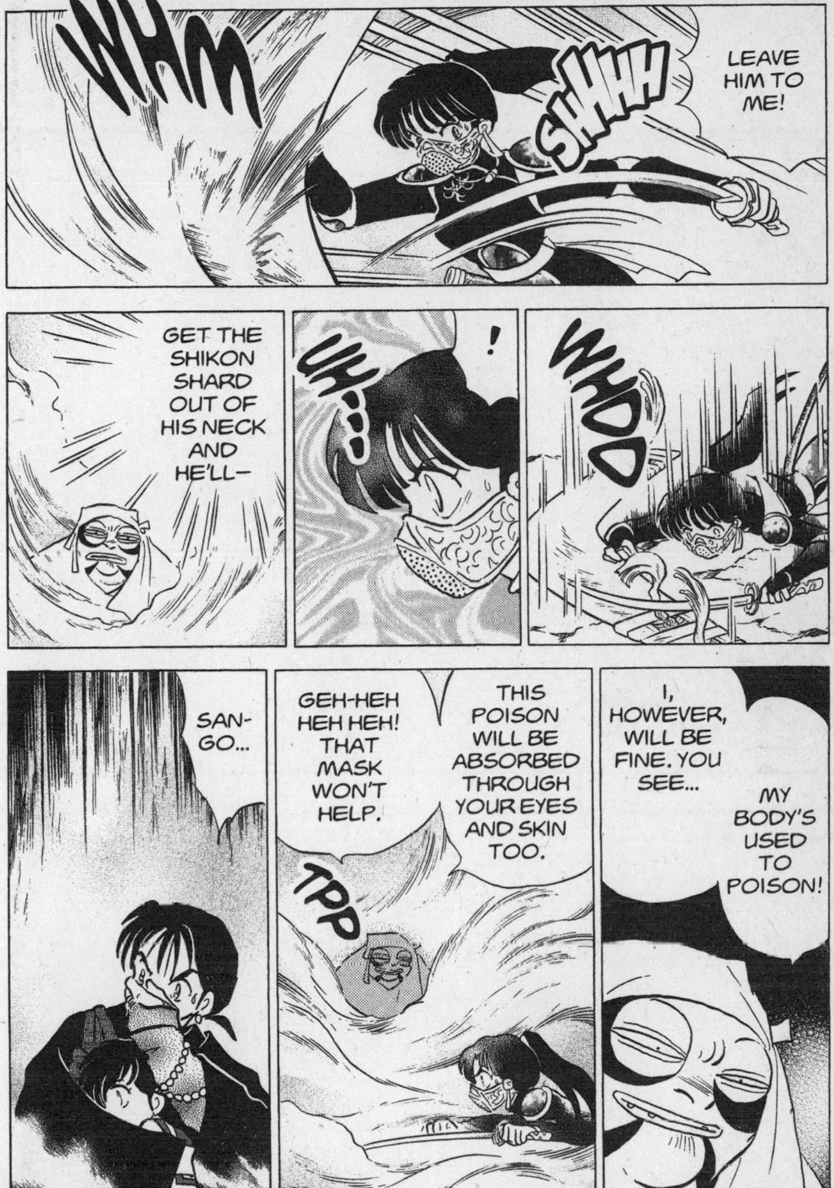
WHM
SHHHH
LEAVE HIM TO ME!
GET THE SHIKON SHARD OUT OF HIS NECK AND HE'LL—
UH...
!
WHDD
SAN-GO...
GEH-HEH HEH HEH! THAT MASK WON'T HELP.
THIS POISON WILL BE ABSORBED THROUGH YOUR EYES AND SKIN TOO.
TPP
I, HOWEVER, WILL BE FINE. YOU SEE...
MY BODY'S USED TO POISON!

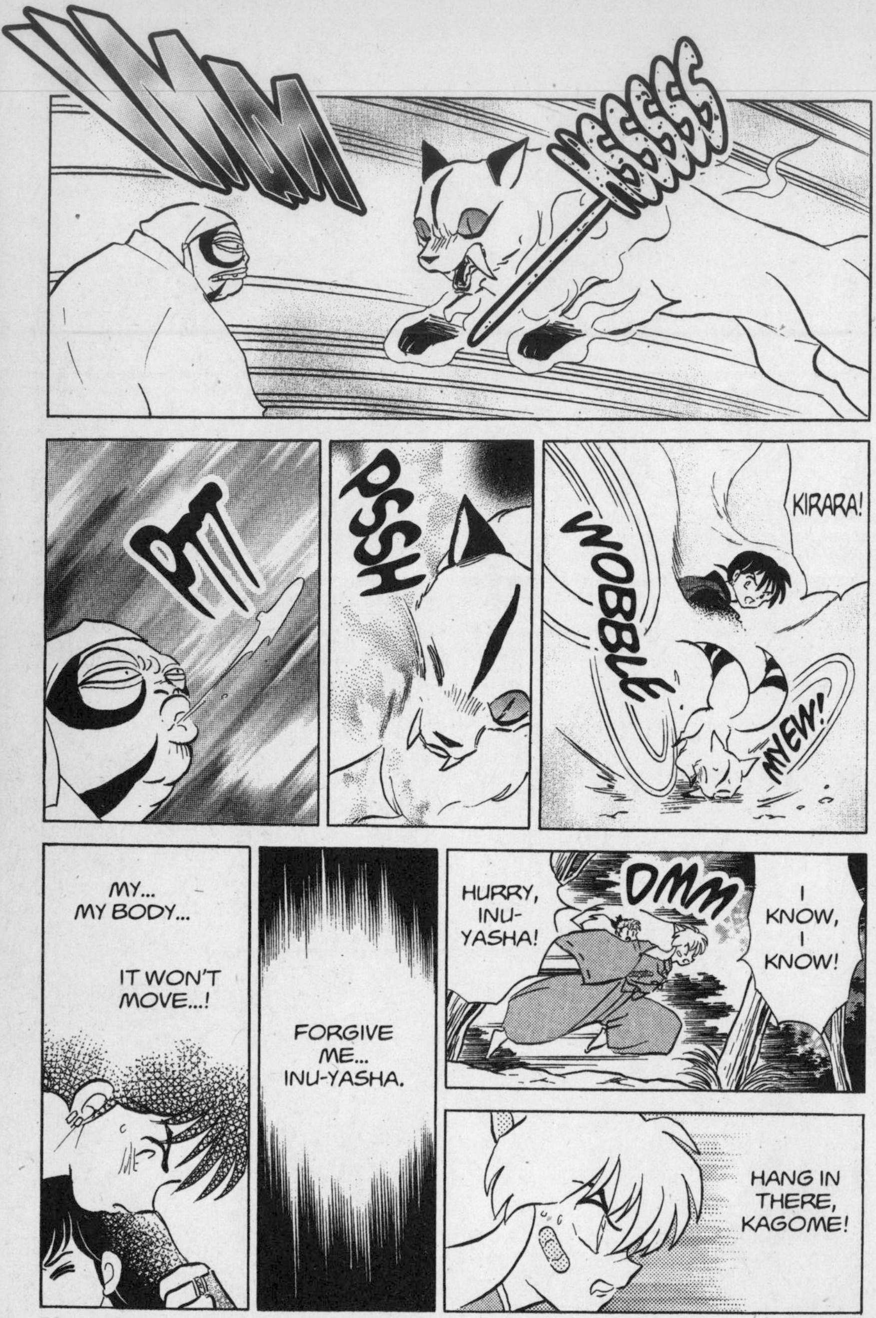
PSSH
WOBBLE
KIRARA!
MYEW!
MY...
MY BODY...
IT WON'T
MOVE...!
FORGIVE
ME...
INU-YASHA.
HURRY,
INU-
YASHA!
DMM
I
KNOW,
I
KNOW!
HANG IN
THERE,
KAGOME!

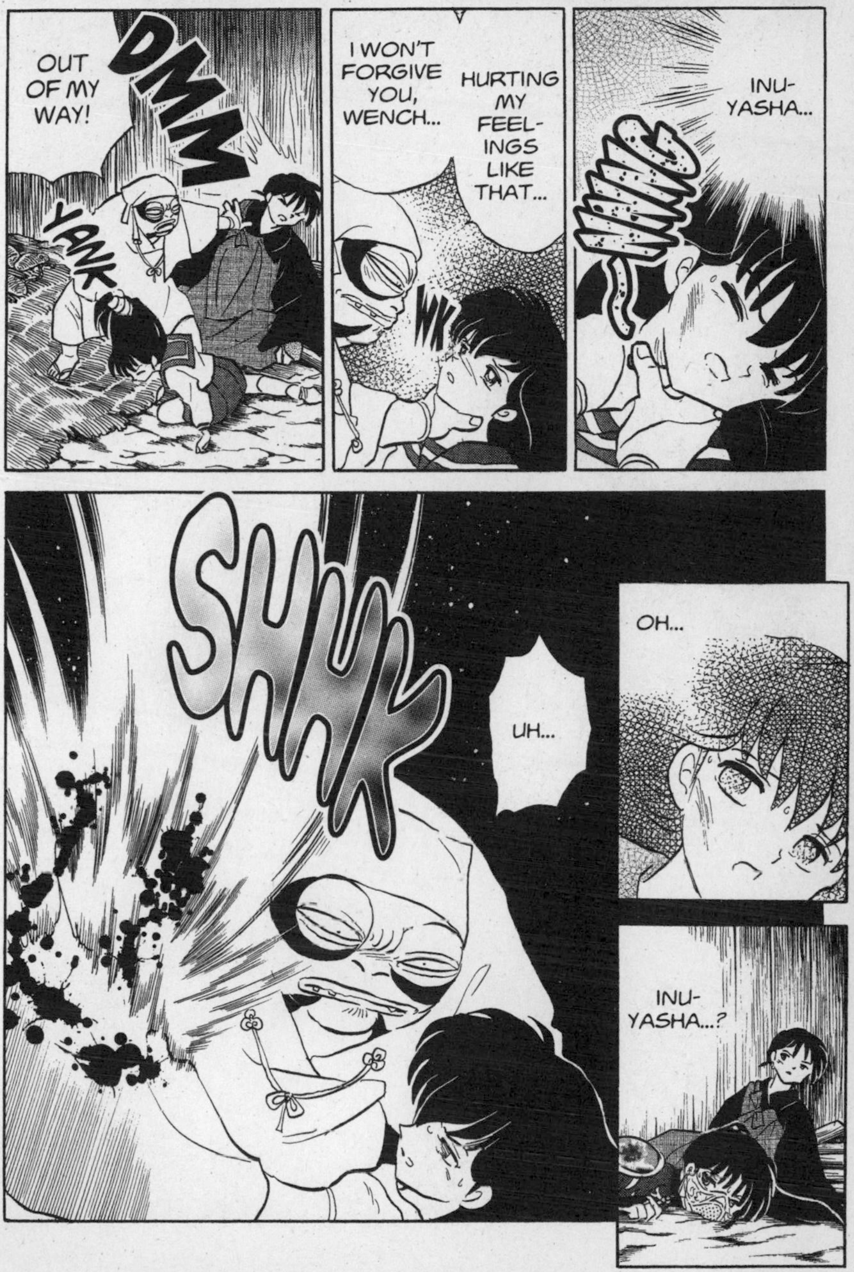
OUT OF MY WAY!
DMM
YANK
I WON'T FORGIVE YOU, WENCH...
HURTING MY FEEL-INGS LIKE THAT...
INU-YASHA...
SHHK
UH...
OH...
INU-YASHA...?

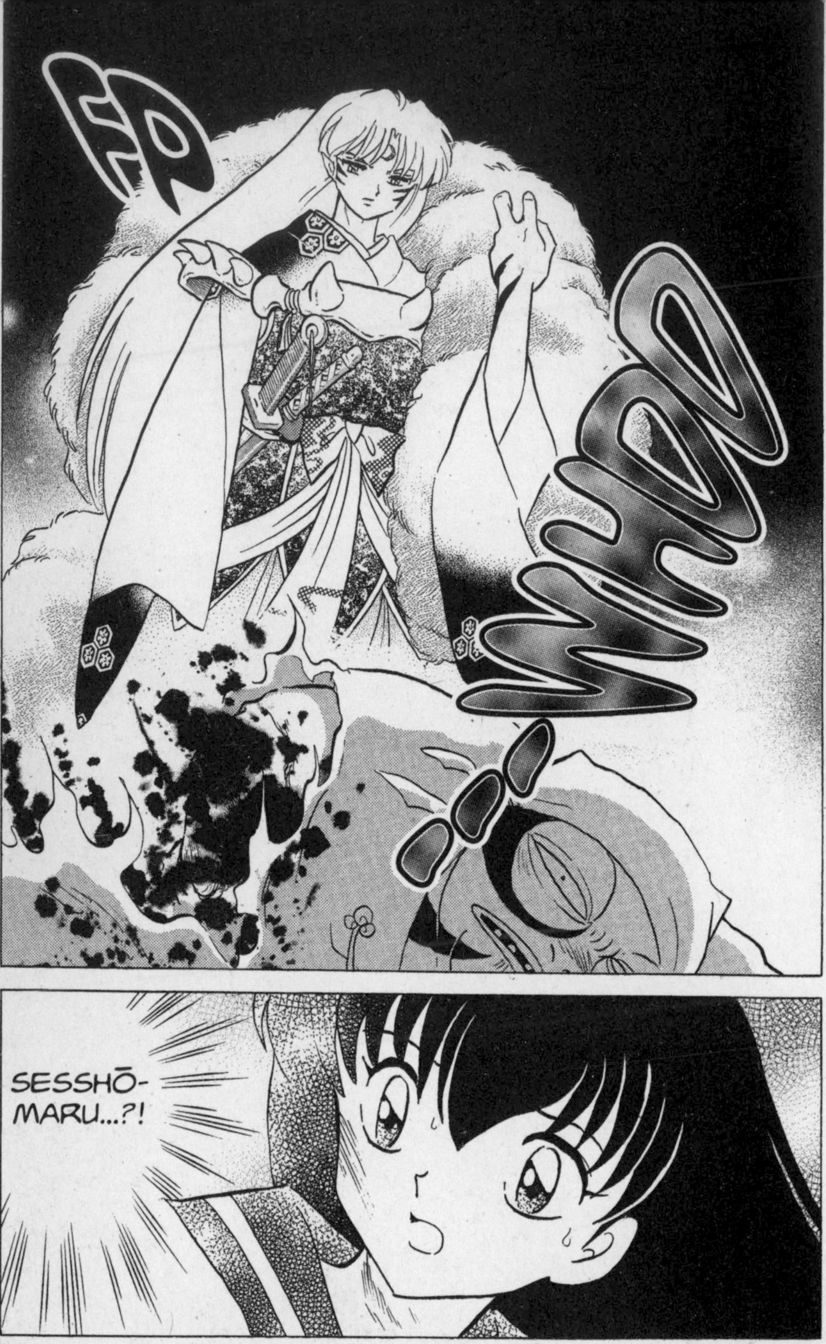
SESSHŌ-
MARU...?!

# SCROLL TWO

# NARAKU'S PURSUERS

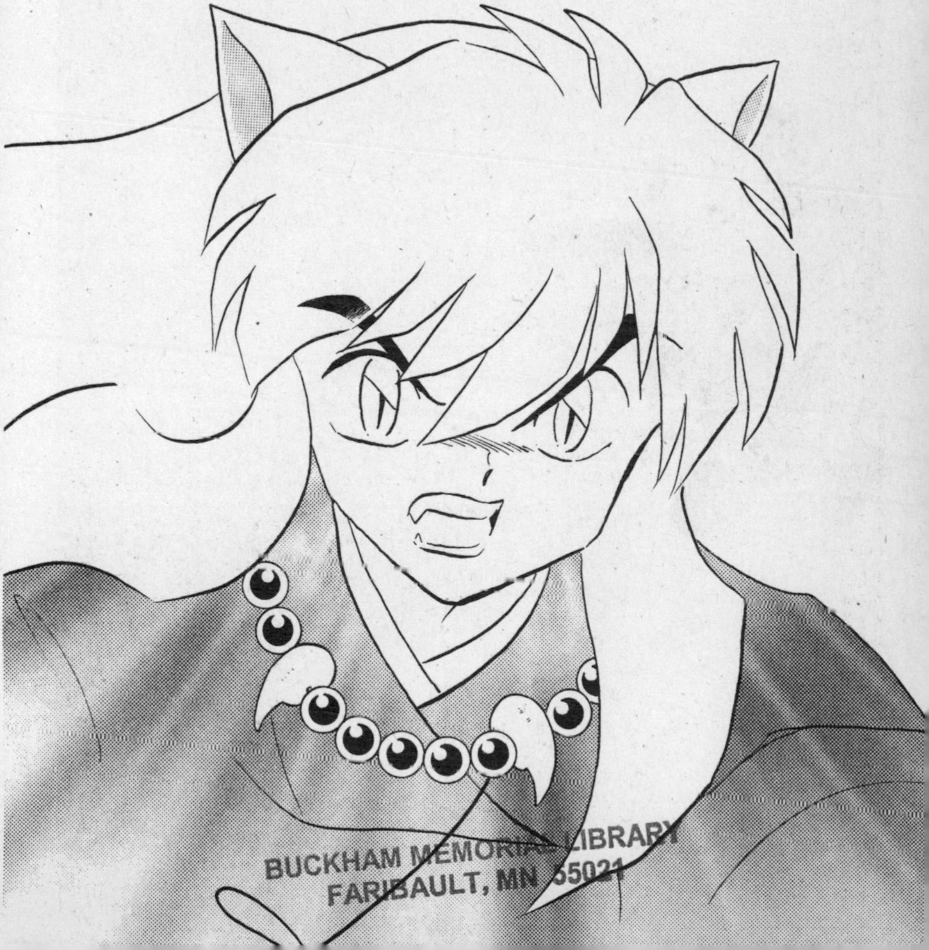

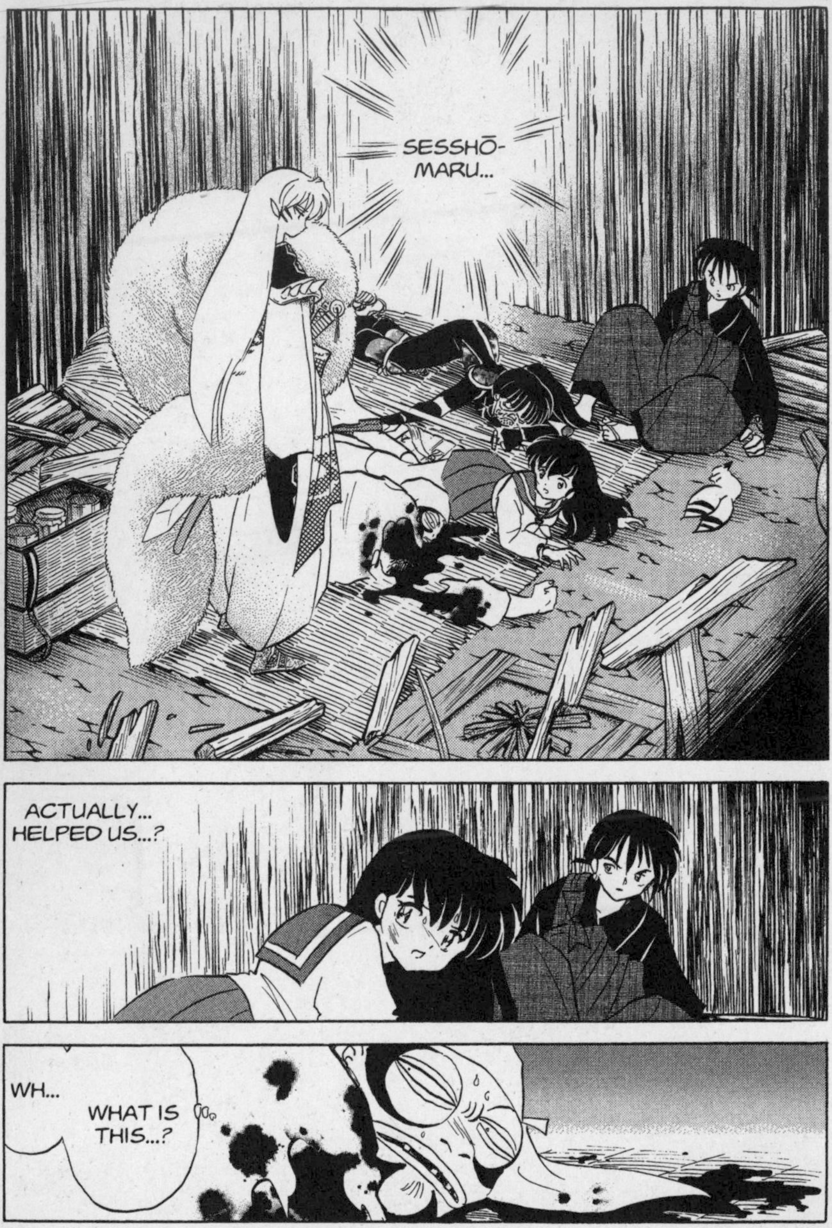
SESSHŌ-
MARU...
ACTUALLY...
HELPED US...?
WH...
WHAT IS
THIS...?

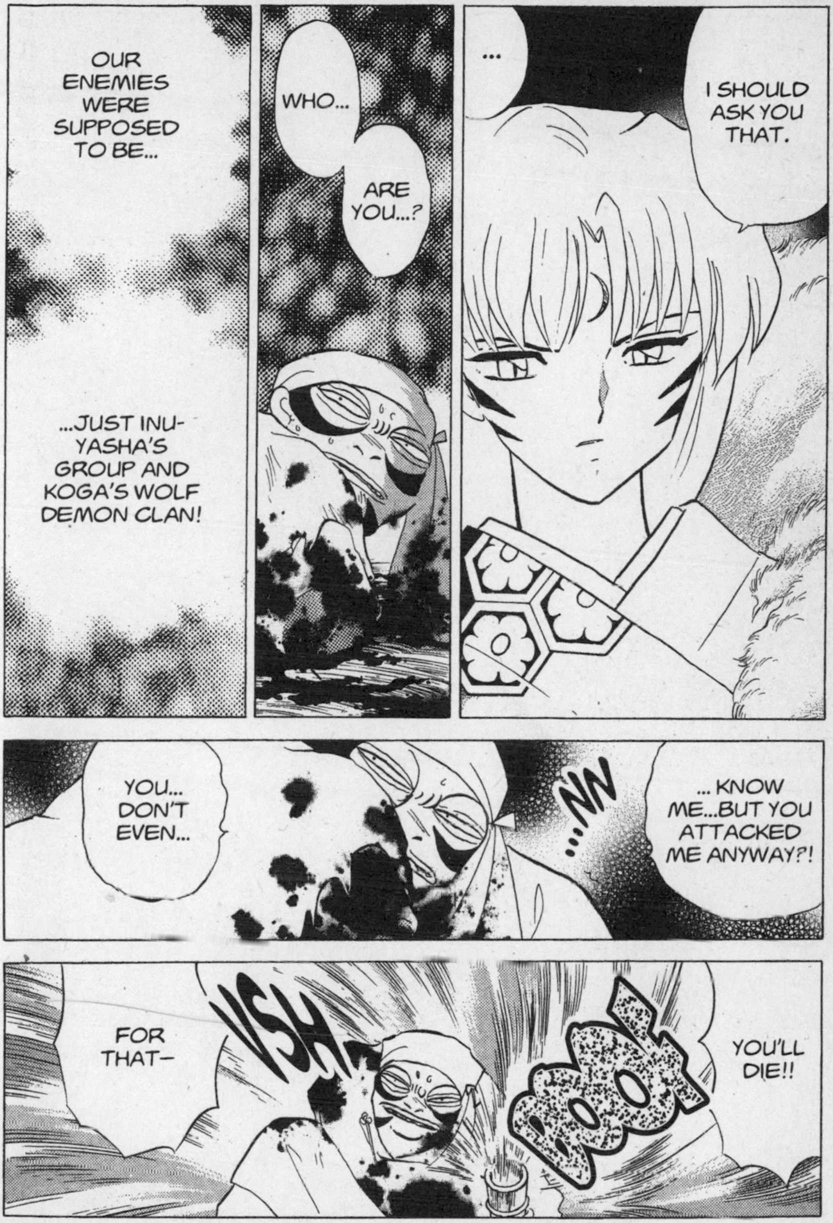
OUR ENEMIES WERE SUPPOSED TO BE...
...JUST INU-YASHA'S GROUP AND KOGA'S WOLF DEMON CLAN!
WHO...
ARE YOU...?
...
I SHOULD ASK YOU THAT.
YOU... DON'T EVEN...
...NN
... KNOW ME...BUT YOU ATTACKED ME ANYWAY?!
FOR THAT–
VSH
BOOF
YOU'LL DIE!!

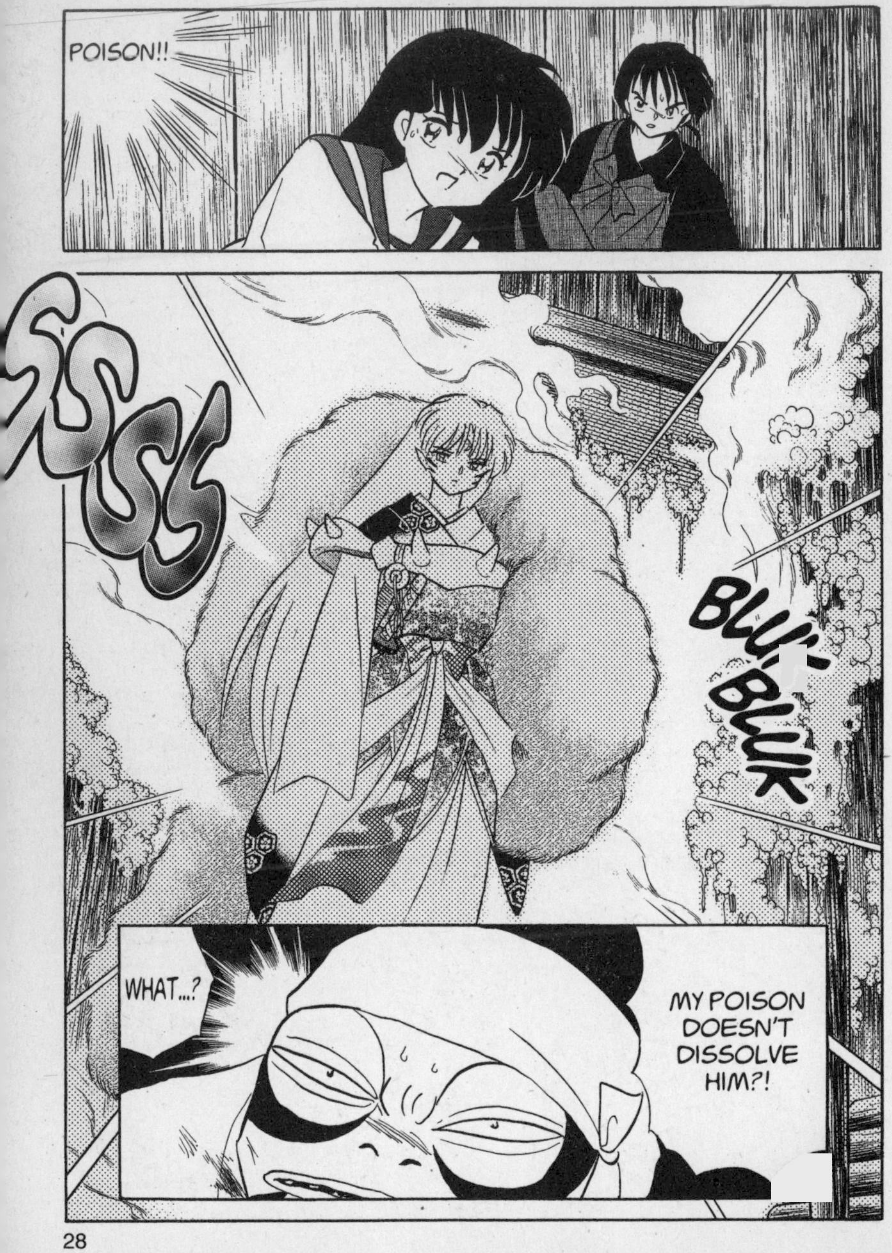
POISON!!
SSSS
BLUK BLUK
WHAT...?
MY POISON DOESN'T DISSOLVE HIM?!

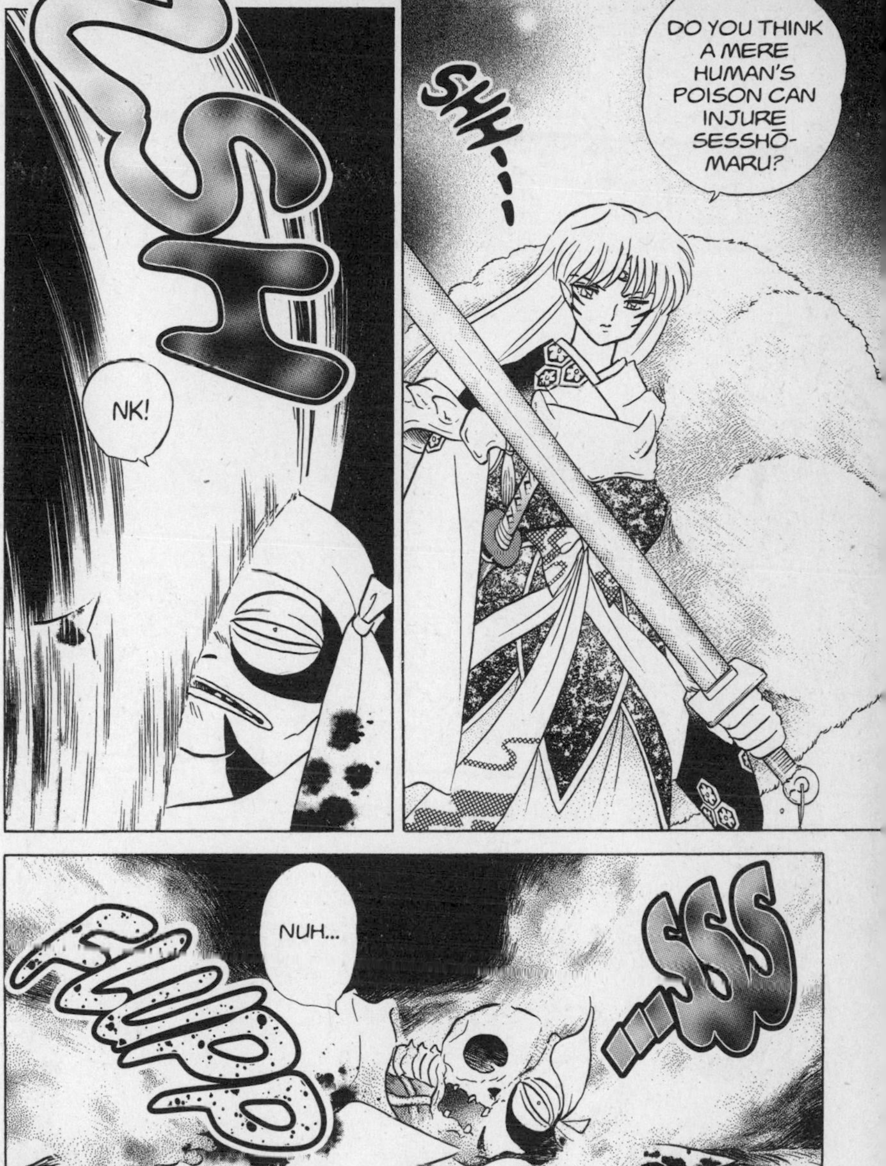
ZSH
NK!
SHH...
DO YOU THINK A MERE HUMAN'S POISON CAN INJURE SESSHŌ-MARU?
FWUPP
NUH...
...SSS

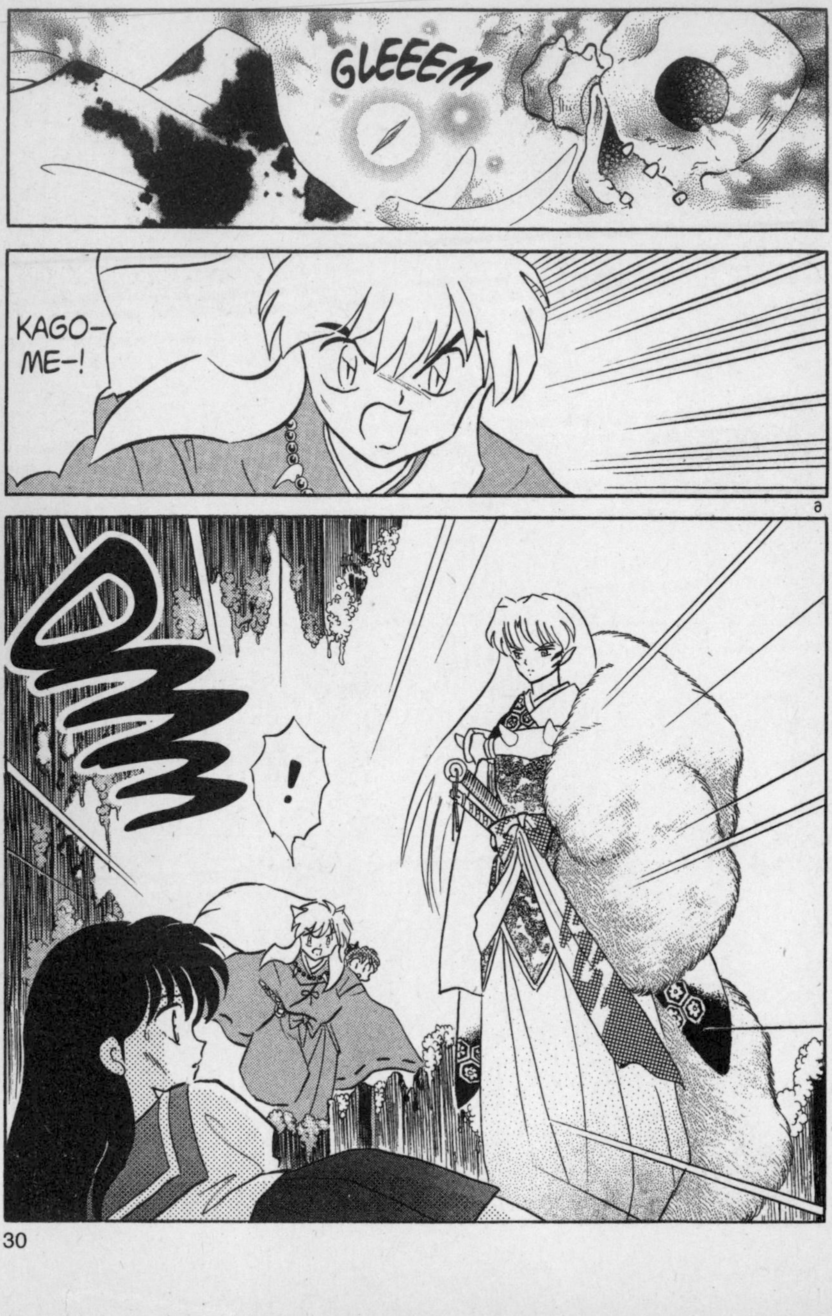
GLEEEM
KAGO-
ME-!
!

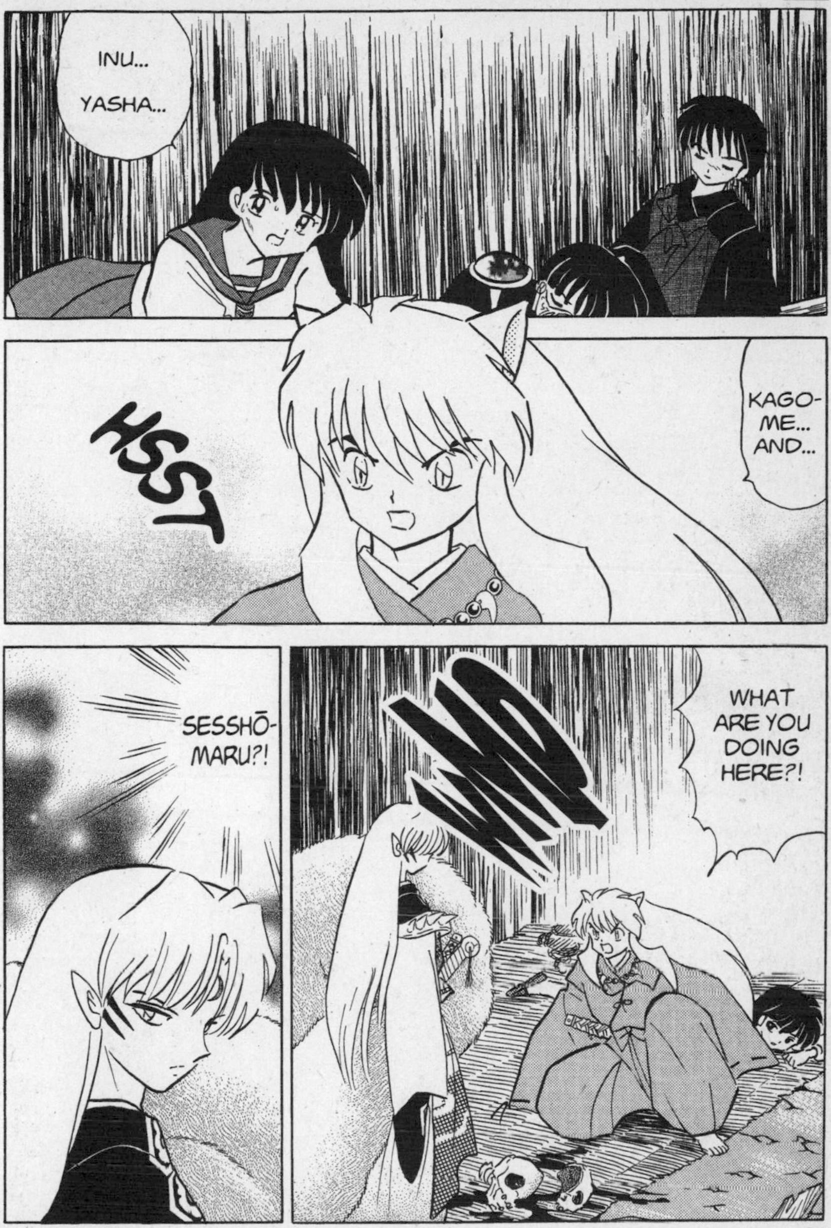
INU...
YASHA...
HSST
KAGO-ME... AND...
SESSHŌ-MARU?!
WMP
WHAT ARE YOU DOING HERE?!

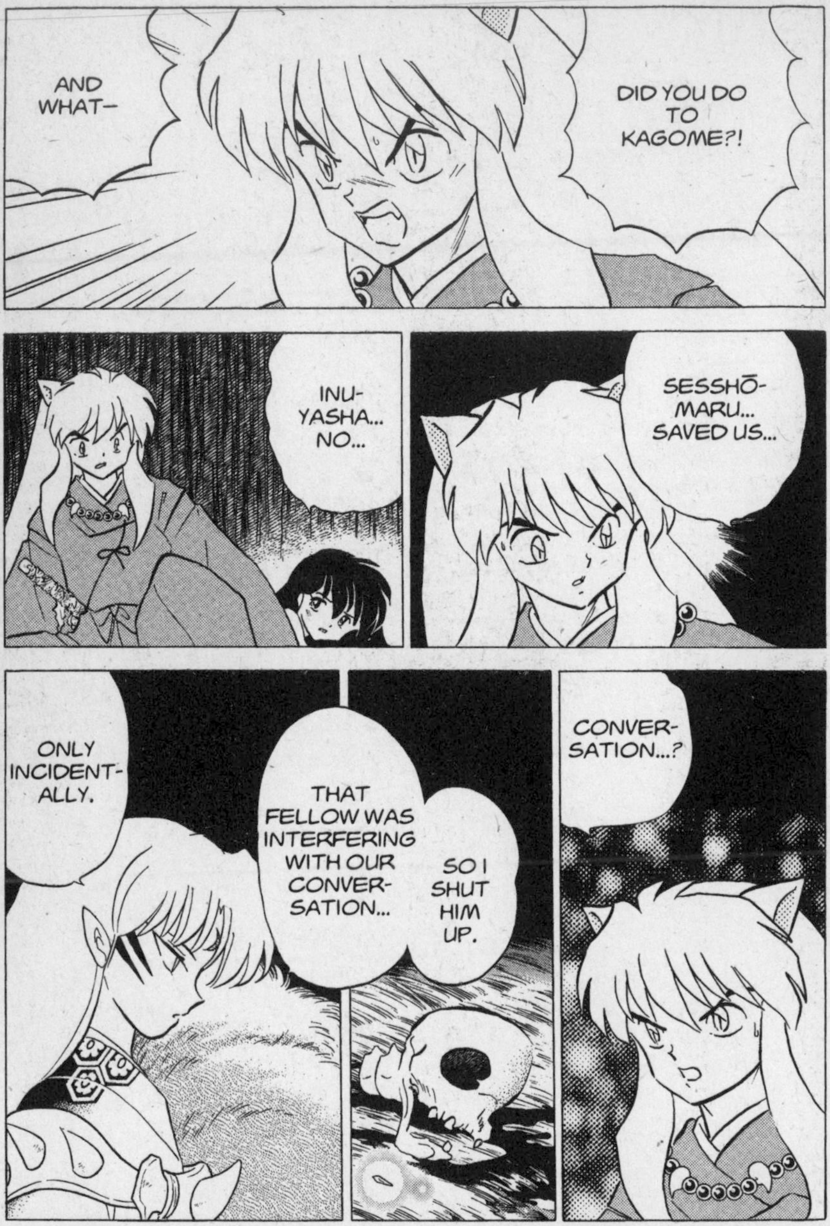
AND WHAT—
DID YOU DO TO KAGOME?!
INU-YASHA... NO...
SESSHŌ-MARU... SAVED US...
ONLY INCIDENT-ALLY.
THAT FELLOW WAS INTERFERING WITH OUR CONVER-SATION...
SO I SHUT HIM UP.
CONVER-SATION...?

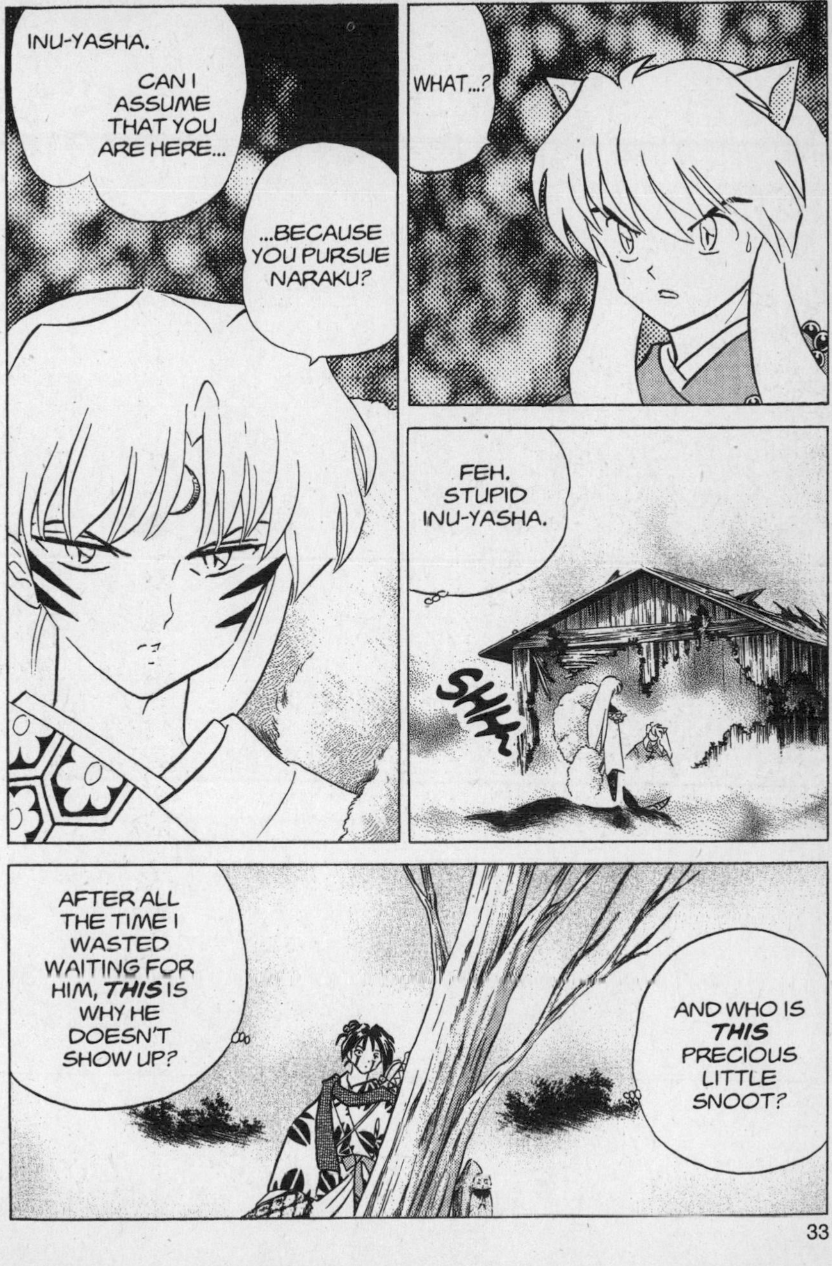
INU-YASHA.
CAN I ASSUME THAT YOU ARE HERE...
...BECAUSE YOU PURSUE NARAKU?
WHAT...?
FEH. STUPID INU-YASHA.
SHHK
AFTER ALL THE TIME I WASTED WAITING FOR HIM, THIS IS WHY HE DOESN'T SHOW UP?
AND WHO IS THIS PRECIOUS LITTLE SNOOT?

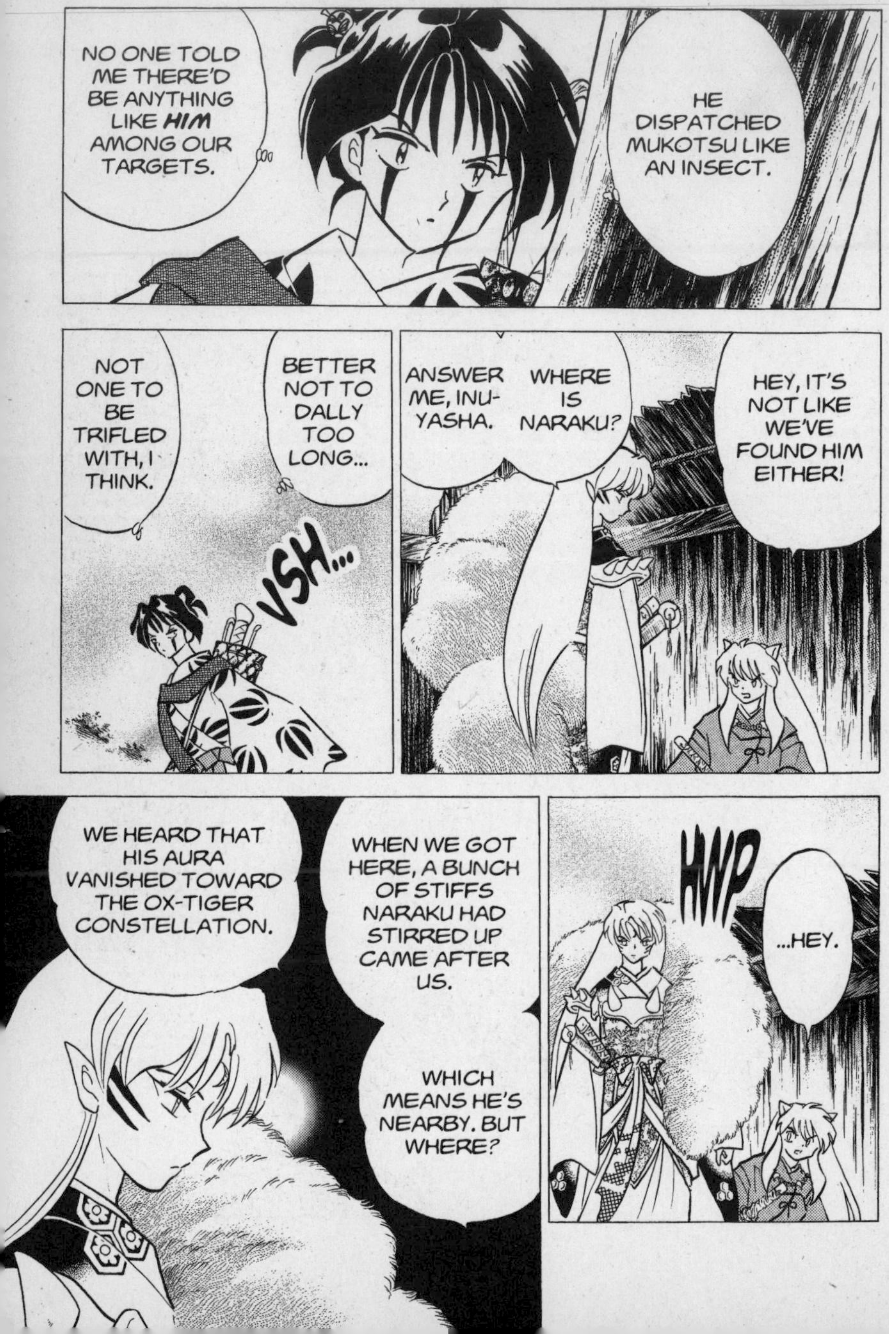
NO ONE TOLD ME THERE'D BE ANYTHING LIKE ***HIM*** AMONG OUR TARGETS.
HE DISPATCHED MUKOTSU LIKE AN INSECT.
NOT ONE TO BE TRIFLED WITH, I THINK.
BETTER NOT TO DALLY TOO LONG...
VSH...
ANSWER ME, INU-YASHA.
WHERE IS NARAKU?
HEY, IT'S NOT LIKE WE'VE FOUND HIM EITHER!
WE HEARD THAT HIS AURA VANISHED TOWARD THE OX-TIGER CONSTELLATION.
WHEN WE GOT HERE, A BUNCH OF STIFFS NARAKU HAD STIRRED UP CAME AFTER US.
WHICH MEANS HE'S NEARBY. BUT WHERE?
HMP
...HEY.

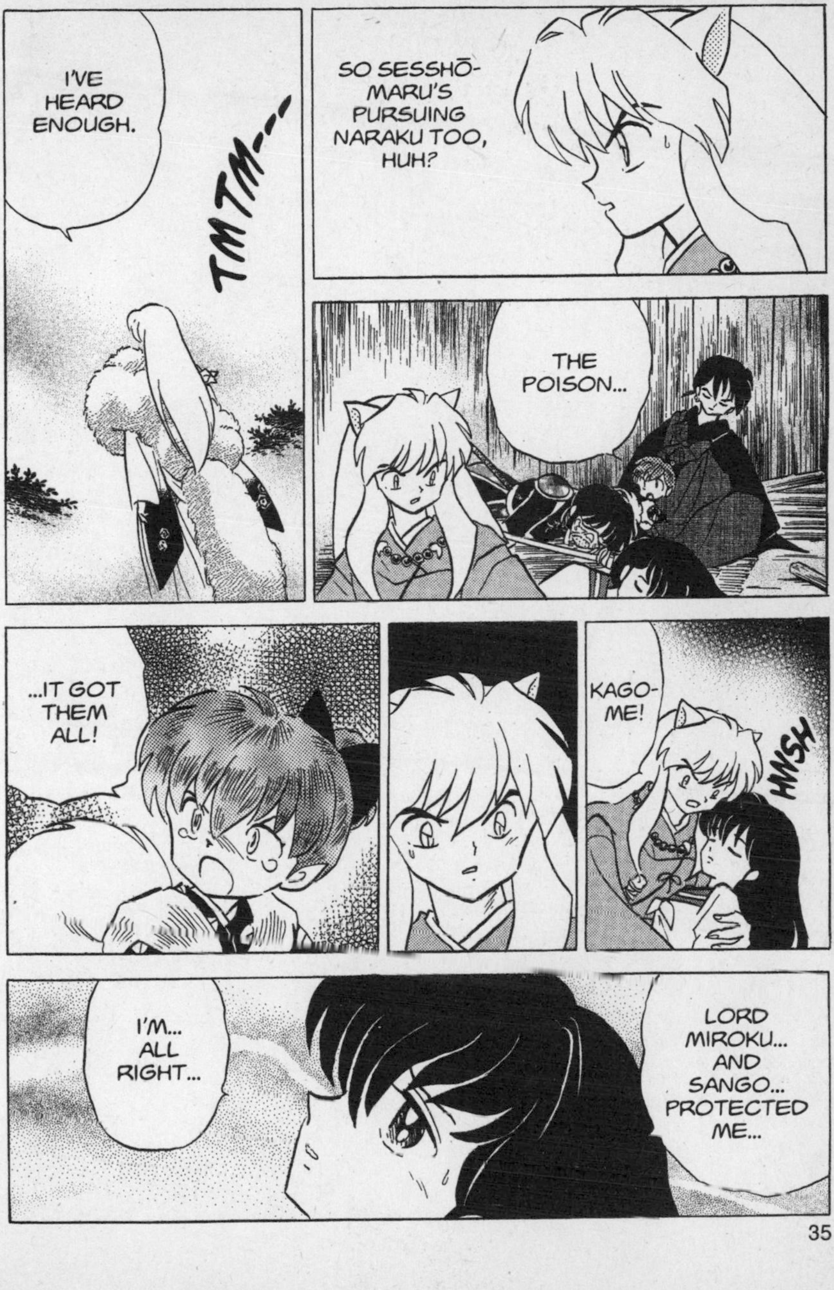
I'VE HEARD ENOUGH.
TMTM...
SO SESSHŌ-MARU'S PURSUING NARAKU TOO, HUH?
THE POISON...
...IT GOT THEM ALL!
KAGO-ME!
HWSH
I'M... ALL RIGHT...
LORD MIROKU... AND SANGO... PROTECTED ME...

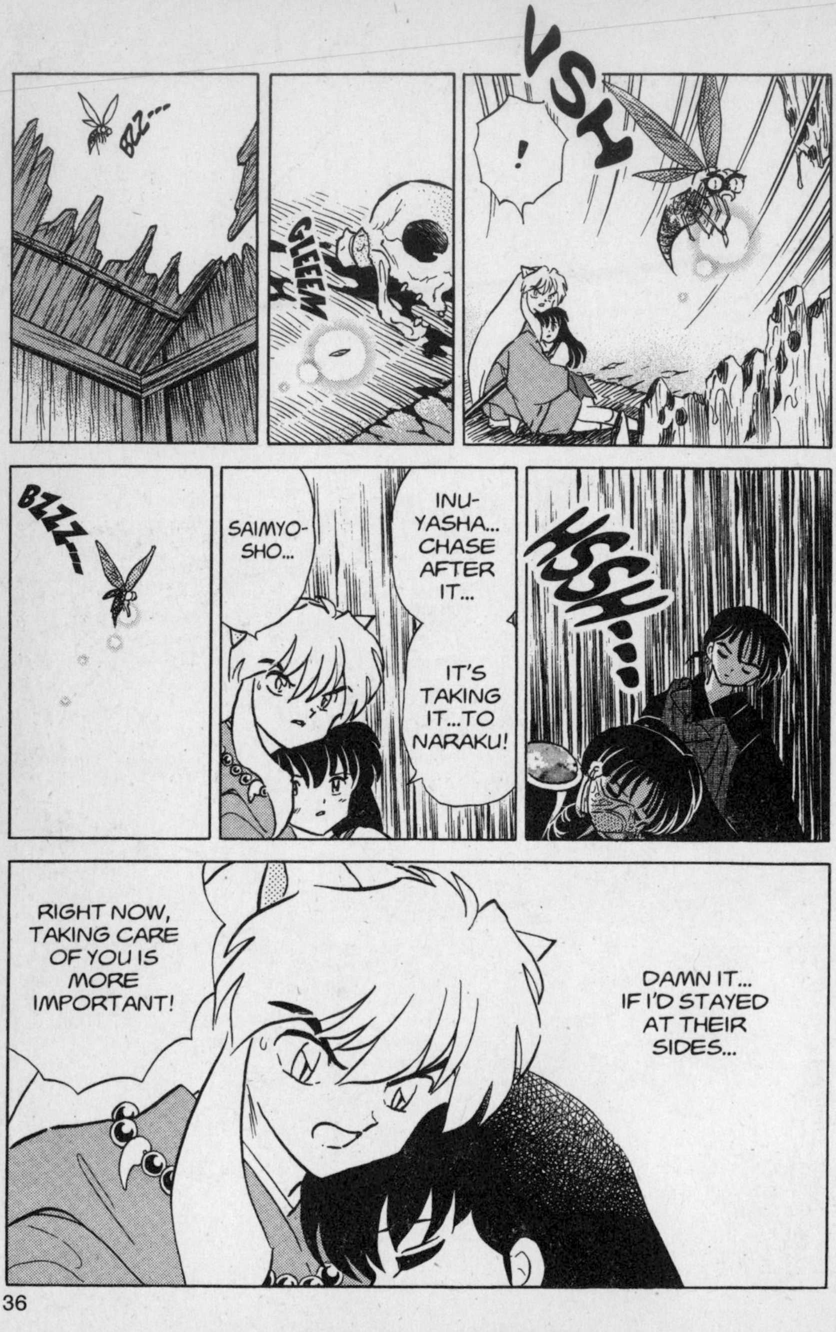
BZZ...
GLEEEM
VSH
!
BZZZ...
SAIMYO-SHO...
INU-YASHA... CHASE AFTER IT...
IT'S TAKING IT...TO NARAKU!
HSSH...
RIGHT NOW, TAKING CARE OF YOU IS MORE IMPORTANT!
DAMN IT... IF I'D STAYED AT THEIR SIDES...

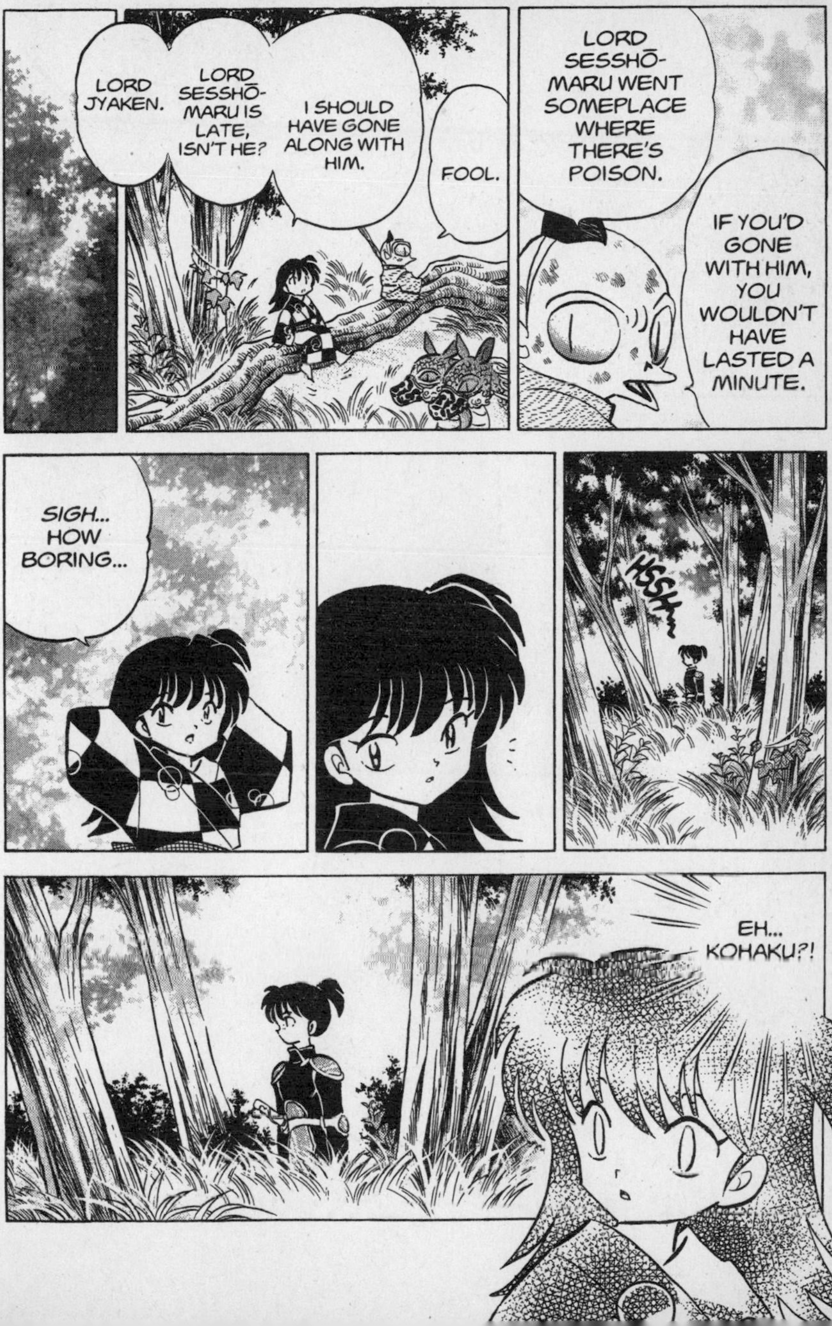
LORD JYAKEN.
LORD SESSHŌ-MARU IS LATE, ISN'T HE?
I SHOULD HAVE GONE ALONG WITH HIM.
FOOL.
LORD SESSHŌ-MARU WENT SOMEPLACE WHERE THERE'S POISON.
IF YOU'D GONE WITH HIM, YOU WOULDN'T HAVE LASTED A MINUTE.
SIGH... HOW BORING...
HSSH
EH... KOHAKU?!

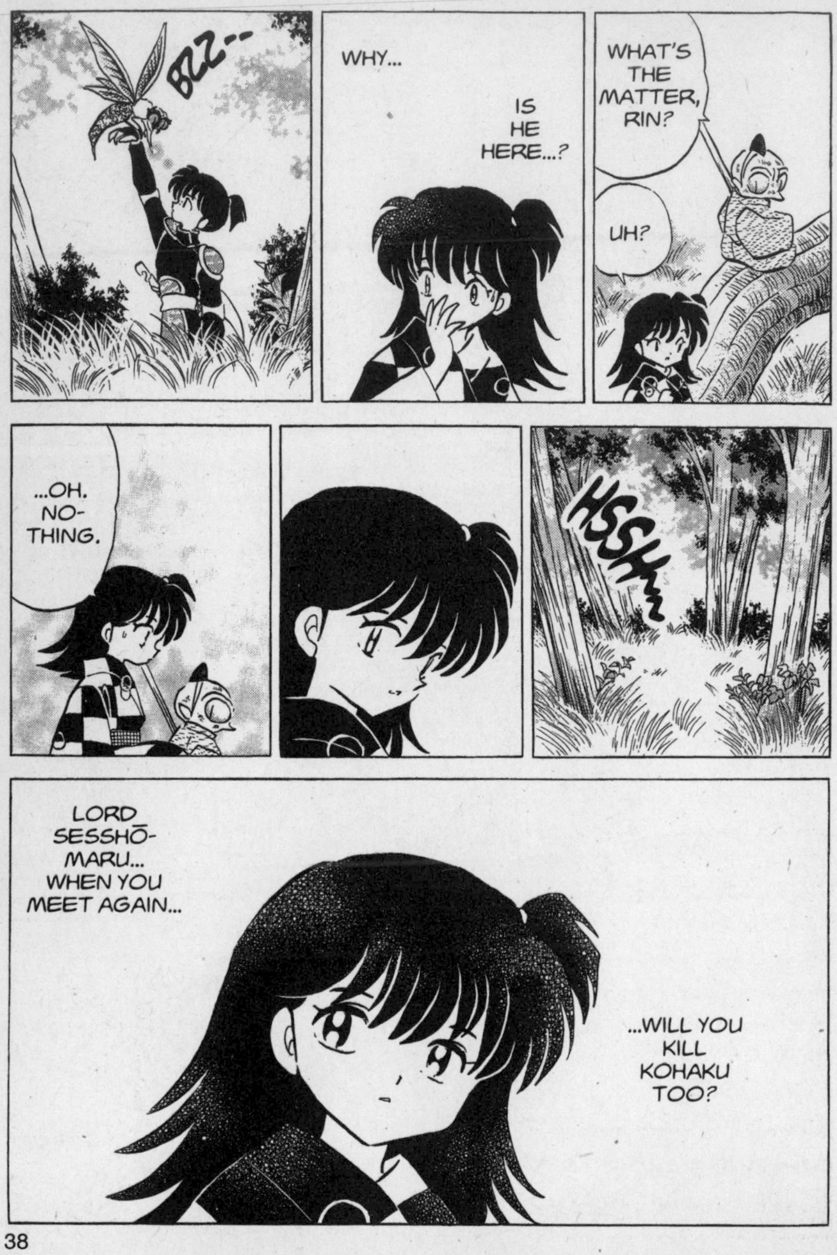
BZZ--
WHY...
IS HE HERE...?
WHAT'S THE MATTER, RIN?
UH?
...OH. NOTHING.
HSSH
LORD SESSHŌMARU... WHEN YOU MEET AGAIN...
...WILL YOU KILL KOHAKU TOO?

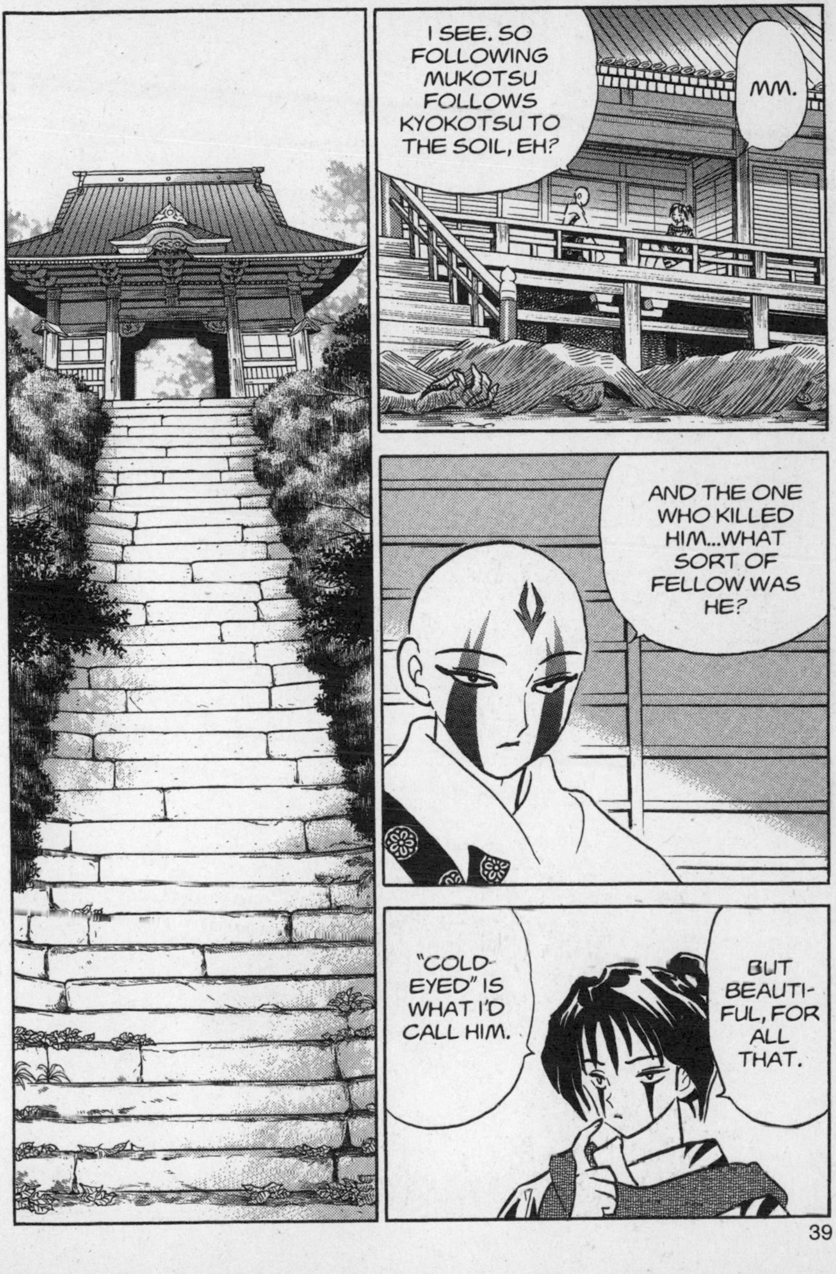
I SEE. SO FOLLOWING MUKOTSU FOLLOWS KYOKOTSU TO THE SOIL, EH?
MM.
AND THE ONE WHO KILLED HIM...WHAT SORT OF FELLOW WAS HE?
"COLD-EYED" IS WHAT I'D CALL HIM.
BUT BEAUTI-FUL, FOR ALL THAT.

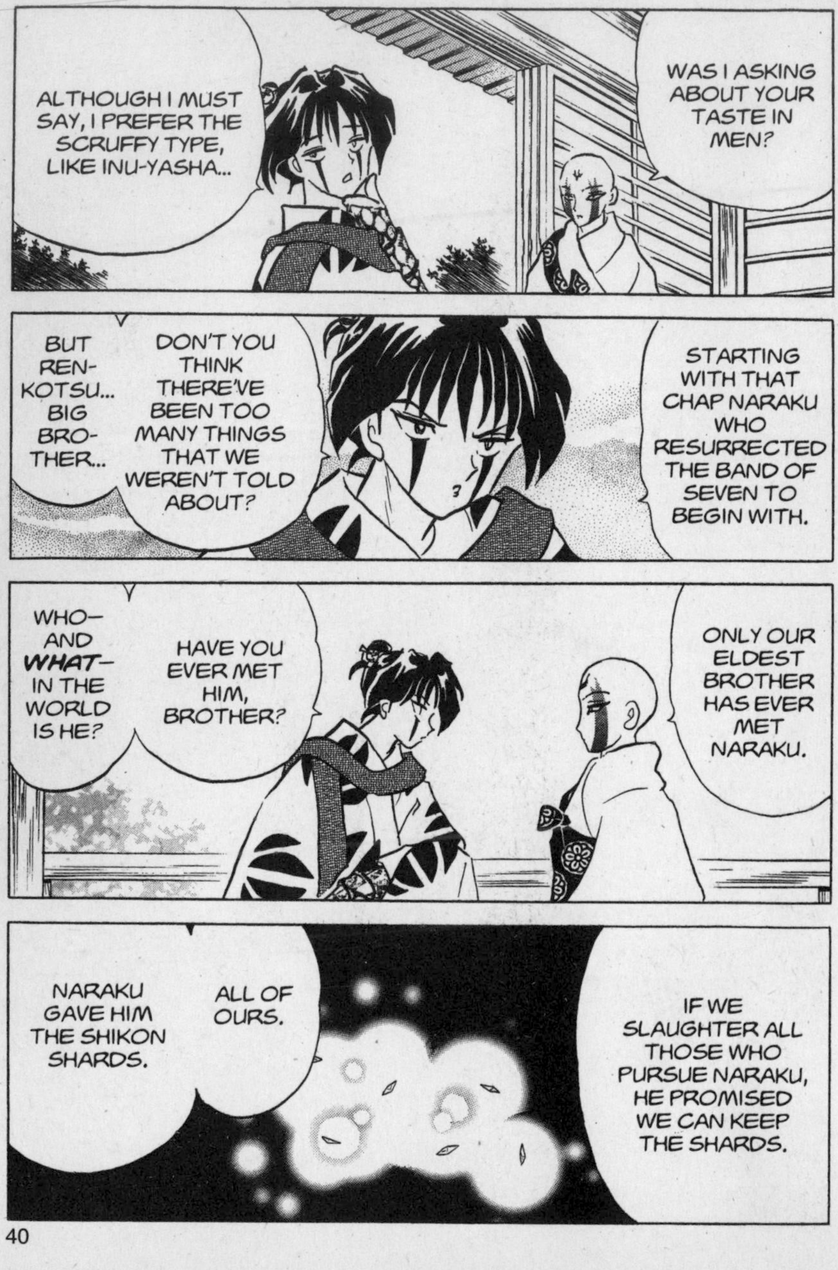
ALTHOUGH I MUST SAY, I PREFER THE SCRUFFY TYPE, LIKE INU-YASHA...
WAS I ASKING ABOUT YOUR TASTE IN MEN?
BUT REN-KOTSU... BIG BROTHER...
DON'T YOU THINK THERE'VE BEEN TOO MANY THINGS THAT WE WEREN'T TOLD ABOUT?
STARTING WITH THAT CHAP NARAKU WHO RESURRECTED THE BAND OF SEVEN TO BEGIN WITH.
WHO—AND ***WHAT***—IN THE WORLD IS HE?
HAVE YOU EVER MET HIM, BROTHER?
ONLY OUR ELDEST BROTHER HAS EVER MET NARAKU.
NARAKU GAVE HIM THE SHIKON SHARDS.
ALL OF OURS.
IF WE SLAUGHTER ALL THOSE WHO PURSUE NARAKU, HE PROMISED WE CAN KEEP THE SHARDS.

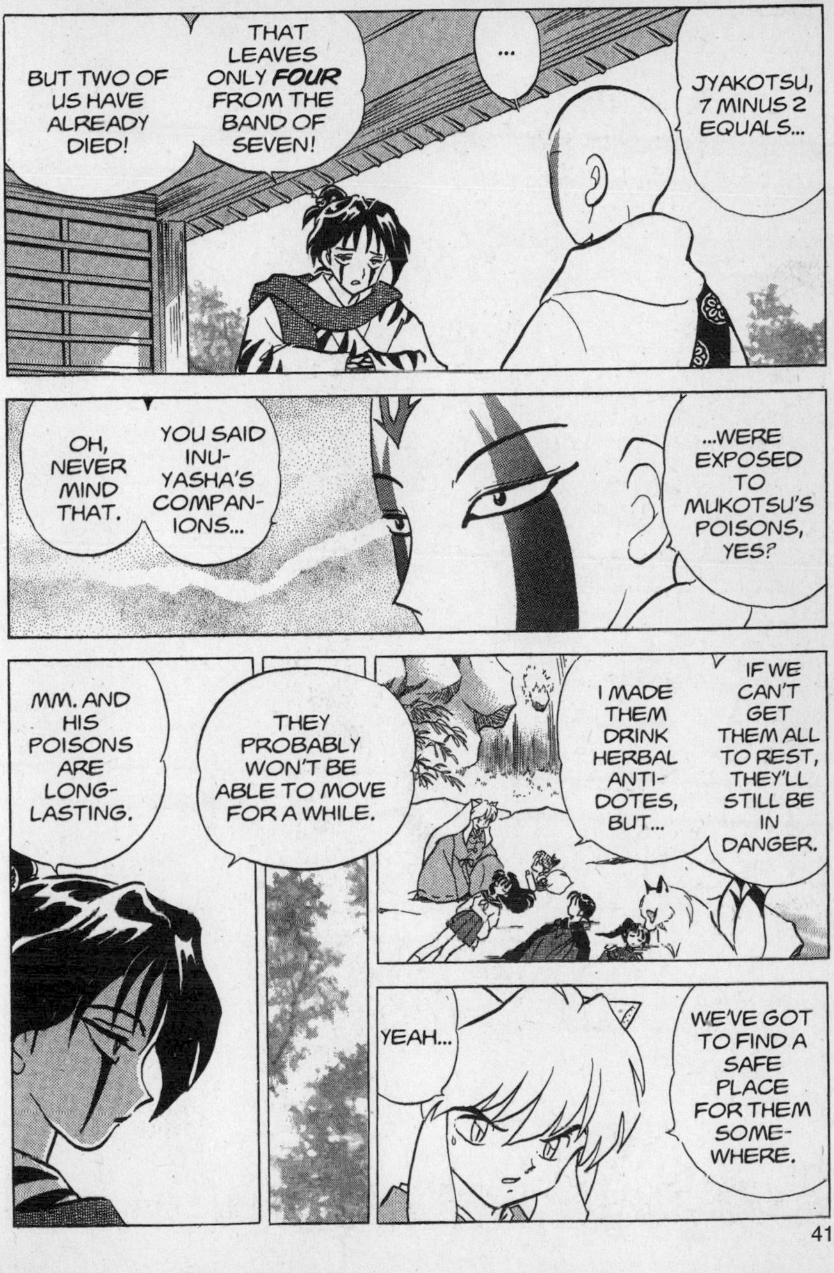
BUT TWO OF US HAVE ALREADY DIED!
THAT LEAVES ONLY **FOUR** FROM THE BAND OF SEVEN!
...
JYAKOTSU, 7 MINUS 2 EQUALS...
OH, NEVER MIND THAT.
YOU SAID INU-YASHA'S COMPANIONS...
...WERE EXPOSED TO MUKOTSU'S POISONS, YES?
MM. AND HIS POISONS ARE LONG-LASTING.
THEY PROBABLY WON'T BE ABLE TO MOVE FOR A WHILE.
I MADE THEM DRINK HERBAL ANTI-DOTES, BUT...
IF WE CAN'T GET THEM ALL TO REST, THEY'LL STILL BE IN DANGER.
YEAH...
WE'VE GOT TO FIND A SAFE PLACE FOR THEM SOME-WHERE.

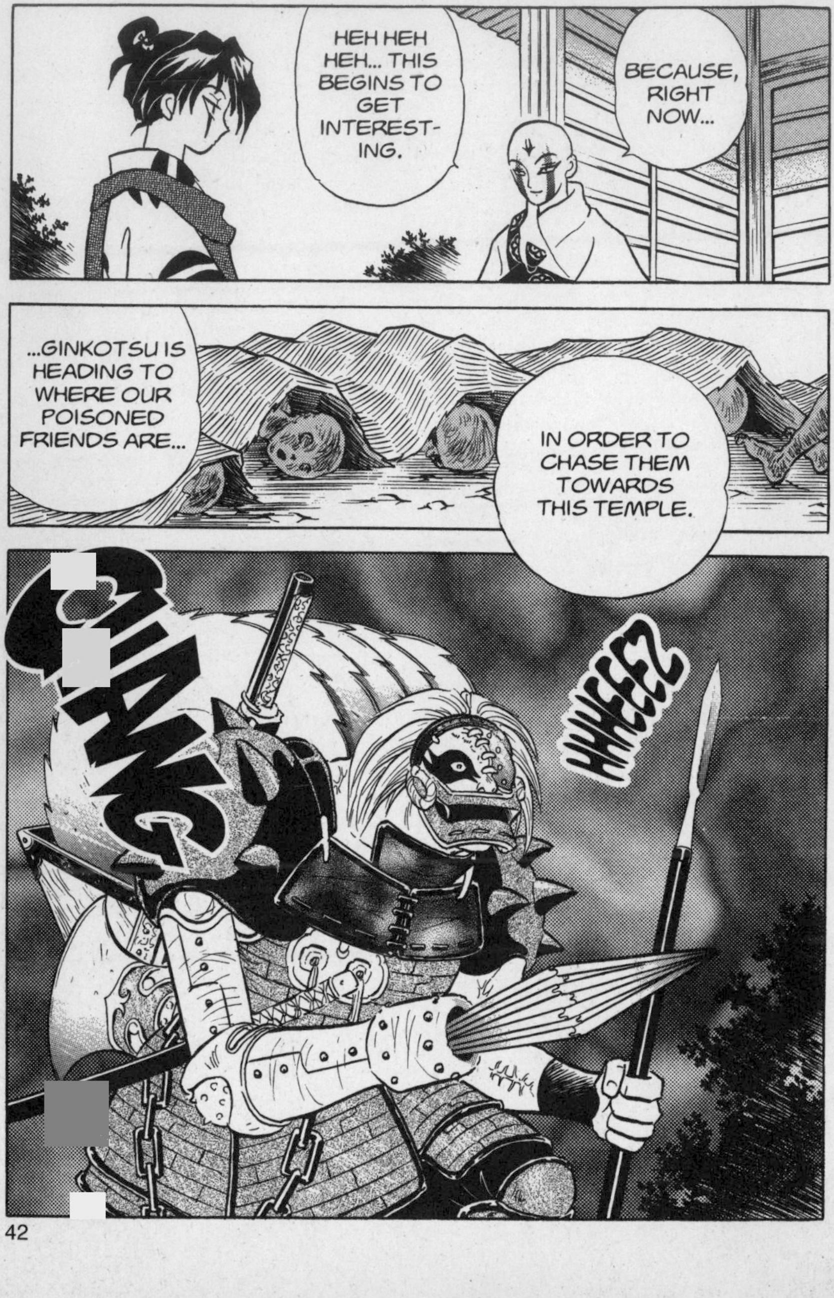
HEH HEH HEH... THIS BEGINS TO GET INTEREST-ING.
BECAUSE, RIGHT NOW...
...GINKOTSU IS HEADING TO WHERE OUR POISONED FRIENDS ARE...
IN ORDER TO CHASE THEM TOWARDS THIS TEMPLE.
CHANG
HHHEEEZ

SCROLL THREE

# GINKOTSU

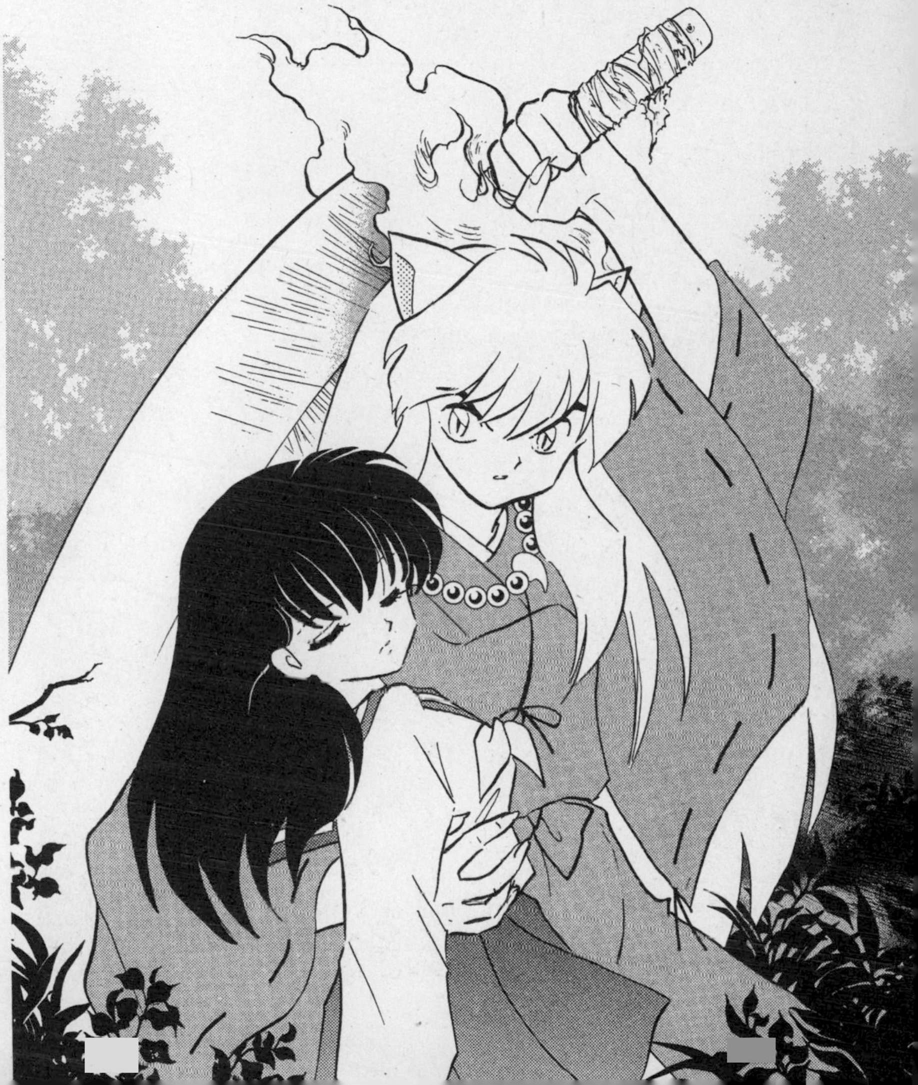

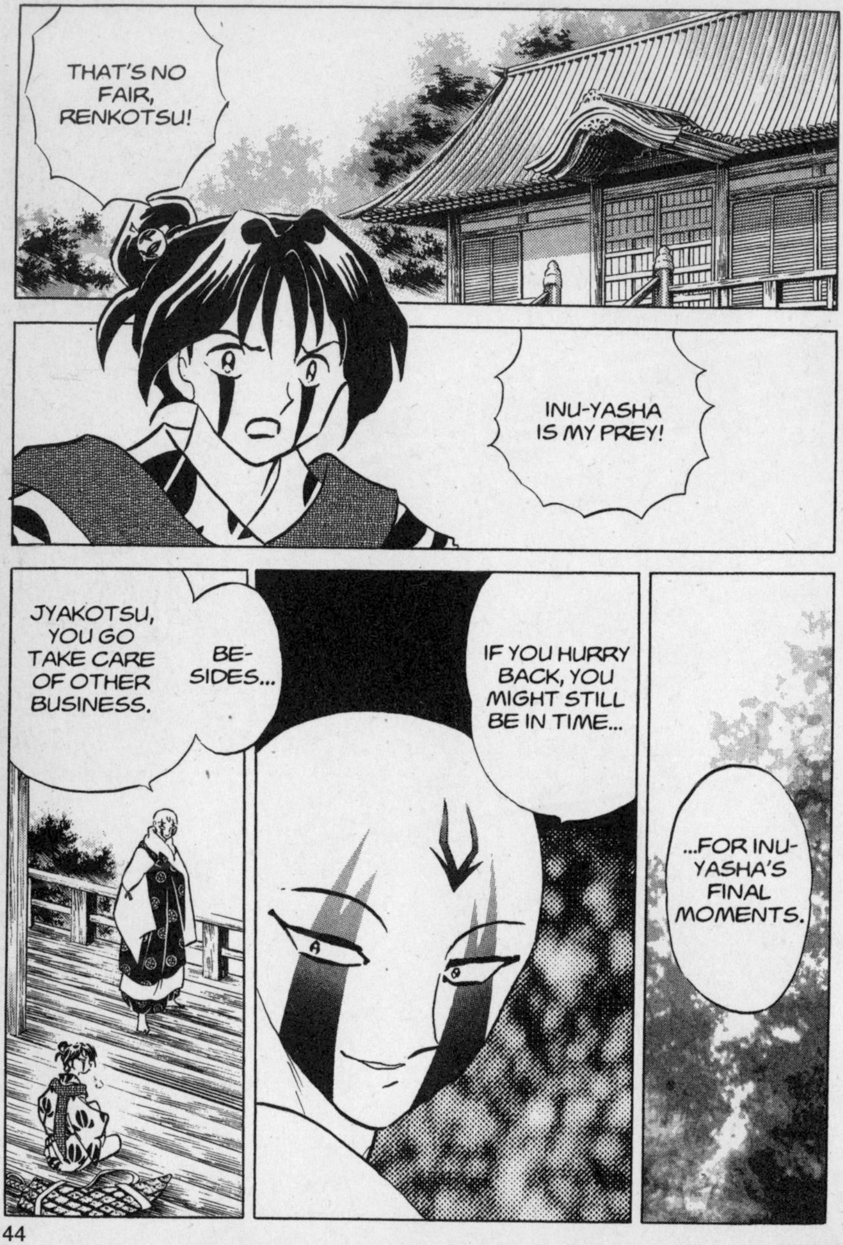
THAT'S NO FAIR, RENKOTSU!
INU-YASHA IS MY PREY!
JYAKOTSU, YOU GO TAKE CARE OF OTHER BUSINESS.
BE-SIDES...
IF YOU HURRY BACK, YOU MIGHT STILL BE IN TIME...
...FOR INU-YASHA'S FINAL MOMENTS.

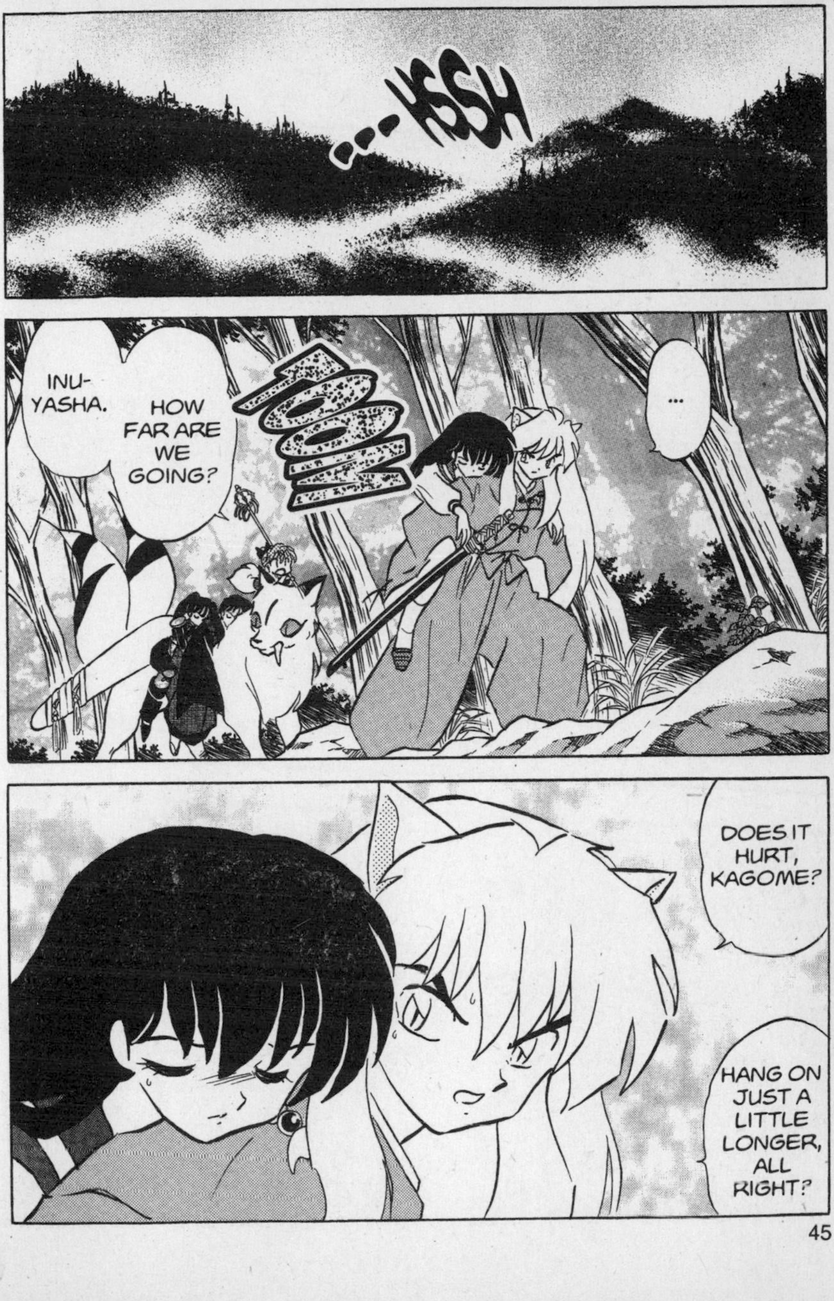

...HSSH
INU-YASHA.
HOW FAR ARE WE GOING?
TOOM
...
DOES IT HURT, KAGOME?
HANG ON JUST A LITTLE LONGER, ALL RIGHT?

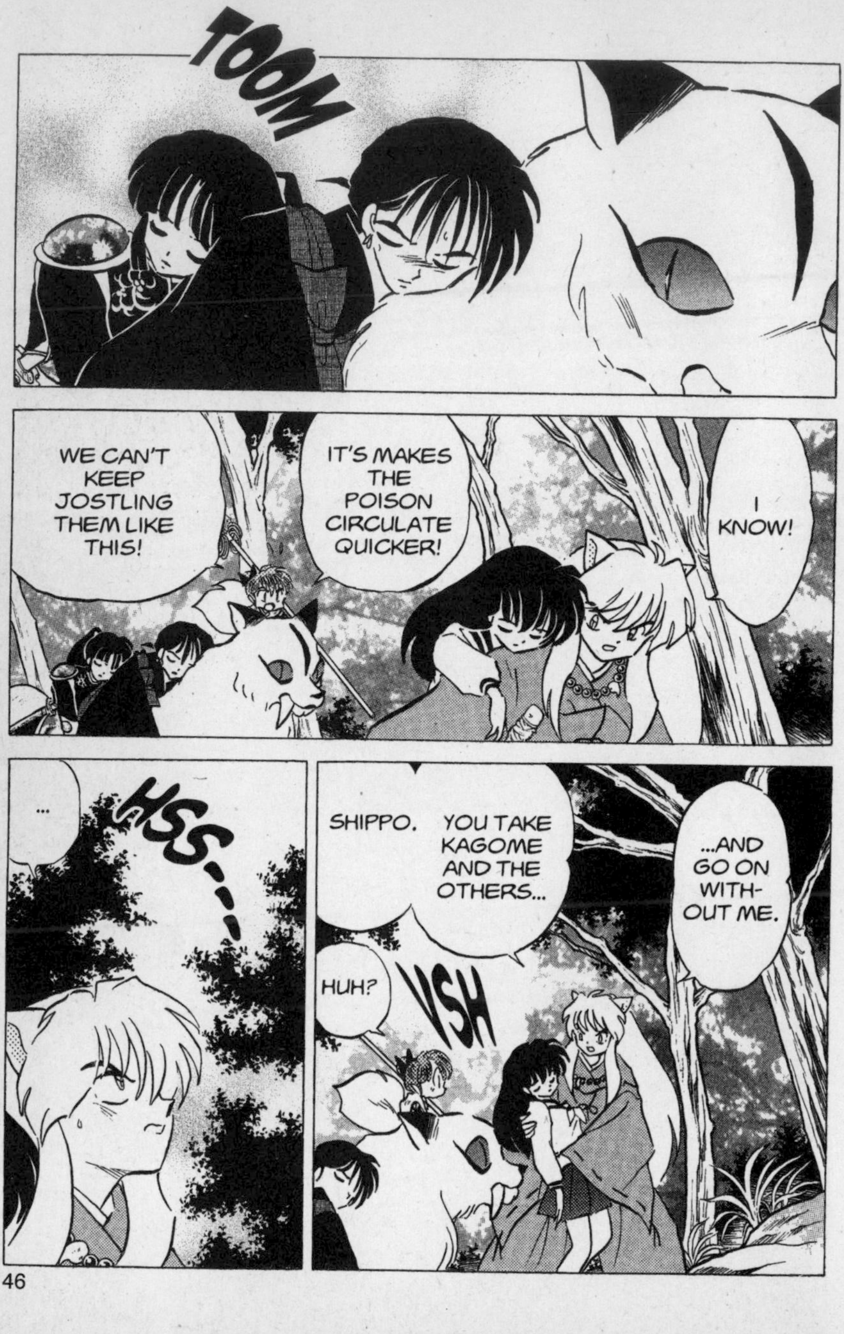
TOOM
WE CAN'T KEEP JOSTLING THEM LIKE THIS!
IT'S MAKES THE POISON CIRCULATE QUICKER!
I KNOW!
...
HSS...
SHIPPO.
YOU TAKE KAGOME AND THE OTHERS...
...AND GO ON WITH-OUT ME.
HUH?
VSH

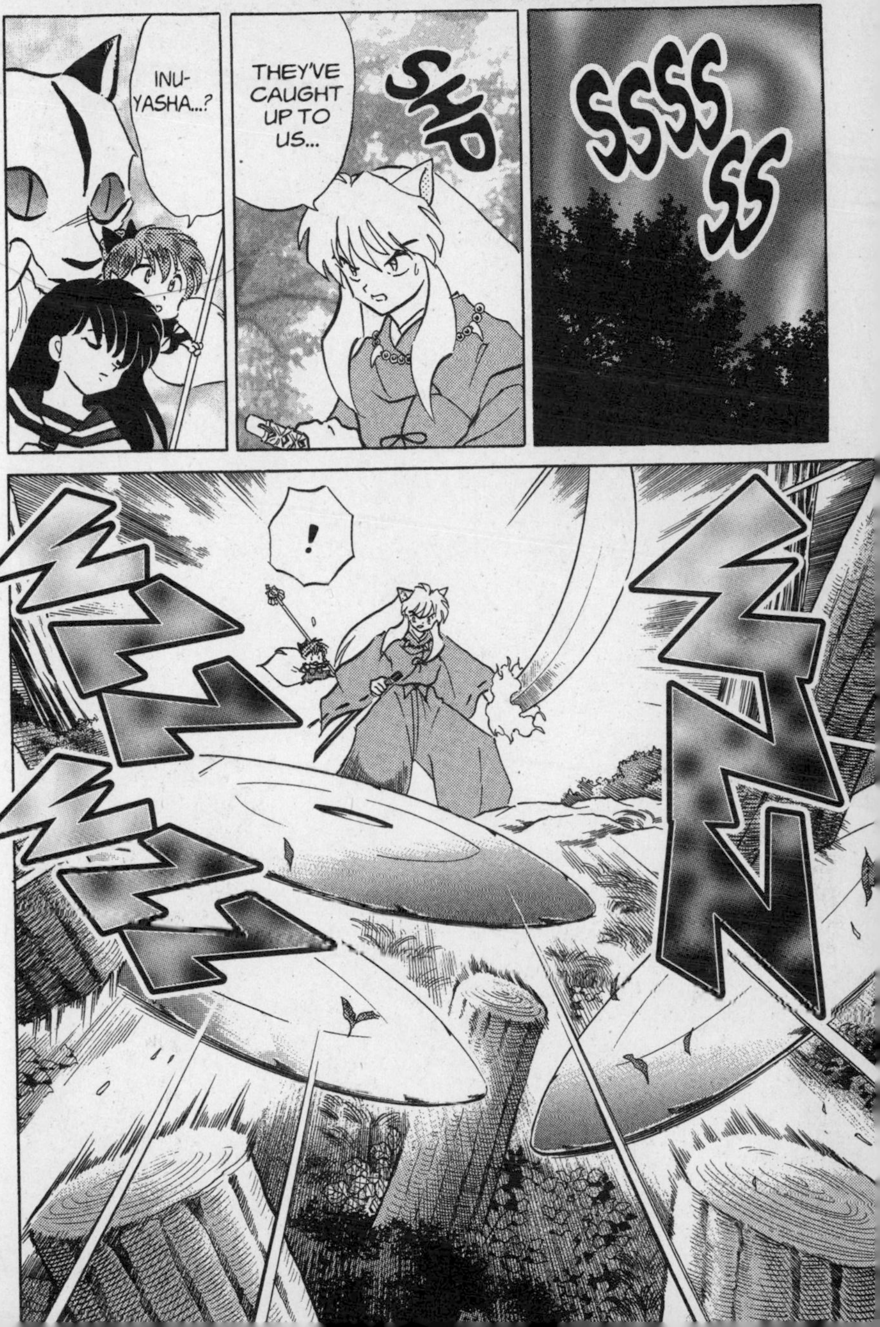
INU-YASHA...?
THEY'VE CAUGHT UP TO US...
SHP
SSSS SS
!

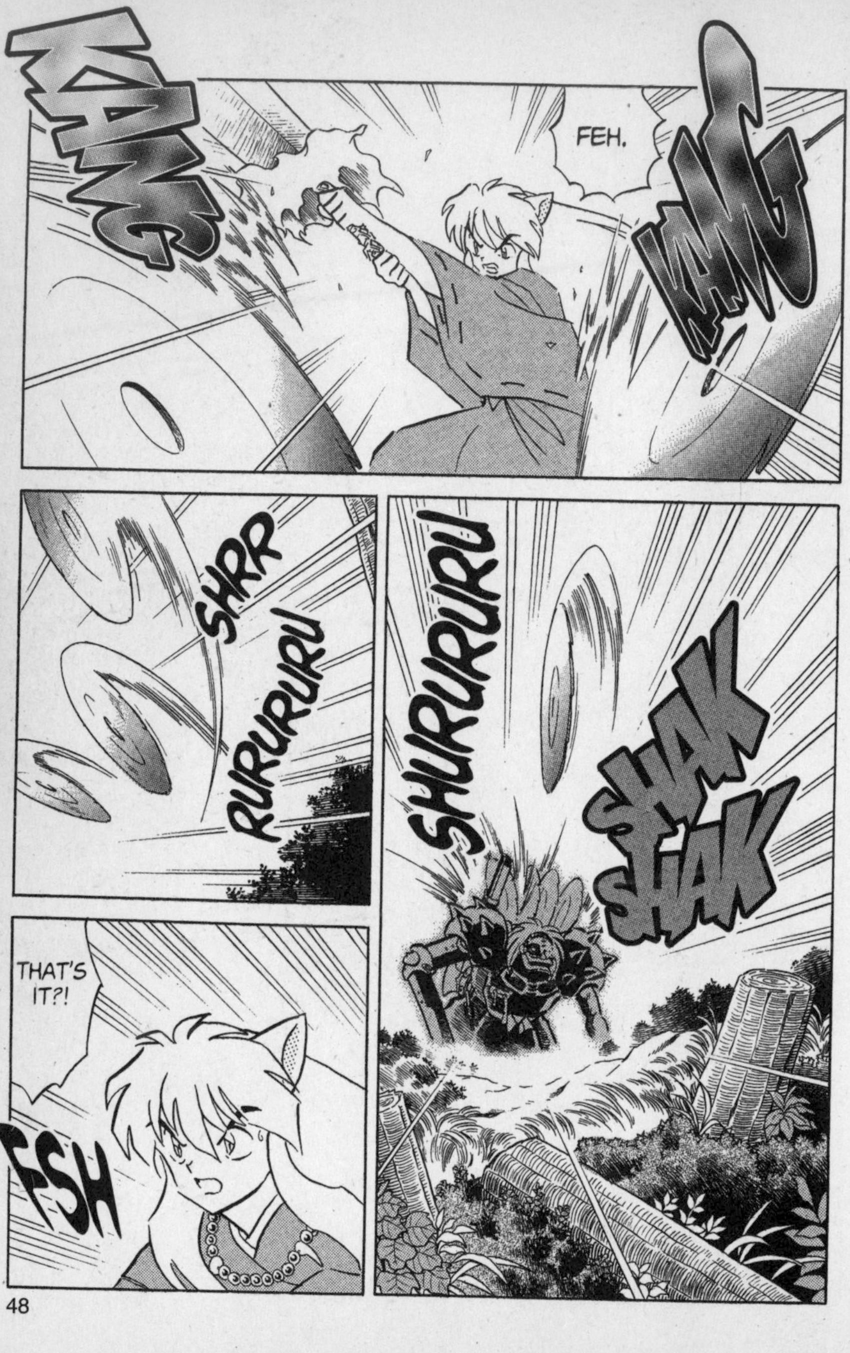
KANG
FEH.
KANG
SHRR RURURURU
SHURURURU
SHAK SHAK
THAT'S IT?!
FSH

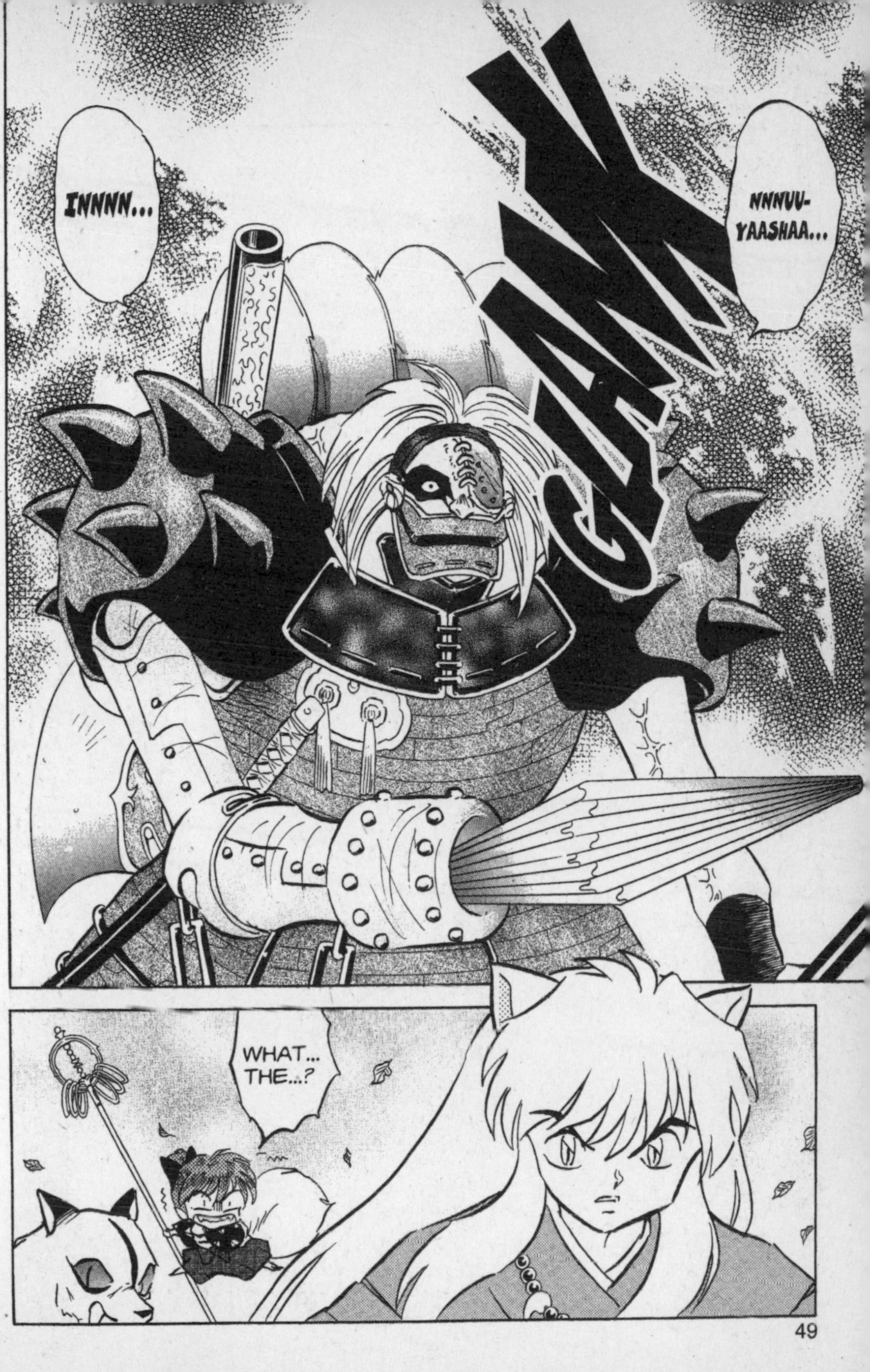
INNNN...
CLANK
NNNUU-YAASHAA...
WHAT... THE...?

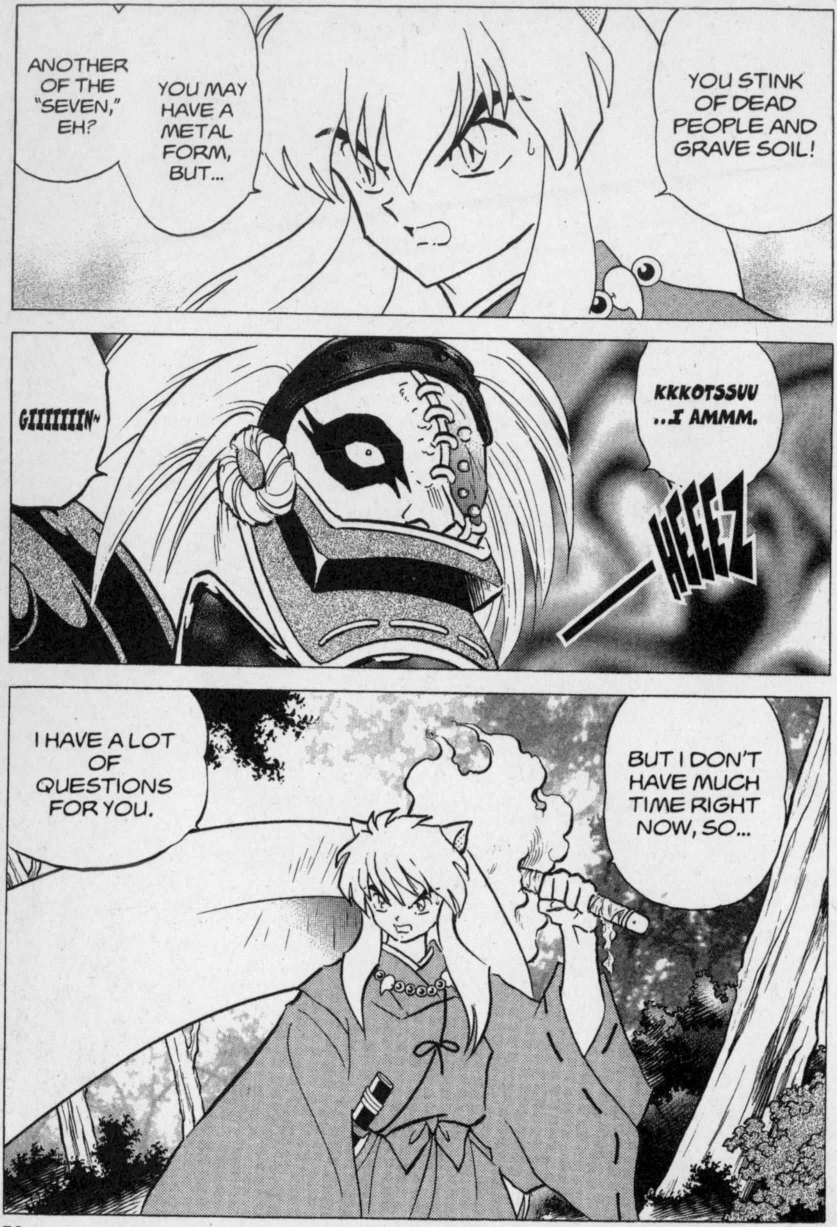

ANOTHER OF THE "SEVEN," EH?
YOU MAY HAVE A METAL FORM, BUT...
YOU STINK OF DEAD PEOPLE AND GRAVE SOIL!
GIIIIIIIN~
KKKOTSSUU ...I AMMM.
HEEEZ
I HAVE A LOT OF QUESTIONS FOR YOU.
BUT I DON'T HAVE MUCH TIME RIGHT NOW, SO...

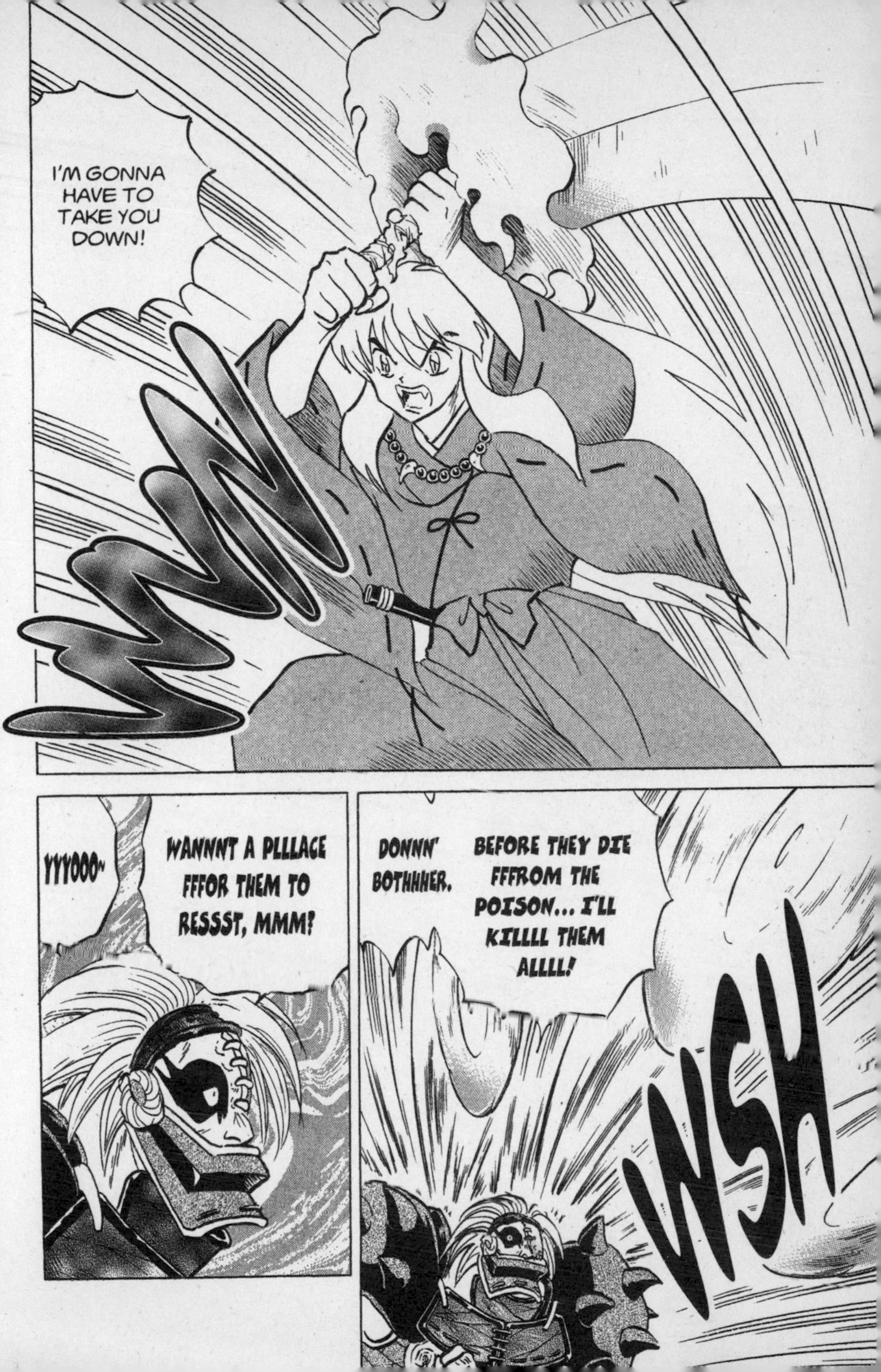
I'M GONNA HAVE TO TAKE YOU DOWN!
YYYOOO~
WANNNT A PLLLACE FFFOR THEM TO RESSST, MMM?
DONNN' BOTHHHER.
BEFORE THEY DIE FFFROM THE POISON... I'LL KILLLL THEM ALLLL!
WSH

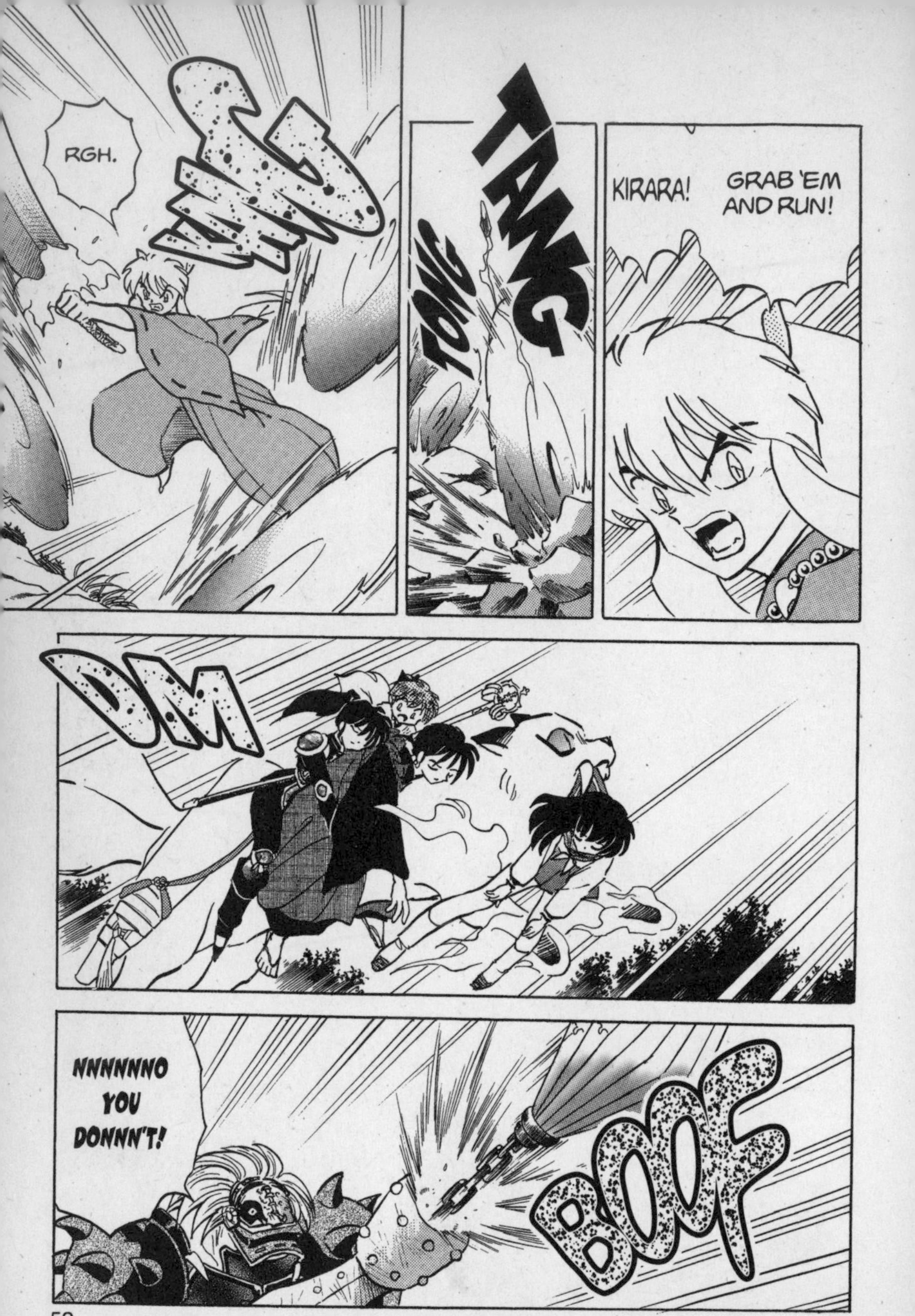
RGH.
TANG
TONG
KIRARA!
GRAB 'EM AND RUN!
NNNNNNO YOU DONNN'T!
BOOF

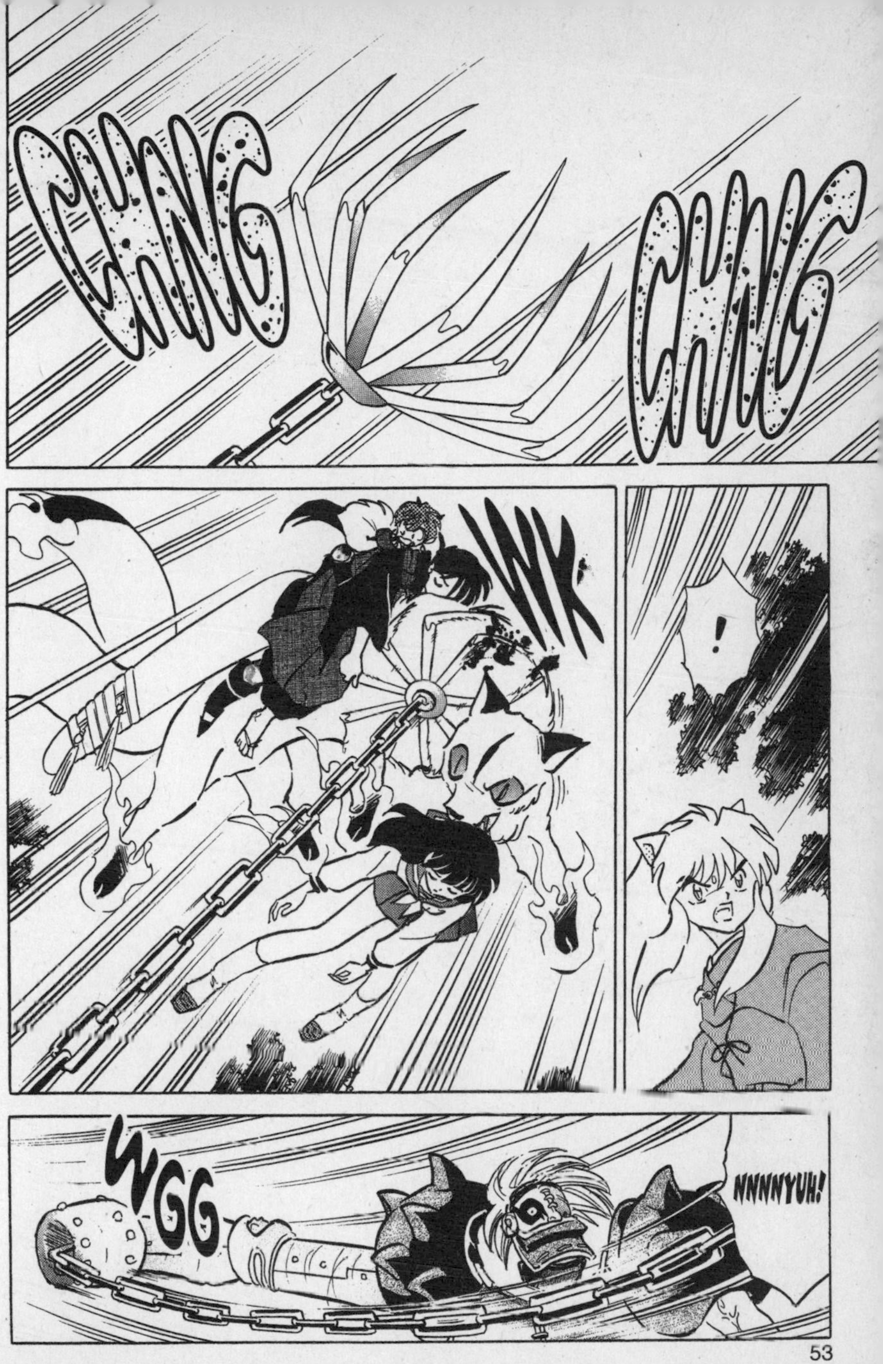
CHING
CHING
WK
!
WGG
NNNNYUH!

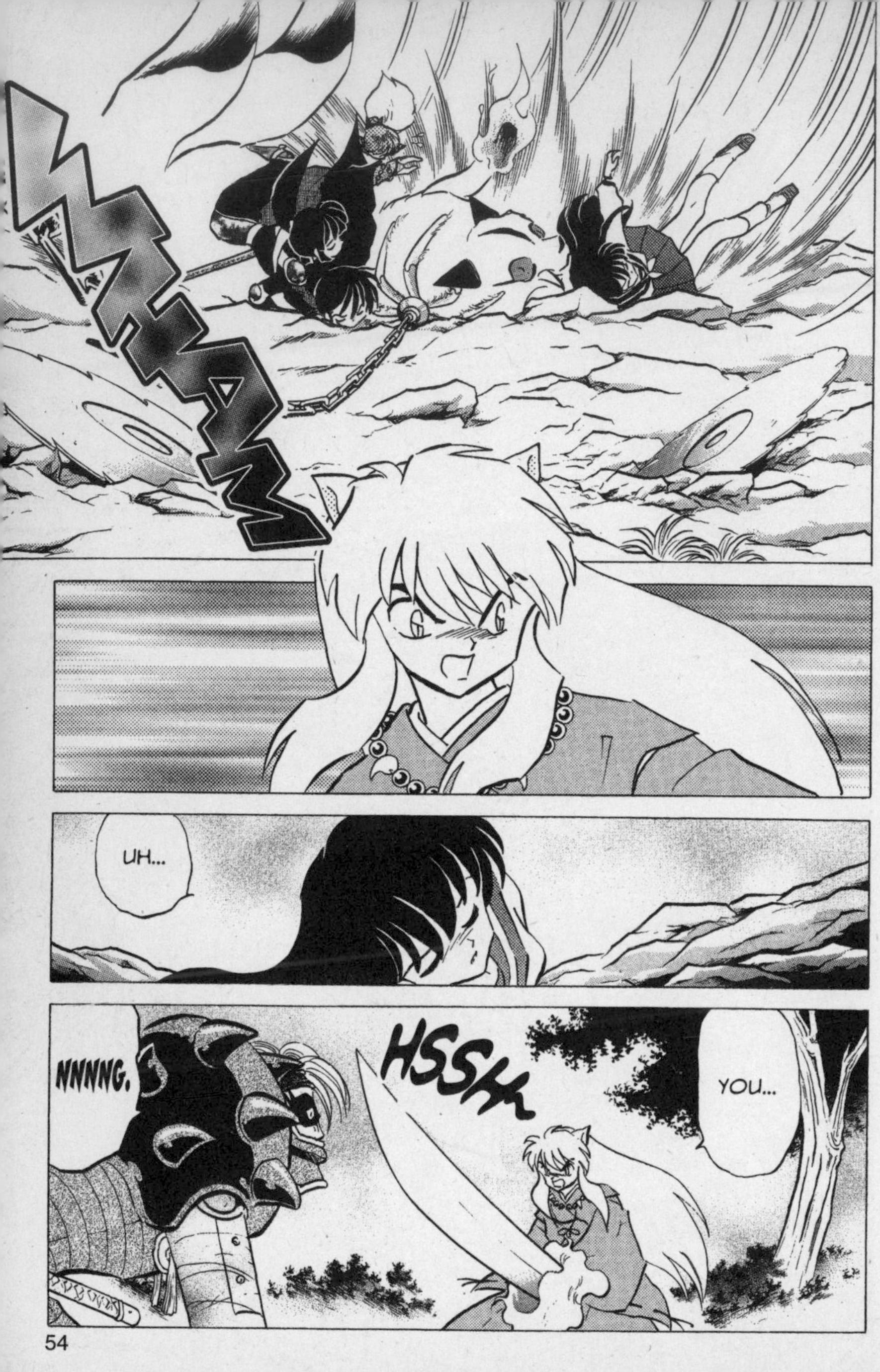
WHAM
UH...
NNNNG.
HSSH
YOU...

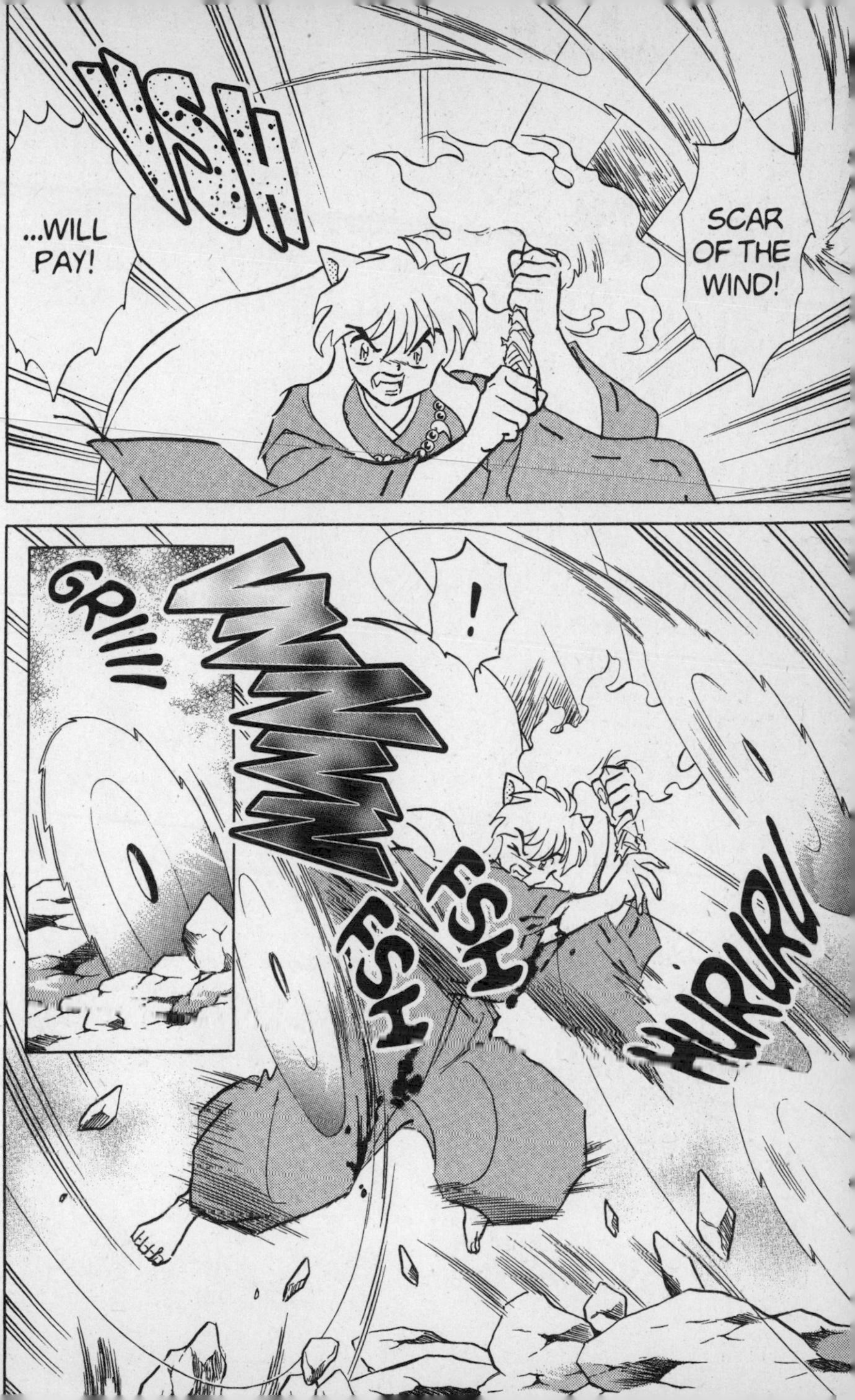
VSH
...WILL PAY!
SCAR OF THE WIND!
GRIIIII
!
VVVVVV
FSH
FSH
HURURU

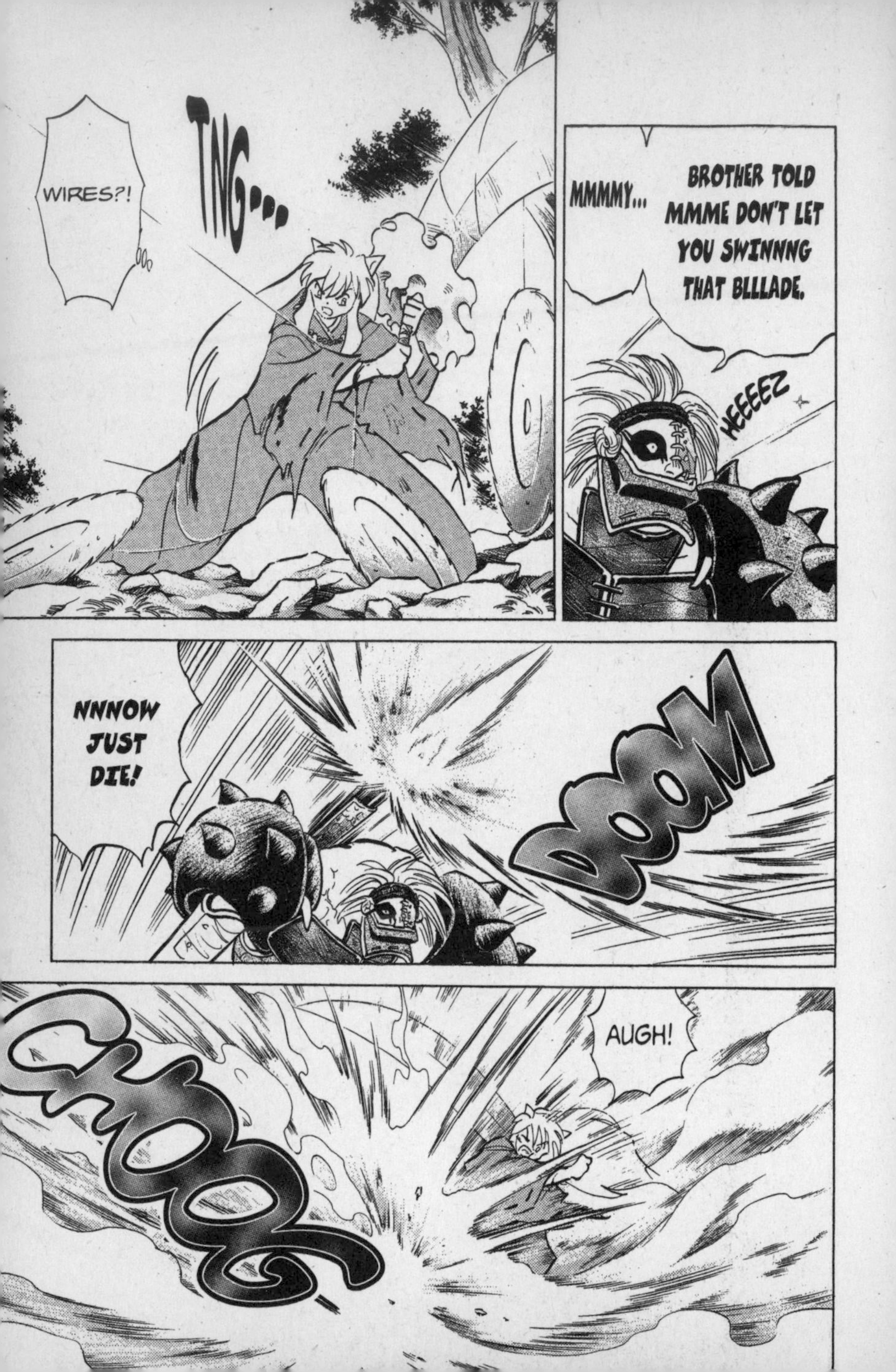
WIRES?!
TNG...
MMMMY...
BROTHER TOLD MMME DON'T LET YOU SWINNNG THAT BLLLADE.
HEEEEZ
NNNOW JUST DIE!
DOOOM
CHOOG
AUGH!

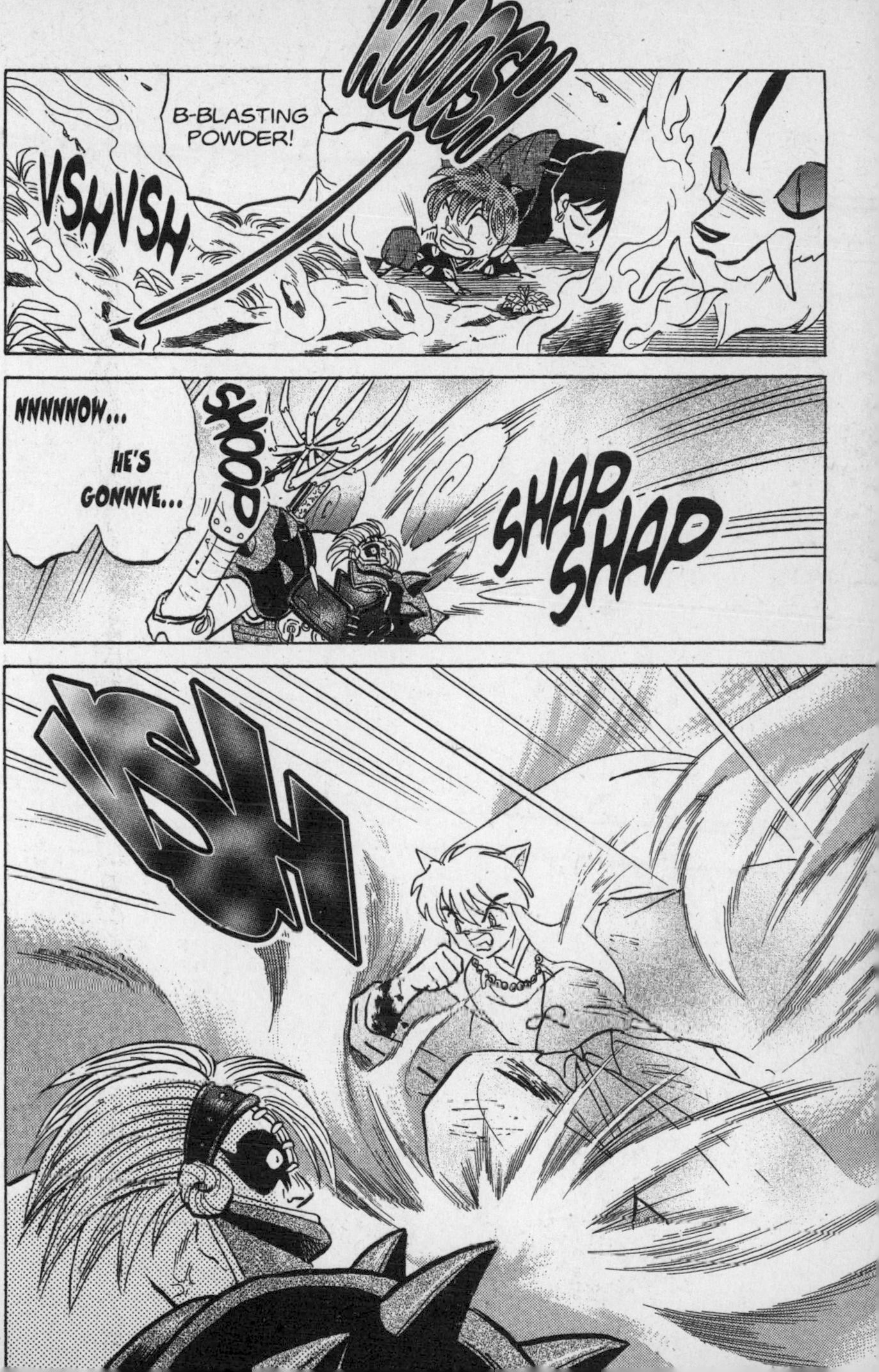
HOOOSH
B-BLASTING POWDER!
VSHVSH
NNNNNOW...
HE'S GONNNE...
SHOOP
SHAP SHAP

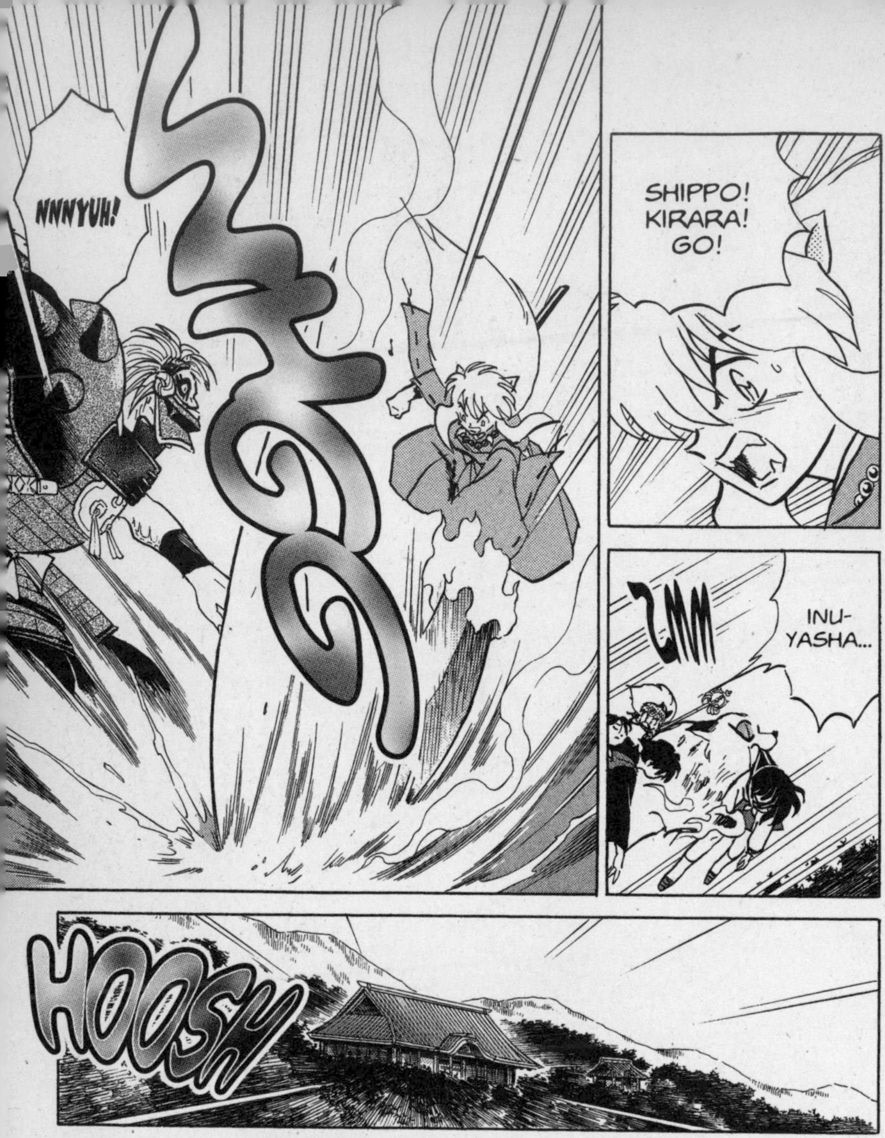
NNNYUH!
SHIPPO! KIRARA! GO!
UMM
INU-YASHA...
HOOSH
A TEMPLE—!
KIRARA— HEAD OVER THERE!

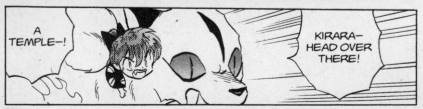

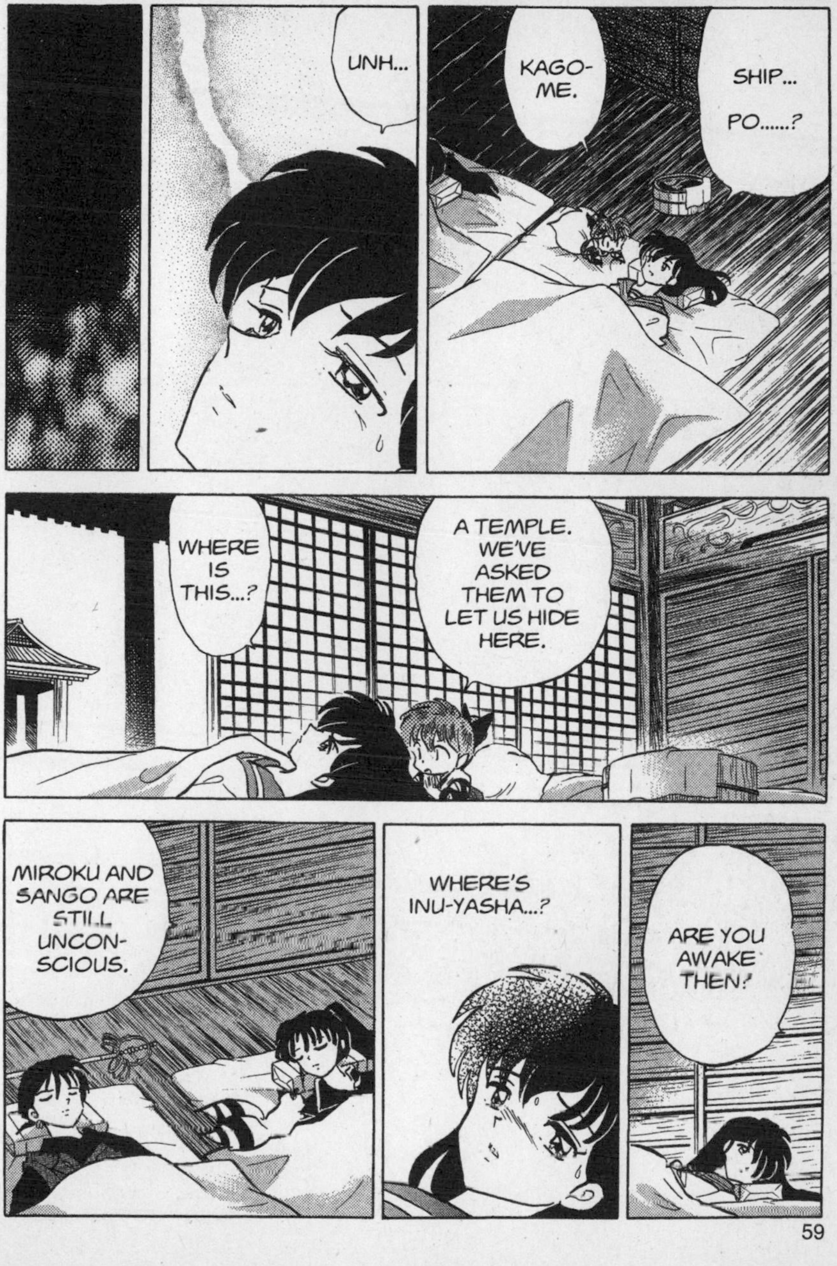
UNH...
KAGO-ME.
SHIP... PO......?
WHERE IS THIS...?
A TEMPLE. WE'VE ASKED THEM TO LET US HIDE HERE.
MIROKU AND SANGO ARE STILL UNCON-SCIOUS.
WHERE'S INU-YASHA...?
ARE YOU AWAKE THEN?

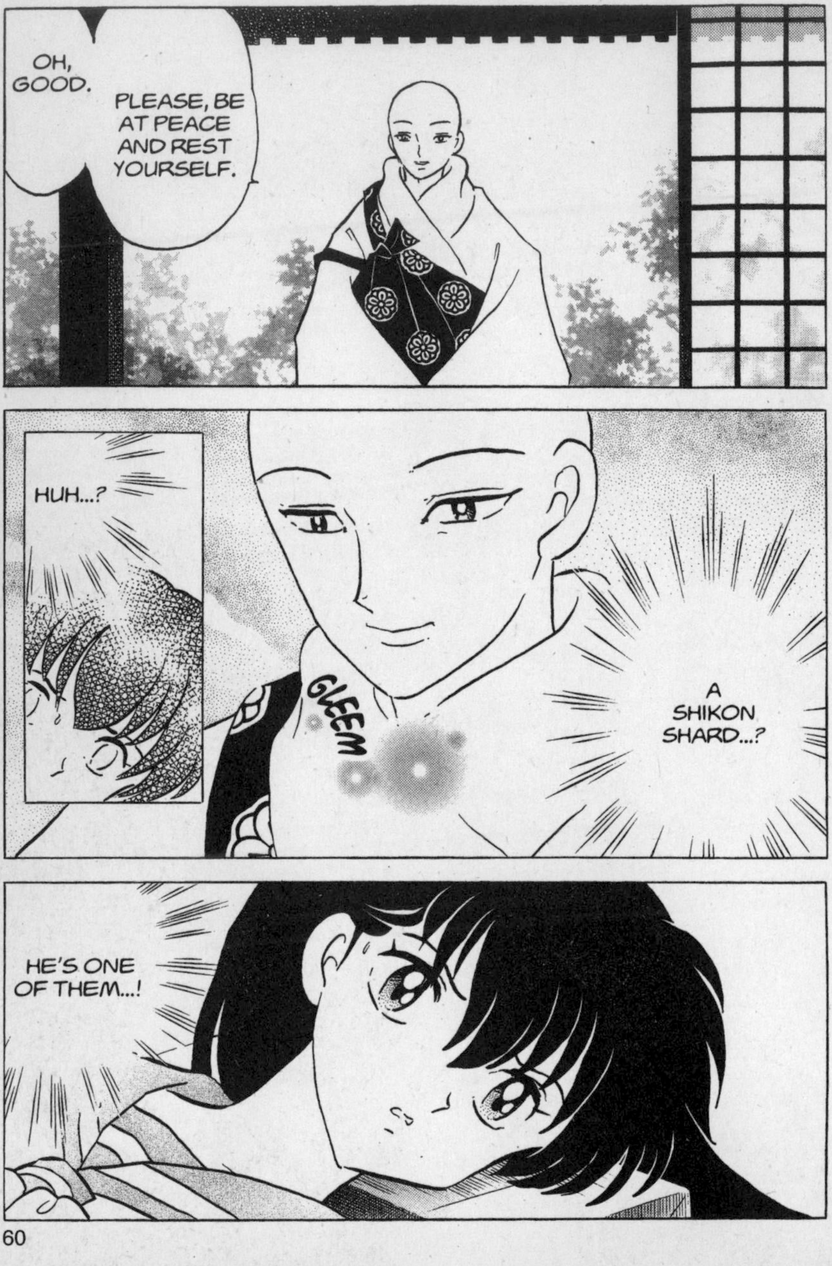
OH, GOOD.
PLEASE, BE AT PEACE AND REST YOURSELF.
HUH...?
GLEEM
A SHIKON SHARD...?
HE'S ONE OF THEM...!

SCROLL FOUR

# RENKOTSU'S TEMPLE

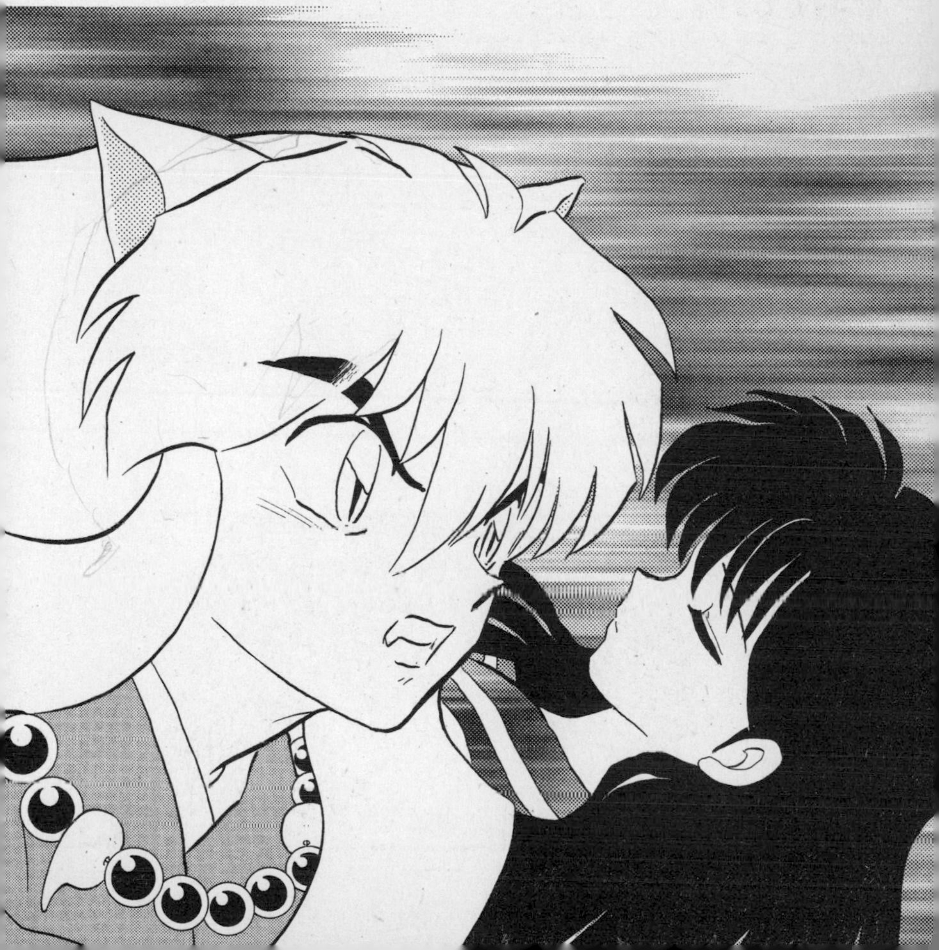

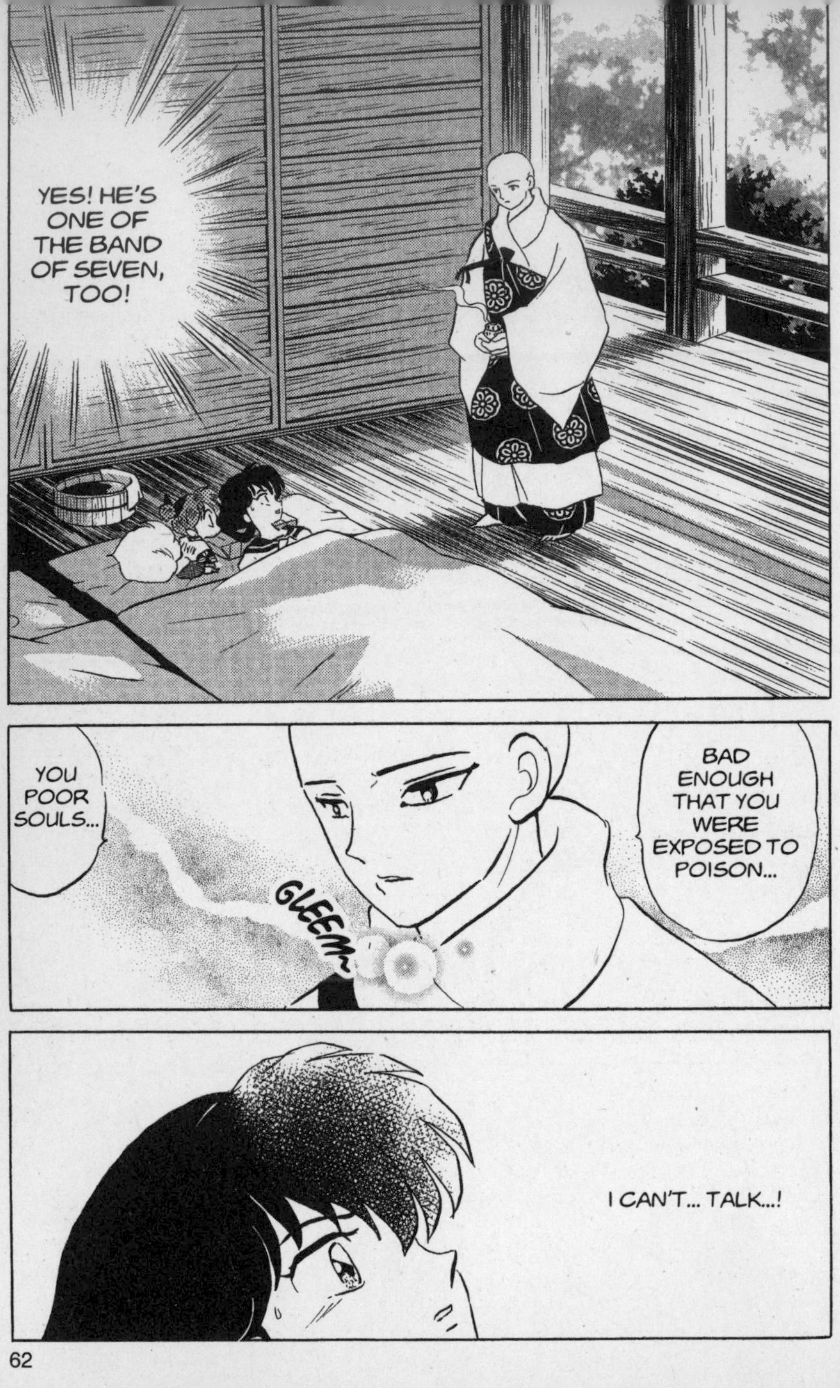
YES! HE'S ONE OF THE BAND OF SEVEN, TOO!
YOU POOR SOULS...
GLEEM~
BAD ENOUGH THAT YOU WERE EXPOSED TO POISON...
I CAN'T... TALK...!

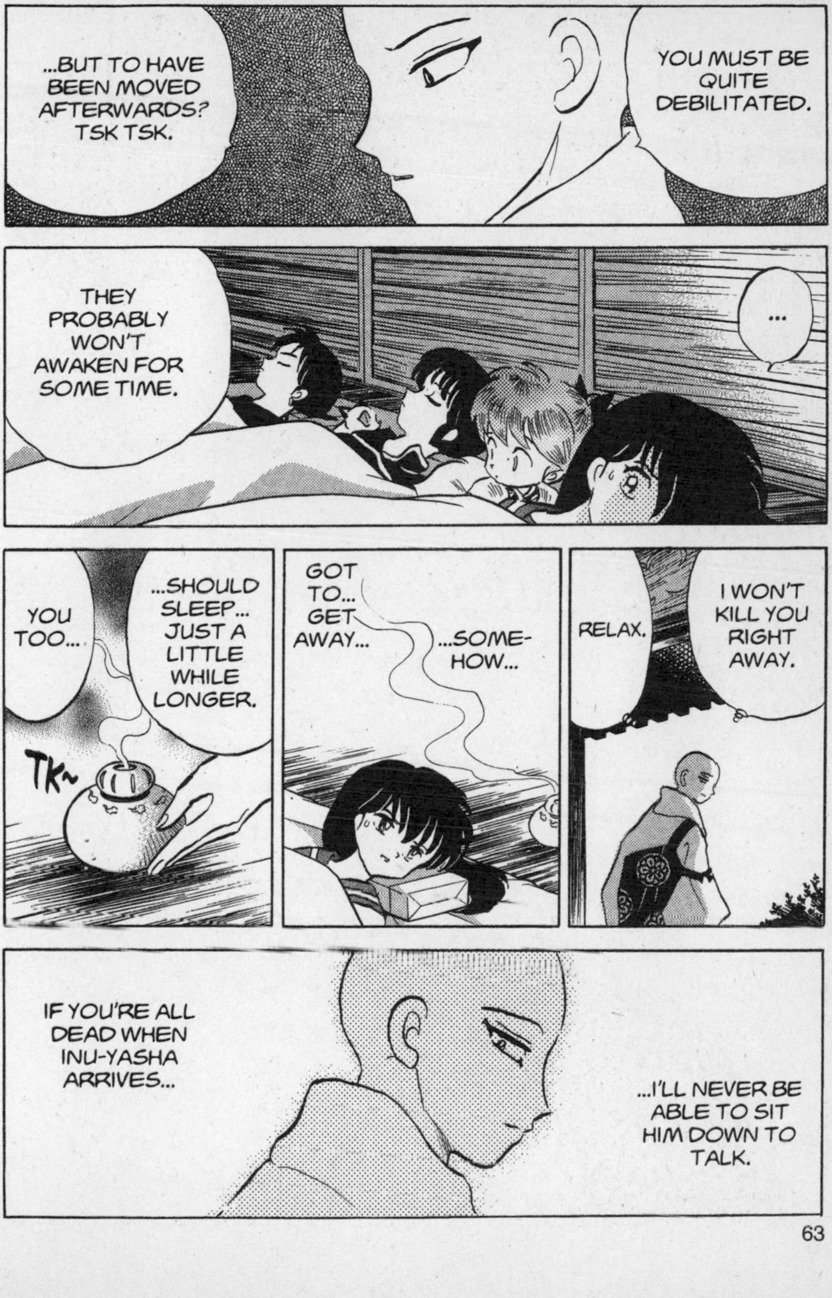
...BUT TO HAVE BEEN MOVED AFTERWARDS? TSK TSK.
YOU MUST BE QUITE DEBILITATED.
THEY PROBABLY WON'T AWAKEN FOR SOME TIME.
...
YOU TOO...
...SHOULD SLEEP... JUST A LITTLE WHILE LONGER.
TK~
GOT TO... GET AWAY...
...SOME-HOW...
RELAX.
I WON'T KILL YOU RIGHT AWAY.
IF YOU'RE ALL DEAD WHEN INU-YASHA ARRIVES...
...I'LL NEVER BE ABLE TO SIT HIM DOWN TO TALK.

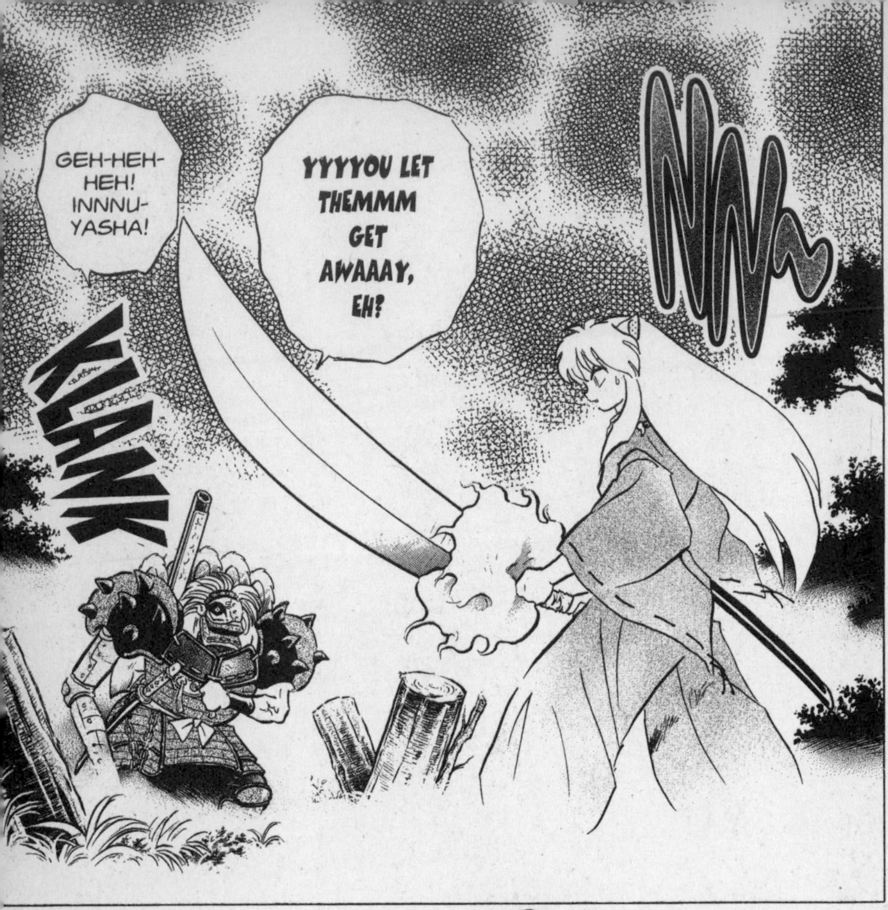
GEH-HEH-HEH! INNNU-YASHA!
YYYYOU LET THEMMM GET AWAAAY, EH?
KLANK
NNN

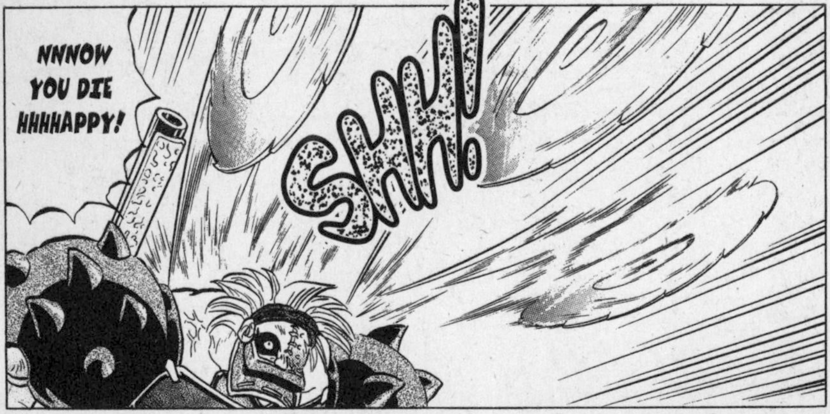
NNNOW YOU DIE HHHHAPPY!
SHH!

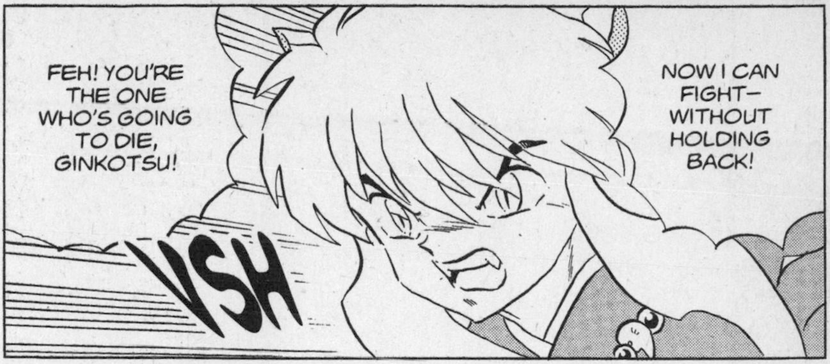
FEH! YOU'RE THE ONE WHO'S GOING TO DIE, GINKOTSU!
NOW I CAN FIGHT—WITHOUT HOLDING BACK!
VSH

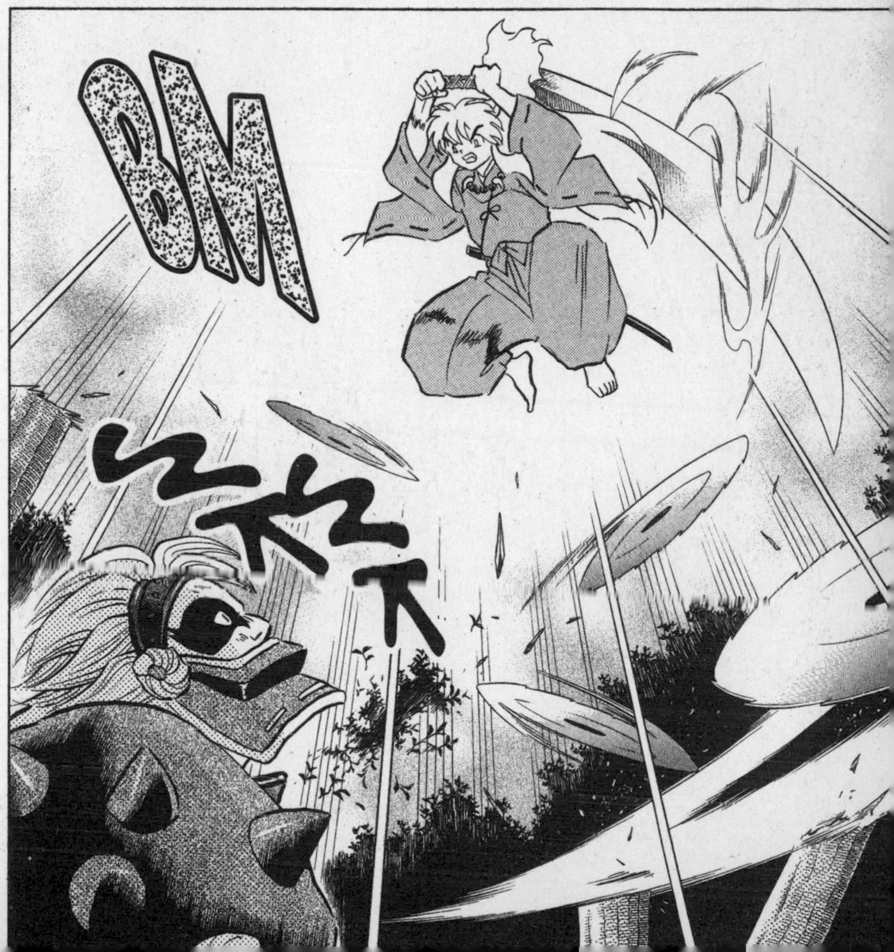
BM
SKKT

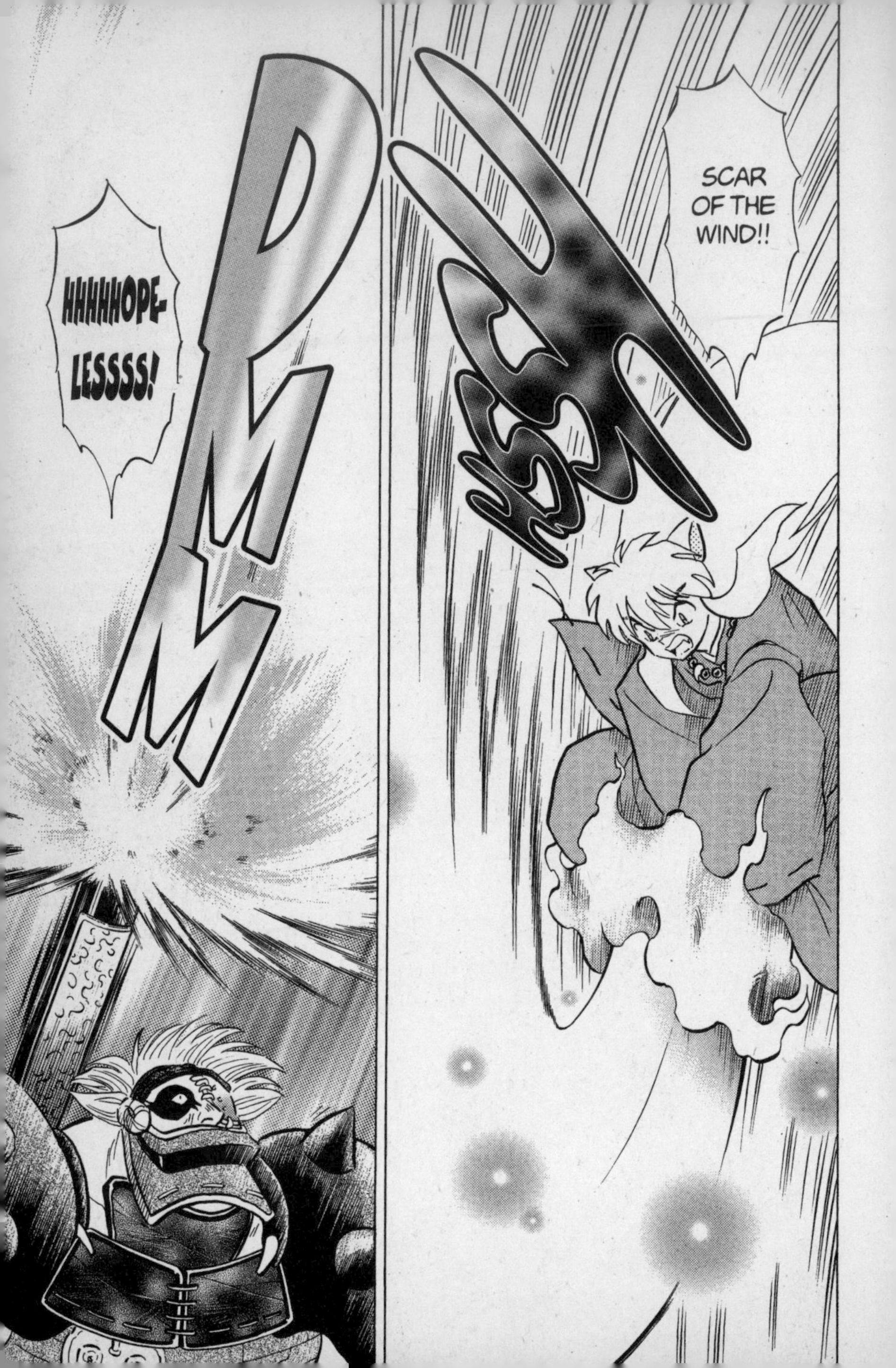
HHHHHOPE-
LESSSS!
DMM
SCAR OF THE WIND!!

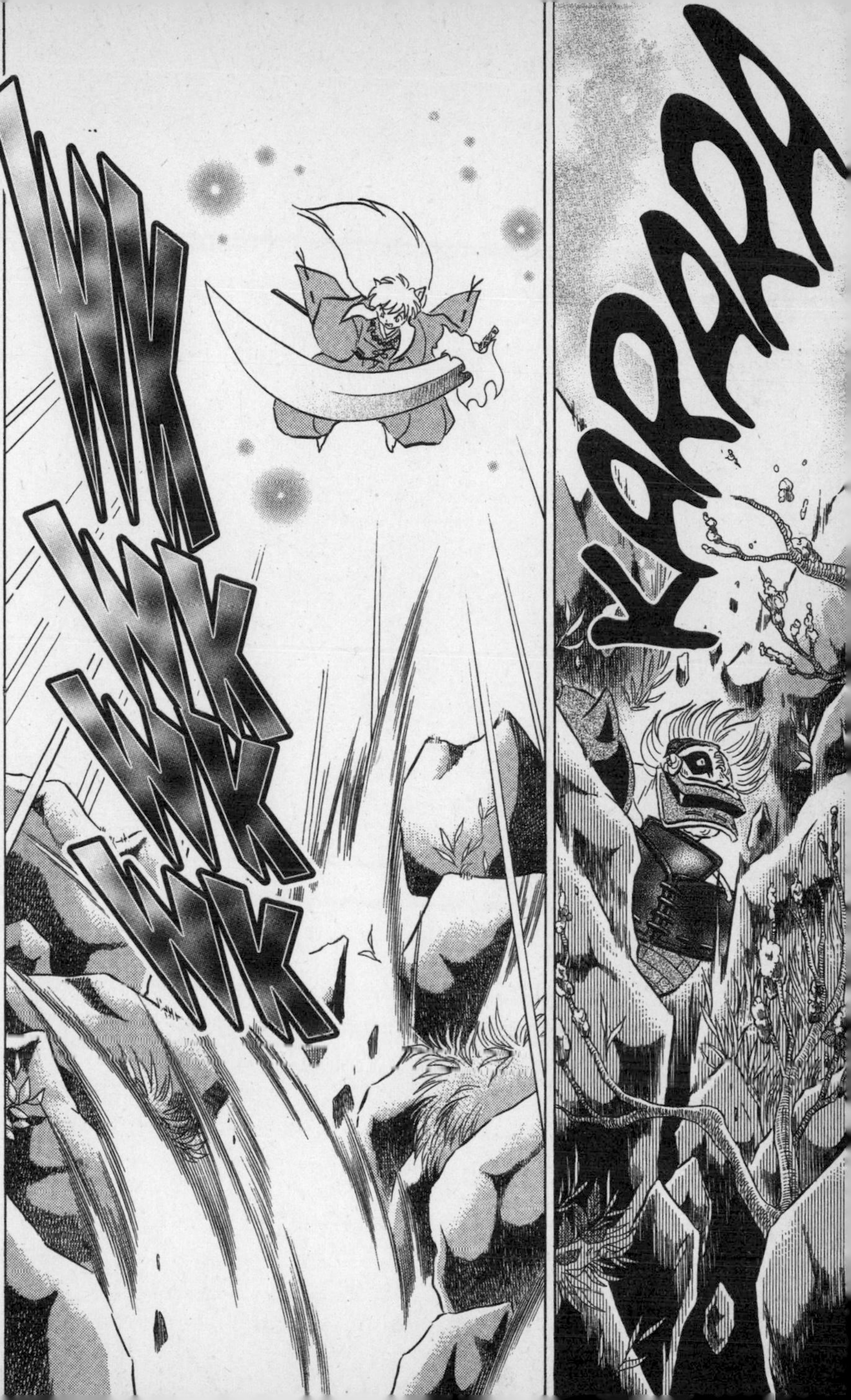
WHK
WHK
WHK
WHK

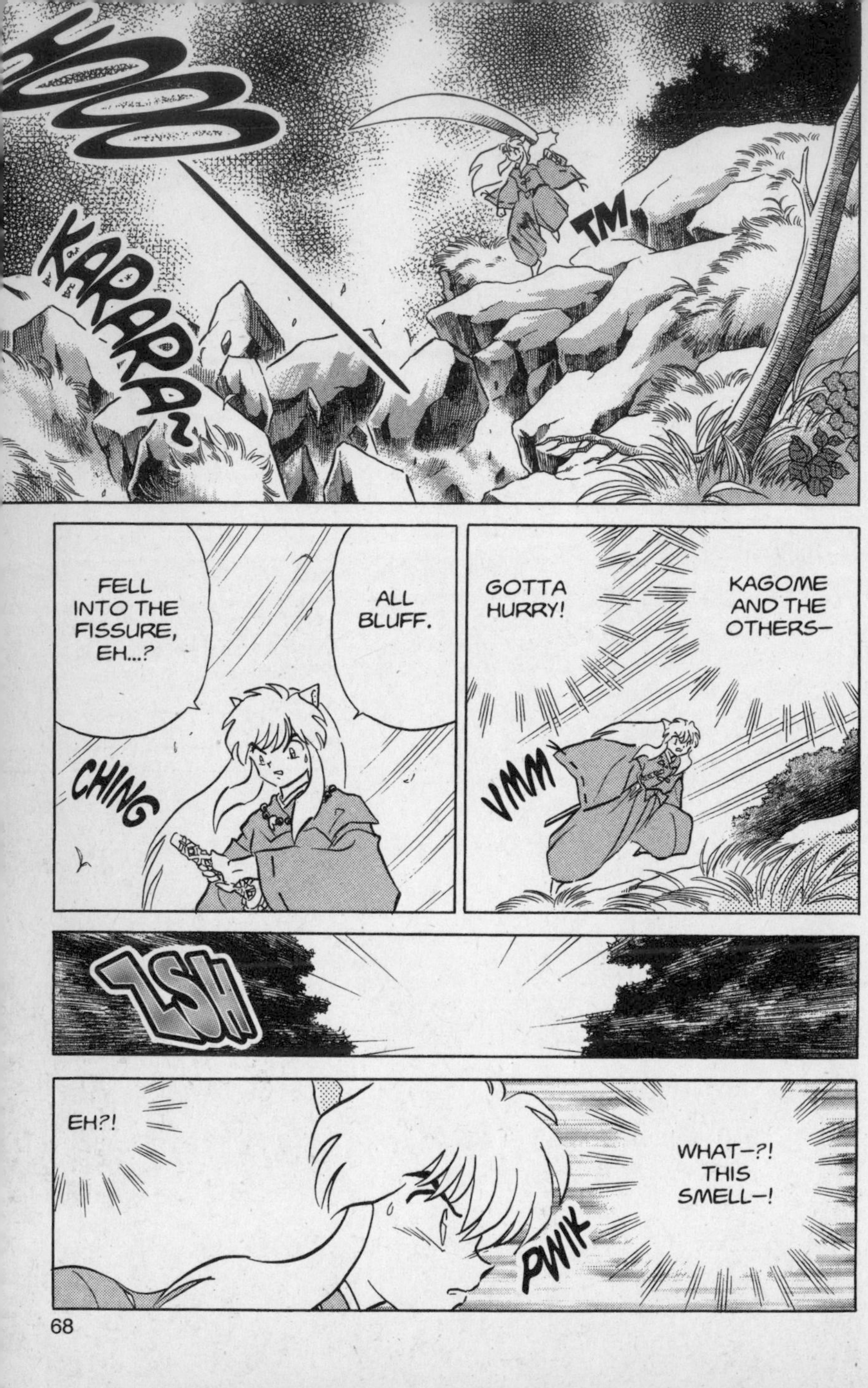
WOOO
KARARA~
TM
FELL INTO THE FISSURE, EH...?
ALL BLUFF.
CHING
GOTTA HURRY!
KAGOME AND THE OTHERS—
VMM
ZSH
EH?!
WHAT—?! THIS SMELL—!
PWIK

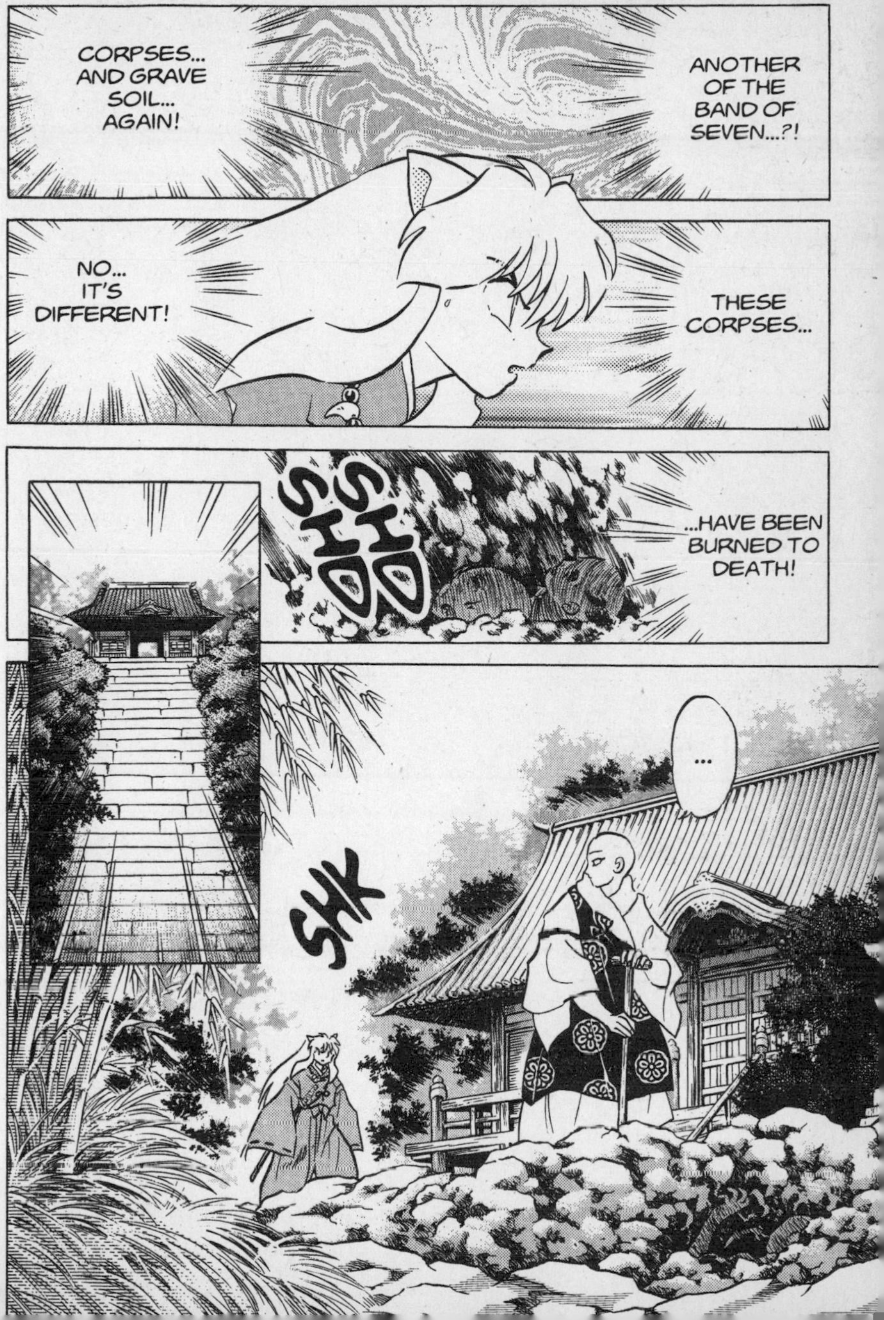
CORPSES... AND GRAVE SOIL... AGAIN!
ANOTHER OF THE BAND OF SEVEN...?!
NO... IT'S DIFFERENT!
THESE CORPSES...
SHOOOO
...HAVE BEEN BURNED TO DEATH!
SHK
...

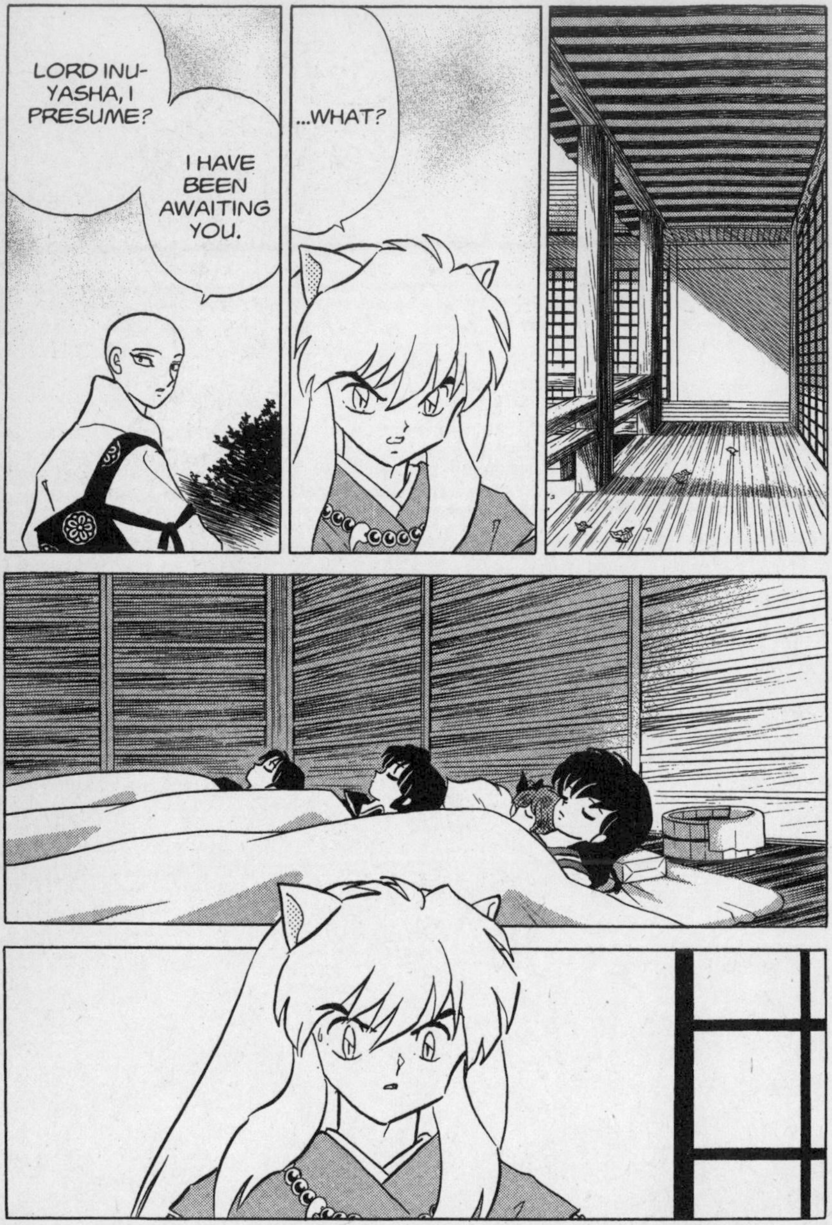
LORD INU-YASHA, I PRESUME?
I HAVE BEEN AWAITING YOU.
...WHAT?

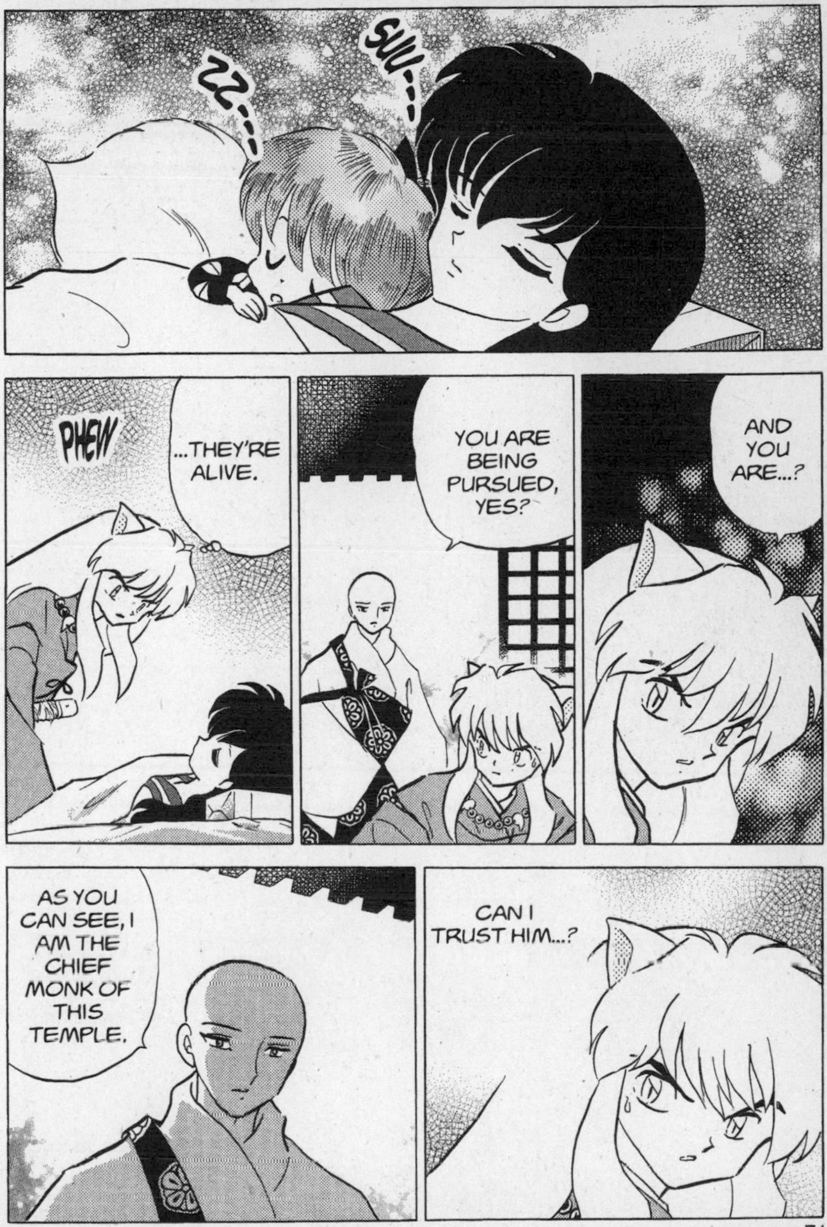
ZZ...
SUU...
PHEW
...THEY'RE ALIVE.
YOU ARE BEING PURSUED, YES?
AND YOU ARE...?
AS YOU CAN SEE, I AM THE CHIEF MONK OF THIS TEMPLE.
CAN I TRUST HIM...?

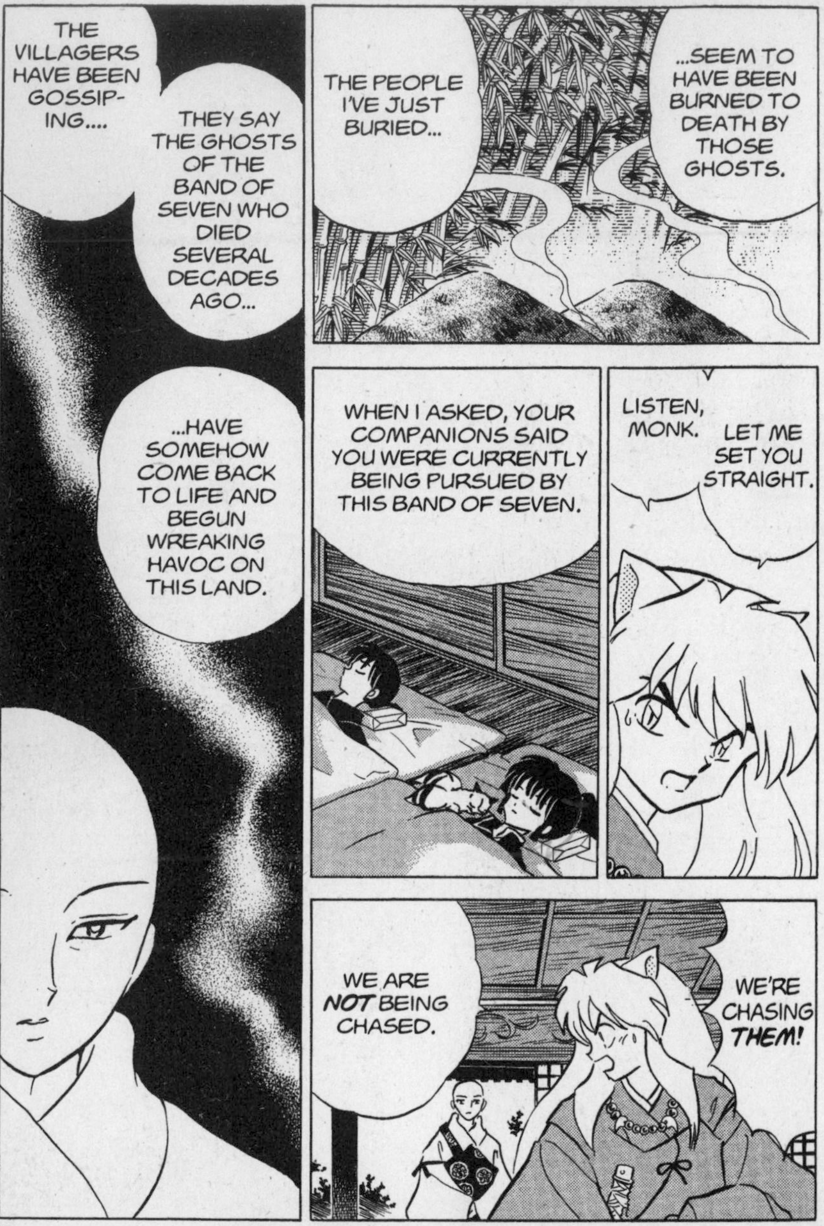
THE VILLAGERS HAVE BEEN GOSSIP-ING....
THEY SAY THE GHOSTS OF THE BAND OF SEVEN WHO DIED SEVERAL DECADES AGO...
...HAVE SOMEHOW COME BACK TO LIFE AND BEGUN WREAKING HAVOC ON THIS LAND.
THE PEOPLE I'VE JUST BURIED...
...SEEM TO HAVE BEEN BURNED TO DEATH BY THOSE GHOSTS.
WHEN I ASKED, YOUR COMPANIONS SAID YOU WERE CURRENTLY BEING PURSUED BY THIS BAND OF SEVEN.
LISTEN, MONK.
LET ME SET YOU STRAIGHT.
WE ARE *NOT* BEING CHASED.
WE'RE CHASING *THEM!*

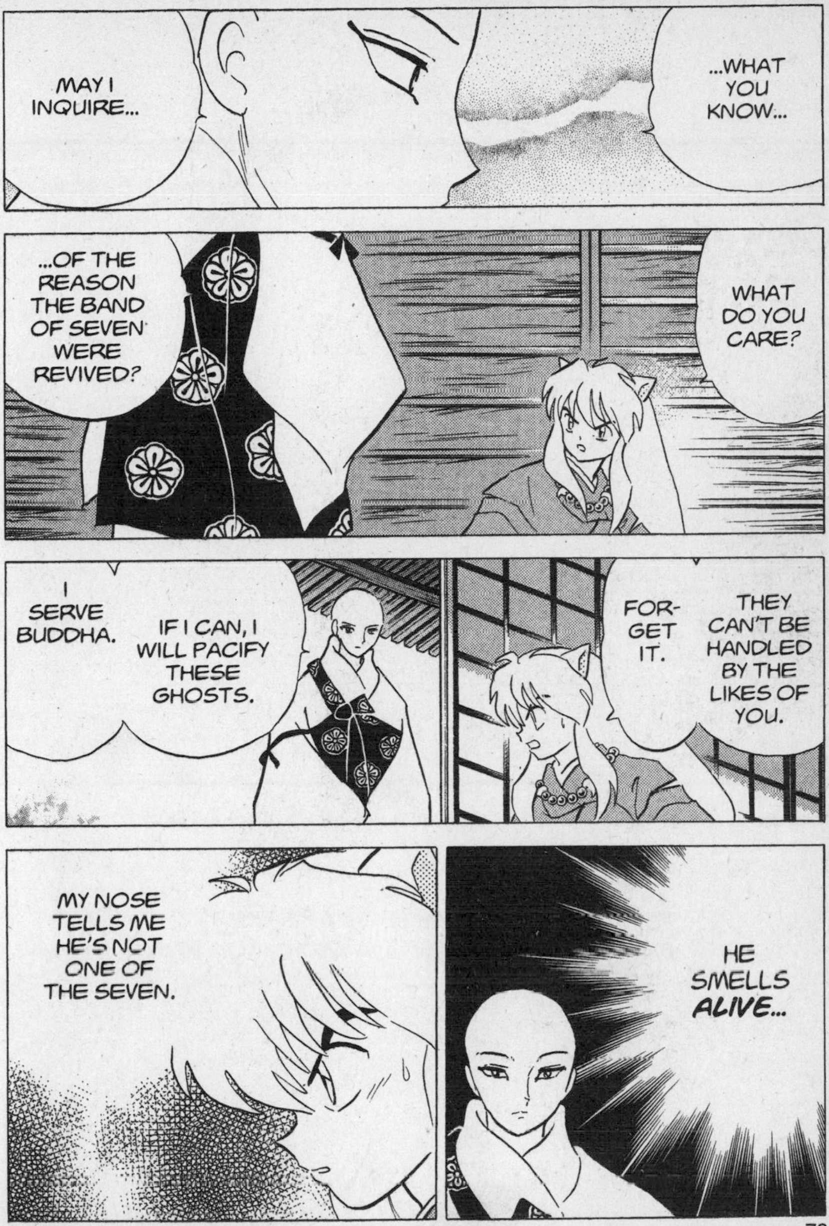
MAY I INQUIRE...
...WHAT YOU KNOW...
...OF THE REASON THE BAND OF SEVEN WERE REVIVED?
WHAT DO YOU CARE?
I SERVE BUDDHA.
IF I CAN, I WILL PACIFY THESE GHOSTS.
FOR-GET IT.
THEY CAN'T BE HANDLED BY THE LIKES OF YOU.
MY NOSE TELLS ME HE'S NOT ONE OF THE SEVEN.
HE SMELLS *ALIVE...*

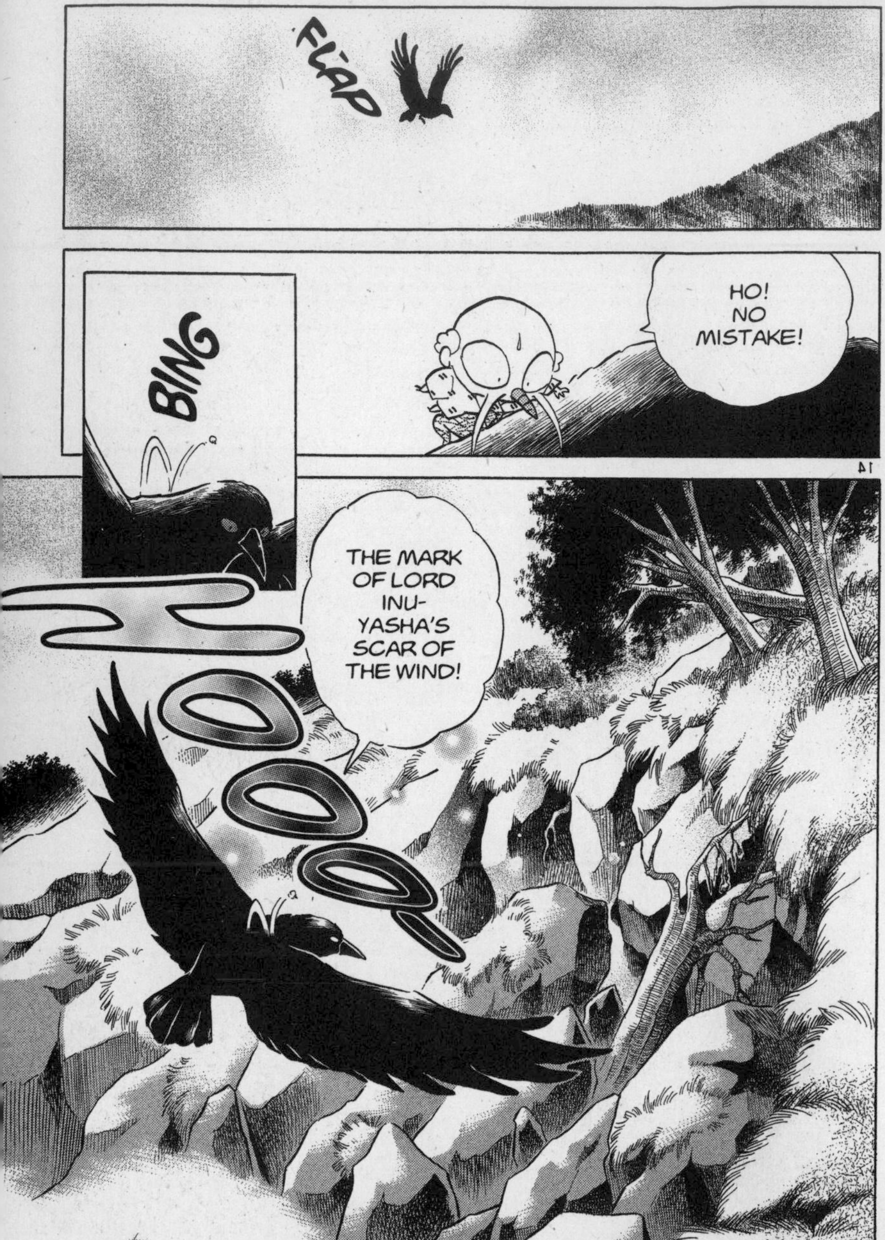

FLAP
BING
HO! NO MISTAKE!
THE MARK OF LORD INU-YASHA'S SCAR OF THE WIND!

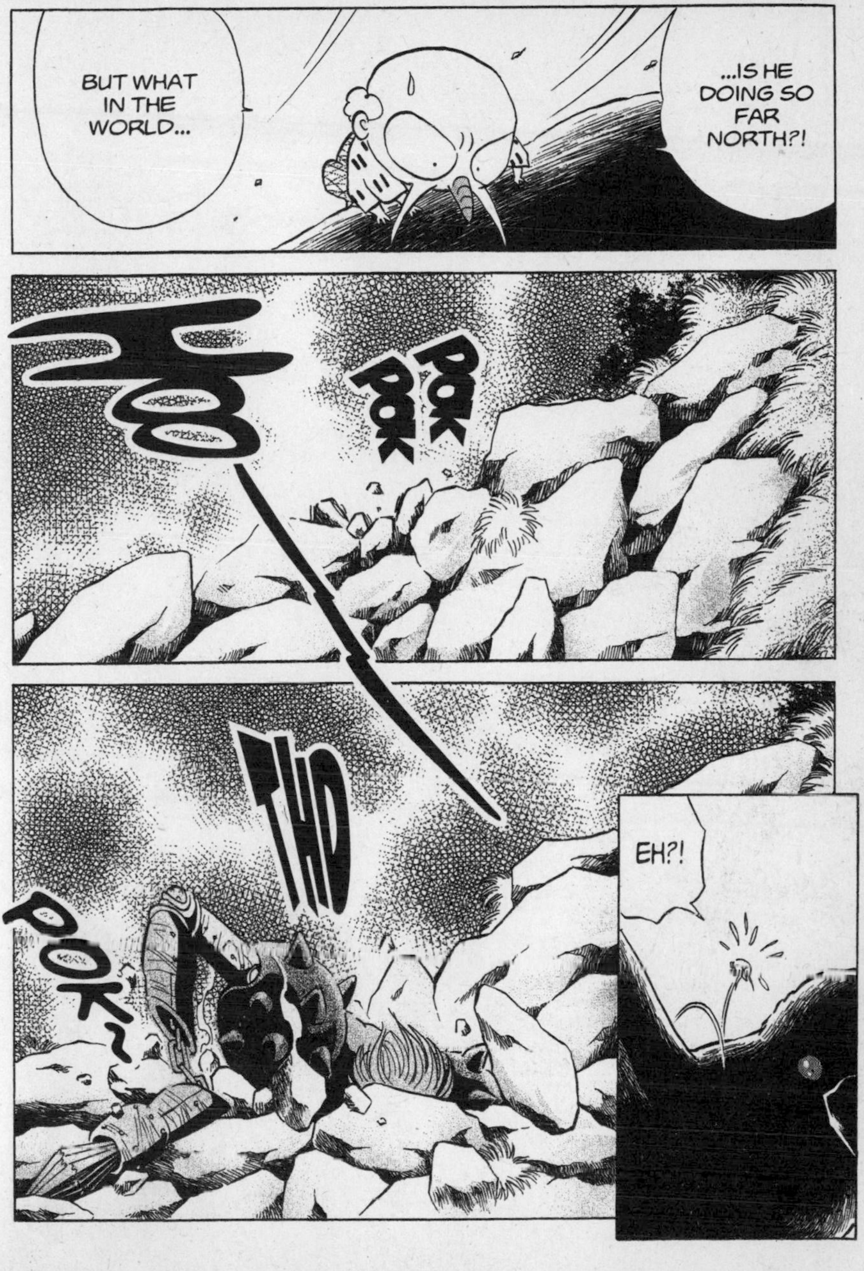

BUT WHAT IN THE WORLD...
...IS HE DOING SO FAR NORTH?!
FOO
POK POK
THD
POK~
EH?!

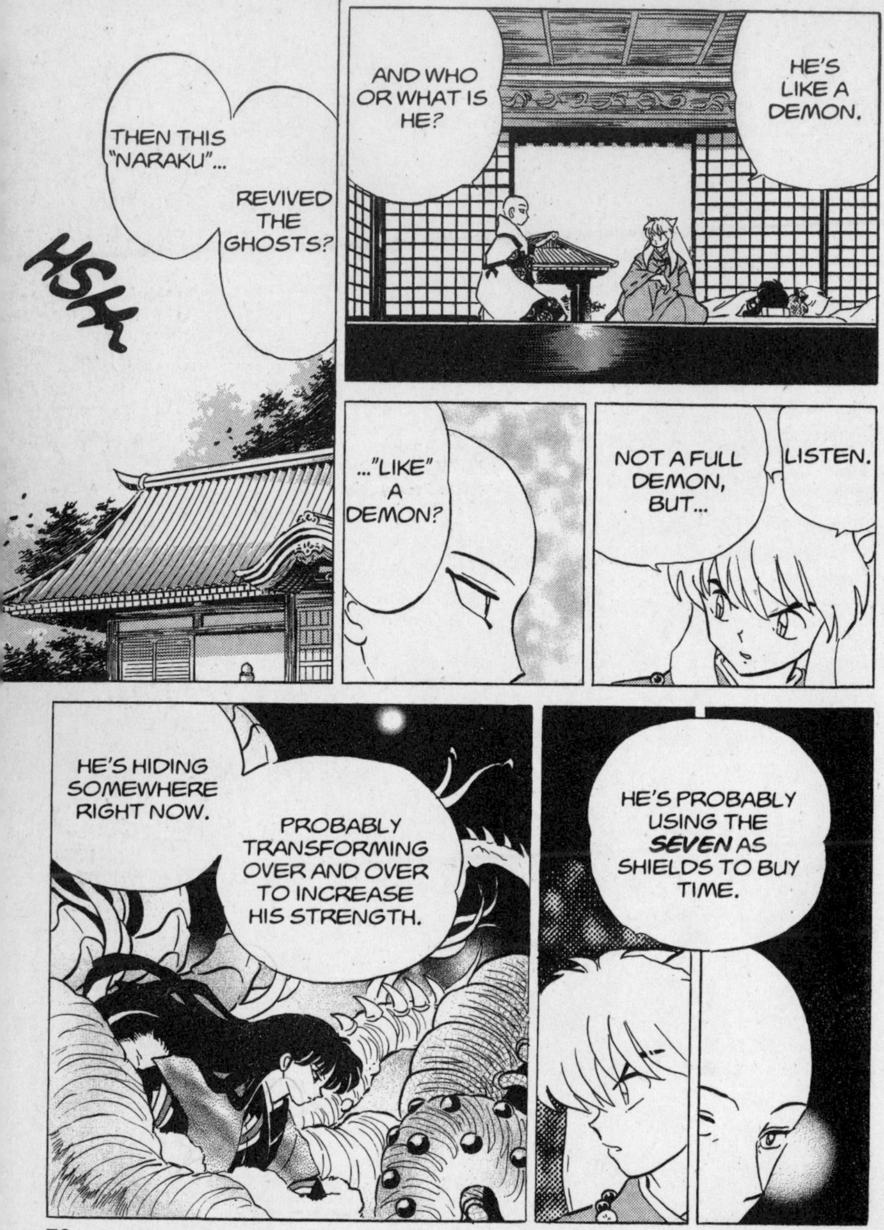
THEN THIS "NARAKU"...
REVIVED THE GHOSTS?
HSH
AND WHO OR WHAT IS HE?
HE'S LIKE A DEMON.
..."LIKE" A DEMON?
NOT A FULL DEMON, BUT...
LISTEN.
HE'S HIDING SOMEWHERE RIGHT NOW.
PROBABLY TRANSFORMING OVER AND OVER TO INCREASE HIS STRENGTH.
HE'S PROBABLY USING THE SEVEN AS SHIELDS TO BUY TIME.

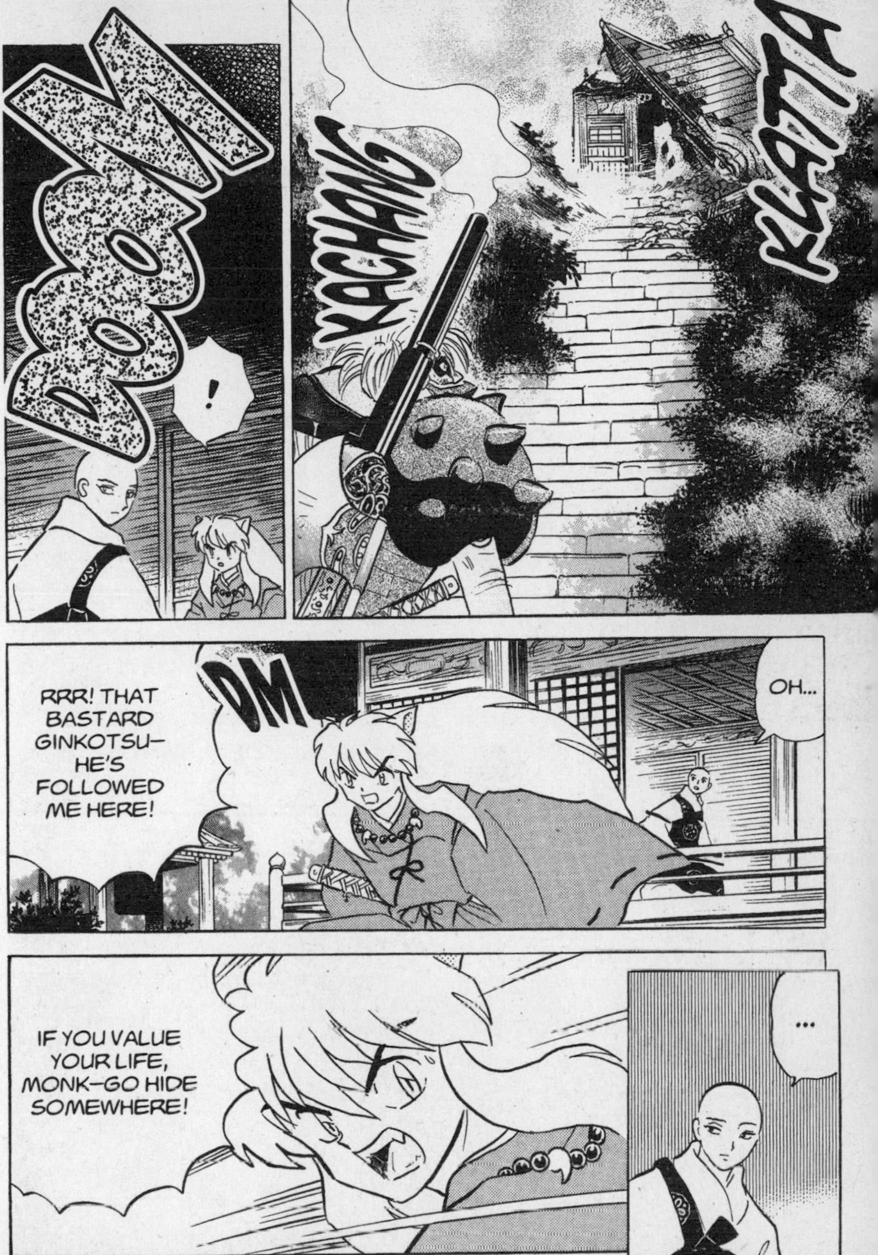
DOOOM
!
KACHANG
KLAPTA
RRR! THAT BASTARD GINKOTSU— HE'S FOLLOWED ME HERE!
DM
OH...
IF YOU VALUE YOUR LIFE, MONK—GO HIDE SOMEWHERE!
...

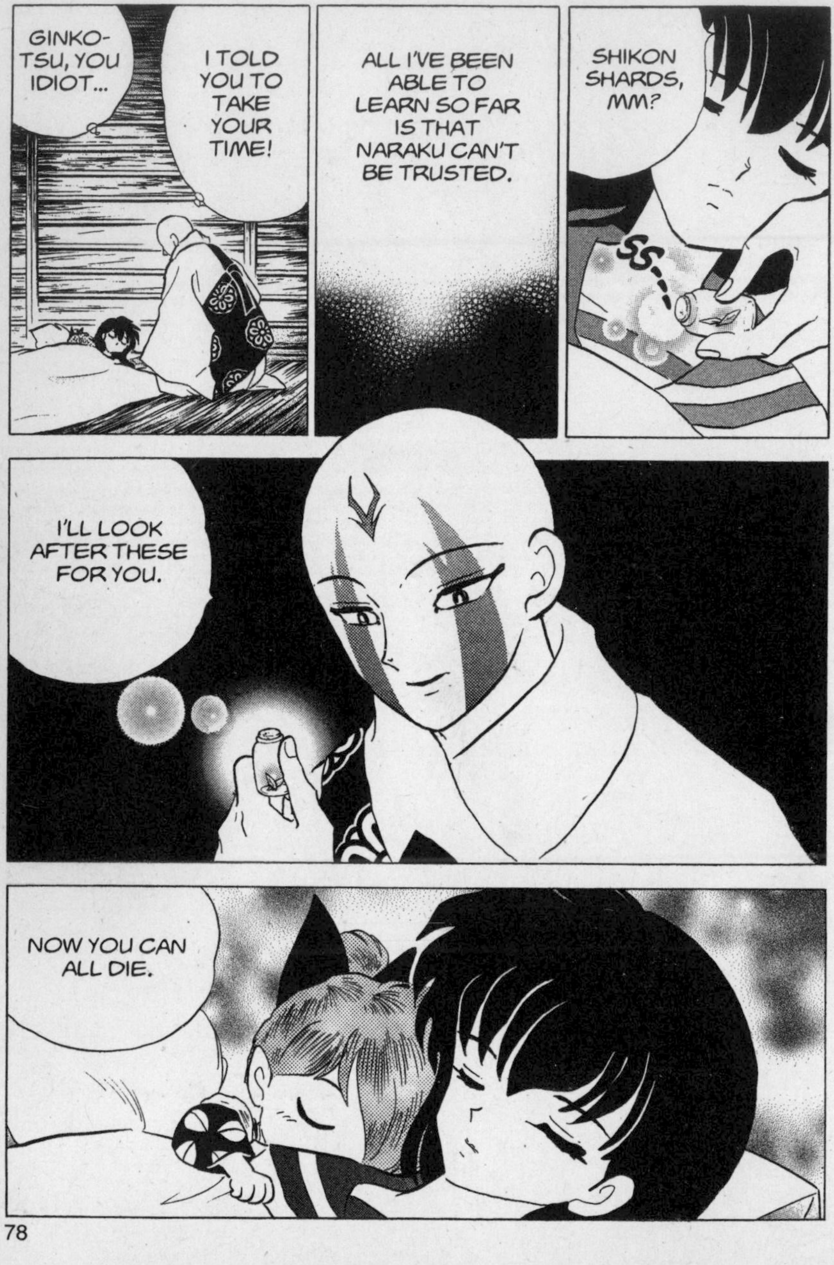
SHIKON SHARDS, MM?
ALL I'VE BEEN ABLE TO LEARN SO FAR IS THAT NARAKU CAN'T BE TRUSTED.
I TOLD YOU TO TAKE YOUR TIME!
GINKO-TSU, YOU IDIOT...
SS...
I'LL LOOK AFTER THESE FOR YOU.
NOW YOU CAN ALL DIE.

SCROLL FIVE

# THE SCENT OF THE SEVEN

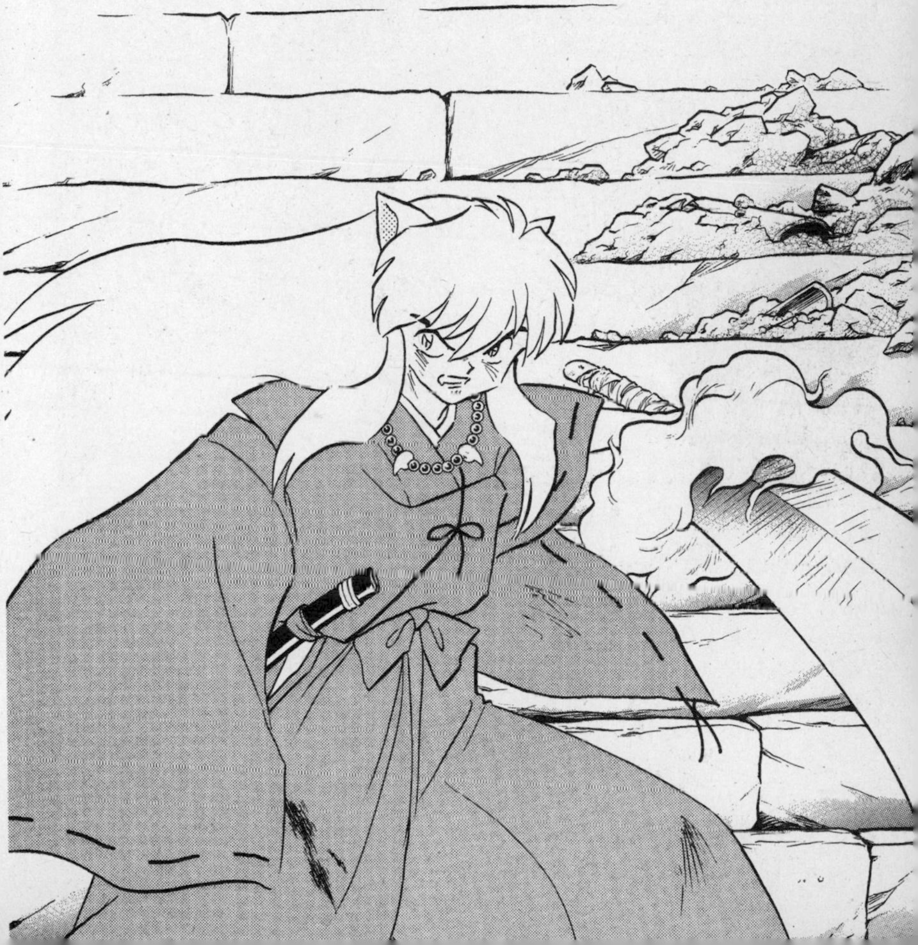

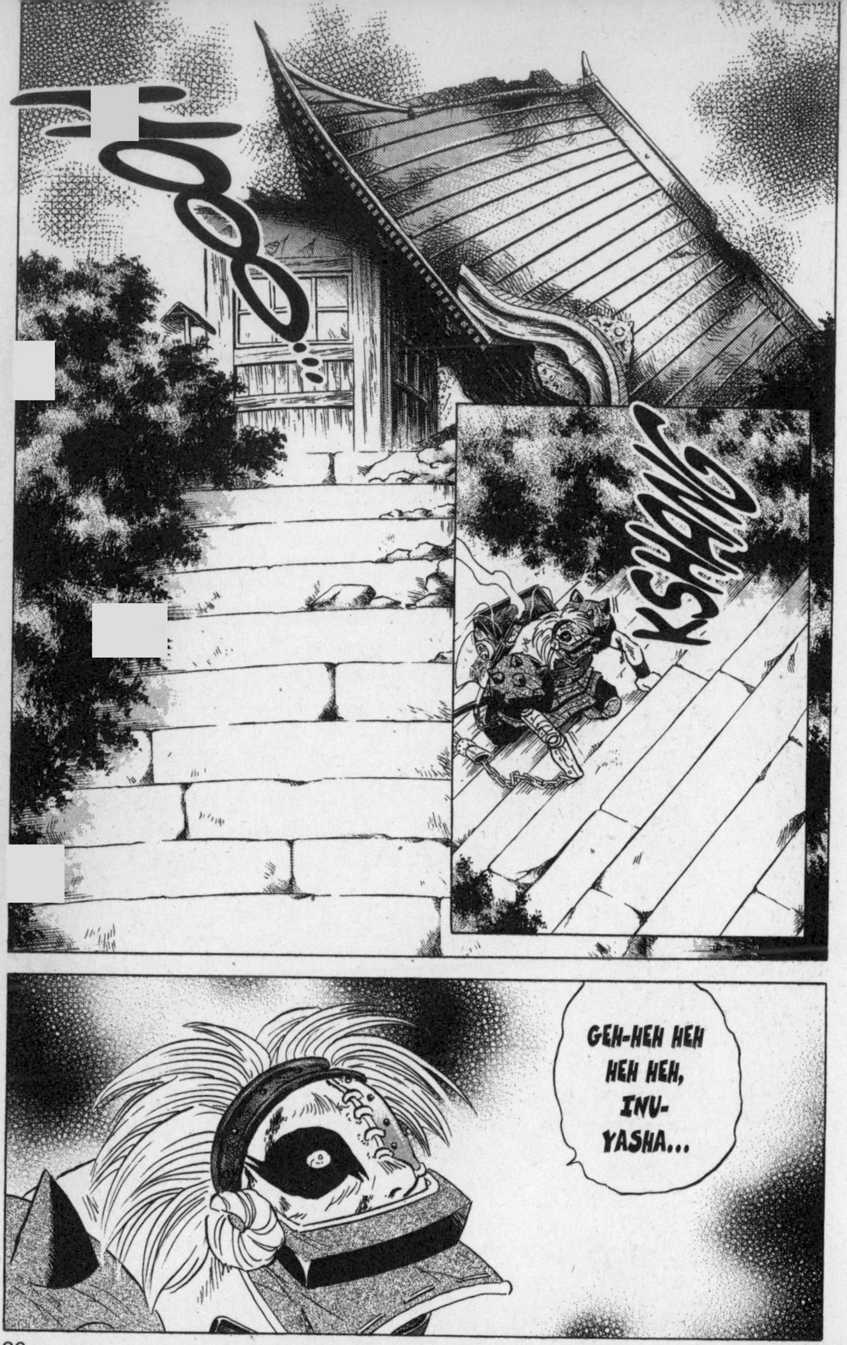
KSHANG
GEH-HEH HEH HEH HEH, INU-YASHA...

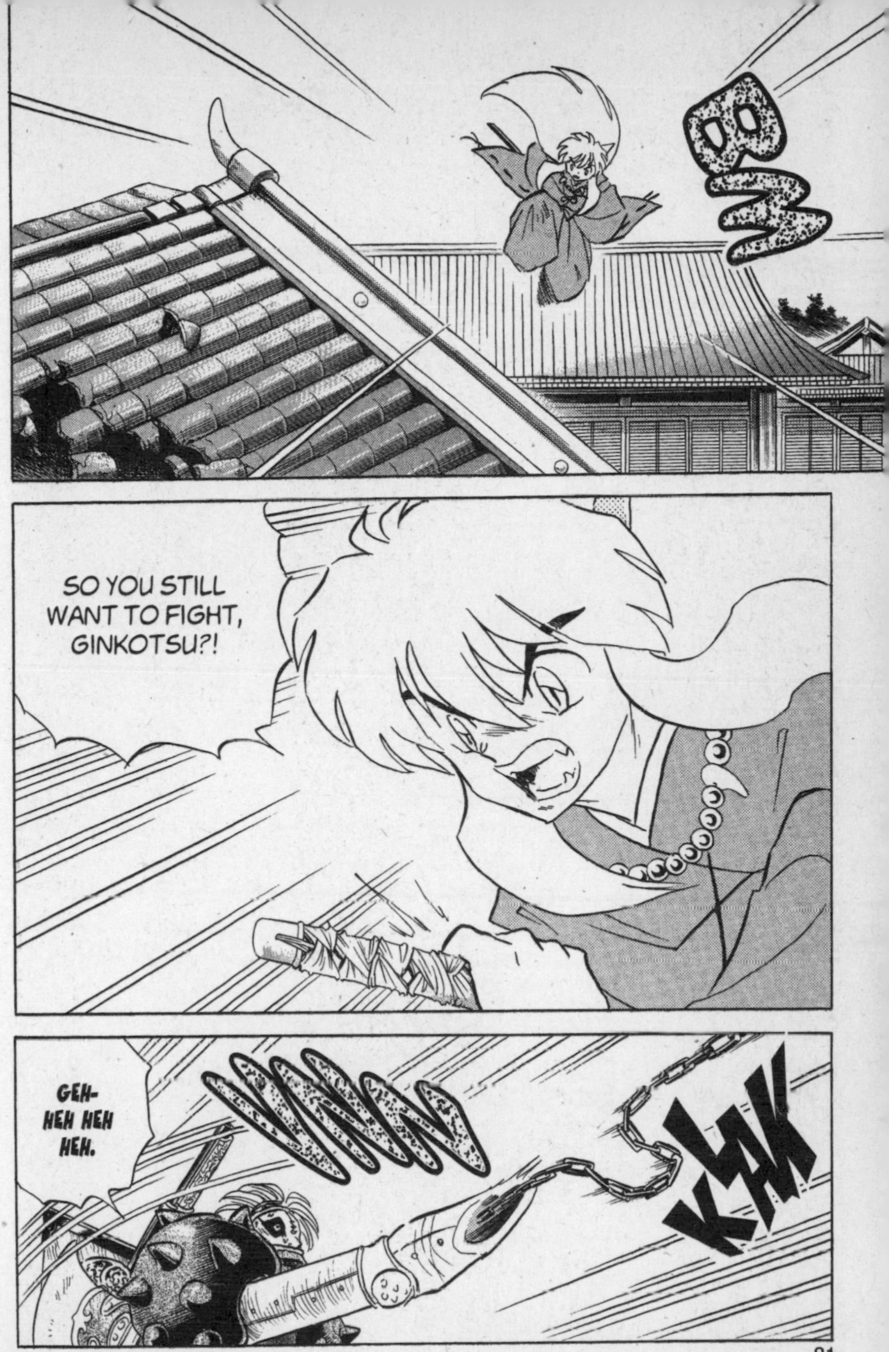
BAM
SO YOU STILL WANT TO FIGHT, GINKOTSU?!
GEH-HEH HEH HEH.
KAK

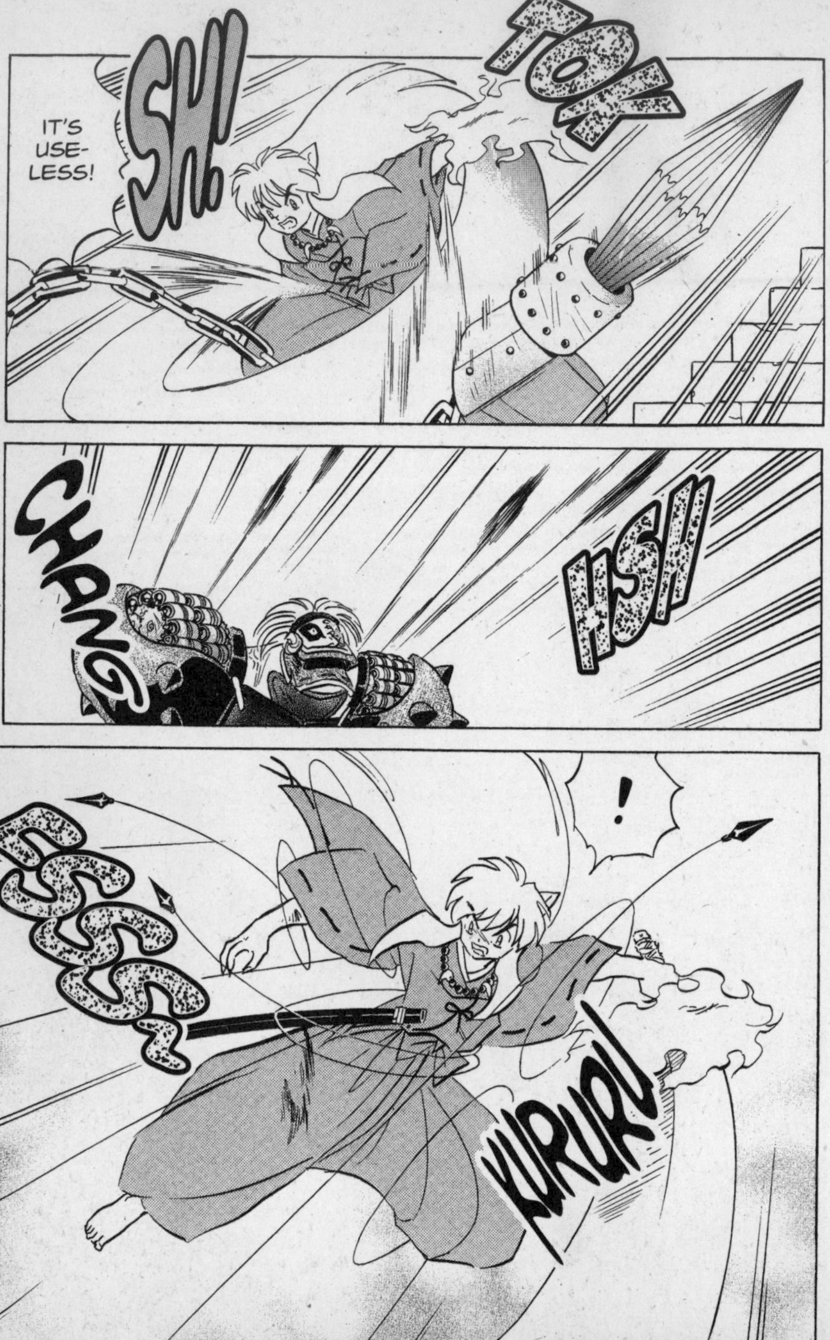

IT'S USE-LESS!
SH!
TOK
CHANG
HSH
FSSSS
!
KURURU

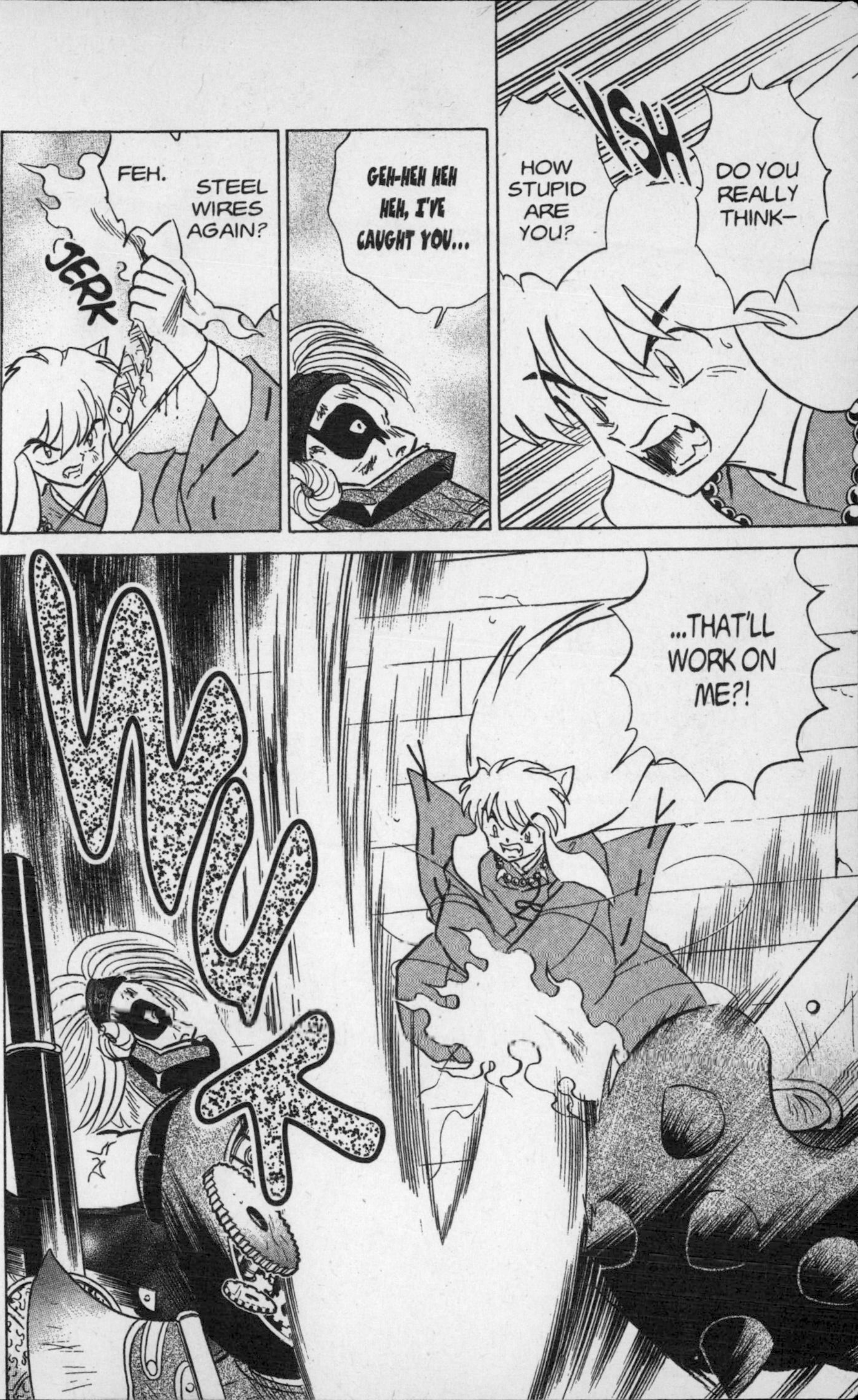

FEH.
STEEL WIRES AGAIN?
JERK
GEH-HEH HEH HEH, I'VE CAUGHT YOU...
HOW STUPID ARE YOU?
VSH
DO YOU REALLY THINK—
...THAT'LL WORK ON ME?!

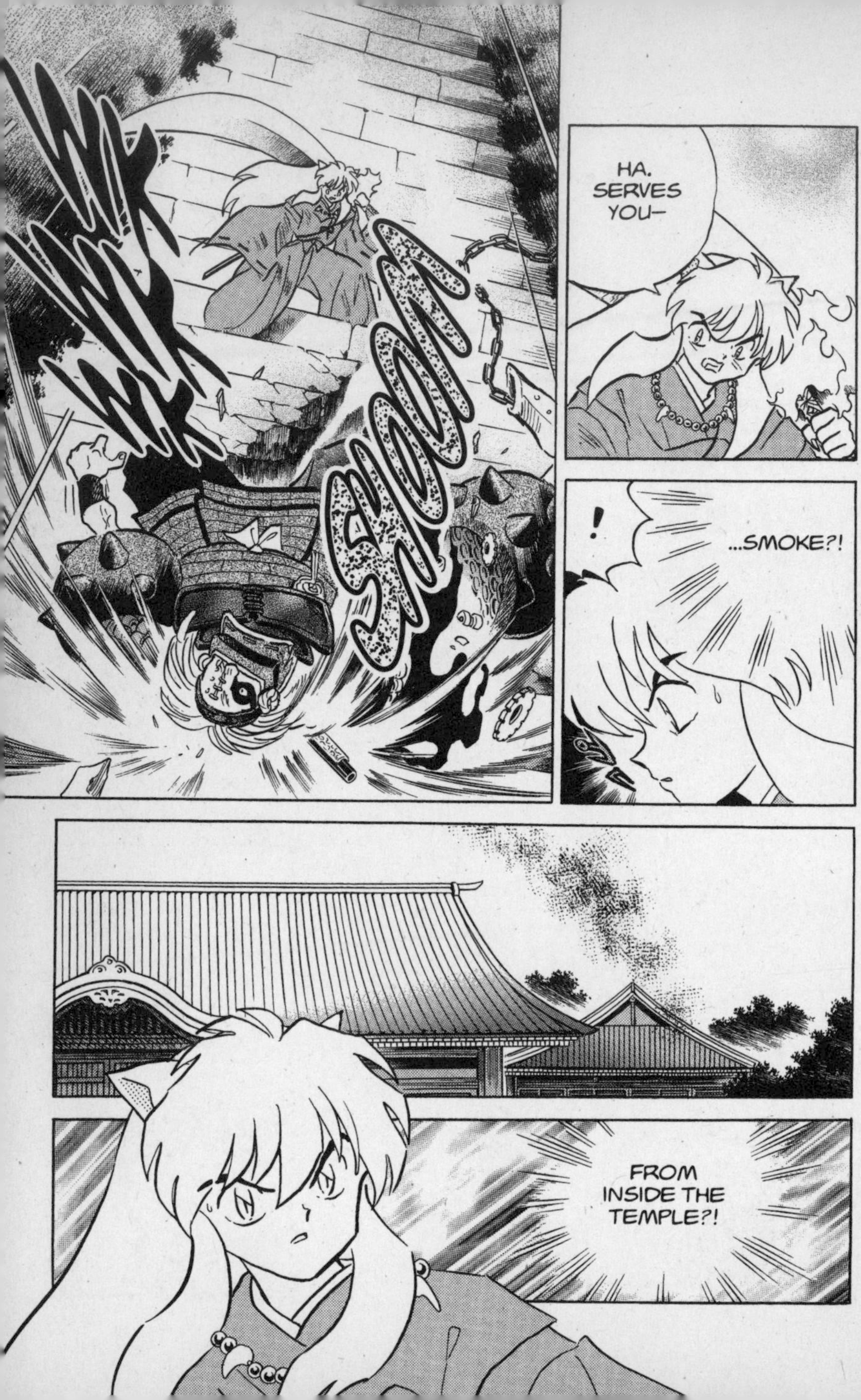
HA.
SERVES
YOU—
!
...SMOKE?!
FROM
INSIDE THE
TEMPLE?!

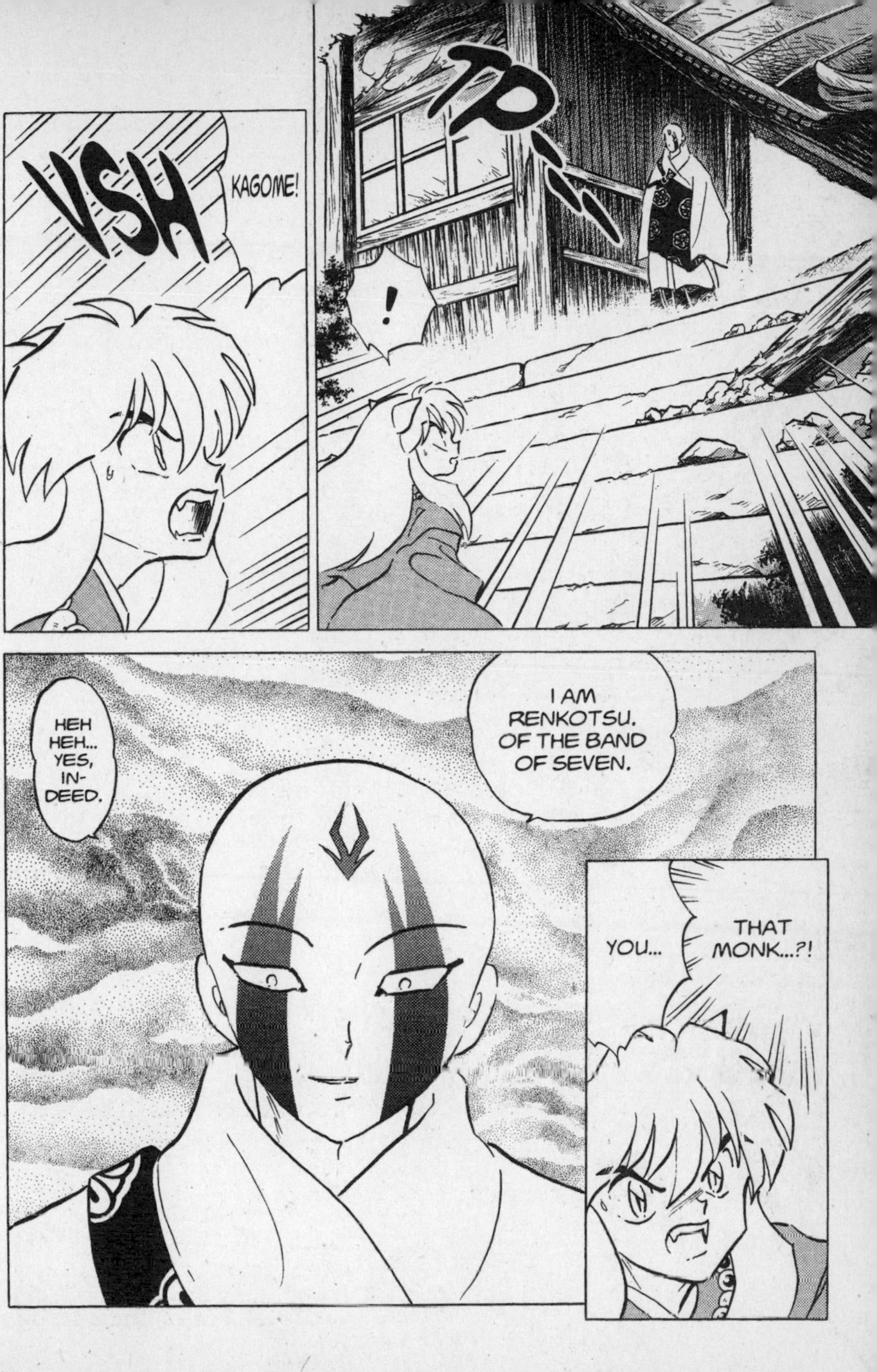
VSH
KAGOME!
TP...
!
HEH HEH... YES, IN-DEED.
I AM RENKOTSU. OF THE BAND OF SEVEN.
YOU...
THAT MONK...?!

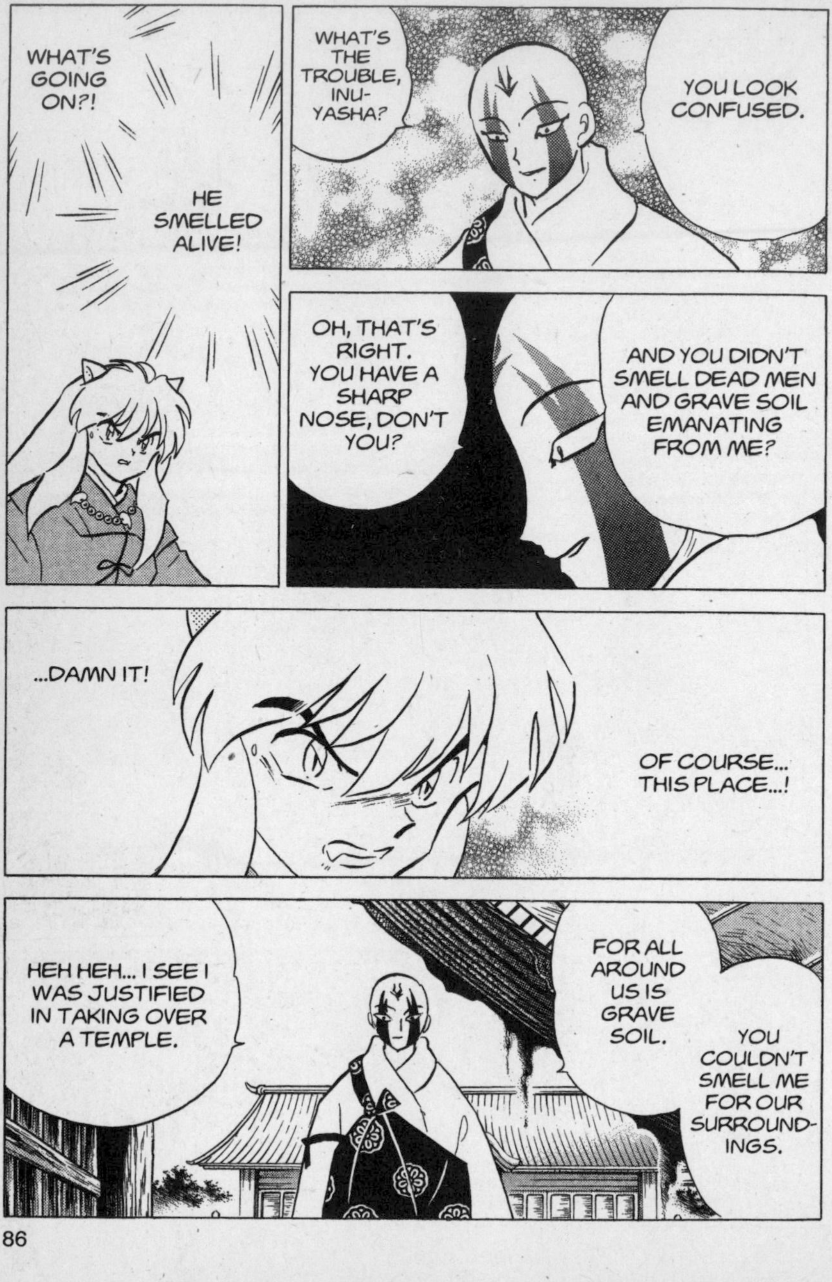
WHAT'S GOING ON?!
HE SMELLED ALIVE!
WHAT'S THE TROUBLE, INU-YASHA?
YOU LOOK CONFUSED.
OH, THAT'S RIGHT. YOU HAVE A SHARP NOSE, DON'T YOU?
AND YOU DIDN'T SMELL DEAD MEN AND GRAVE SOIL EMANATING FROM ME?
...DAMN IT!
OF COURSE... THIS PLACE...!
HEH HEH... I SEE I WAS JUSTIFIED IN TAKING OVER A TEMPLE.
FOR ALL AROUND US IS GRAVE SOIL.
YOU COULDN'T SMELL ME FOR OUR SURROUND-INGS.

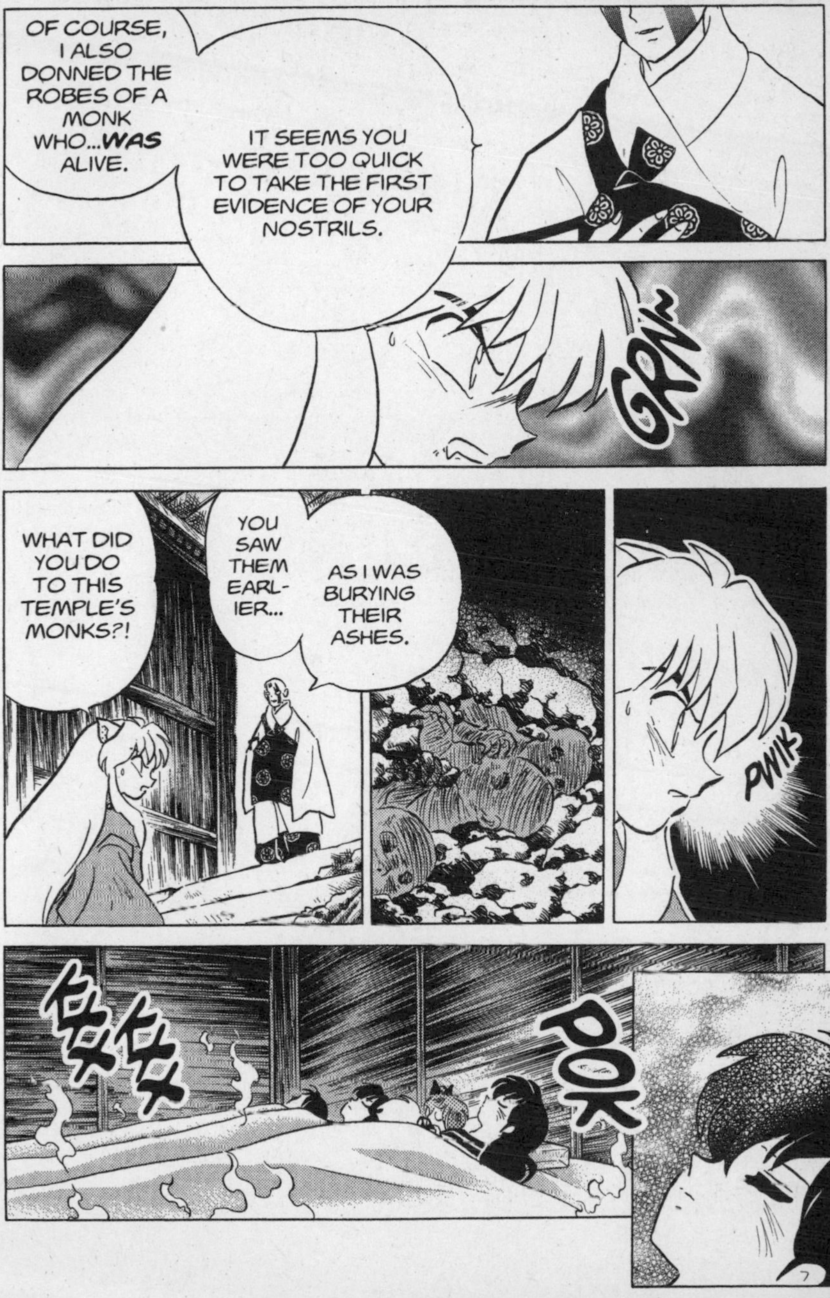
OF COURSE, I ALSO DONNED THE ROBES OF A MONK WHO...WAS ALIVE.
IT SEEMS YOU WERE TOO QUICK TO TAKE THE FIRST EVIDENCE OF YOUR NOSTRILS.
GRN
WHAT DID YOU DO TO THIS TEMPLE'S MONKS?!
YOU SAW THEM EARL-IER...
AS I WAS BURYING THEIR ASHES.
PWIK
KKK KKK
POK

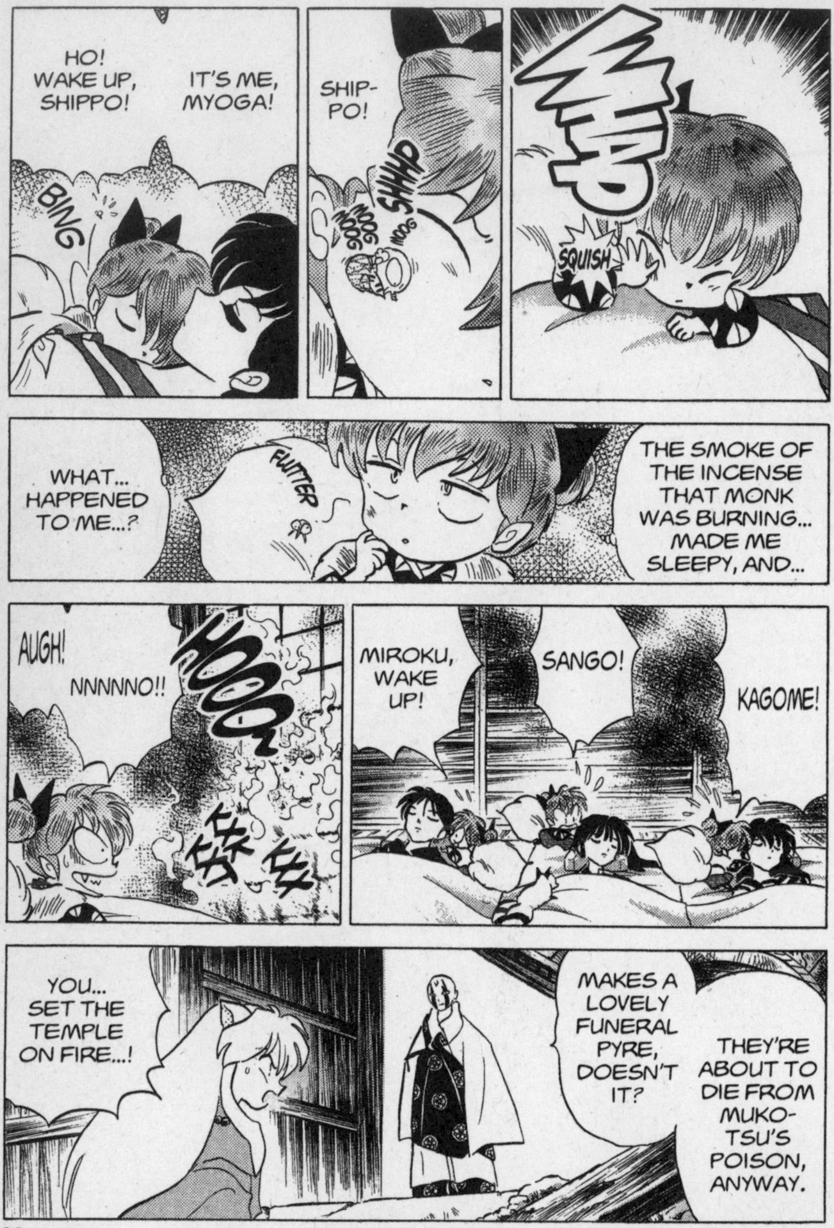
HO! WAKE UP, SHIPPO!
IT'S ME, MYOGA!
BING
SHIP-PO!
SHHHP
MOOG MOOG MOOG
SQUISH
WHAT... HAPPENED TO ME...?
FLUTTER
THE SMOKE OF THE INCENSE THAT MONK WAS BURNING... MADE ME SLEEPY, AND...
AUGH!
NNNNNO!!
MIROKU, WAKE UP!
SANGO!
KAGOME!
YOU... SET THE TEMPLE ON FIRE...!
MAKES A LOVELY FUNERAL PYRE, DOESN'T IT?
THEY'RE ABOUT TO DIE FROM MUKO-TSU'S POISON, ANYWAY.

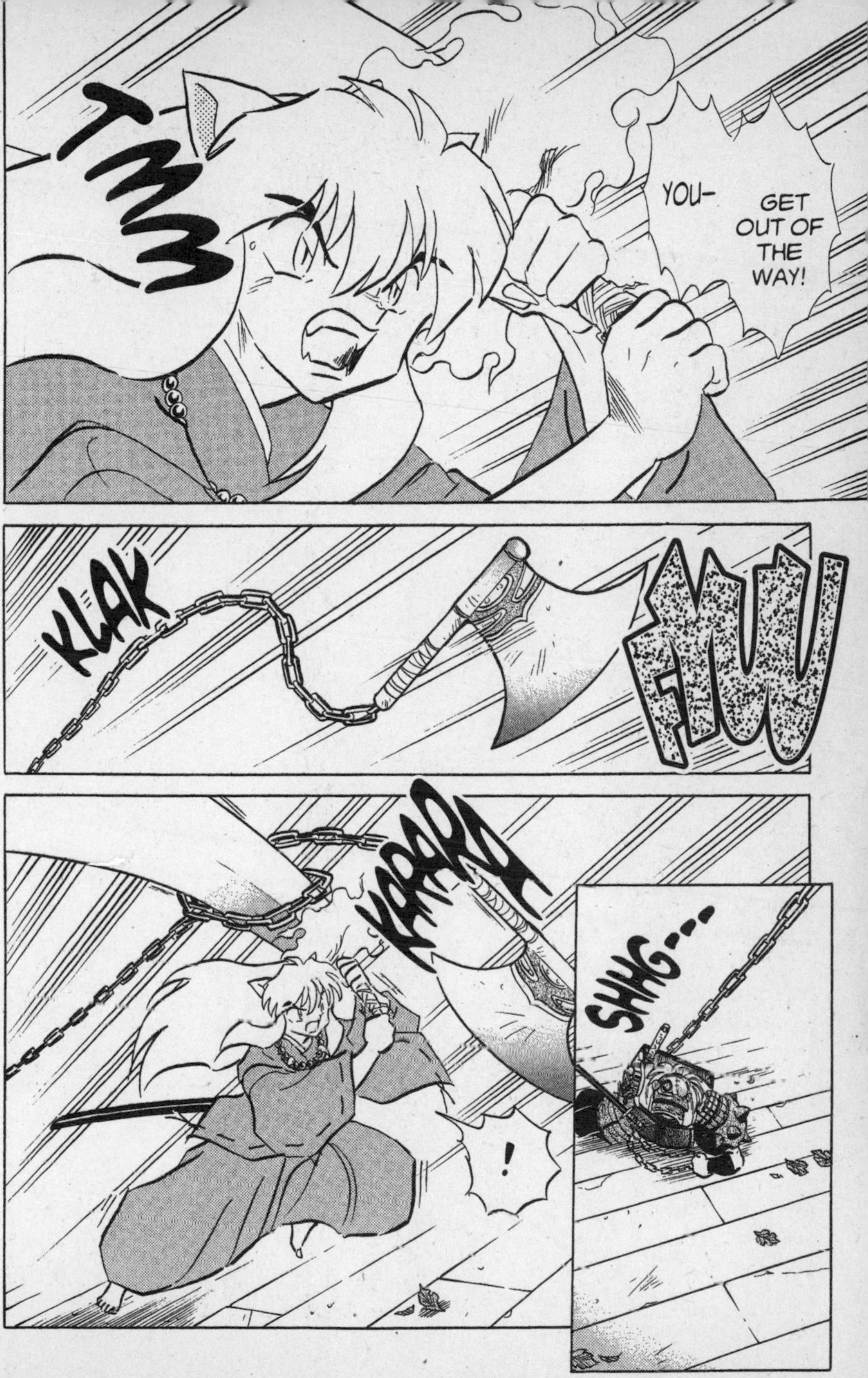
TMM
YOU-
GET OUT OF THE WAY!
KLAK
FWU
KARARA
!
SHHG...

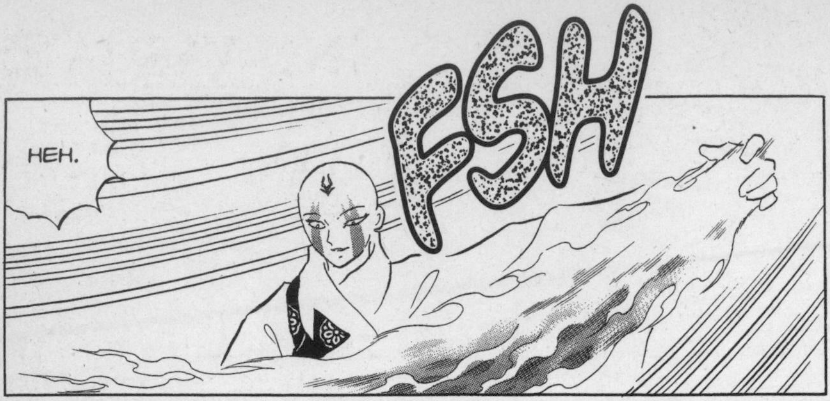
HEH.
FSH
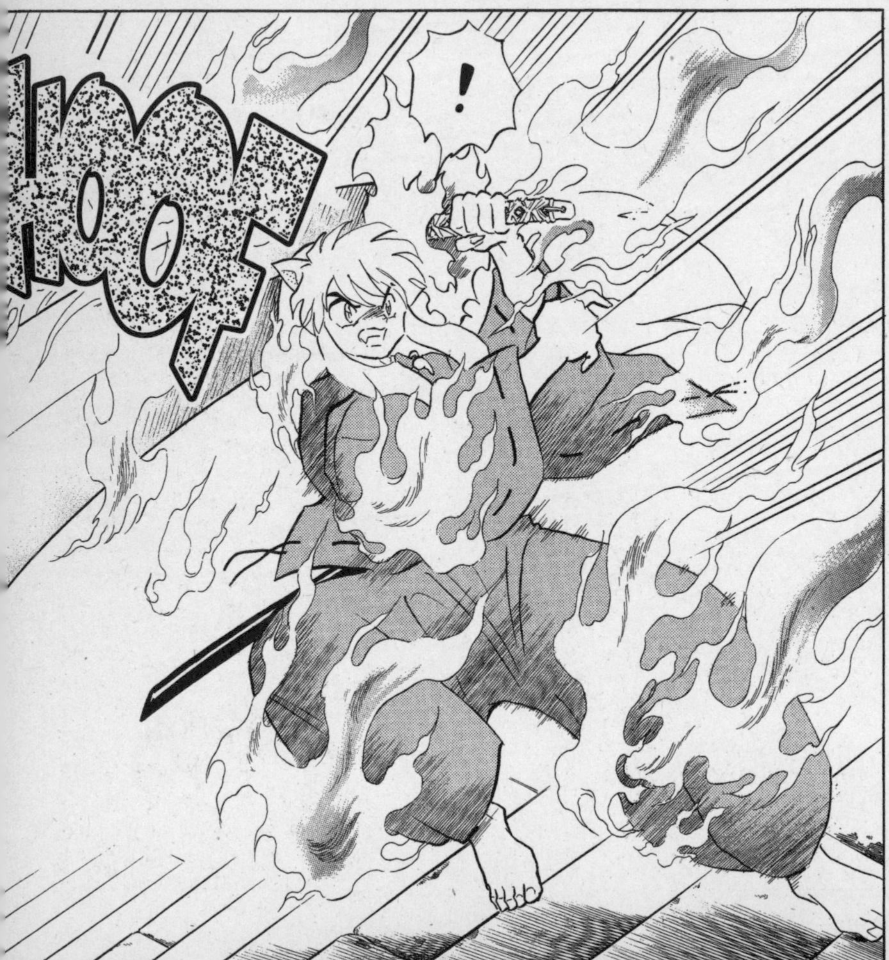
!
WHOOF

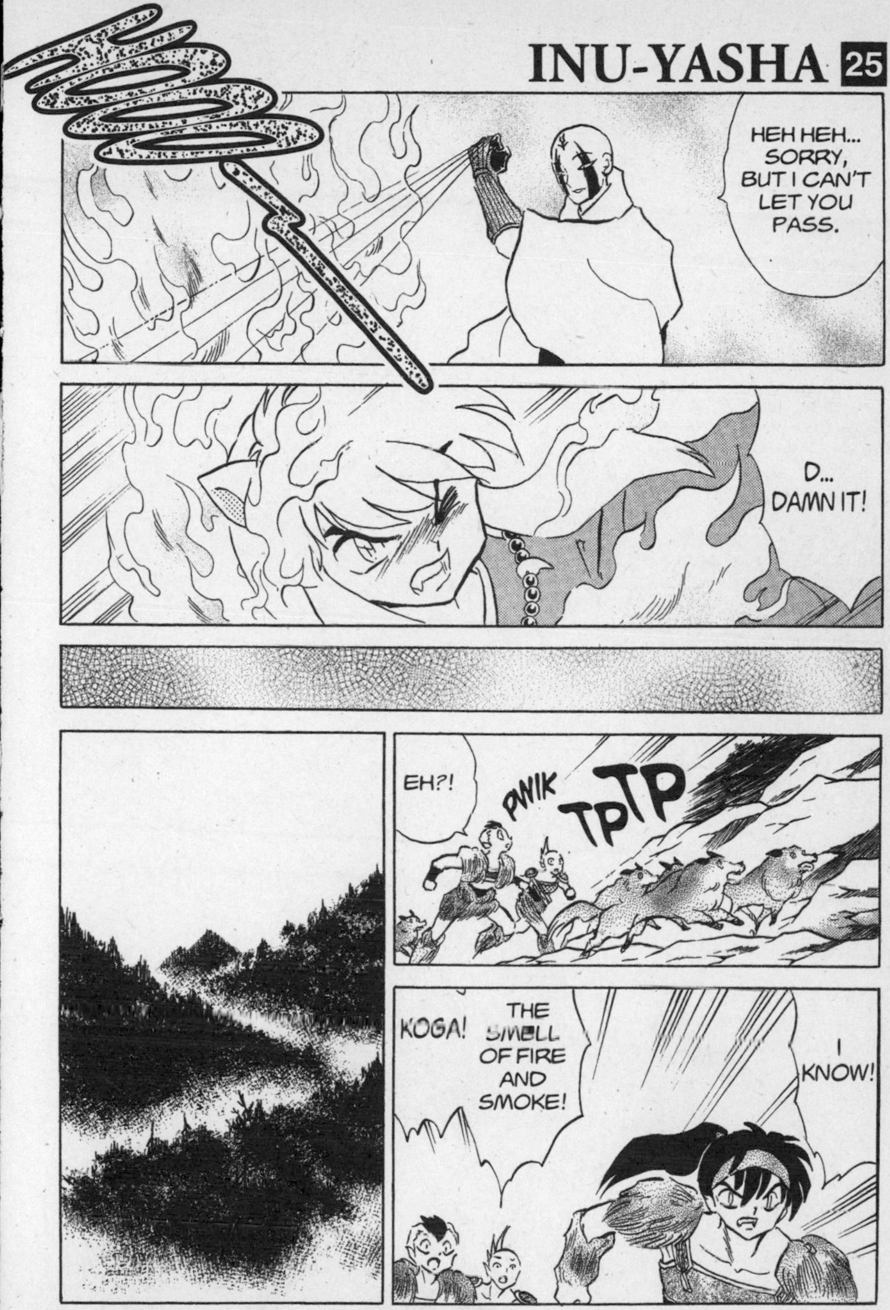
HEH HEH... SORRY, BUT I CAN'T LET YOU PASS.
D... DAMN IT!
EH?!
PWIK
TPTP
KOGA!
THE SMELL OF FIRE AND SMOKE!
I KNOW!

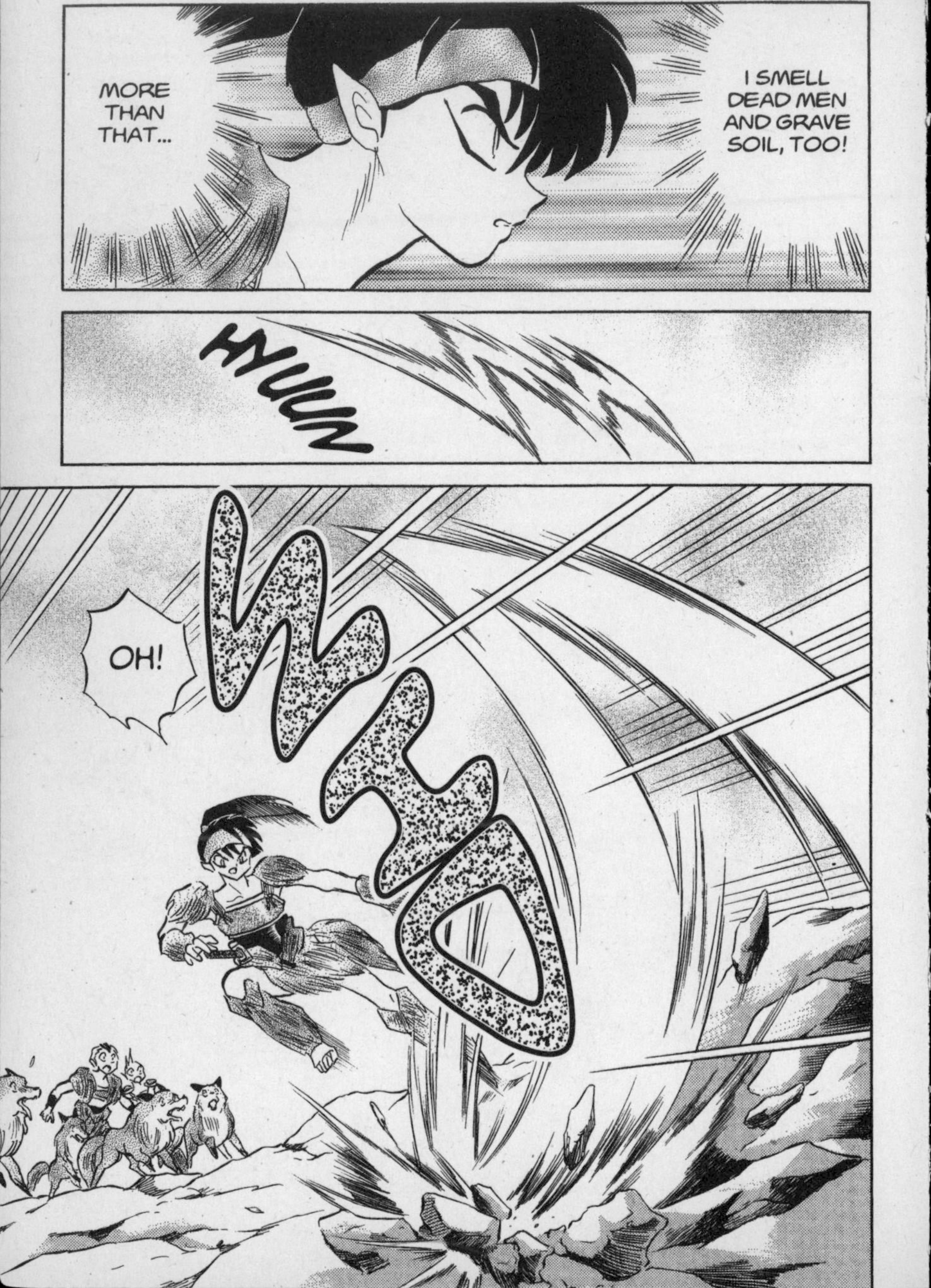
MORE THAN THAT...
I SMELL DEAD MEN AND GRAVE SOIL, TOO!
HYUUN
OH!
SHHO

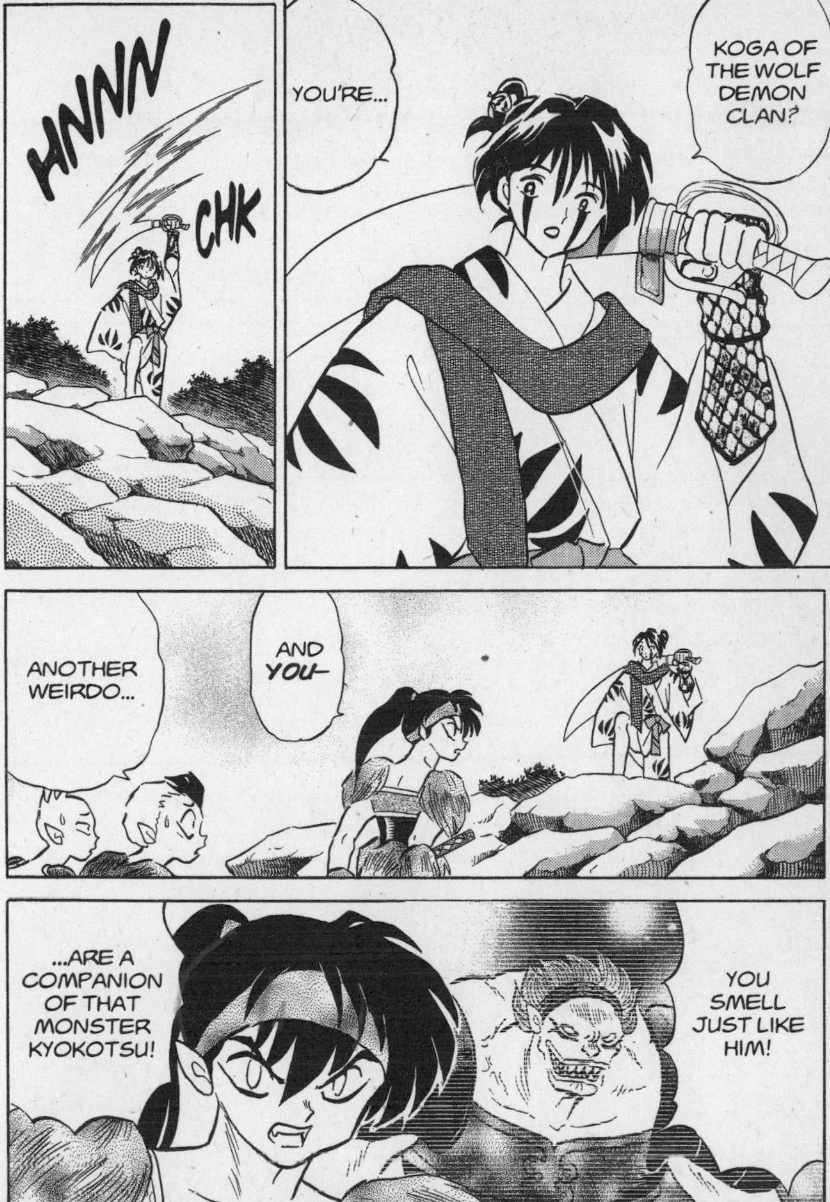
HNNN
CHK
YOU'RE...
KOGA OF THE WOLF DEMON CLAN?
ANOTHER WEIRDO...
AND YOU—
...ARE A COMPANION OF THAT MONSTER KYOKOTSU!
YOU SMELL JUST LIKE HIM!

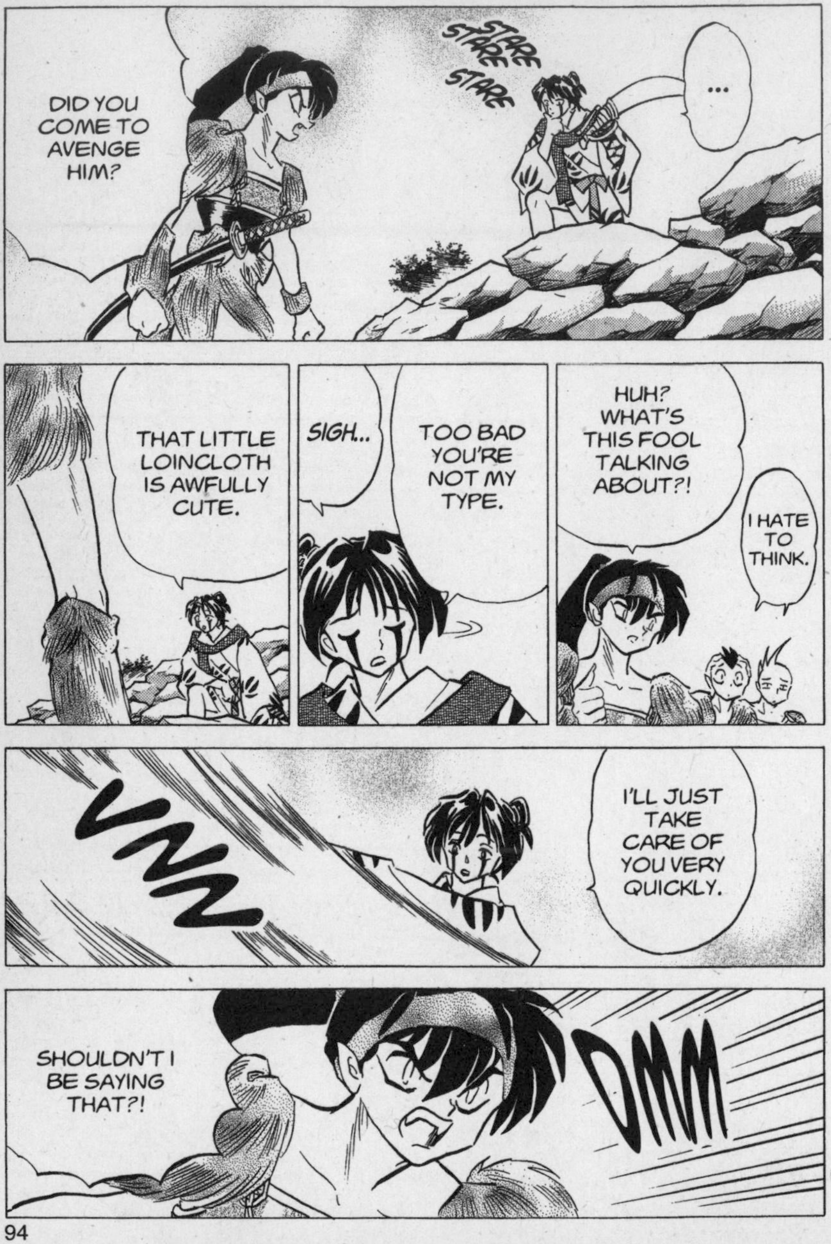
DID YOU COME TO AVENGE HIM?
STARE STARE STARE
...
THAT LITTLE LOINCLOTH IS AWFULLY CUTE.
SIGH...
TOO BAD YOU'RE NOT MY TYPE.
HUH? WHAT'S THIS FOOL TALKING ABOUT?!
I HATE TO THINK.
VNN
I'LL JUST TAKE CARE OF YOU VERY QUICKLY.
SHOULDN'T I BE SAYING THAT?!
DMM

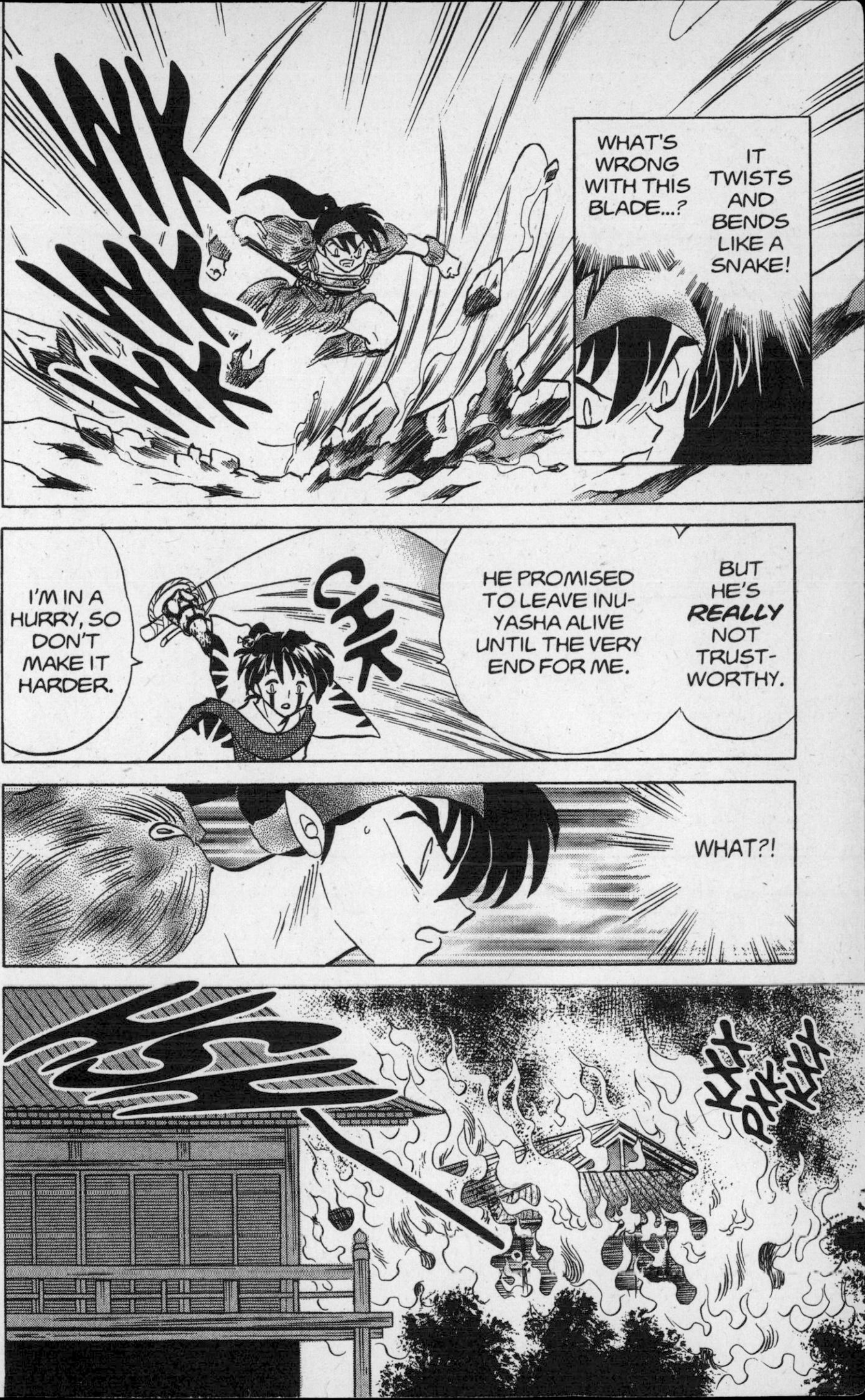
WHAT'S WRONG WITH THIS BLADE...?
IT TWISTS AND BENDS LIKE A SNAKE!
I'M IN A HURRY, SO DON'T MAKE IT HARDER.
CHK
HE PROMISED TO LEAVE INU-YASHA ALIVE UNTIL THE VERY END FOR ME.
BUT HE'S **REALLY** NOT TRUST-WORTHY.
WHAT?!

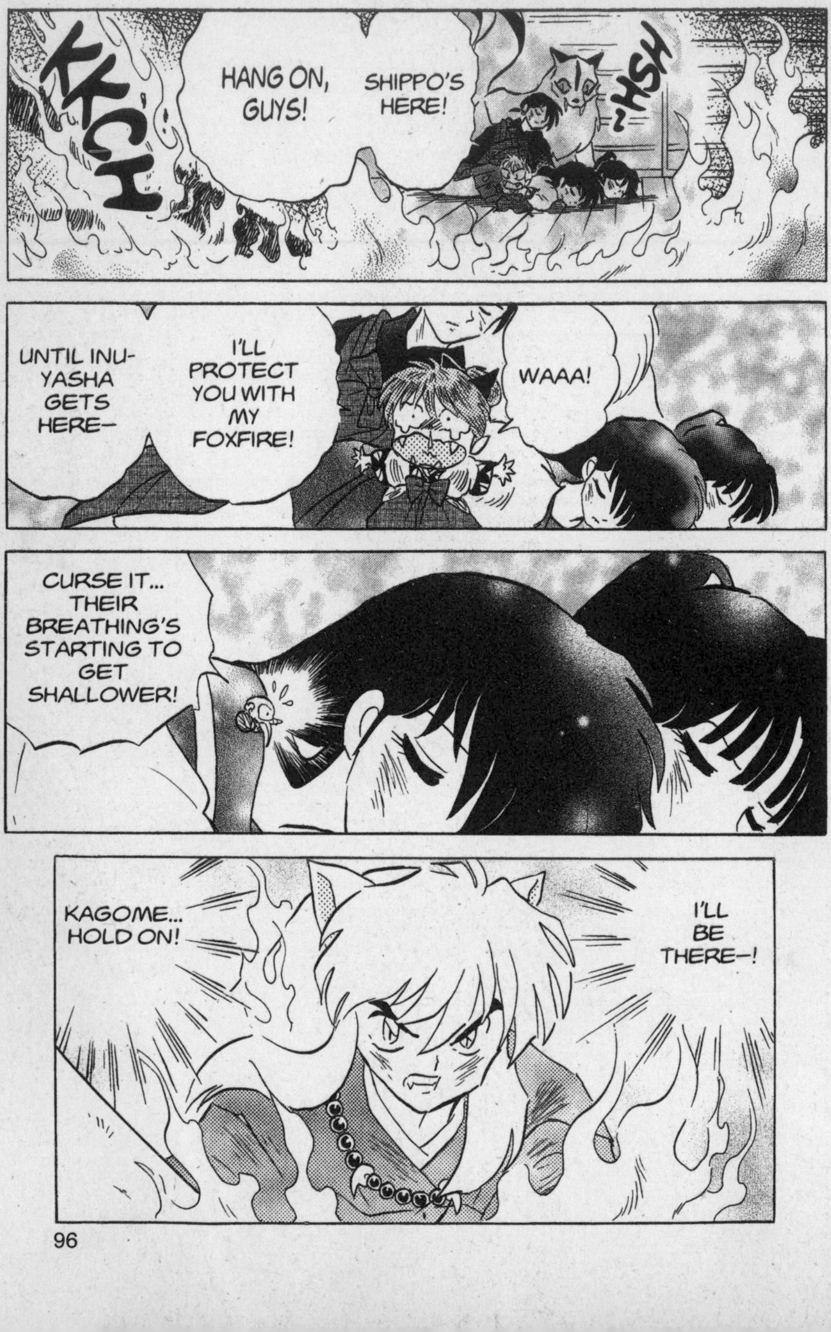
KKCH
HANG ON, GUYS!
SHIPPO'S HERE!
HSH?
UNTIL INU-YASHA GETS HERE—
I'LL PROTECT YOU WITH MY FOXFIRE!
WAAA!
CURSE IT... THEIR BREATHING'S STARTING TO GET SHALLOWER!
KAGOME... HOLD ON!
I'LL BE THERE—!

SCROLL SIX

# THE LIVES OF ONE'S COMPANIONS

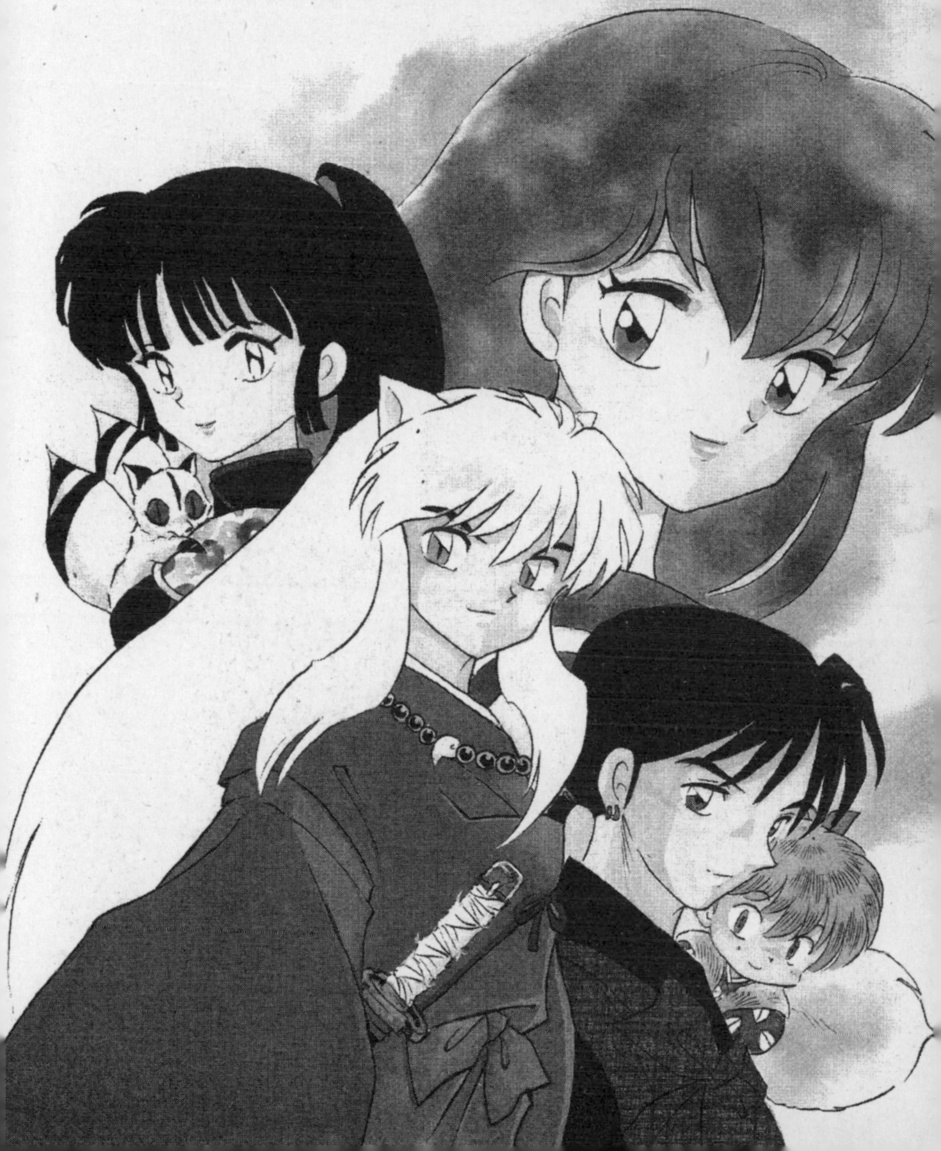

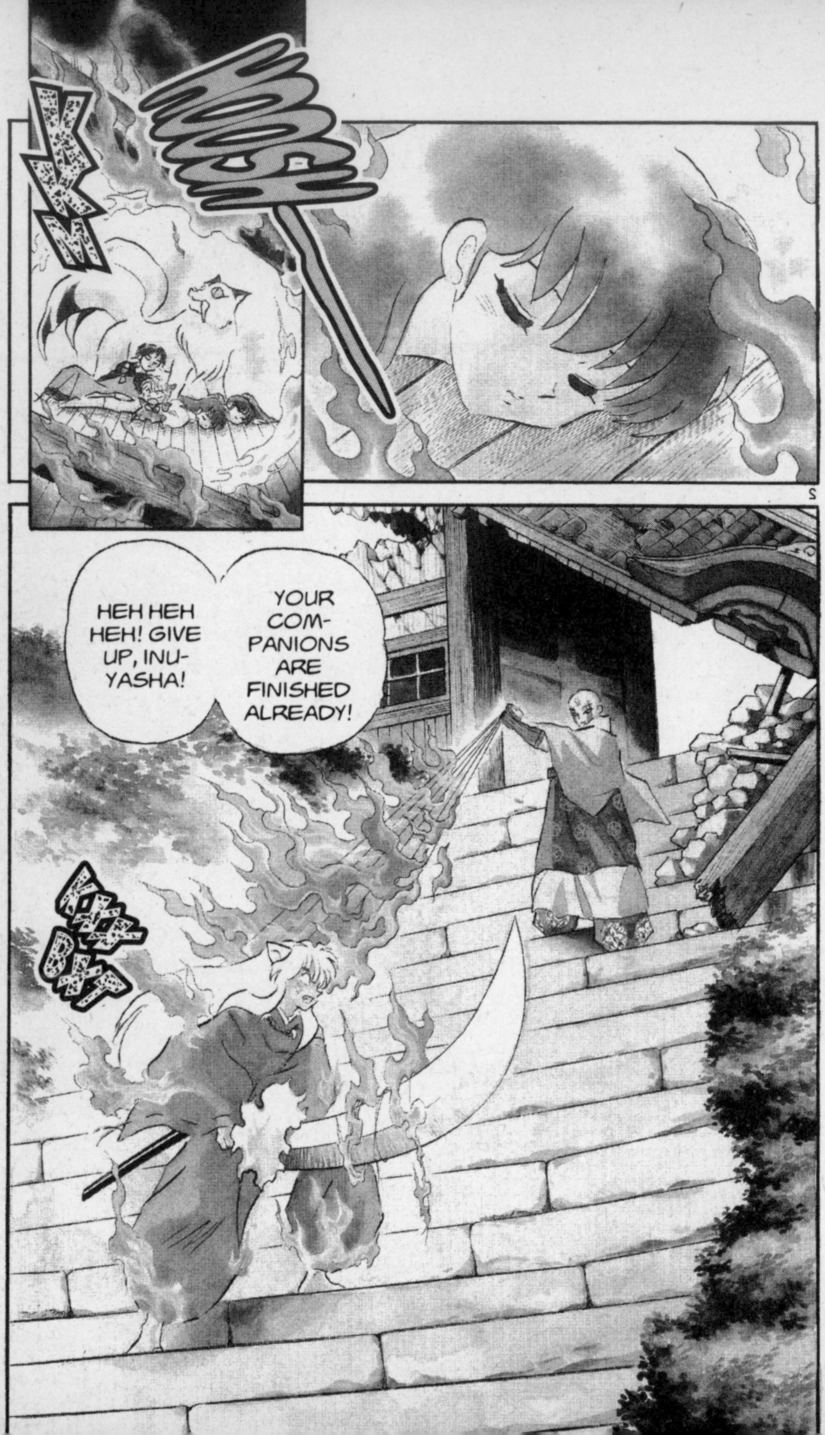
HEH HEH HEH! GIVE UP, INU-YASHA!
YOUR COM-PANIONS ARE FINISHED ALREADY!

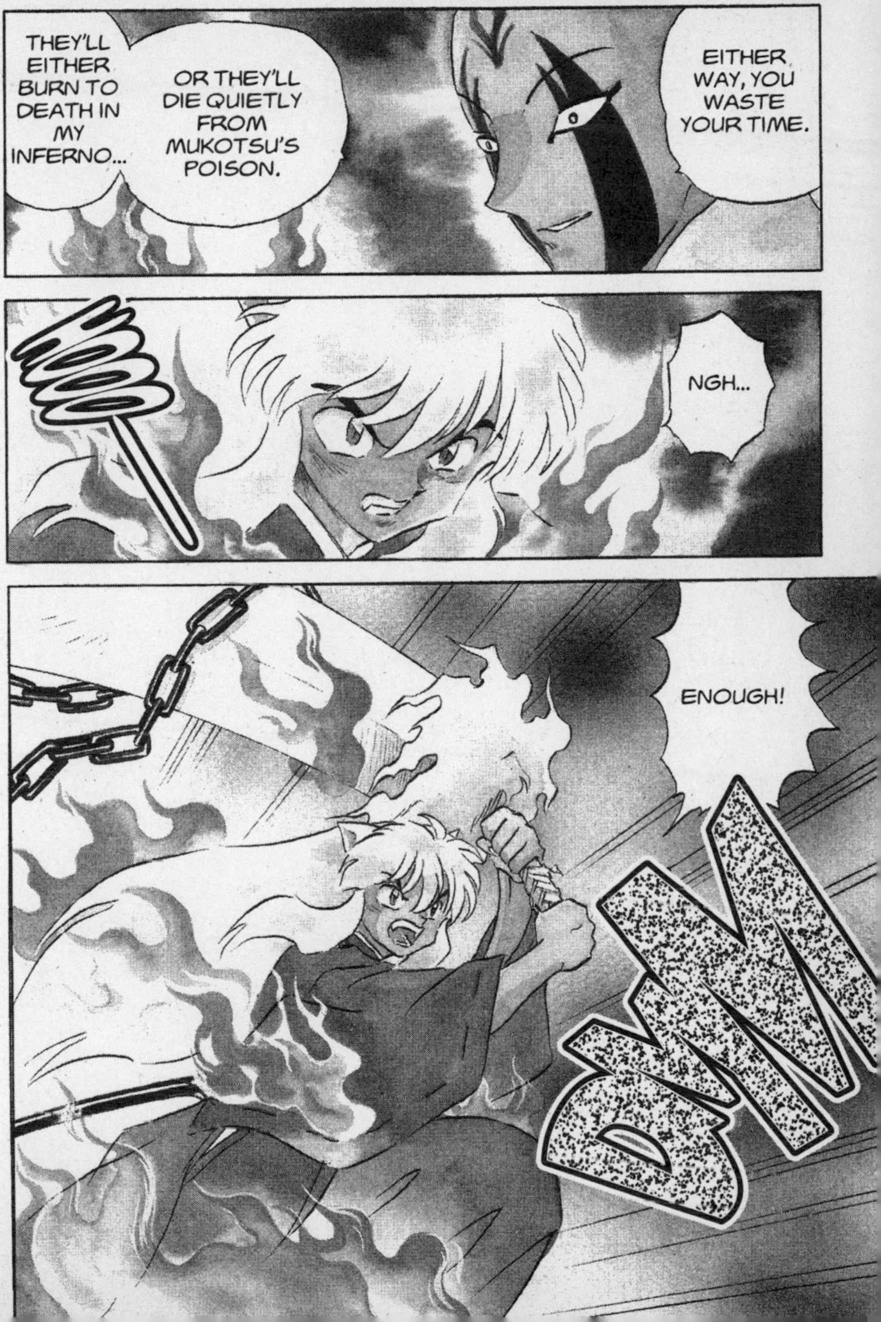
THEY'LL EITHER BURN TO DEATH IN MY INFERNO...
OR THEY'LL DIE QUIETLY FROM MUKOTSU'S POISON.
EITHER WAY, YOU WASTE YOUR TIME.
NGH...
ENOUGH!

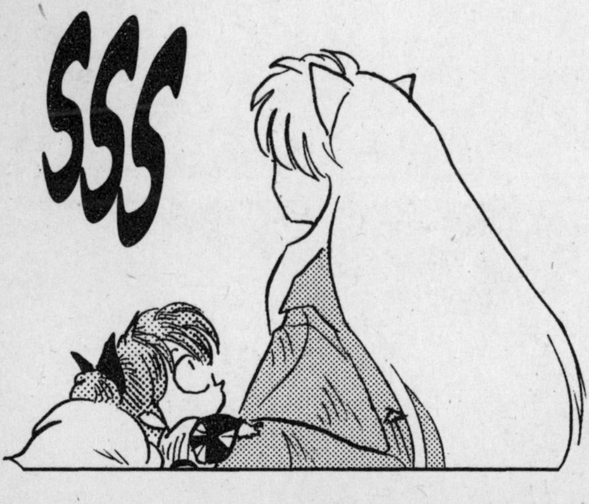
SSS

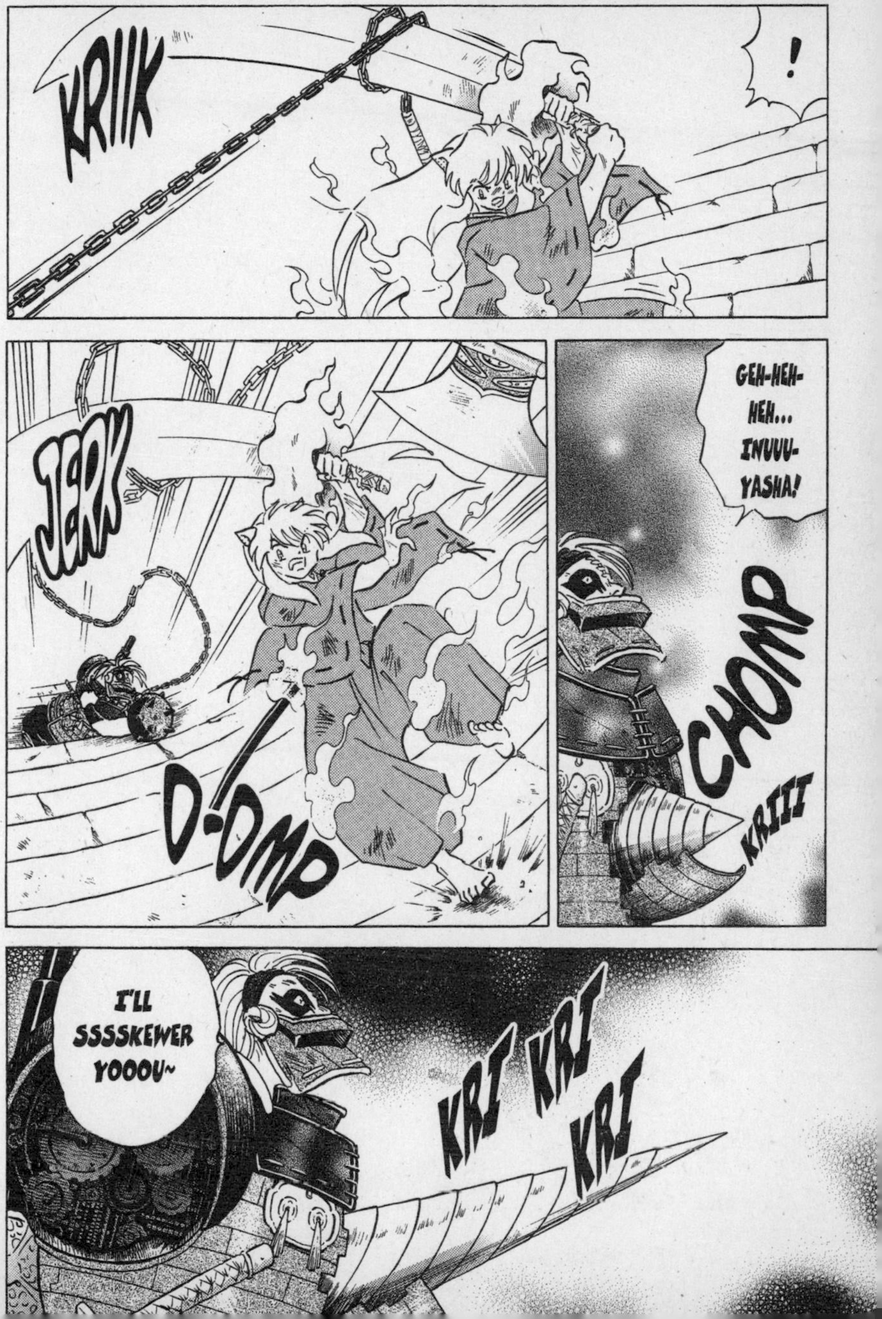
KRIIK
!
JERK
D-DOMP
GEH-HEH-HEH... INUUU-YASHA!
CHOMP
KRIII
I'LL SSSSKEWER YOOOU~
KRI KRI
KRI

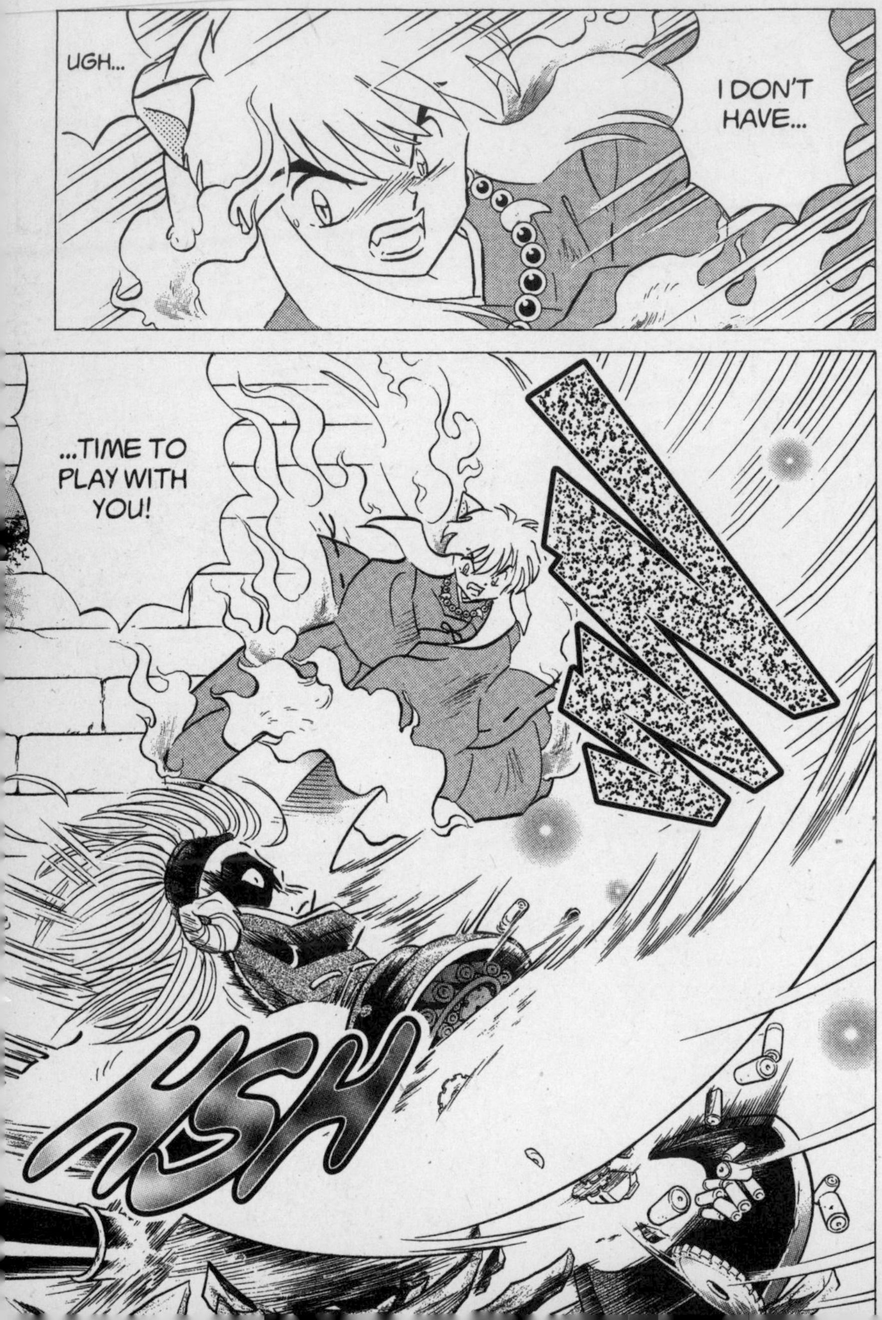
UGH...
I DON'T HAVE...
...TIME TO PLAY WITH YOU!
HSH

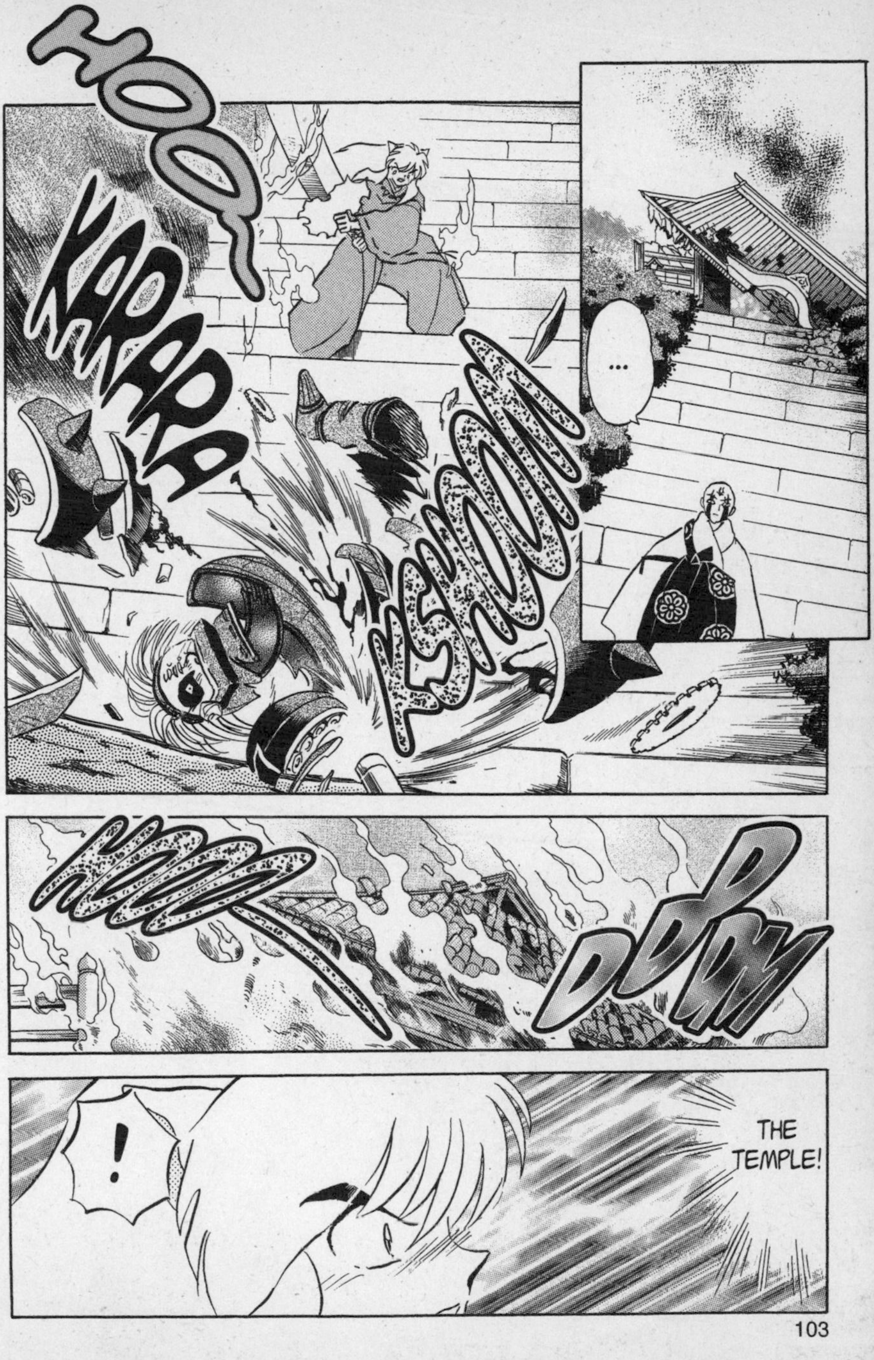
HOOO
KARARA
KSHOOM
...
!
THE TEMPLE!

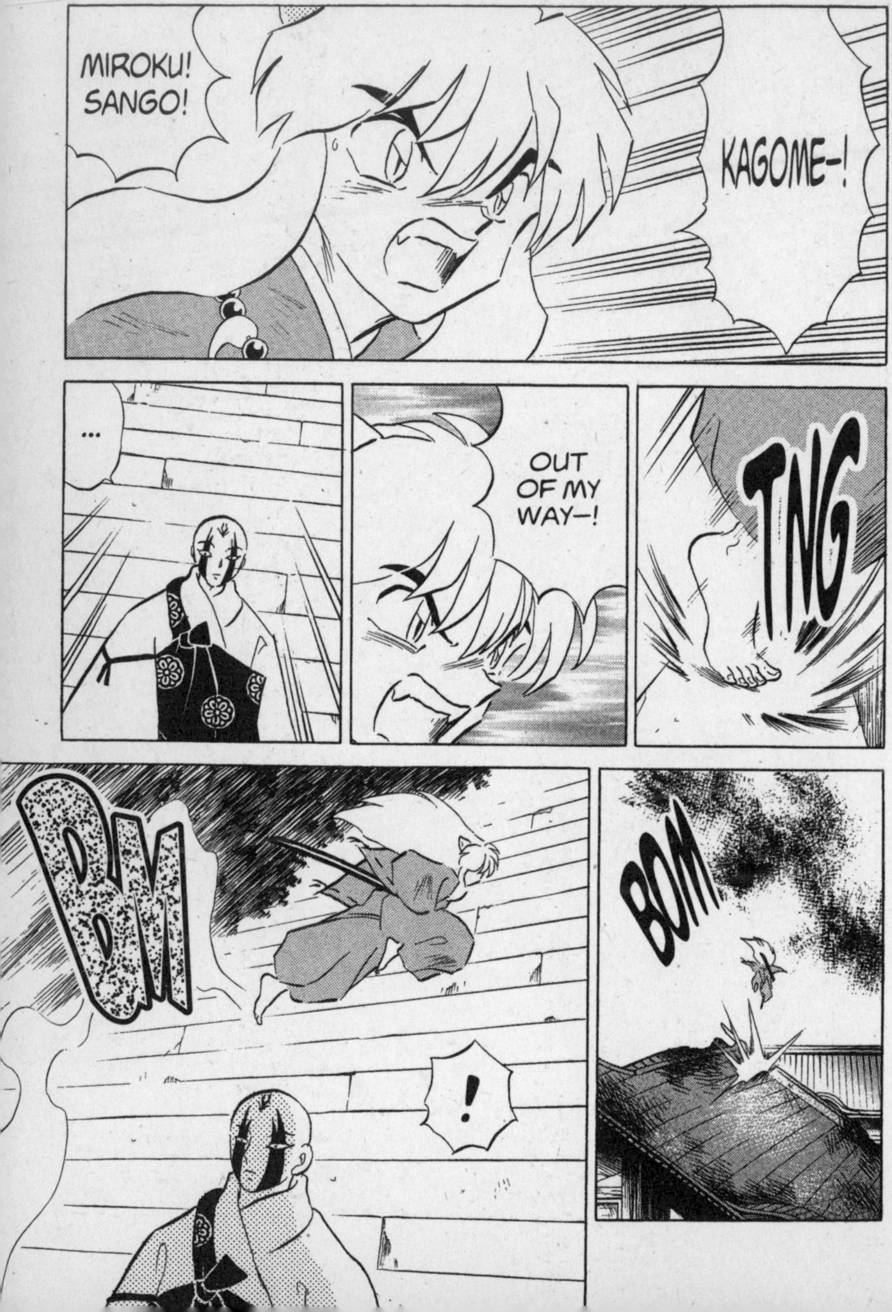
MIROKU! SANGO!
KAGOME--!
...
OUT OF MY WAY--!
TNG
BM
!
BOM

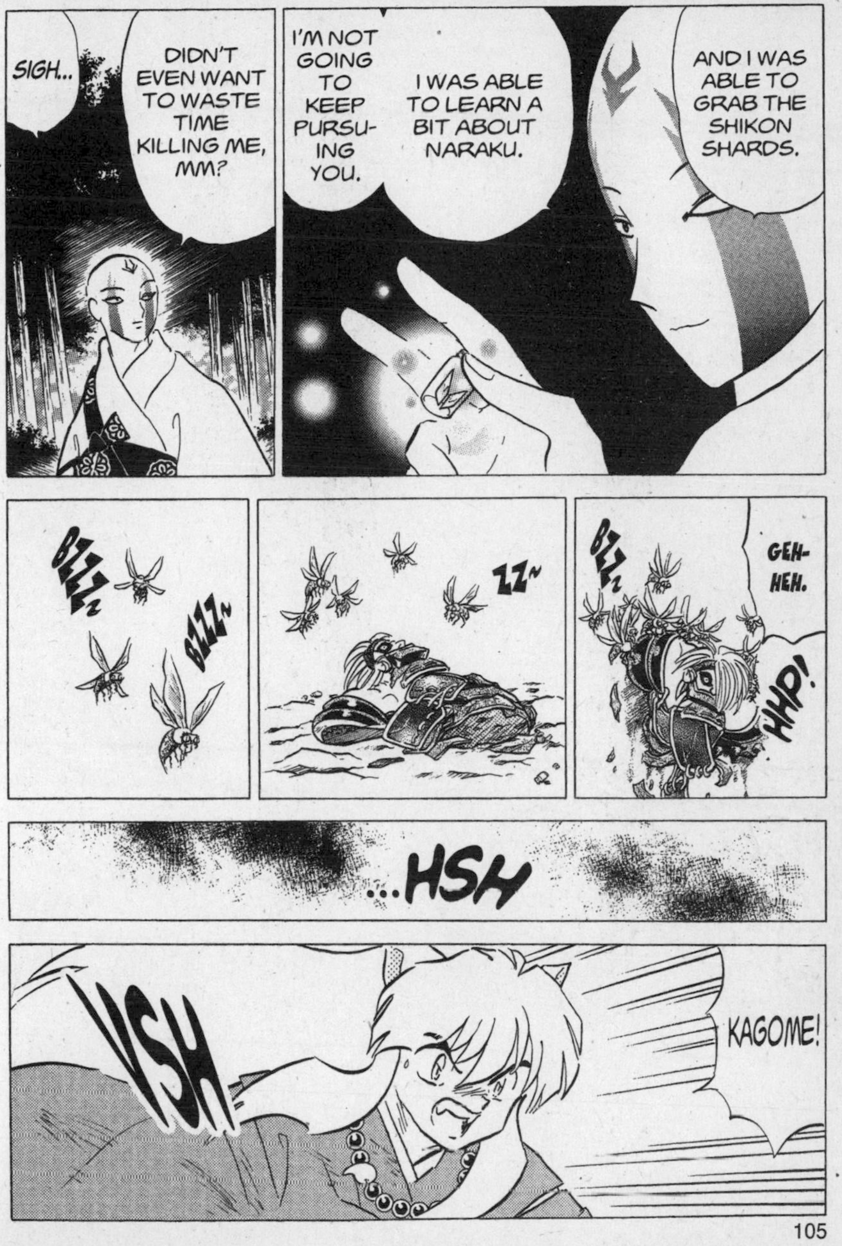
SIGH...
DIDN'T EVEN WANT TO WASTE TIME KILLING ME, MM?
I'M NOT GOING TO KEEP PURSU-ING YOU.
I WAS ABLE TO LEARN A BIT ABOUT NARAKU.
AND I WAS ABLE TO GRAB THE SHIKON SHARDS.
BZZZz
BZZZ~
ZZ~
BZZz
GEH-HEH.
HHP!
...HSH
VSH
KAGOME!

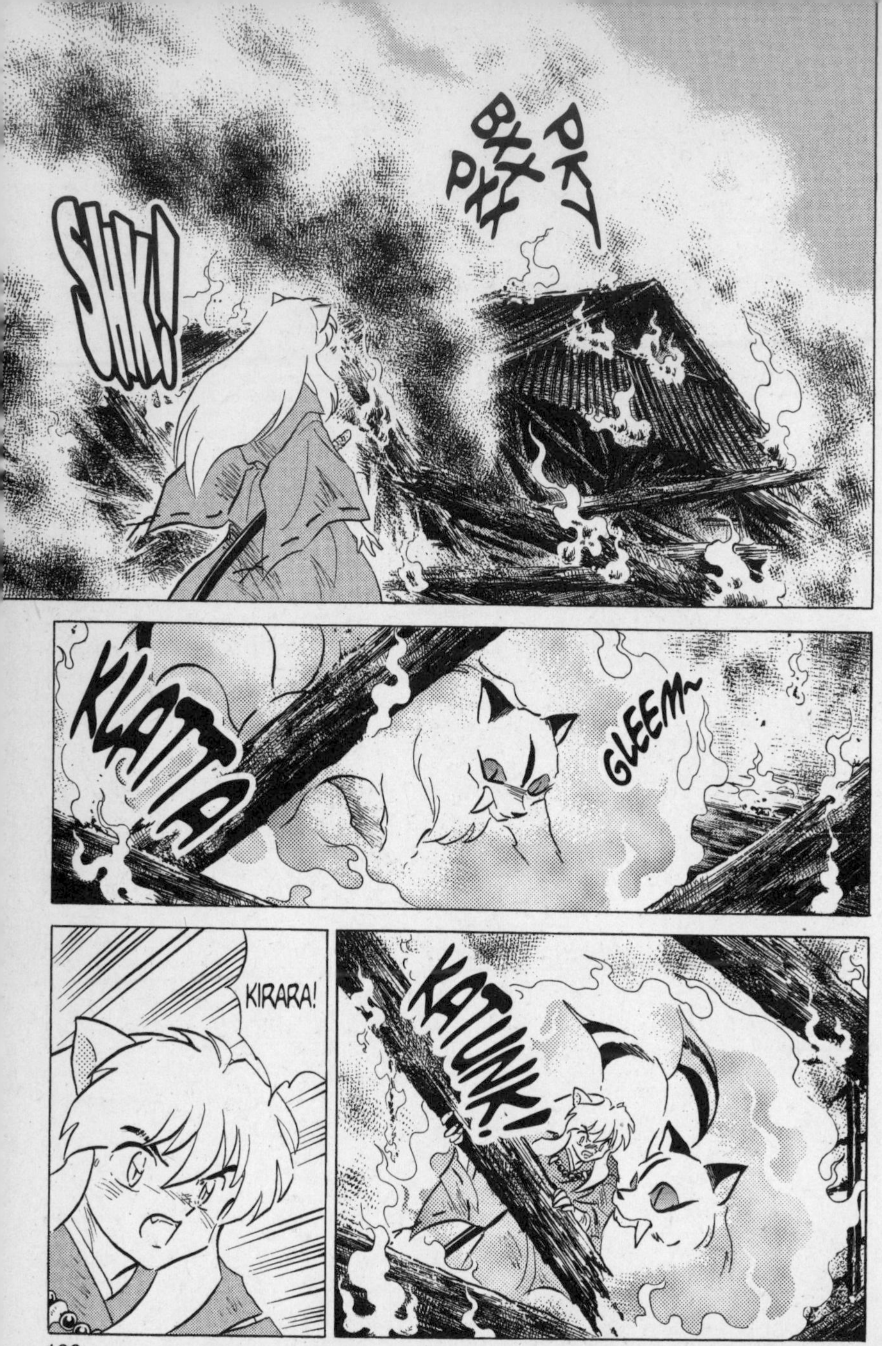
SHNK!
PKT
KLATTA
GLEEM~
KIRARA!
KATUNK!

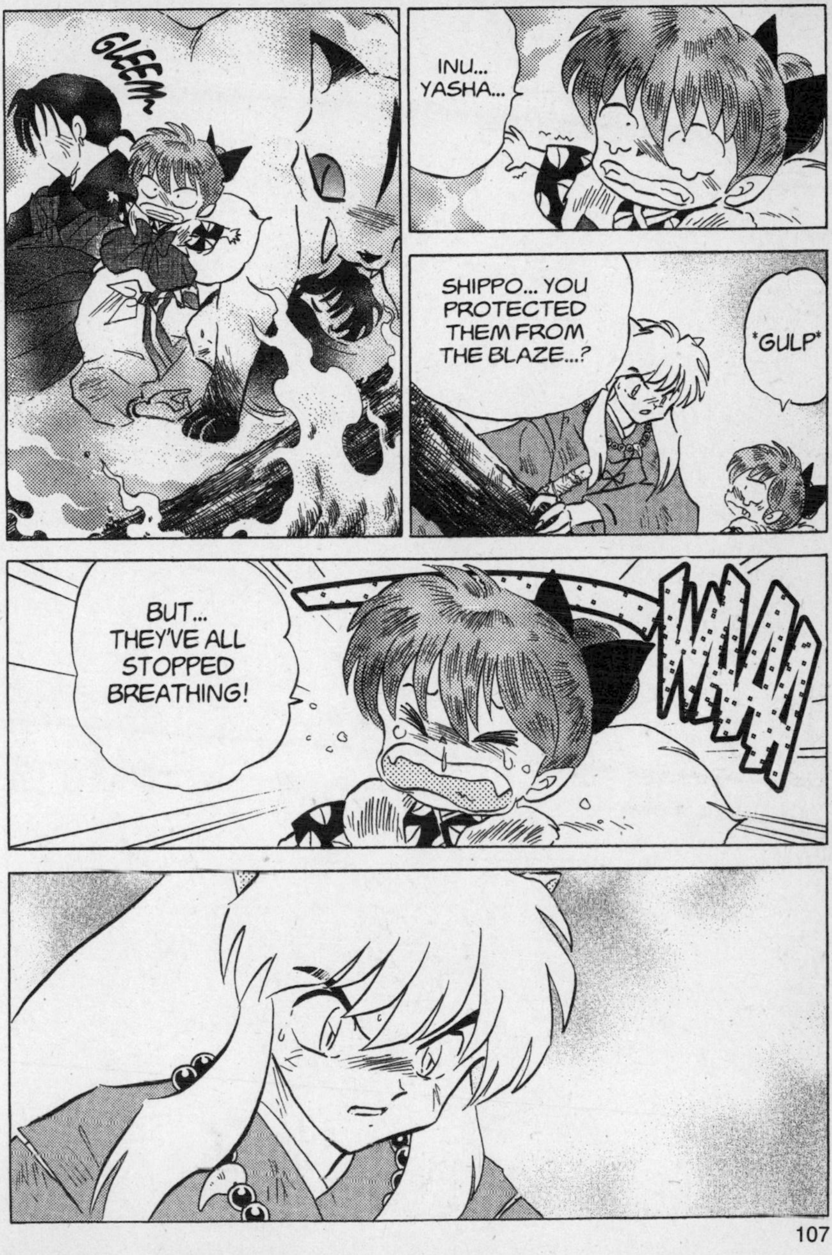
GLEEM~
INU... YASHA...
SHIPPO... YOU PROTECTED THEM FROM THE BLAZE...?
*GULP*
BUT... THEY'VE ALL STOPPED BREATHING!
WAA

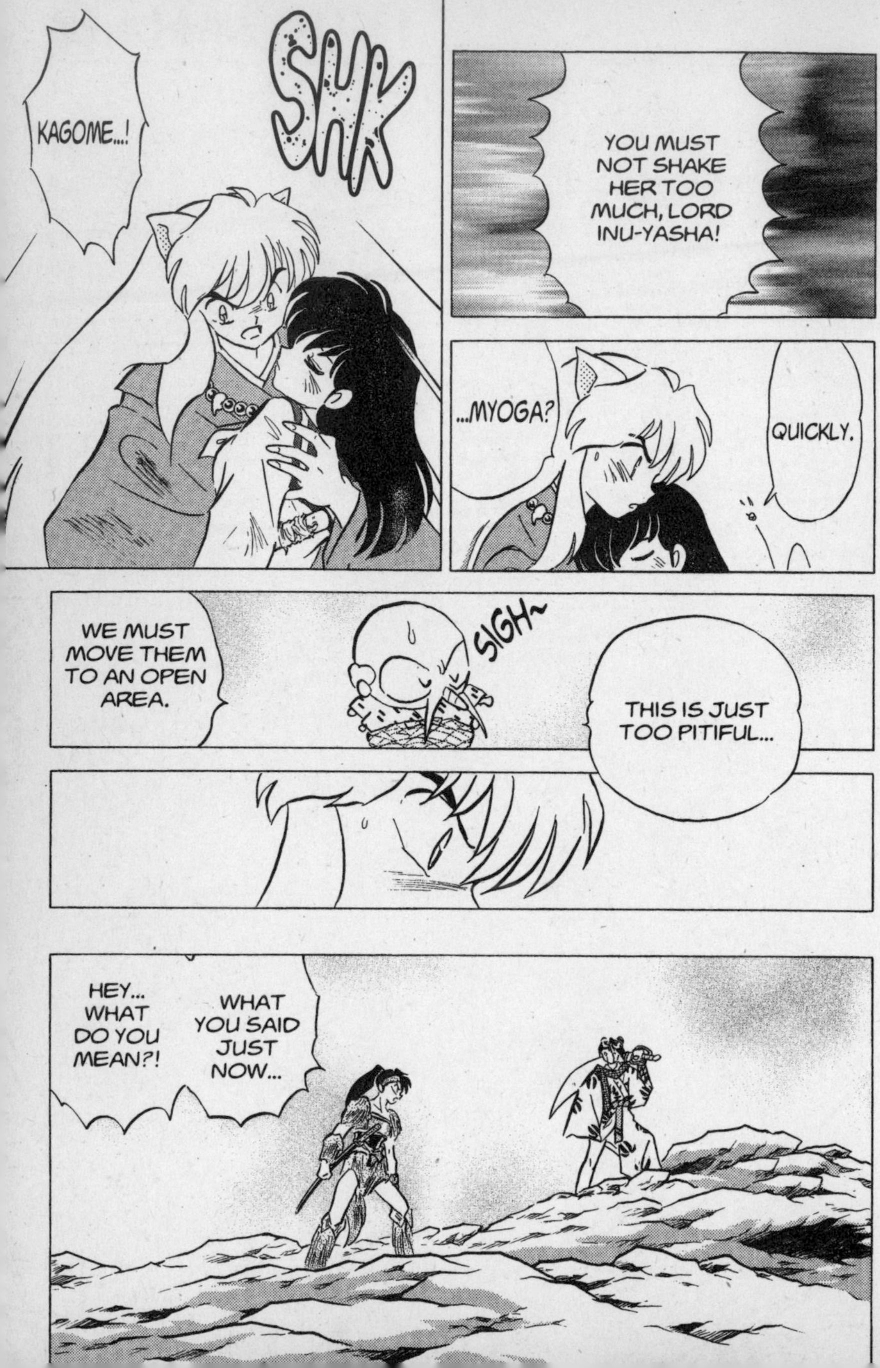
KAGOME...!
SHK
YOU MUST NOT SHAKE HER TOO MUCH, LORD INU-YASHA!
...MYOGA?
QUICKLY.
WE MUST MOVE THEM TO AN OPEN AREA.
SIGH~
THIS IS JUST TOO PITIFUL...
HEY... WHAT DO YOU MEAN?!
WHAT YOU SAID JUST NOW...

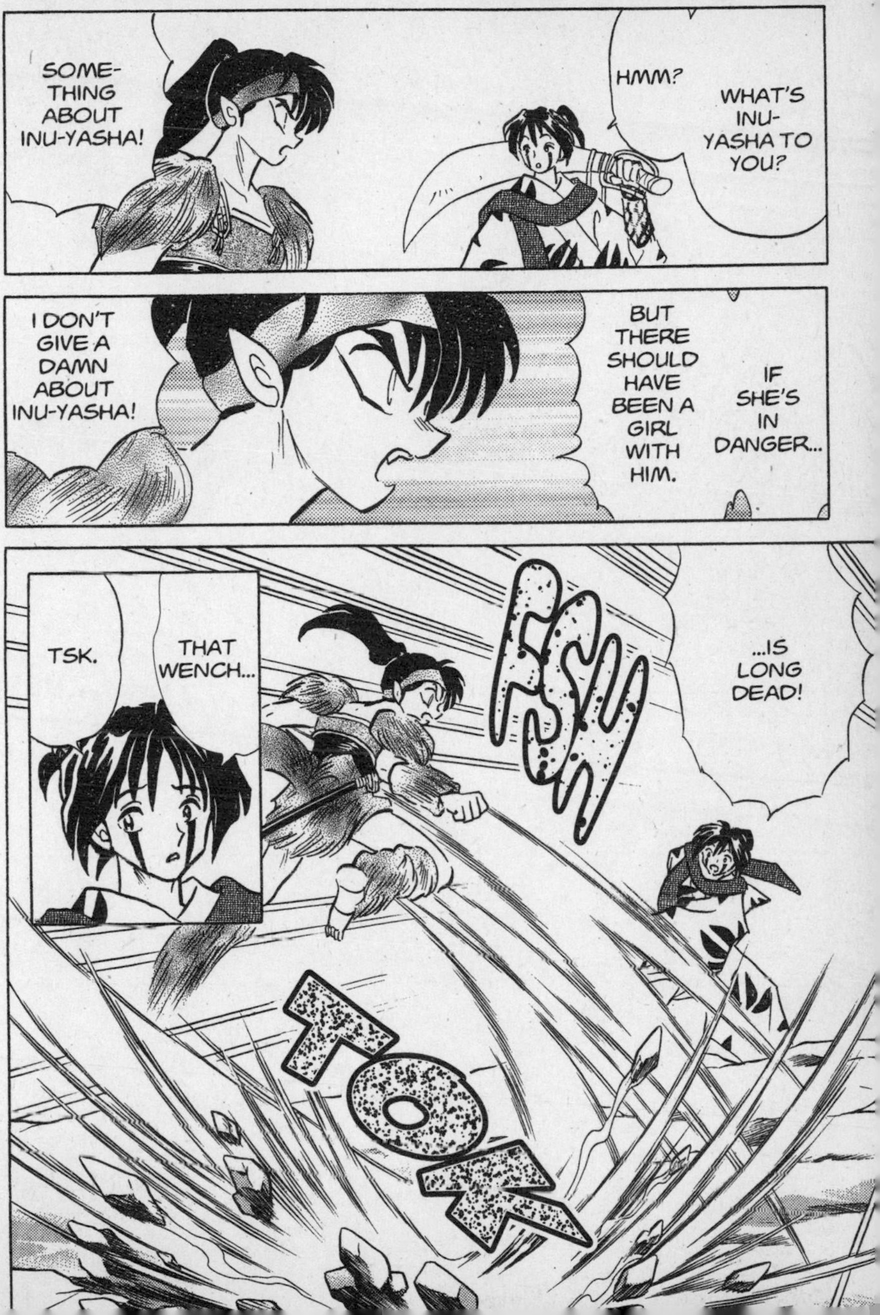
SOME-
THING
ABOUT
INU-YASHA!
HMM?
WHAT'S
INU-
YASHA TO
YOU?
I DON'T
GIVE A
DAMN
ABOUT
INU-YASHA!
BUT
THERE
SHOULD
HAVE
BEEN A
GIRL
WITH
HIM.
IF
SHE'S
IN
DANGER...
TSK.
THAT
WENCH...
FSSH
...IS
LONG
DEAD!
TOK

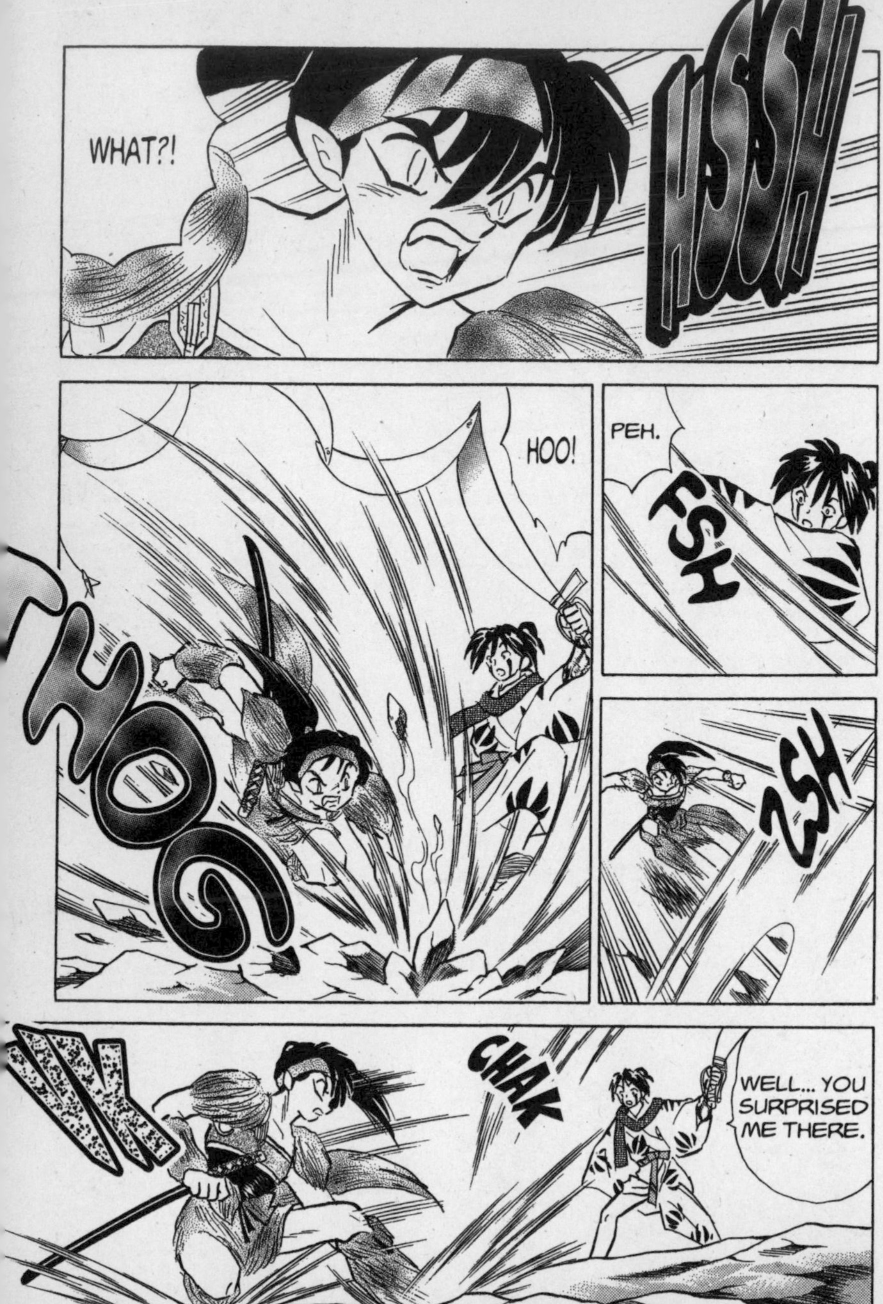
WHAT?!
HSSH
HOO!
PEH.
FSH
ZSH
CHAK
WELL... YOU SURPRISED ME THERE.

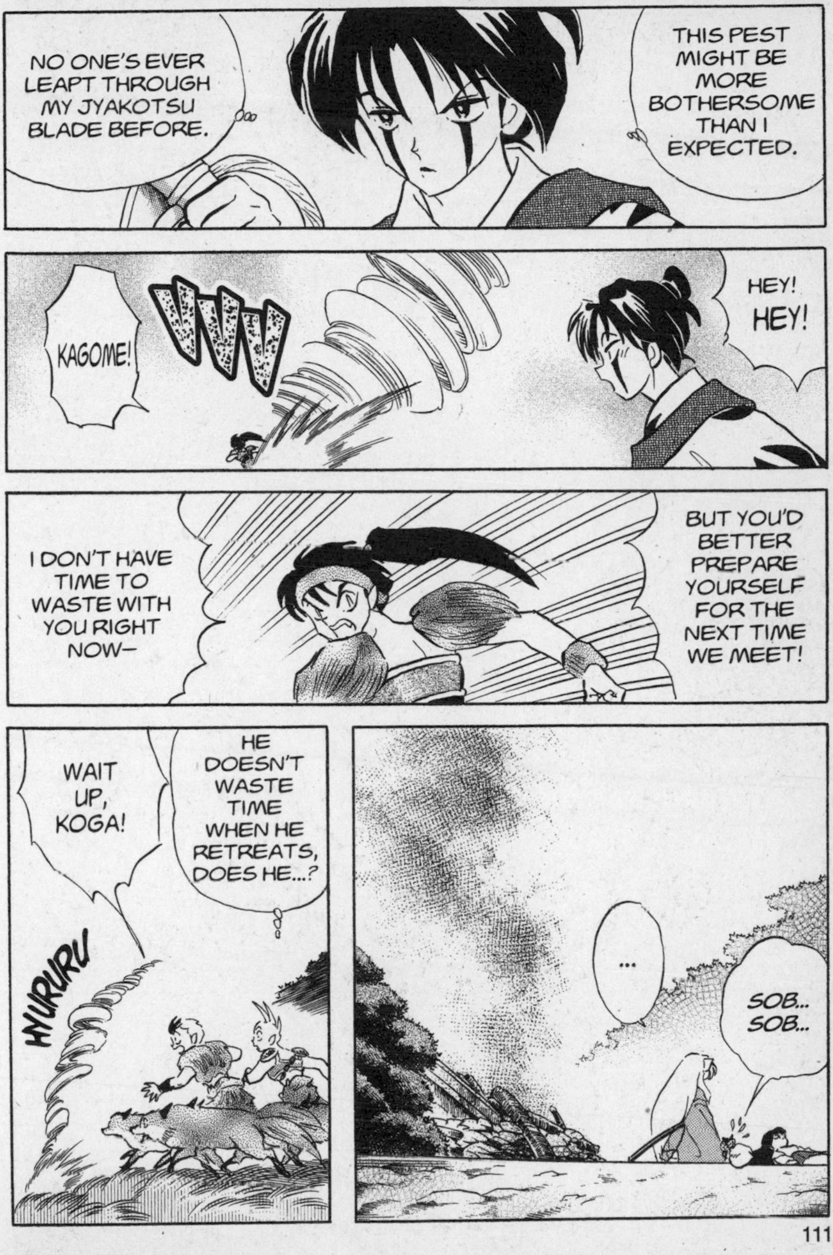
NO ONE'S EVER LEAPT THROUGH MY JYAKOTSU BLADE BEFORE.
THIS PEST MIGHT BE MORE BOTHERSOME THAN I EXPECTED.
KAGOME!
HEY! HEY!
I DON'T HAVE TIME TO WASTE WITH YOU RIGHT NOW–
BUT YOU'D BETTER PREPARE YOURSELF FOR THE NEXT TIME WE MEET!
WAIT UP, KOGA!
HE DOESN'T WASTE TIME WHEN HE RETREATS, DOES HE...?
HYURURU
...
SOB... SOB...

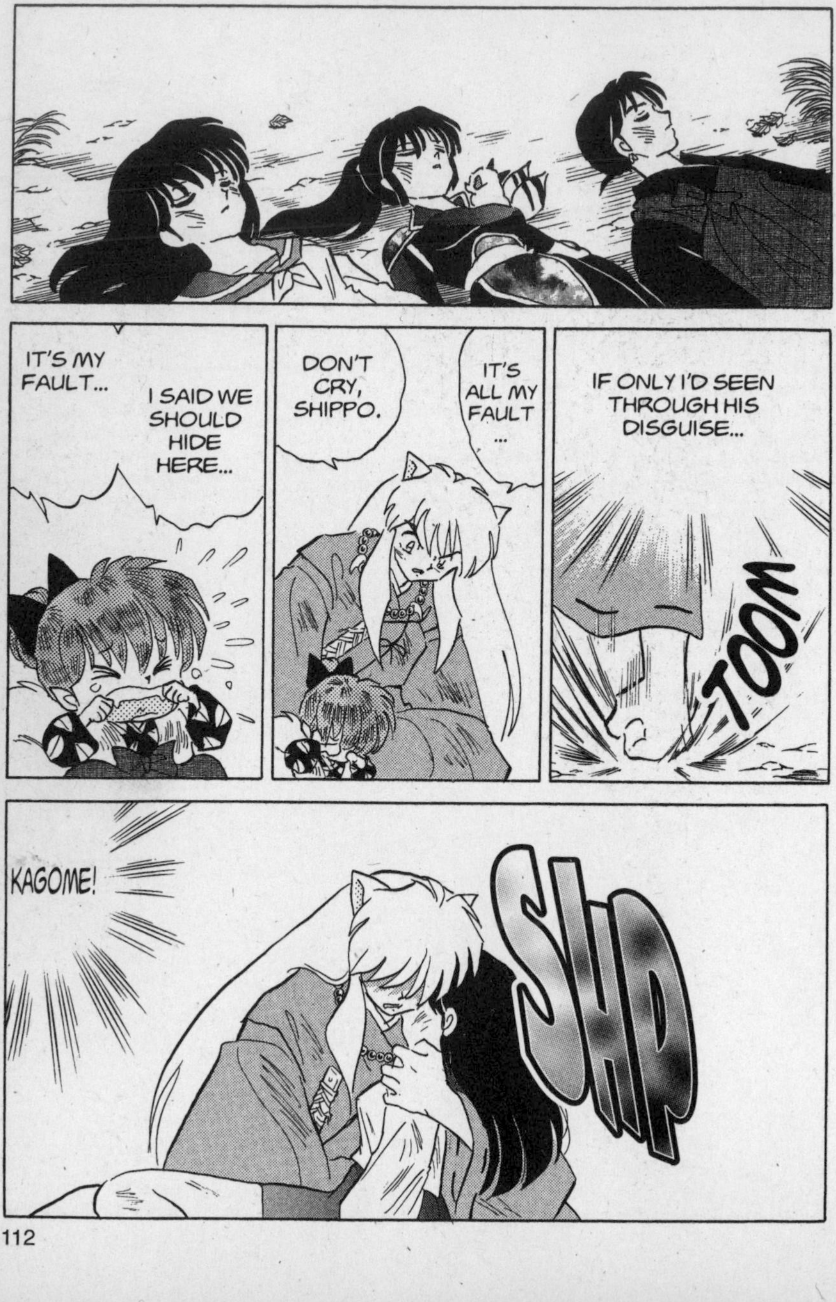
IT'S MY FAULT...
I SAID WE SHOULD HIDE HERE...
DON'T CRY, SHIPPO.
IT'S ALL MY FAULT ...
IF ONLY I'D SEEN THROUGH HIS DISGUISE...
TOOM
KAGOME!
SHP

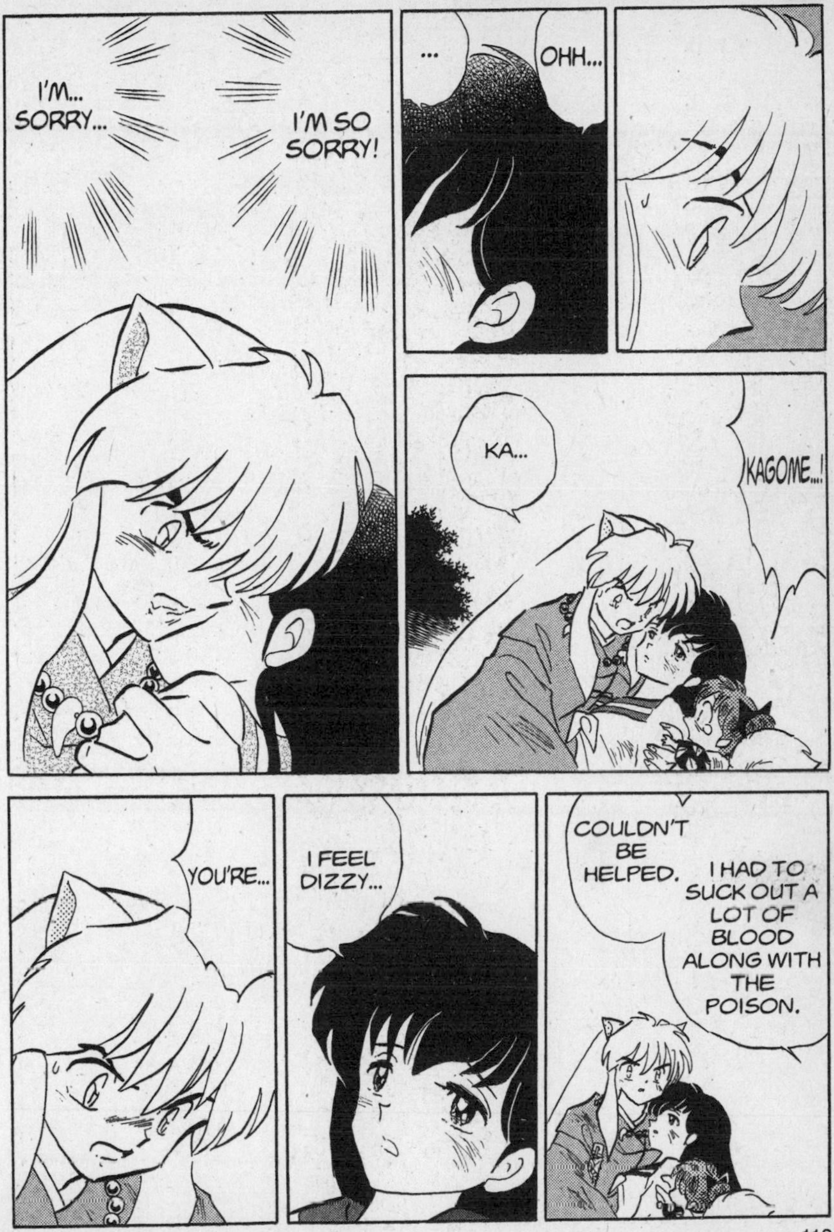
I'M... SORRY...
I'M SO SORRY!
...
OHH...
KA...
KAGOME...!
YOU'RE...
I FEEL DIZZY...
COULDN'T BE HELPED.
I HAD TO SUCK OUT A LOT OF BLOOD ALONG WITH THE POISON.

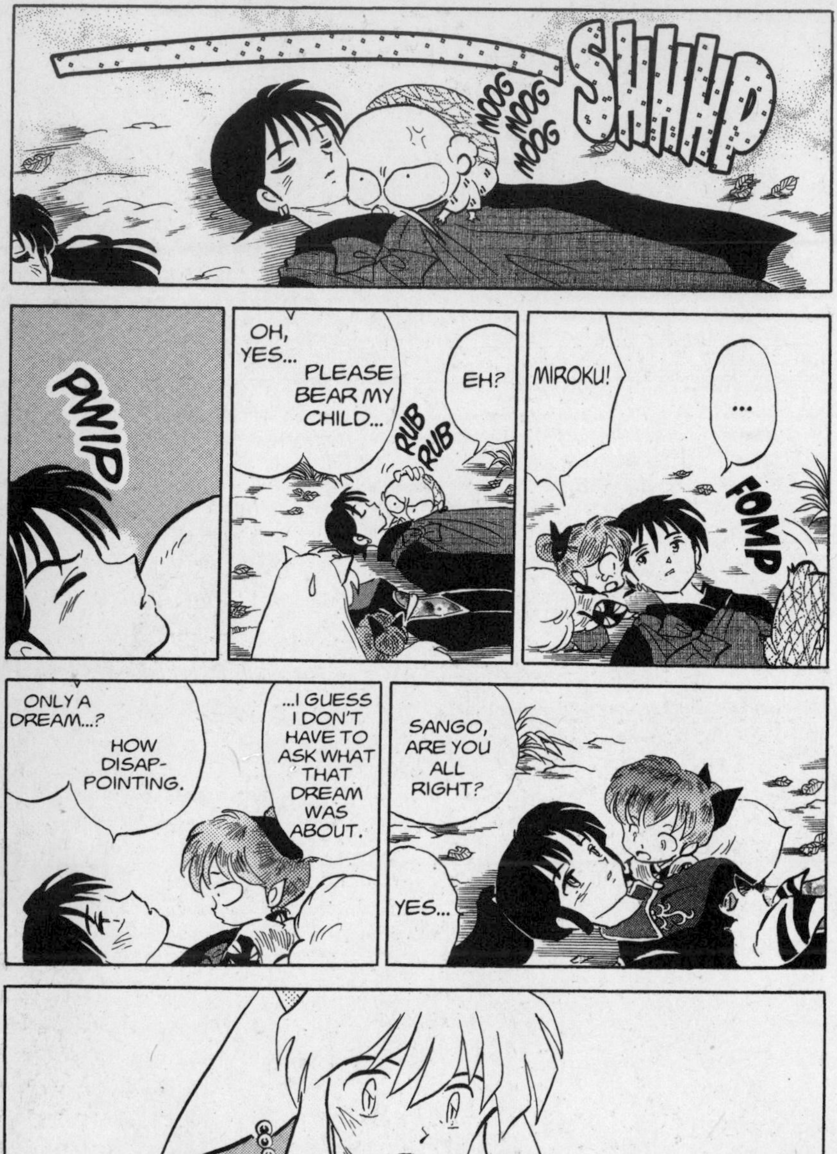
SHHHP
MOOG MOOG MOOG
PWIP
OH, YES... PLEASE BEAR MY CHILD...
RUB RUB
EH?
MIROKU!
...
FOMP
ONLY A DREAM...? HOW DISAP-POINTING.
...I GUESS I DON'T HAVE TO ASK WHAT THAT DREAM WAS ABOUT.
SANGO, ARE YOU ALL RIGHT?
YES...

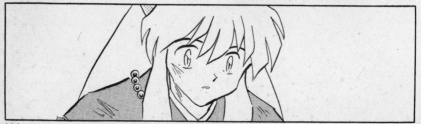

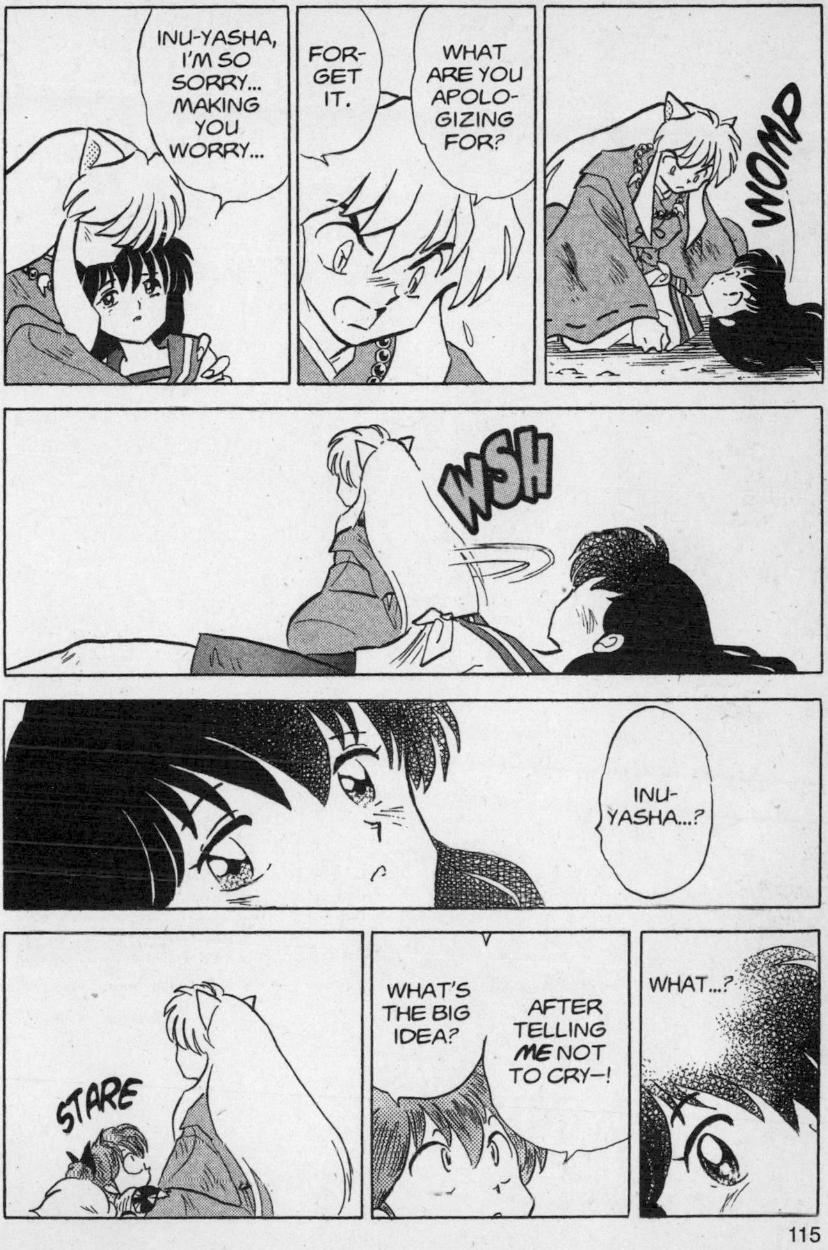
INU-YASHA, I'M SO SORRY... MAKING YOU WORRY...
FOR-GET IT.
WHAT ARE YOU APOLO-GIZING FOR?
WOMP
WSH
INU-YASHA...?
STARE
WHAT'S THE BIG IDEA?
AFTER TELLING *ME* NOT TO CRY—!
WHAT...?

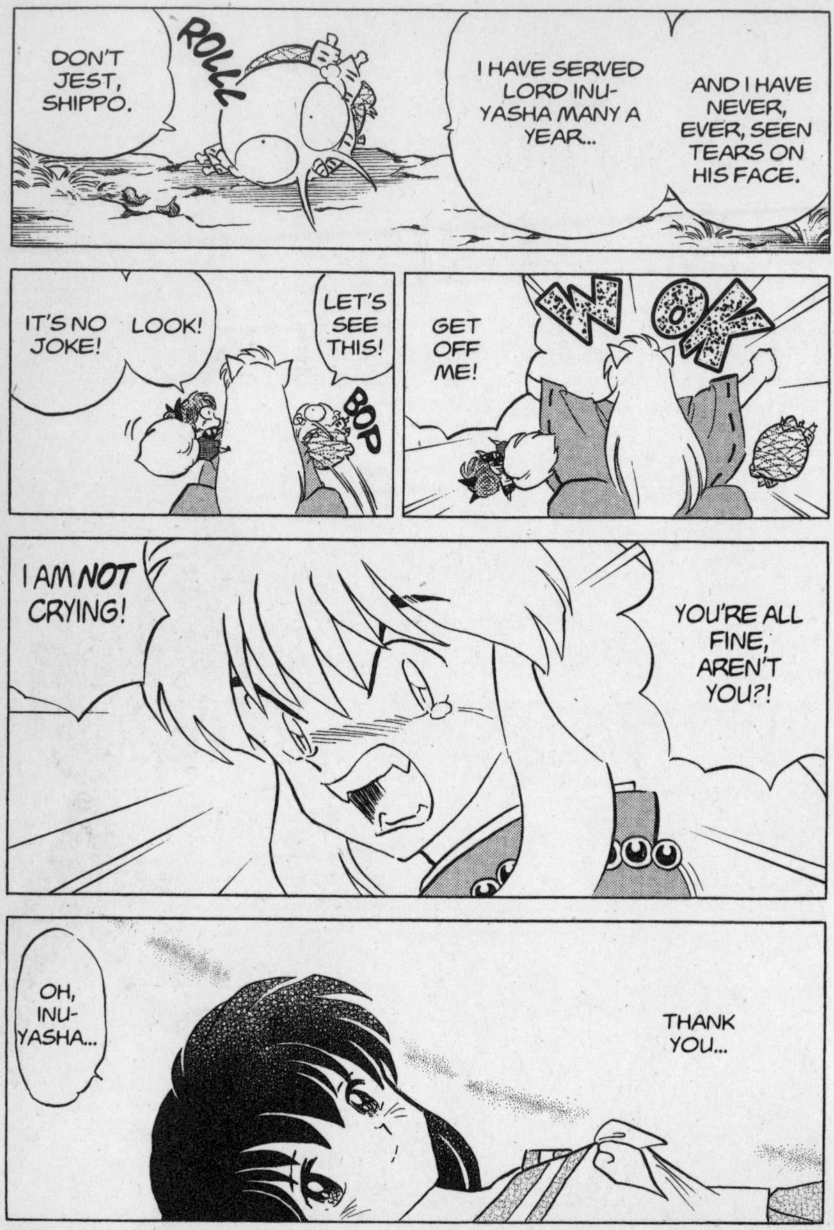

DON'T JEST, SHIPPO.
ROLL
I HAVE SERVED LORD INU-YASHA MANY A YEAR...
AND I HAVE NEVER, EVER, SEEN TEARS ON HIS FACE.
IT'S NO JOKE!
LOOK!
LET'S SEE THIS!
BOP
GET OFF ME!
WOK
I AM **NOT** CRYING!
YOU'RE ALL FINE, AREN'T YOU?!
OH, INU-YASHA...
THANK YOU...

SCROLL SEVEN

# THE BURIAL MOUND

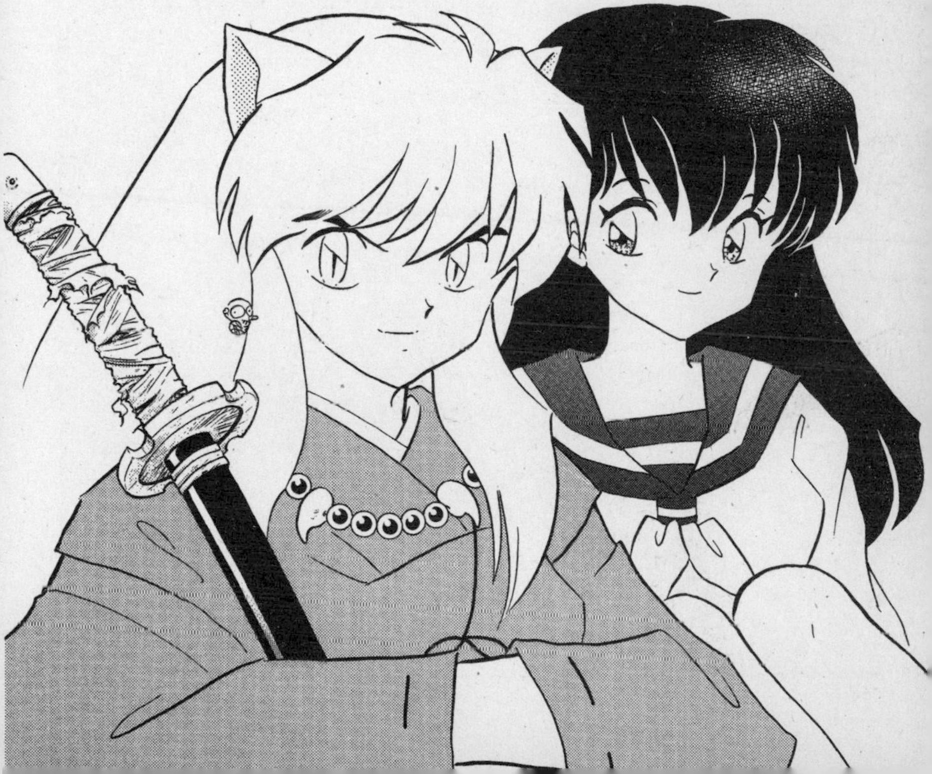

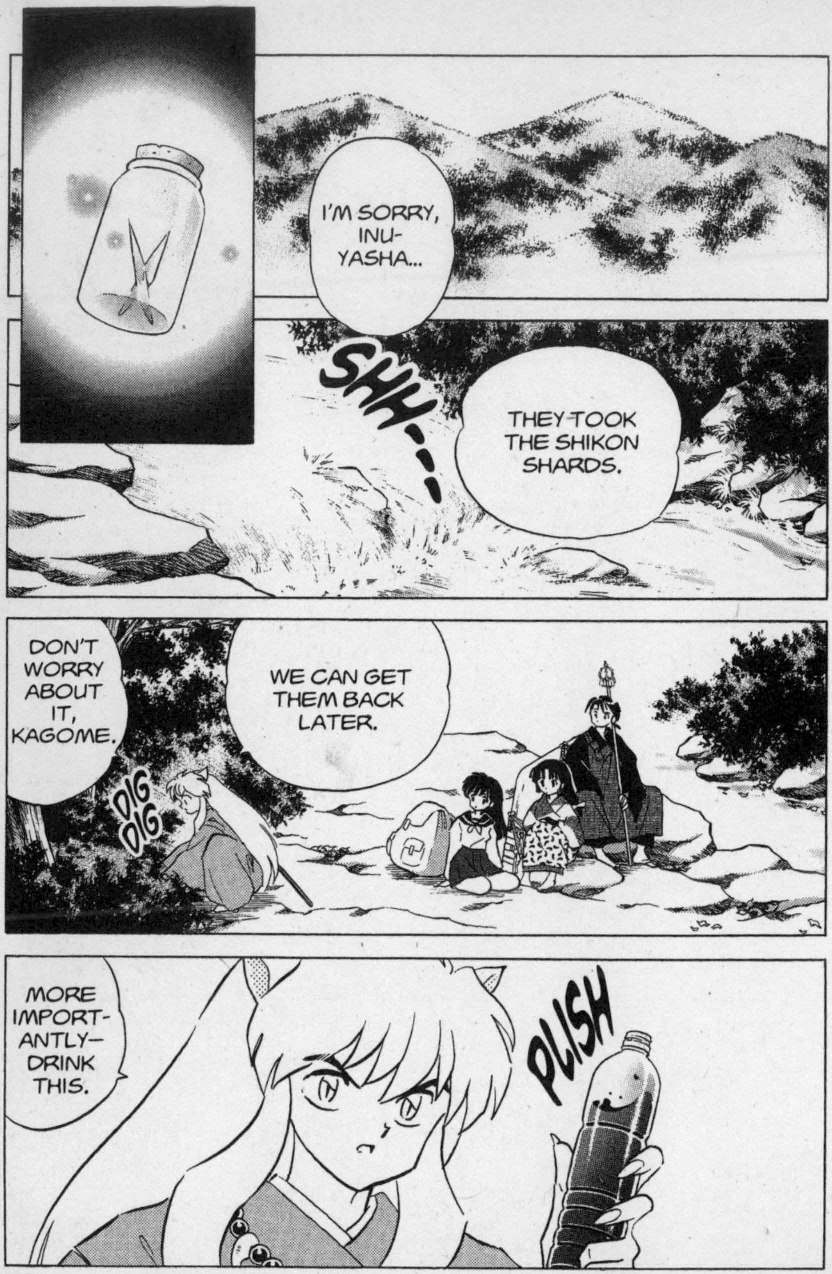
I'M SORRY, INU-YASHA...
SHHH...
THEY TOOK THE SHIKON SHARDS.
DON'T WORRY ABOUT IT, KAGOME.
WE CAN GET THEM BACK LATER.
DIG DIG
MORE IMPORT-ANTLY— DRINK THIS.
PLISH

MIROKU, SANGO, YOU TOO!

FAP

FAP

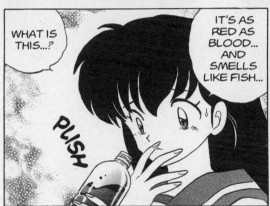

WHAT IS THIS...?

IT'S AS RED AS BLOOD... AND SMELLS LIKE FISH...

PUSH

JUST DRINK IT.

IT'S MYOGA'S SPECIAL HEALING ELIXIR!

PING

FOR IN ORDER TO SAVE YOUR LIVES, I HAD TO SUCK OUT QUITE A LARGE AMOUNT OF BLOOD ALONG WITH THE POISONS.

DRINK THIS ELIXIR AND YOUR BODY WILL RESTORE THE BLOOD QUICKLY. YOU'LL FEEL BETTER IN NO TIME.

DAMN, FLEA...IT'S SO BITTER!

GUG

I'M AFRAID WE MUST GRIN AND BEAR IT.

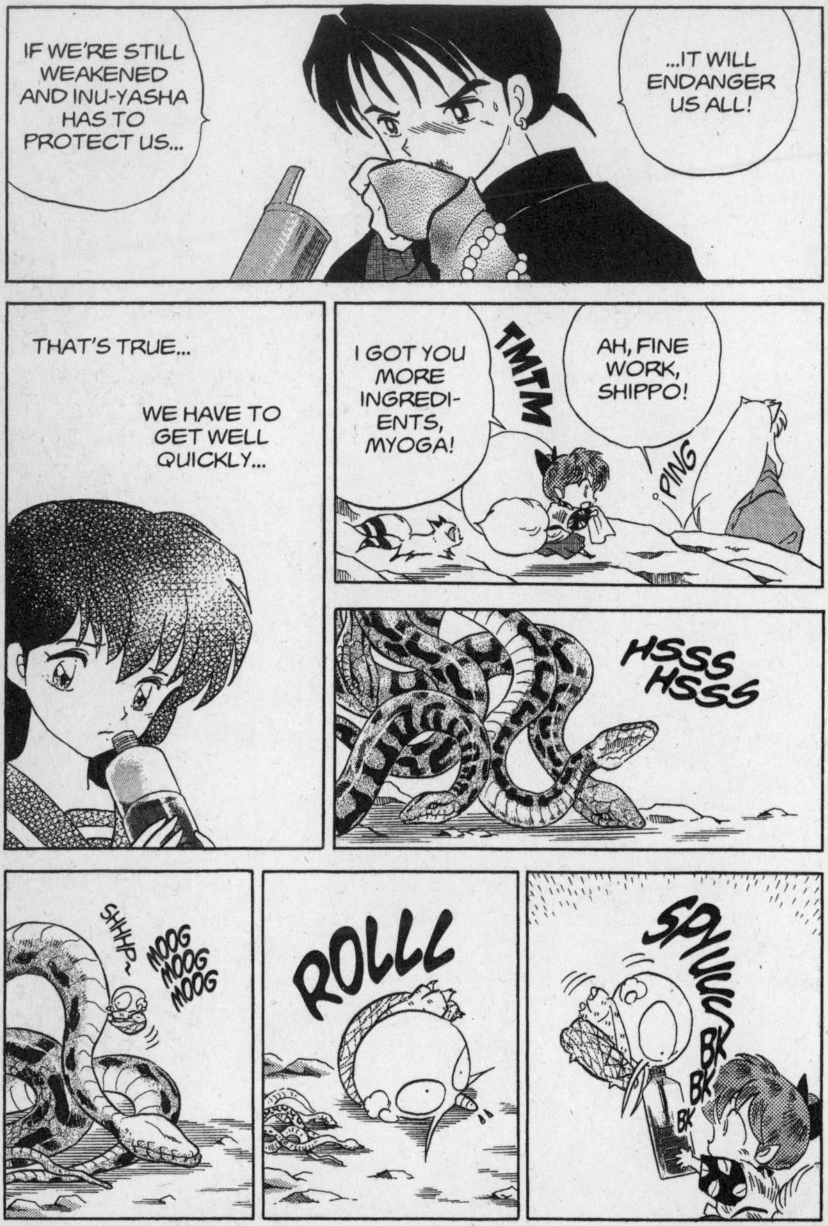

IF WE'RE STILL WEAKENED AND INU-YASHA HAS TO PROTECT US...
...IT WILL ENDANGER US ALL!
THAT'S TRUE...
WE HAVE TO GET WELL QUICKLY...
I GOT YOU MORE INGREDI-ENTS, MYOGA!
TMTM
AH, FINE WORK, SHIPPO!
PING
HSSS HSSS
SHHHP~
MOOG MOOG MOOG
ROLLL
SPYUUU
BK BK BK BK

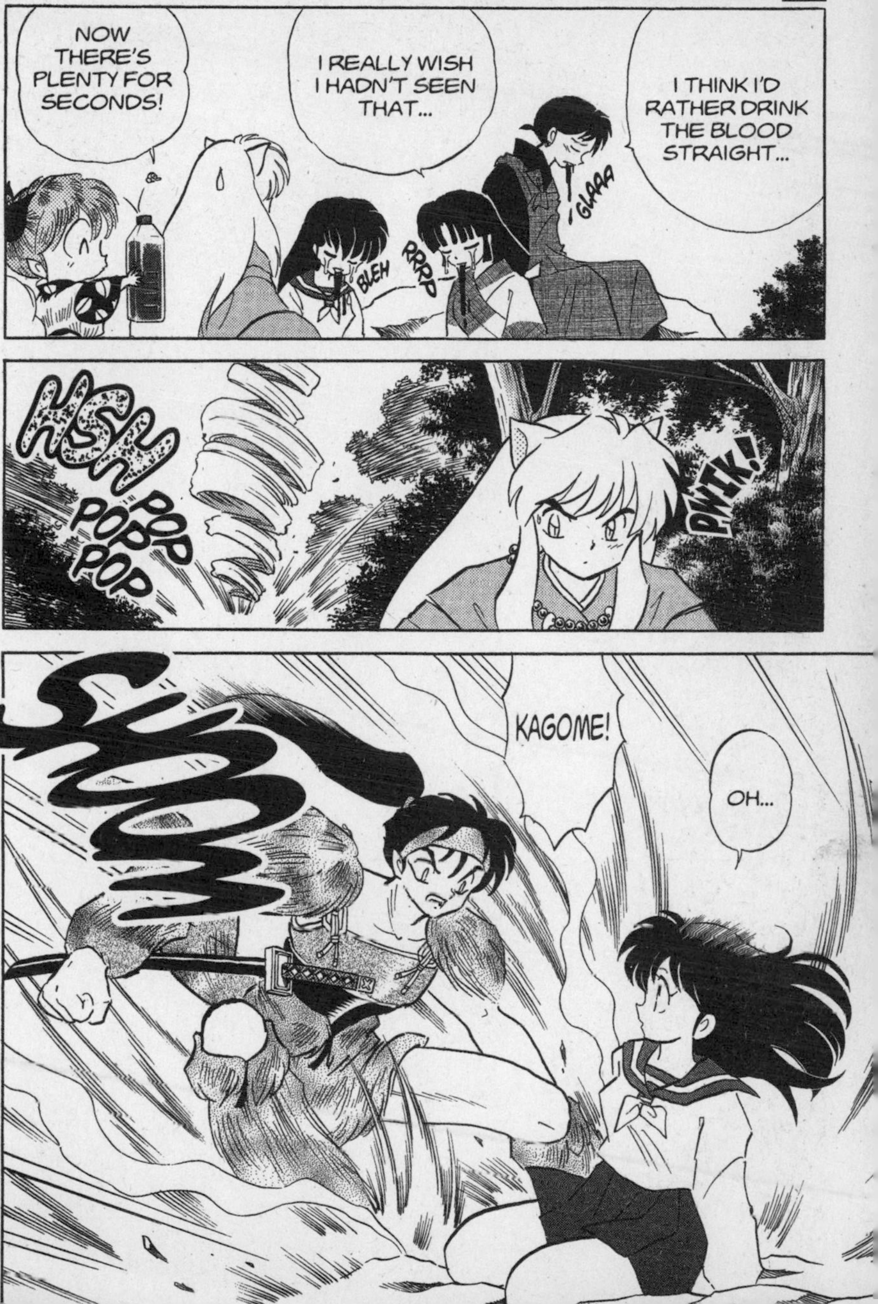
NOW THERE'S PLENTY FOR SECONDS!
I REALLY WISH I HADN'T SEEN THAT...
BLEH
RRRP
GLAAA
I THINK I'D RATHER DRINK THE BLOOD STRAIGHT...
HSH
POP POP POP
PWIK!
SHOOM
KAGOME!
OH...

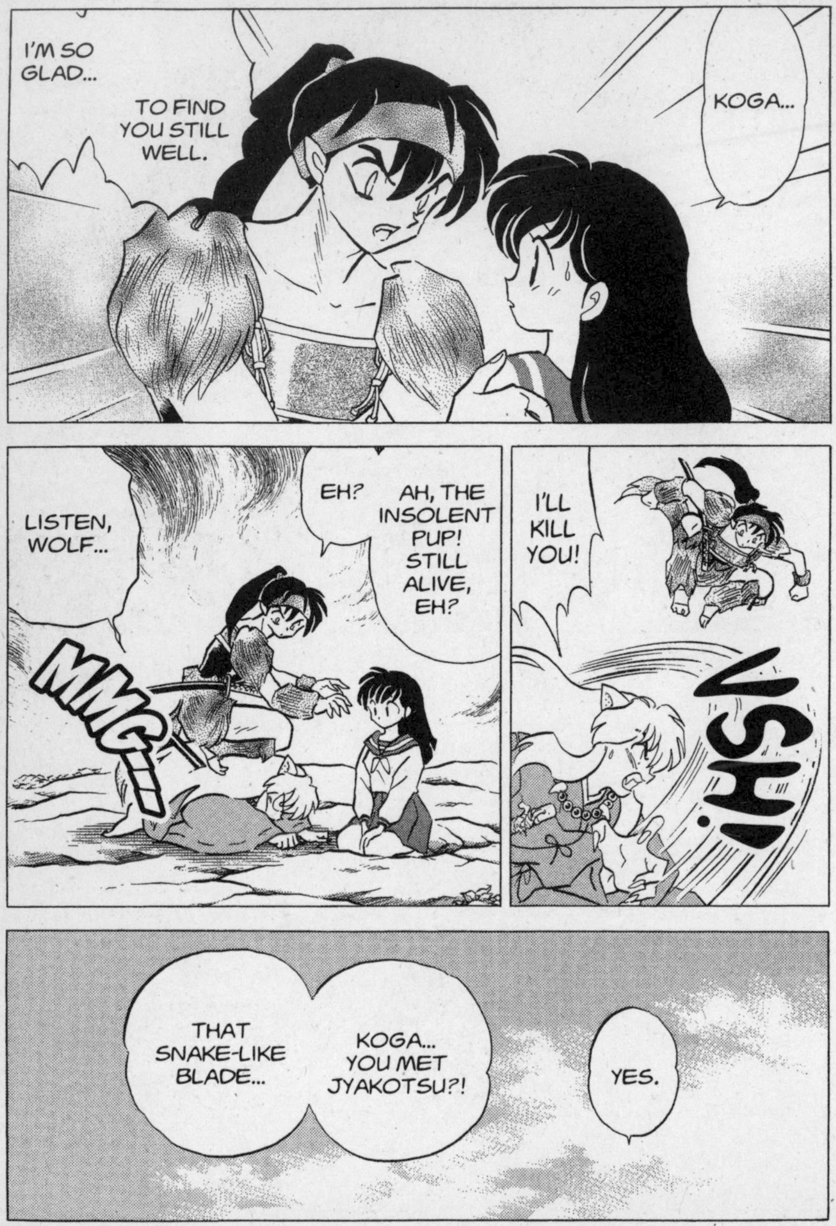
I'M SO GLAD...
TO FIND YOU STILL WELL.
KOGA...
LISTEN, WOLF...
MMG...
EH?
AH, THE INSOLENT PUP! STILL ALIVE, EH?
I'LL KILL YOU!
VSH!
THAT SNAKE-LIKE BLADE...
KOGA... YOU MET JYAKOTSU?!
YES.

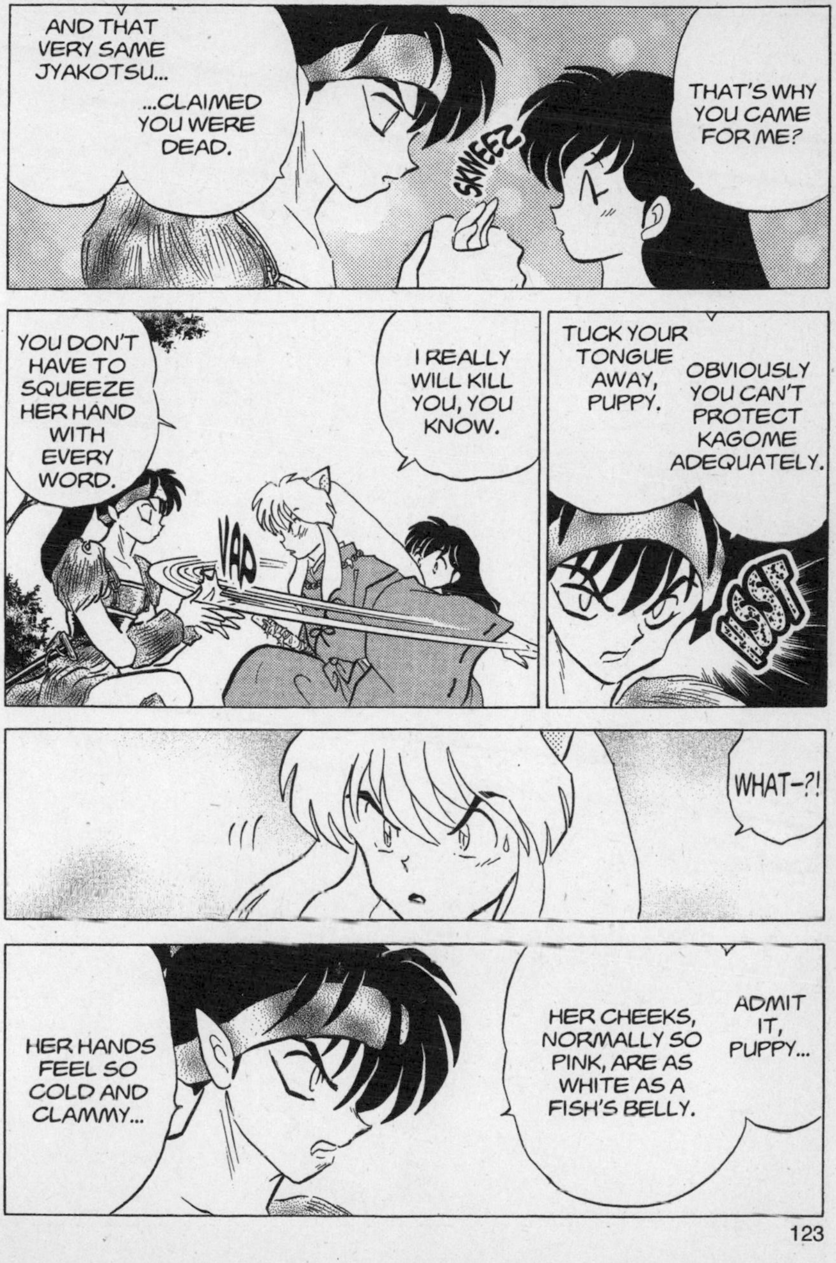
AND THAT VERY SAME JYAKOTSU...
...CLAIMED YOU WERE DEAD.
SKWEEZ
THAT'S WHY YOU CAME FOR ME?
YOU DON'T HAVE TO SQUEEZE HER HAND WITH EVERY WORD.
VAP
I REALLY WILL KILL YOU, YOU KNOW.
TUCK YOUR TONGUE AWAY, PUPPY.
OBVIOUSLY YOU CAN'T PROTECT KAGOME ADEQUATELY.
HISST
WHAT-?!
HER HANDS FEEL SO COLD AND CLAMMY...
HER CHEEKS, NORMALLY SO PINK, ARE AS WHITE AS A FISH'S BELLY.
ADMIT IT, PUPPY...

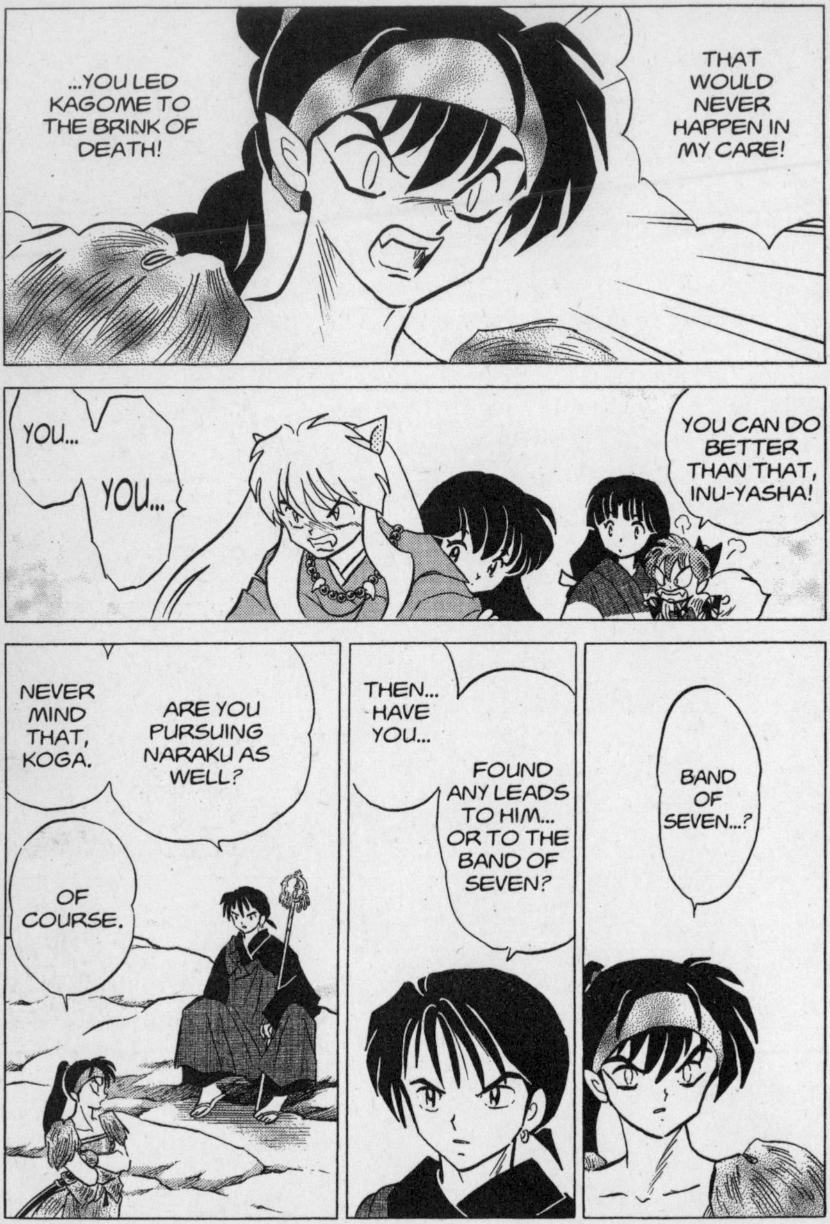
...YOU LED KAGOME TO THE BRINK OF DEATH!
THAT WOULD NEVER HAPPEN IN MY CARE!
YOU...
YOU...
YOU CAN DO BETTER THAN THAT, INU-YASHA!
NEVER MIND THAT, KOGA.
ARE YOU PURSUING NARAKU AS WELL?
OF COURSE.
THEN... HAVE YOU...
FOUND ANY LEADS TO HIM... OR TO THE BAND OF SEVEN?
BAND OF SEVEN...?

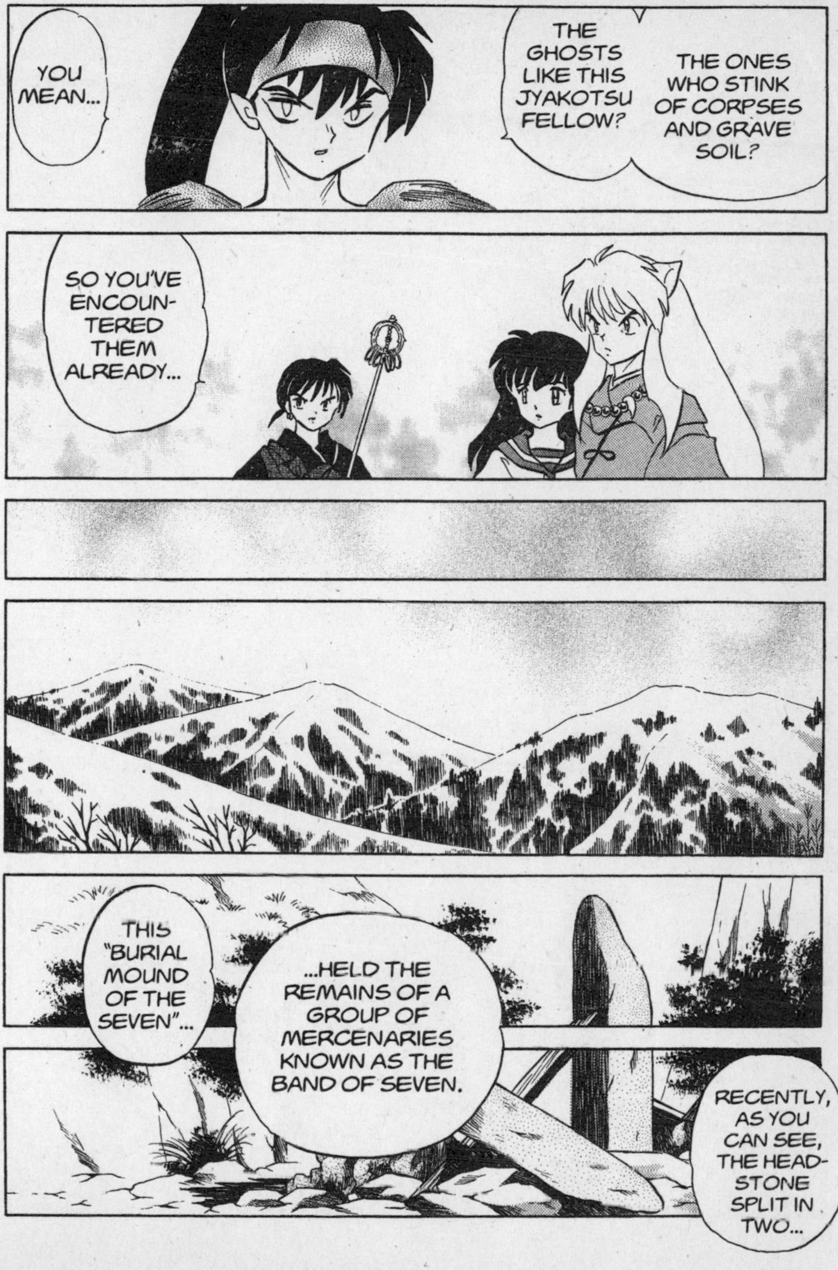
YOU MEAN...
THE GHOSTS LIKE THIS JYAKOTSU FELLOW?
THE ONES WHO STINK OF CORPSES AND GRAVE SOIL?
SO YOU'VE ENCOUN-TERED THEM ALREADY...
THIS "BURIAL MOUND OF THE SEVEN"...
...HELD THE REMAINS OF A GROUP OF MERCENARIES KNOWN AS THE BAND OF SEVEN.
RECENTLY, AS YOU CAN SEE, THE HEAD-STONE SPLIT IN TWO...

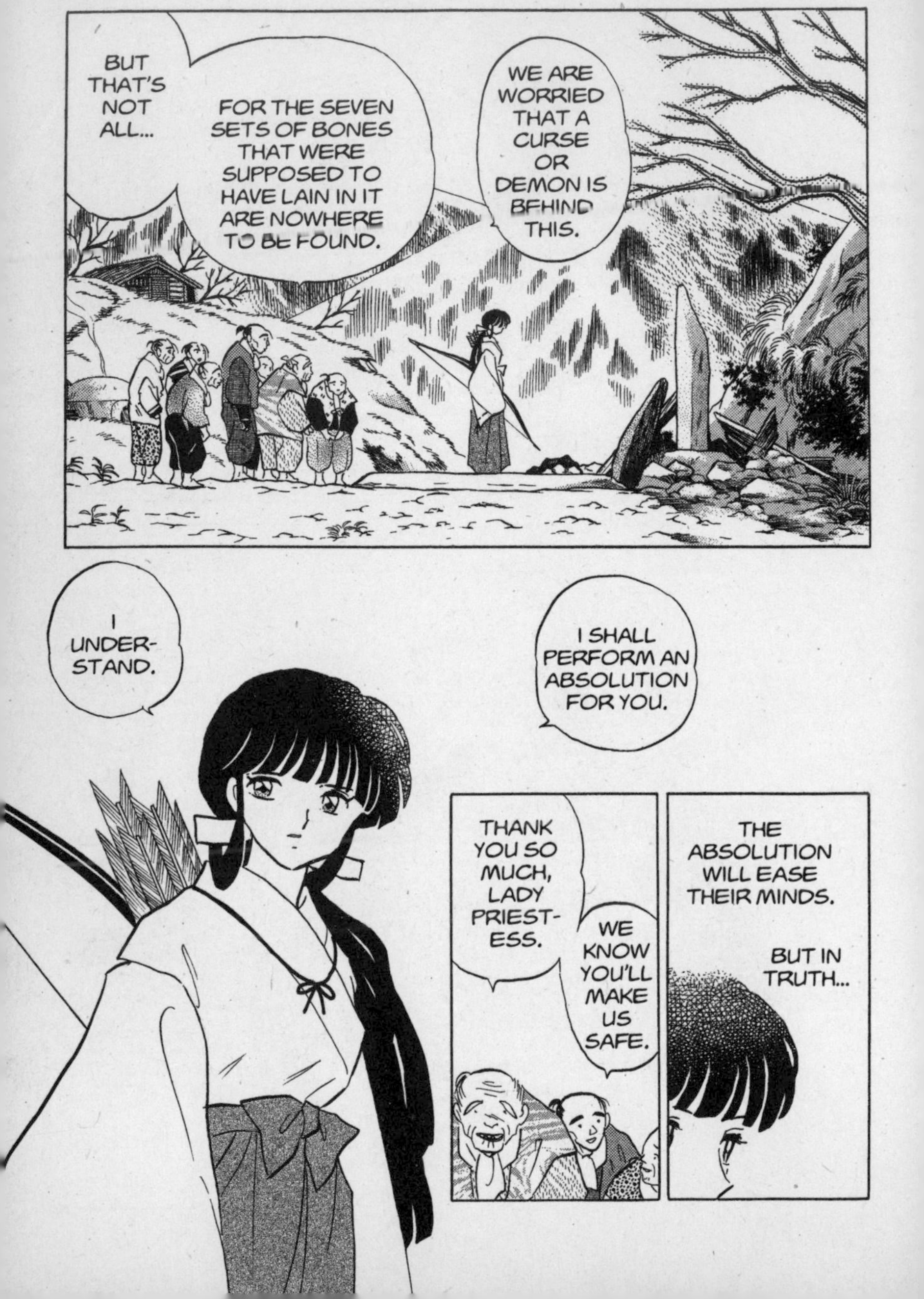
BUT THAT'S NOT ALL...
FOR THE SEVEN SETS OF BONES THAT WERE SUPPOSED TO HAVE LAIN IN IT ARE NOWHERE TO BE FOUND.
WE ARE WORRIED THAT A CURSE OR DEMON IS BEHIND THIS.
I UNDERSTAND.
I SHALL PERFORM AN ABSOLUTION FOR YOU.
THANK YOU SO MUCH, LADY PRIESTESS.
WE KNOW YOU'LL MAKE US SAFE.
THE ABSOLUTION WILL EASE THEIR MINDS.
BUT IN TRUTH...

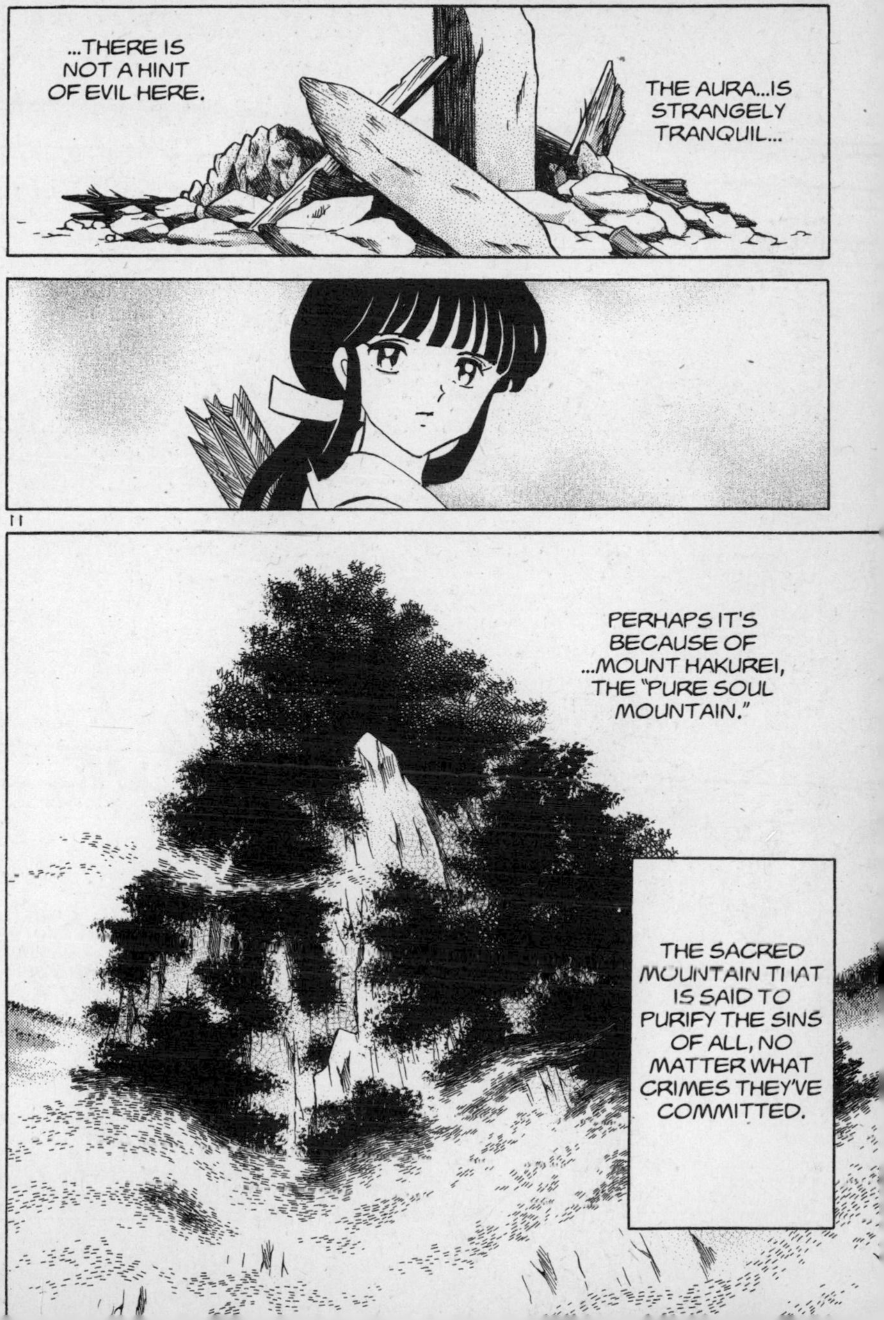
...THERE IS NOT A HINT OF EVIL HERE.
THE AURA...IS STRANGELY TRANQUIL...
PERHAPS IT'S BECAUSE OF ...MOUNT HAKUREI, THE "PURE SOUL MOUNTAIN."
THE SACRED MOUNTAIN THAT IS SAID TO PURIFY THE SINS OF ALL, NO MATTER WHAT CRIMES THEY'VE COMMITTED.

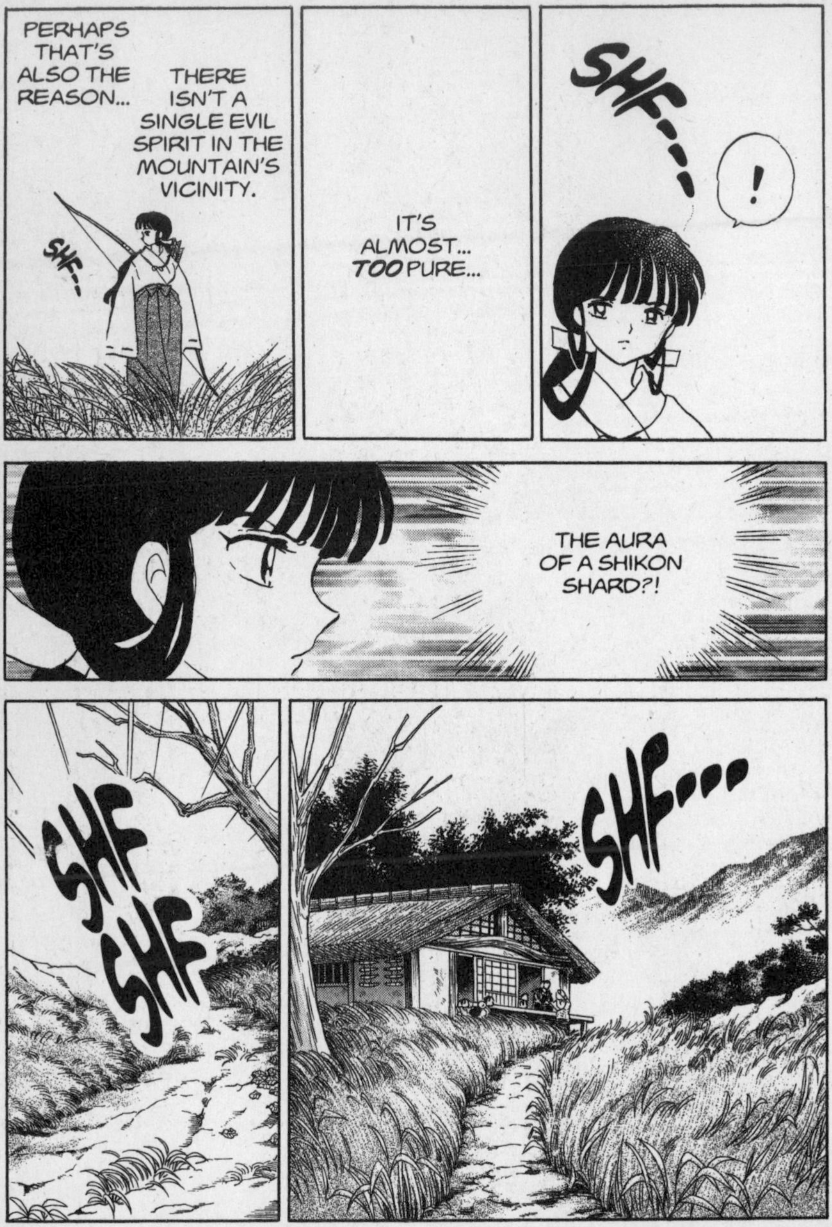

PERHAPS THAT'S ALSO THE REASON...
THERE ISN'T A SINGLE EVIL SPIRIT IN THE MOUNTAIN'S VICINITY.
SHF...
IT'S ALMOST... TOO PURE...
SHF...
!
THE AURA OF A SHIKON SHARD?!
SHF SHF
SHF...

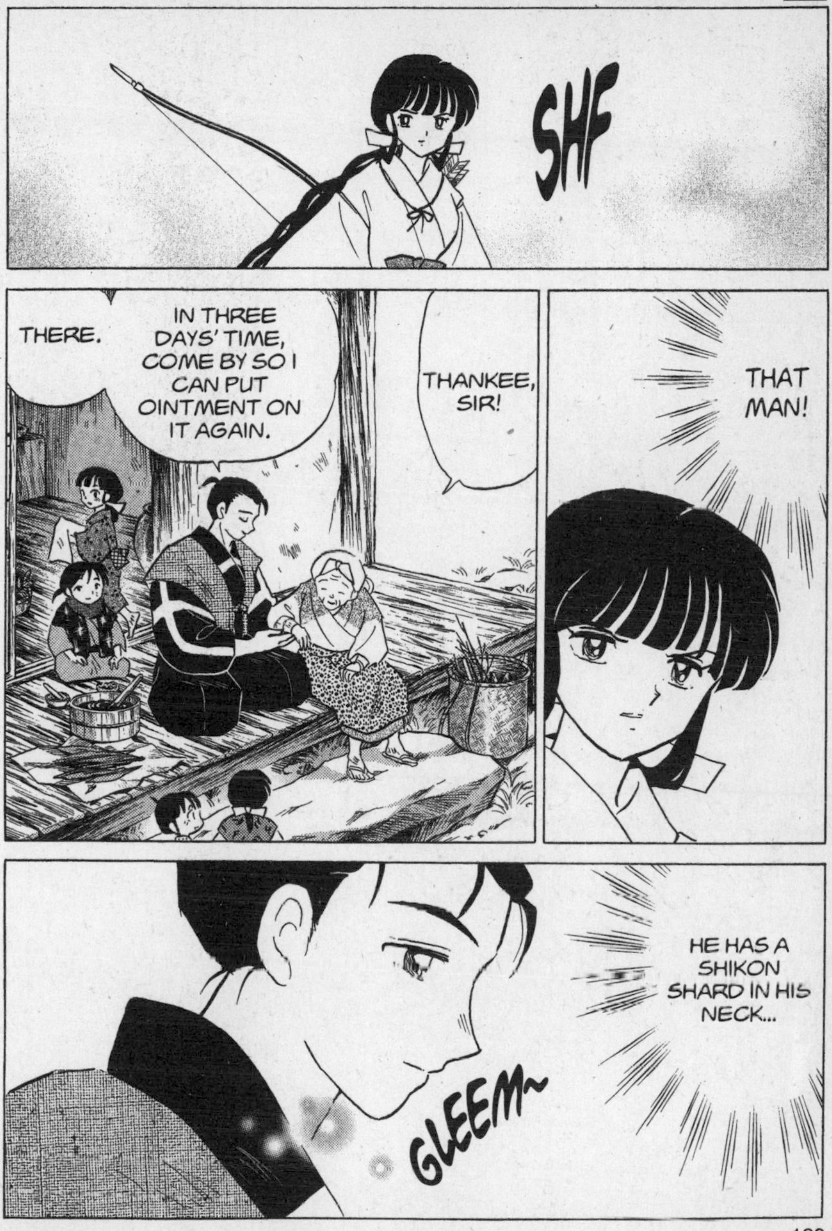
SHF
IN THREE DAYS' TIME, COME BY SO I CAN PUT OINTMENT ON IT AGAIN.
THERE.
THAT MAN!
THANKEE, SIR!
HE HAS A SHIKON SHARD IN HIS NECK...
GLEEM~

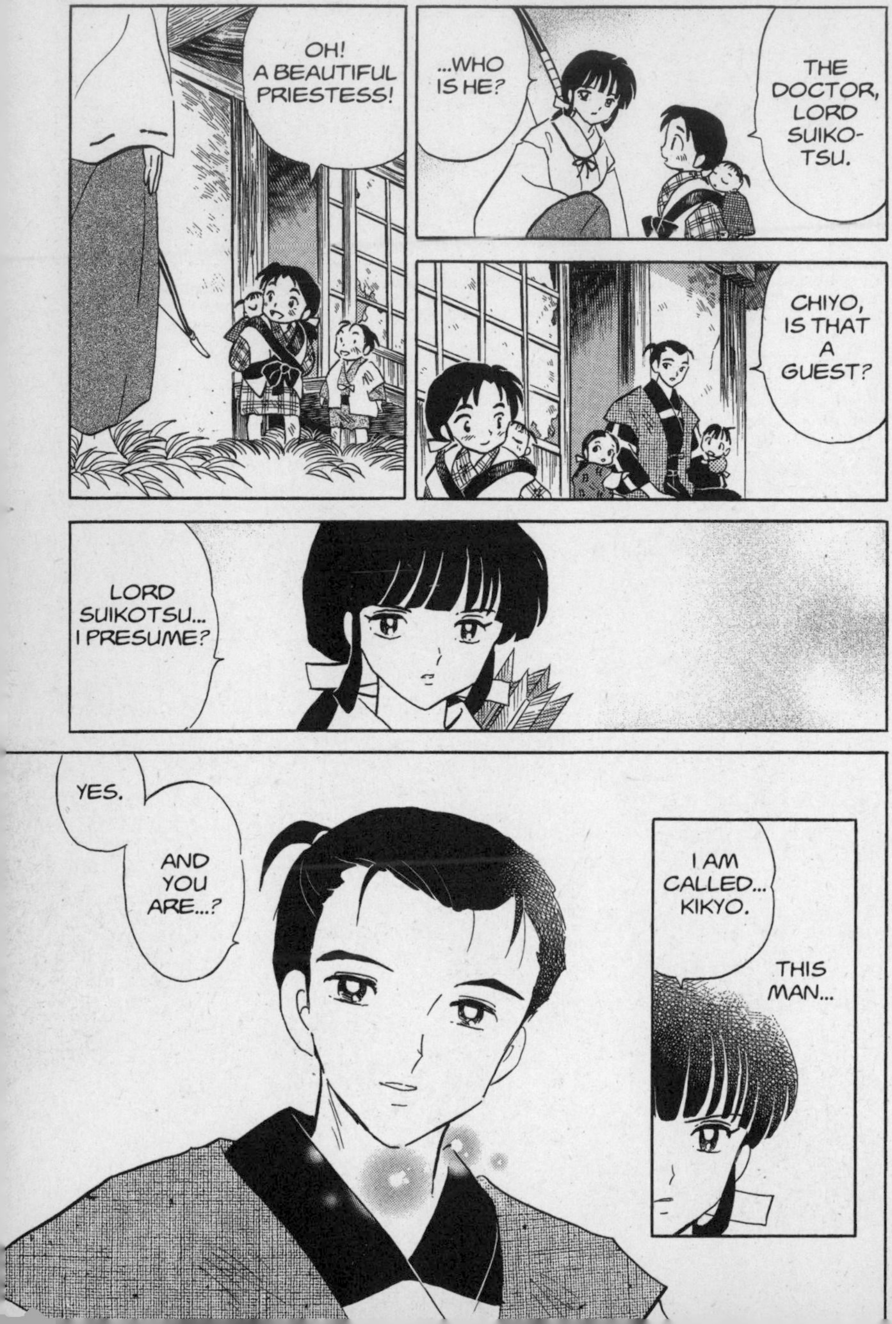
OH! A BEAUTIFUL PRIESTESS!
...WHO IS HE?
THE DOCTOR, LORD SUIKO-TSU.
CHIYO, IS THAT A GUEST?
LORD SUIKOTSU... I PRESUME?
YES.
AND YOU ARE...?
I AM CALLED... KIKYO.
THIS MAN...

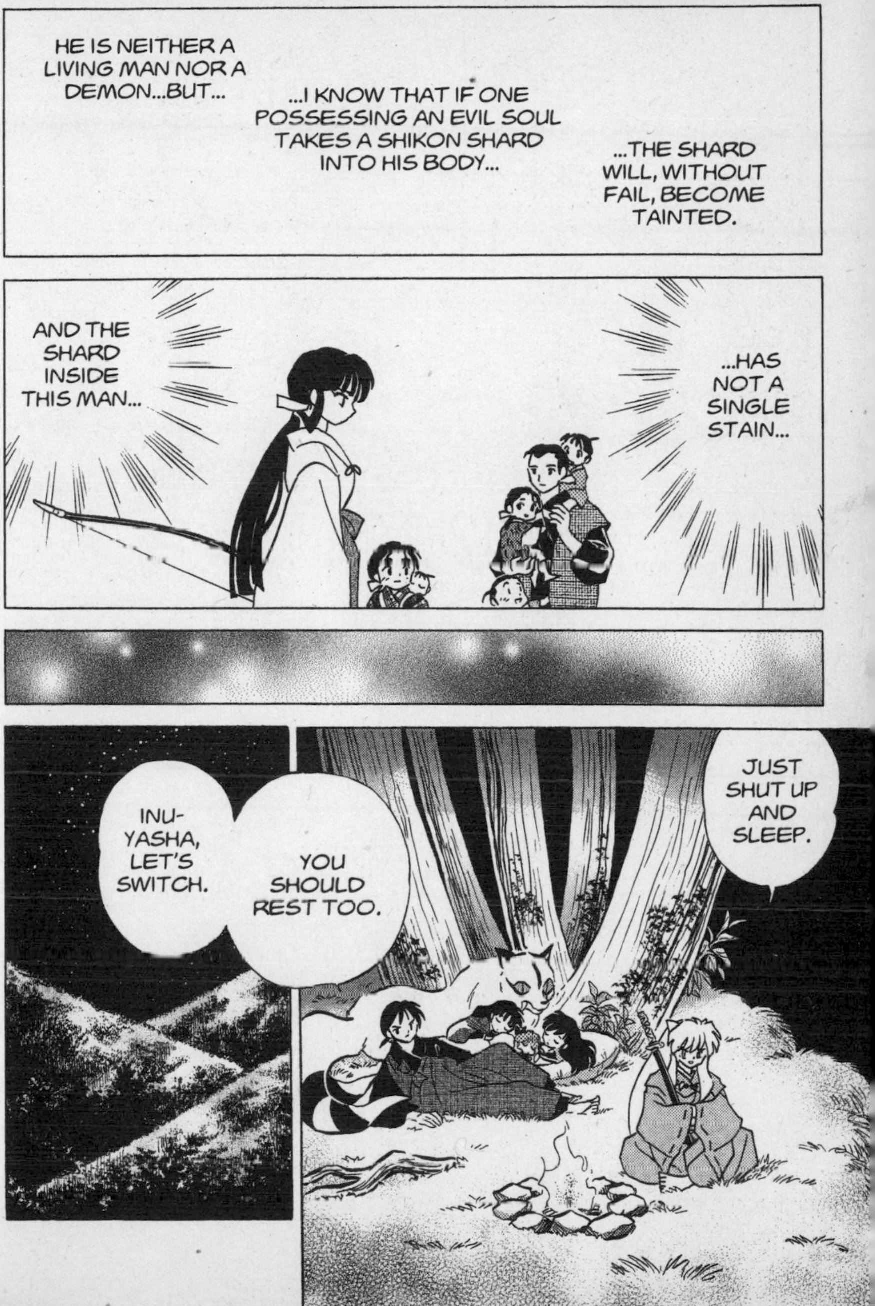
HE IS NEITHER A LIVING MAN NOR A DEMON...BUT...
...I KNOW THAT IF ONE POSSESSING AN EVIL SOUL TAKES A SHIKON SHARD INTO HIS BODY...
...THE SHARD WILL, WITHOUT FAIL, BECOME TAINTED.
AND THE SHARD INSIDE THIS MAN...
...HAS NOT A SINGLE STAIN...
INU-YASHA, LET'S SWITCH.
YOU SHOULD REST TOO.
JUST SHUT UP AND SLEEP.

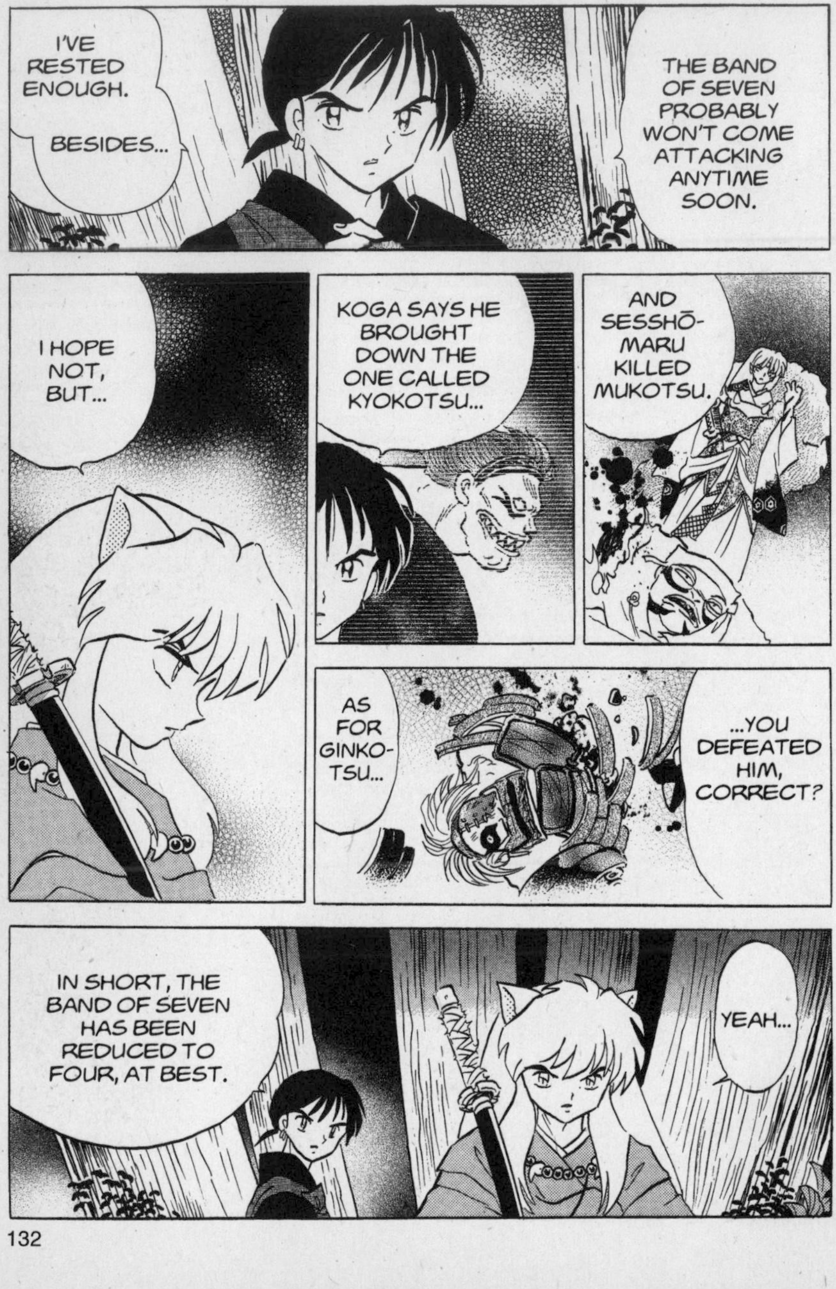
I'VE RESTED ENOUGH.
BESIDES...
THE BAND OF SEVEN PROBABLY WON'T COME ATTACKING ANYTIME SOON.
I HOPE NOT, BUT...
KOGA SAYS HE BROUGHT DOWN THE ONE CALLED KYOKOTSU...
AND SESSHŌ-MARU KILLED MUKOTSU.
AS FOR GINKO-TSU...
...YOU DEFEATED HIM, CORRECT?
IN SHORT, THE BAND OF SEVEN HAS BEEN REDUCED TO FOUR, AT BEST.
YEAH...

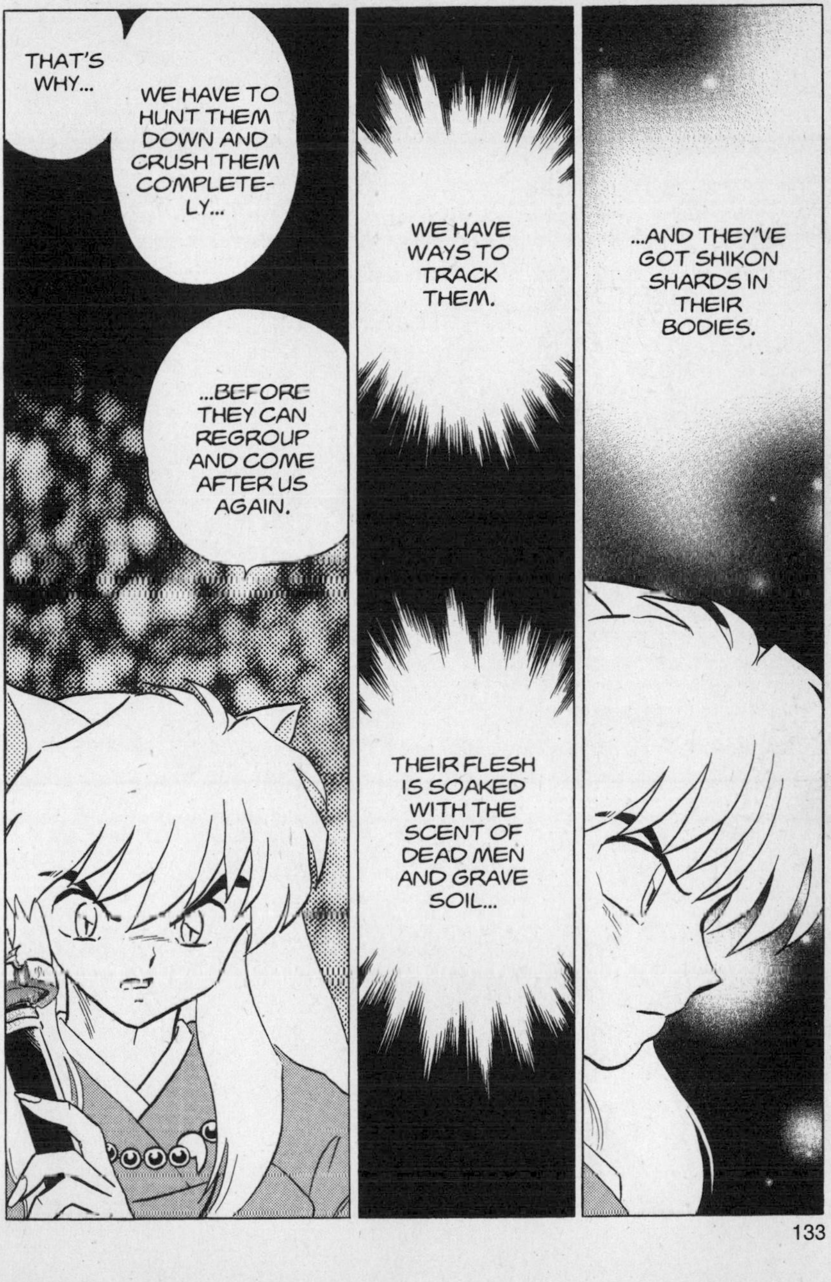
THAT'S WHY...
WE HAVE TO HUNT THEM DOWN AND CRUSH THEM COMPLETE-LY...
...BEFORE THEY CAN REGROUP AND COME AFTER US AGAIN.
WE HAVE WAYS TO TRACK THEM.
THEIR FLESH IS SOAKED WITH THE SCENT OF DEAD MEN AND GRAVE SOIL...
...AND THEY'VE GOT SHIKON SHARDS IN THEIR BODIES.

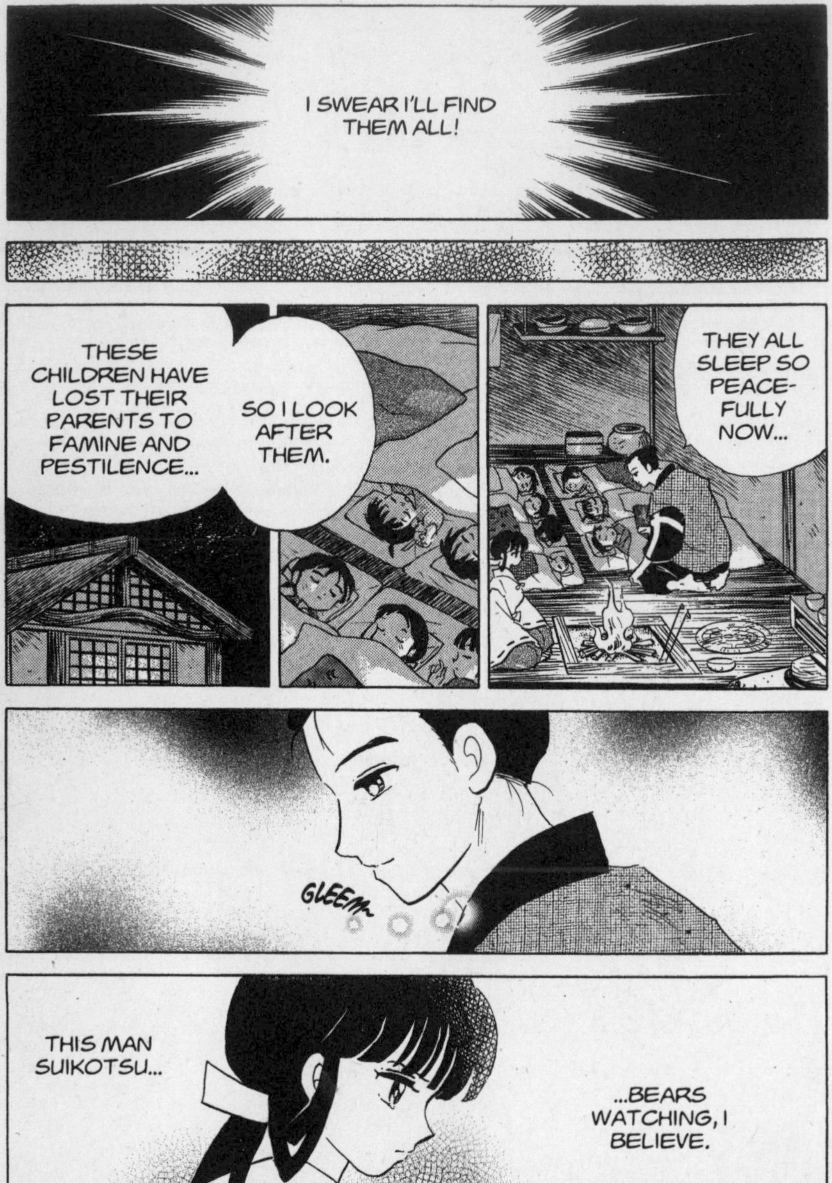
I SWEAR I'LL FIND THEM ALL!
THESE CHILDREN HAVE LOST THEIR PARENTS TO FAMINE AND PESTILENCE...
SO I LOOK AFTER THEM.
THEY ALL SLEEP SO PEACE-FULLY NOW...
GLEEM
THIS MAN SUIKOTSU...
...BEARS WATCHING, I BELIEVE.

SCROLL EIGHT

# THE UNSULLIED LIGHT

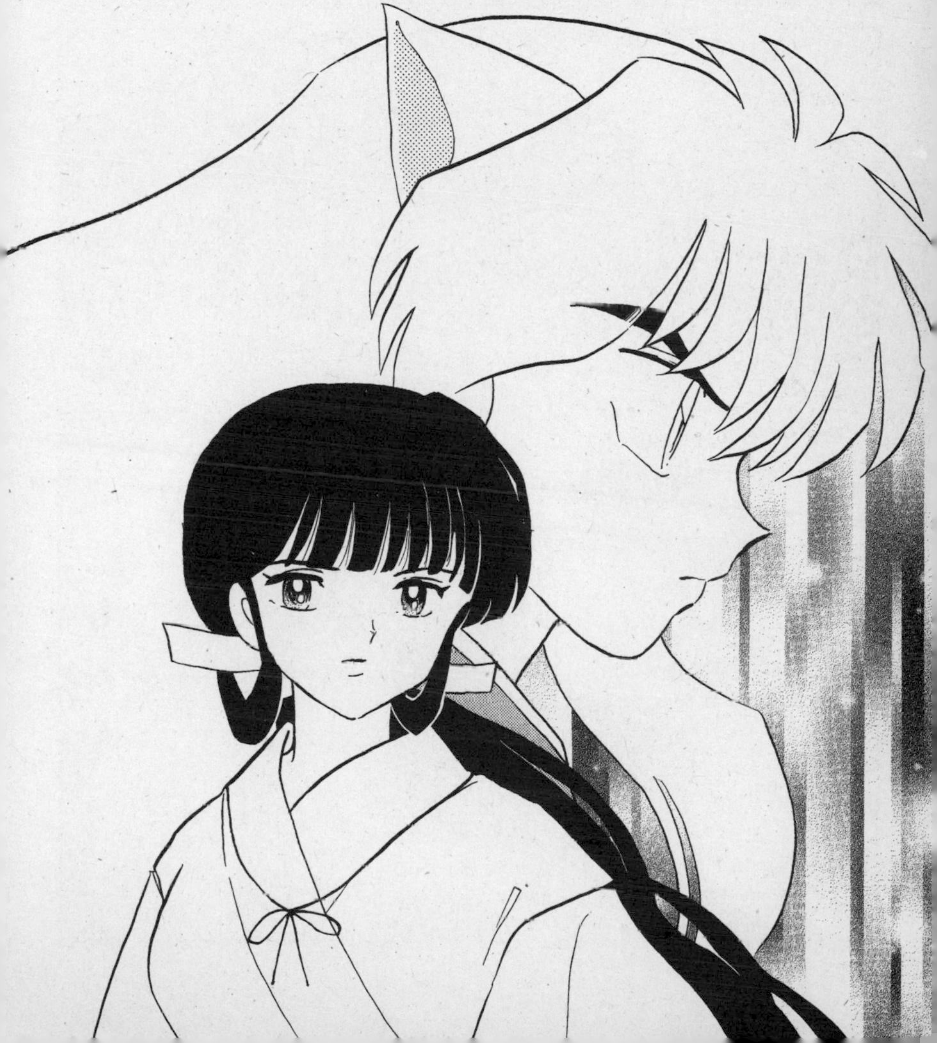

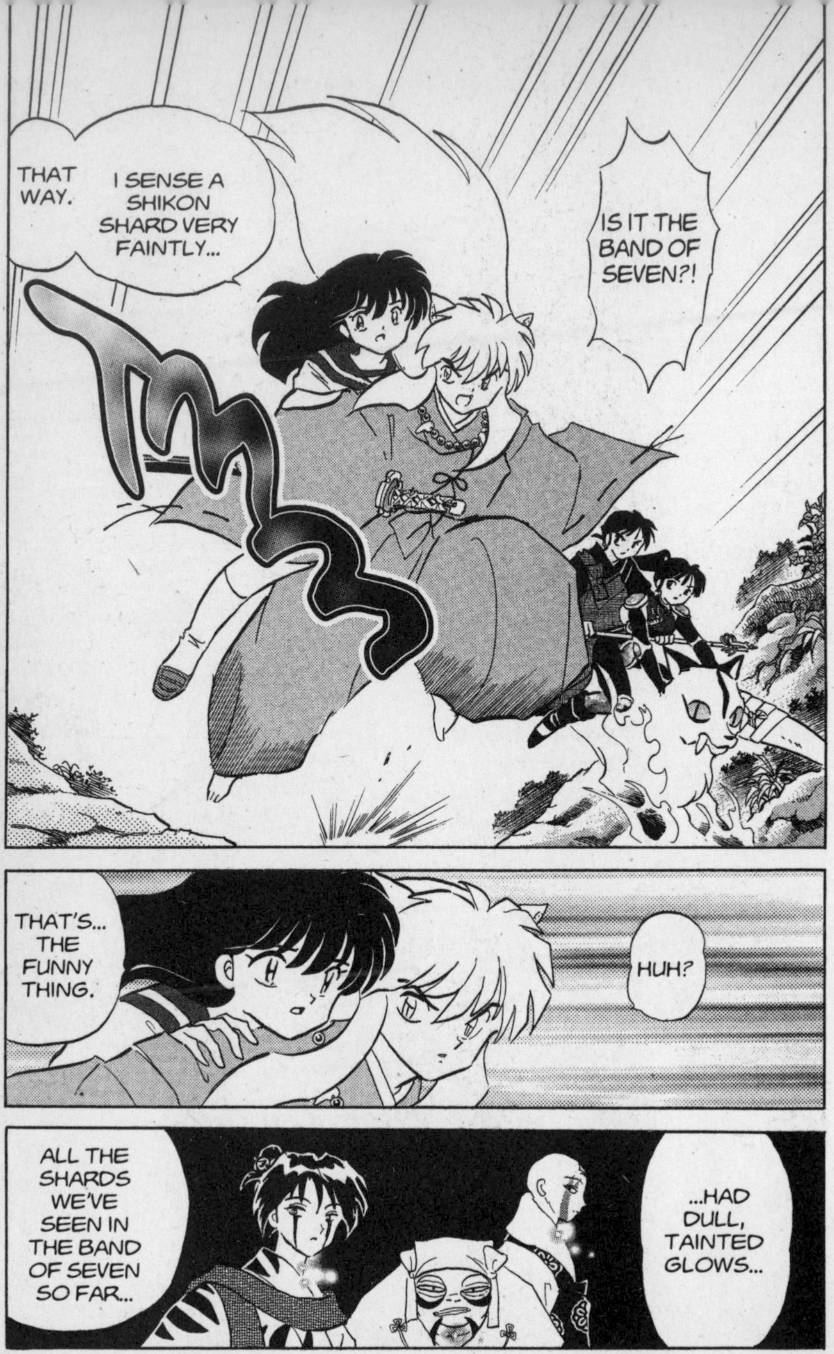
IS IT THE BAND OF SEVEN?!
THAT WAY.
I SENSE A SHIKON SHARD VERY FAINTLY...
HUH?
THAT'S... THE FUNNY THING.
...HAD DULL, TAINTED GLOWS...
ALL THE SHARDS WE'VE SEEN IN THE BAND OF SEVEN SO FAR...

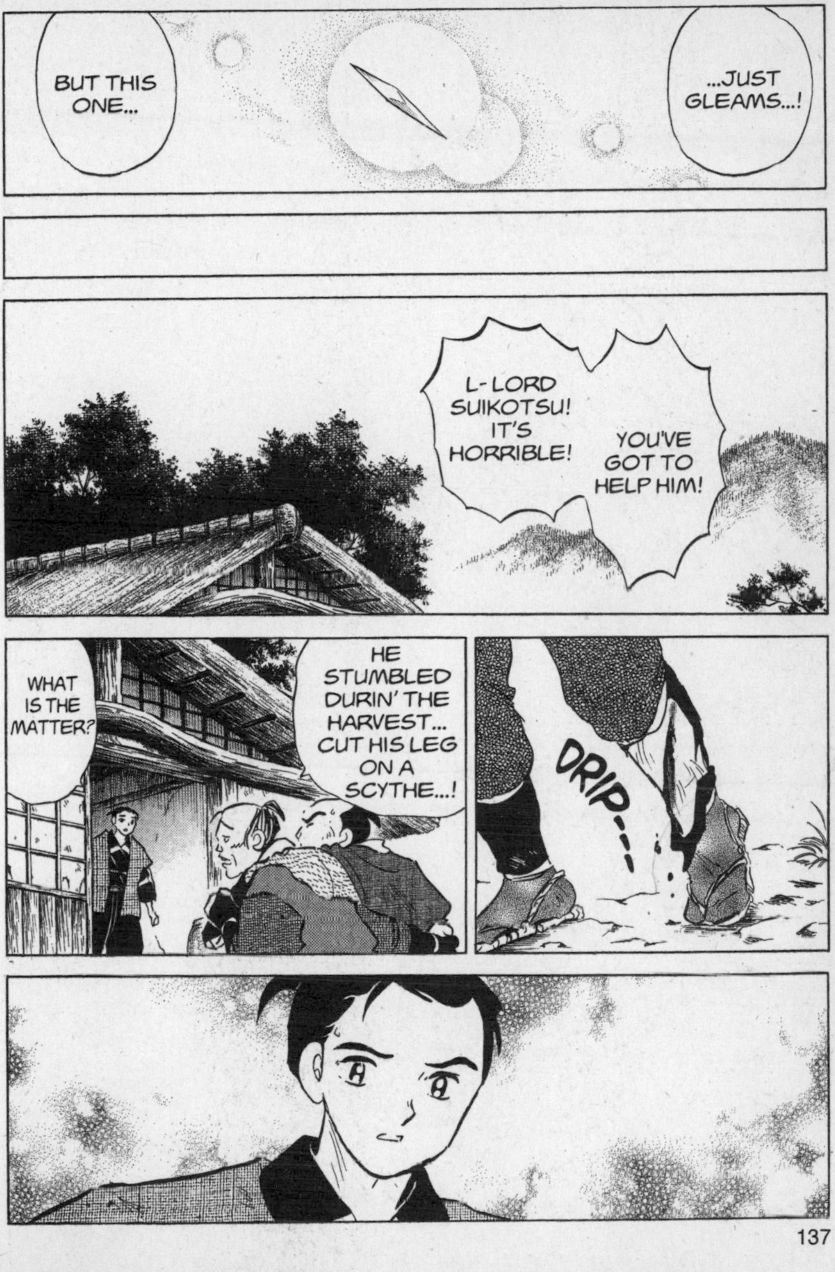
...JUST GLEAMS...!
BUT THIS ONE...
L-LORD SUIKOTSU! IT'S HORRIBLE!
YOU'VE GOT TO HELP HIM!
DRIP...
HE STUMBLED DURIN' THE HARVEST... CUT HIS LEG ON A SCYTHE...!
WHAT IS THE MATTER?

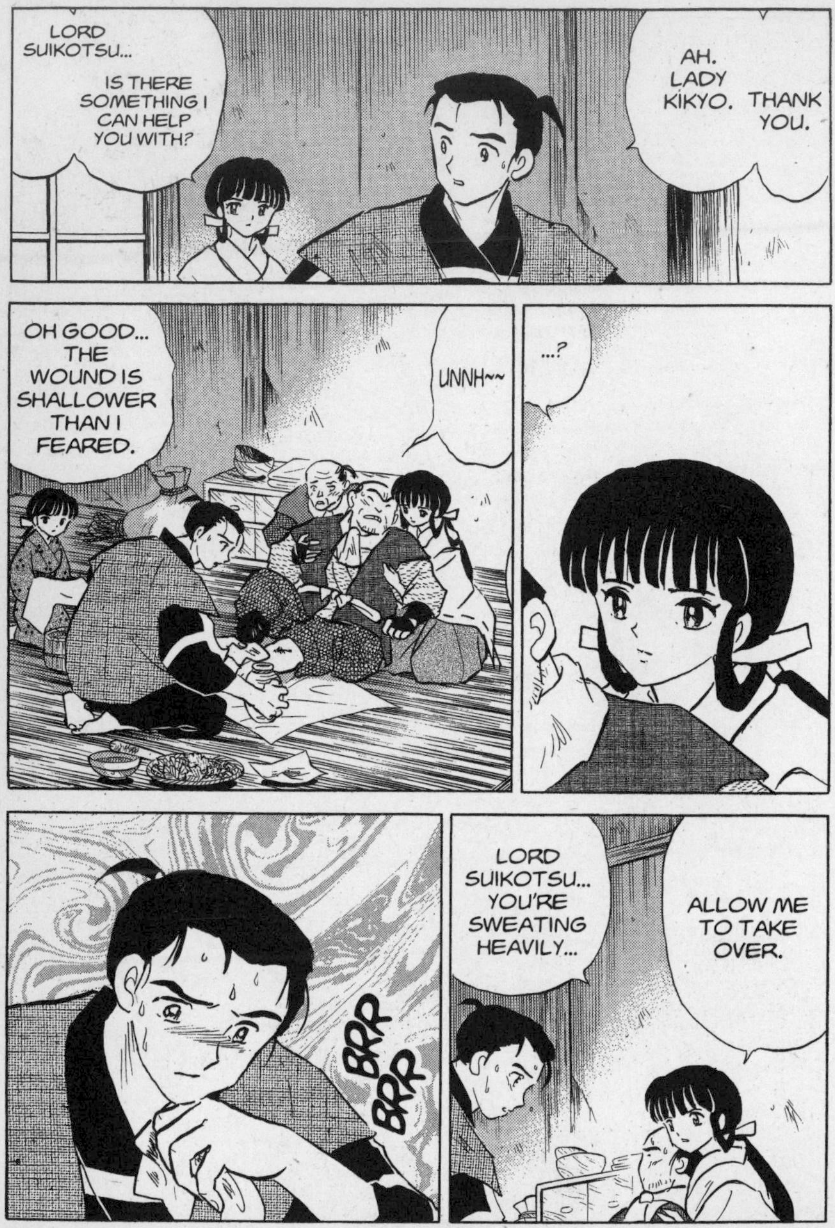
LORD SUIKOTSU... IS THERE SOMETHING I CAN HELP YOU WITH?
AH. LADY KIKYO. THANK YOU.
OH GOOD... THE WOUND IS SHALLOWER THAN I FEARED.
UNNH~~
...?
BRR BRR
LORD SUIKOTSU... YOU'RE SWEATING HEAVILY...
ALLOW ME TO TAKE OVER.

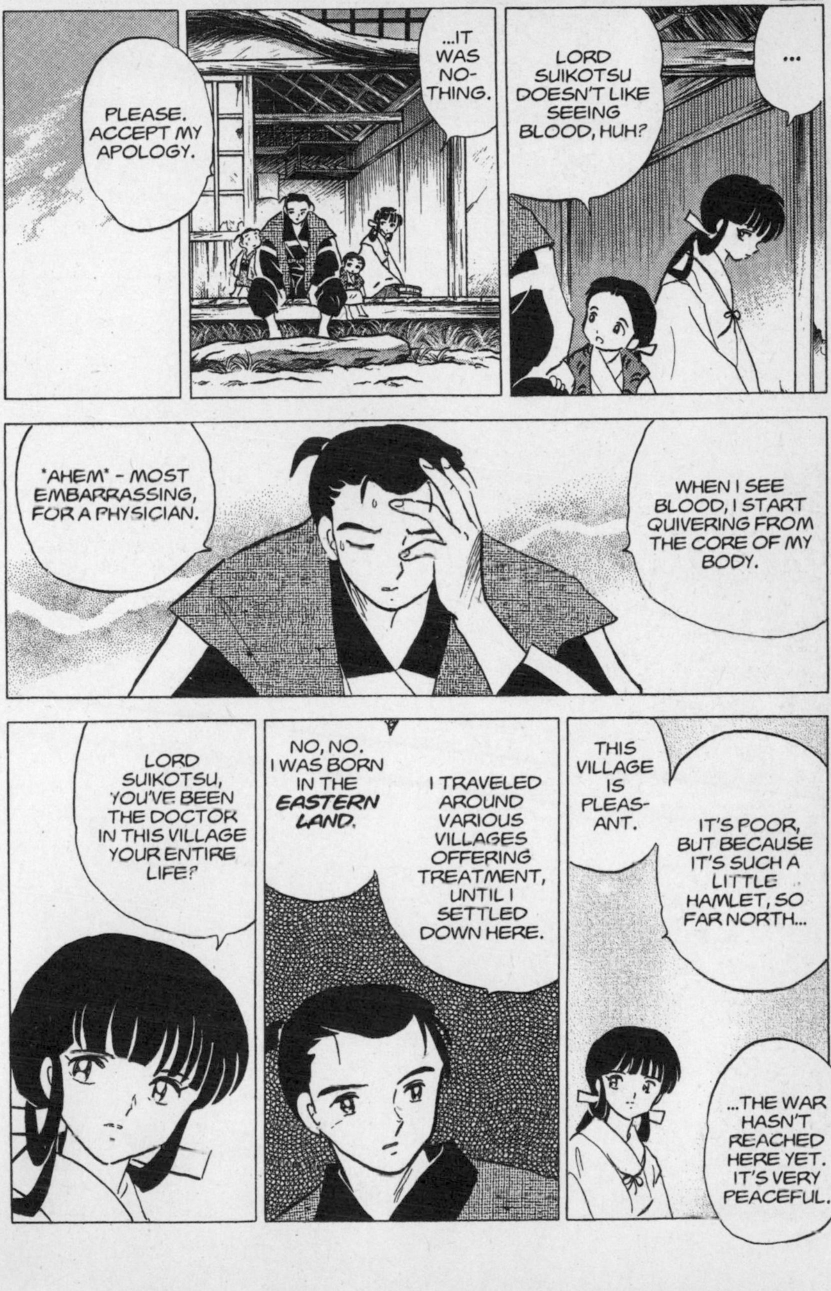
PLEASE. ACCEPT MY APOLOGY.
...IT WAS NO-THING.
LORD SUIKOTSU DOESN'T LIKE SEEING BLOOD, HUH?
...
*AHEM* - MOST EMBARRASSING, FOR A PHYSICIAN.
WHEN I SEE BLOOD, I START QUIVERING FROM THE CORE OF MY BODY.
LORD SUIKOTSU, YOU'VE BEEN THE DOCTOR IN THIS VILLAGE YOUR ENTIRE LIFE?
NO, NO. I WAS BORN IN THE *EASTERN LAND*.
I TRAVELED AROUND VARIOUS VILLAGES OFFERING TREATMENT, UNTIL I SETTLED DOWN HERE.
THIS VILLAGE IS PLEAS-ANT.
IT'S POOR, BUT BECAUSE IT'S SUCH A LITTLE HAMLET, SO FAR NORTH...
...THE WAR HASN'T REACHED HERE YET. IT'S VERY PEACEFUL.

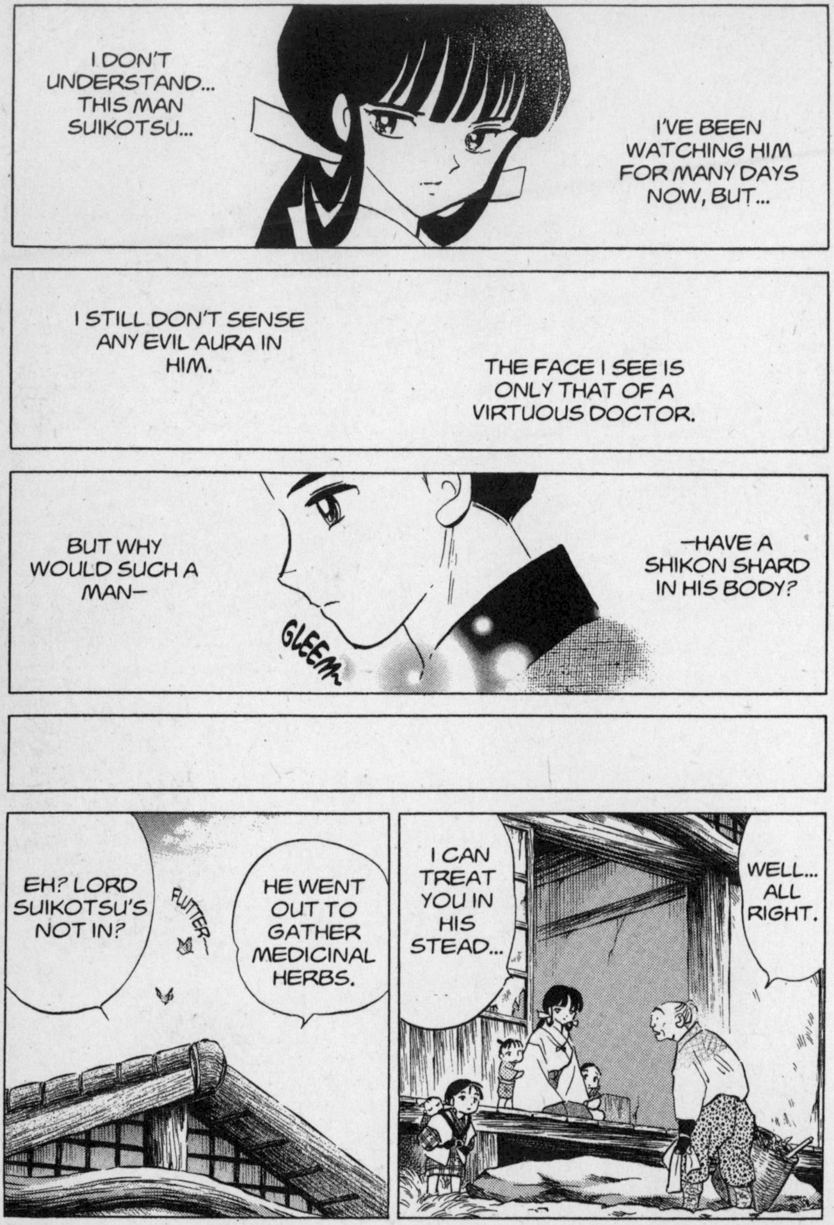
I DON'T UNDERSTAND... THIS MAN SUIKOTSU...
I'VE BEEN WATCHING HIM FOR MANY DAYS NOW, BUT...
I STILL DON'T SENSE ANY EVIL AURA IN HIM.
THE FACE I SEE IS ONLY THAT OF A VIRTUOUS DOCTOR.
BUT WHY WOULD SUCH A MAN—
GLEEM
—HAVE A SHIKON SHARD IN HIS BODY?
EH? LORD SUIKOTSU'S NOT IN?
FLUTTER—
HE WENT OUT TO GATHER MEDICINAL HERBS.
I CAN TREAT YOU IN HIS STEAD...
WELL... ALL RIGHT.

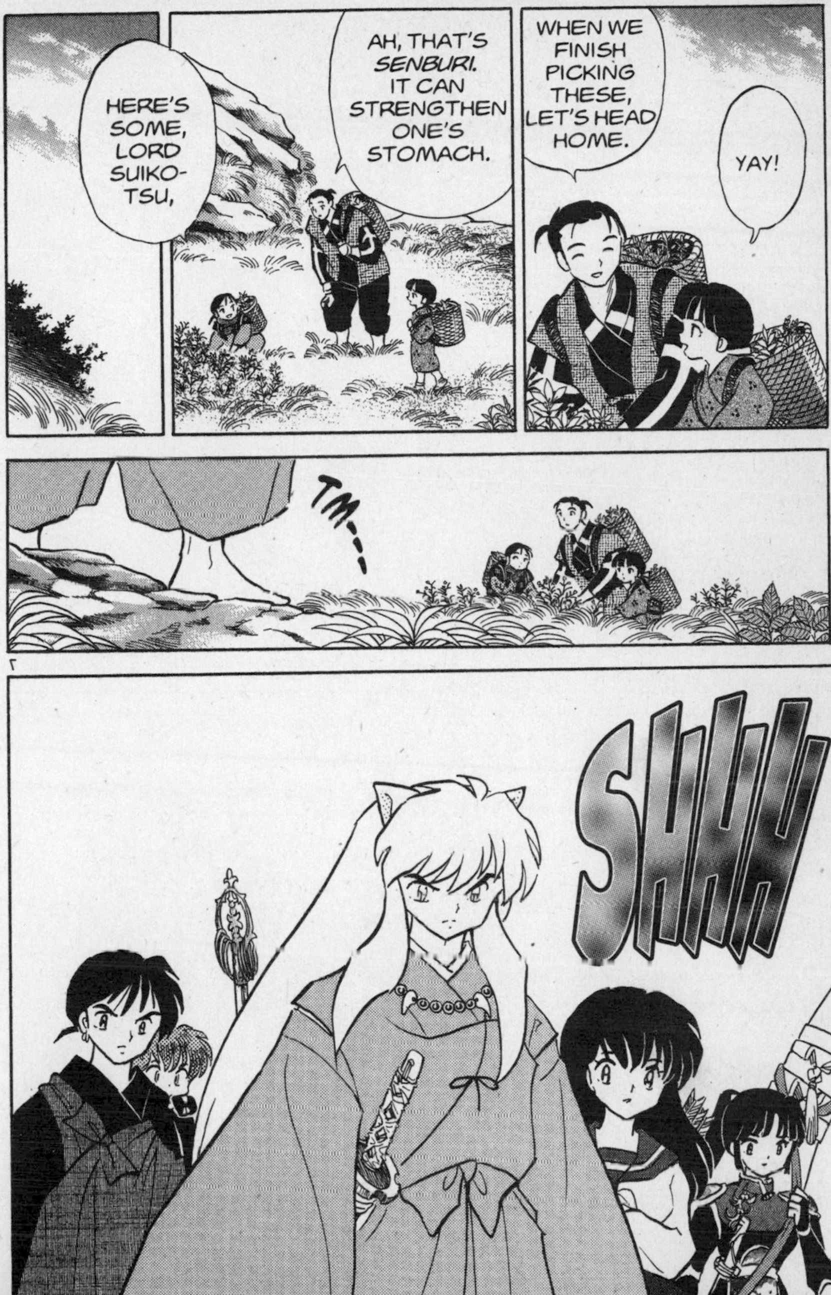
HERE'S SOME, LORD SUIKO-TSU,
AH, THAT'S *SENBURI*. IT CAN STRENGTHEN ONE'S STOMACH.
WHEN WE FINISH PICKING THESE, LET'S HEAD HOME.
YAY!
TM...
SHHH

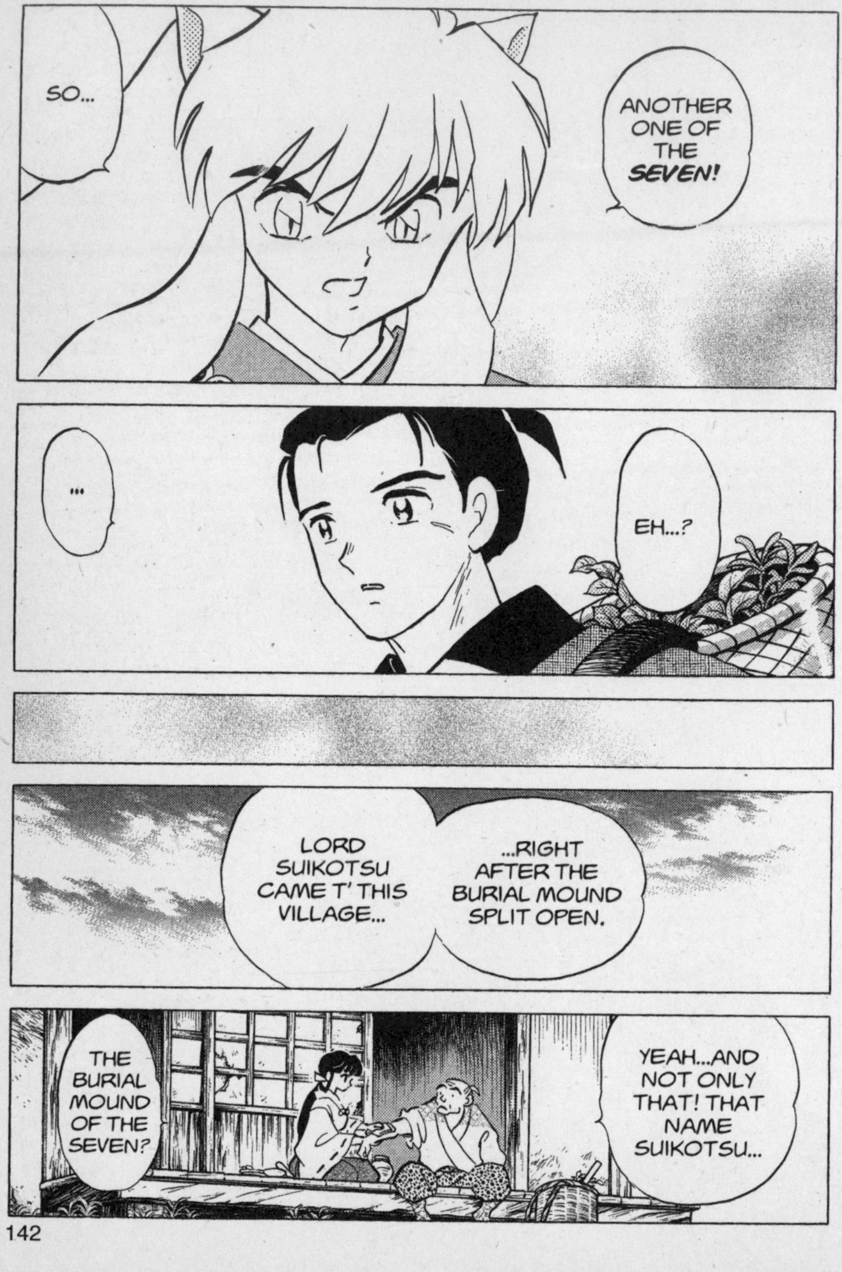
SO...
ANOTHER ONE OF THE SEVEN!
...
EH...?
LORD SUIKOTSU CAME T' THIS VILLAGE...
...RIGHT AFTER THE BURIAL MOUND SPLIT OPEN.
THE BURIAL MOUND OF THE SEVEN?
YEAH...AND NOT ONLY THAT! THAT NAME SUIKOTSU...

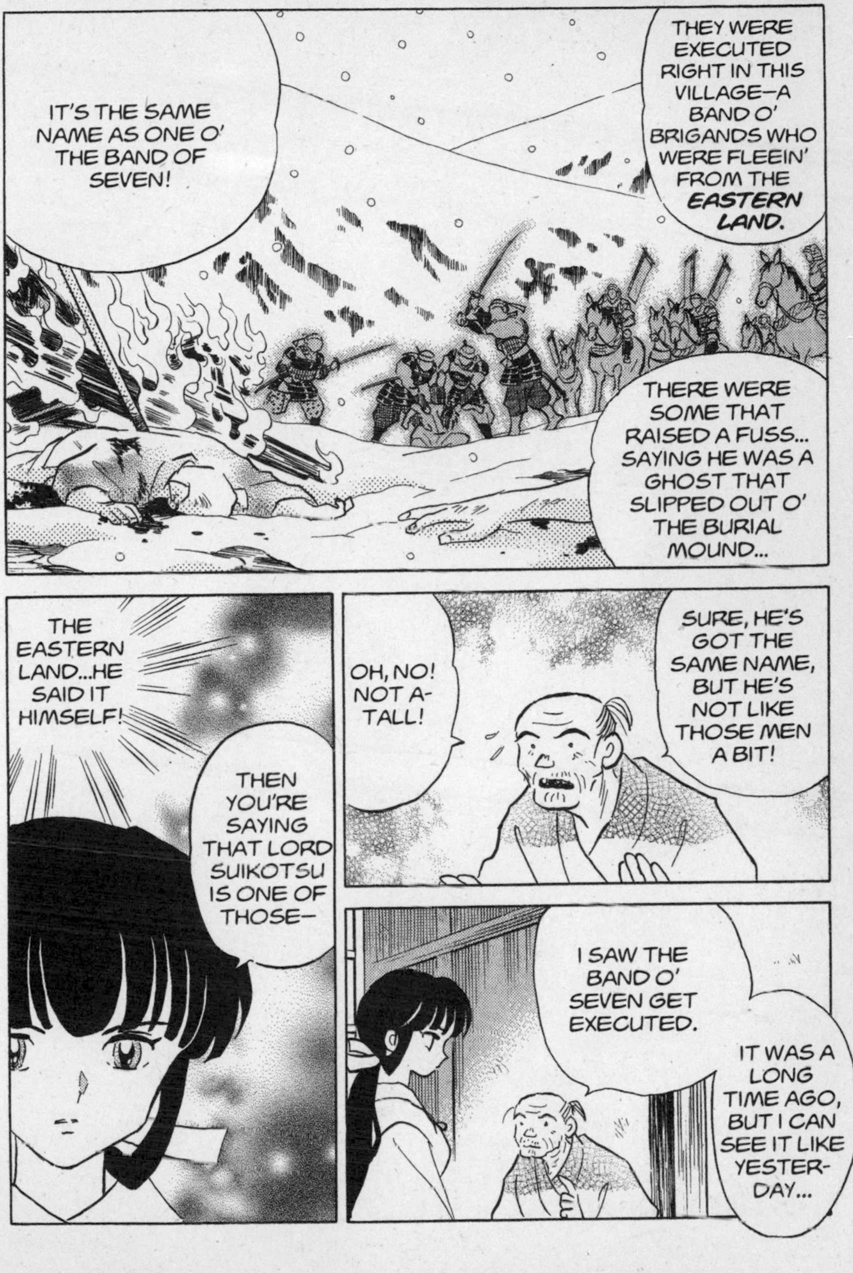
IT'S THE SAME NAME AS ONE O' THE BAND OF SEVEN!
THEY WERE EXECUTED RIGHT IN THIS VILLAGE—A BAND O' BRIGANDS WHO WERE FLEEIN' FROM THE ***EASTERN LAND.***
THERE WERE SOME THAT RAISED A FUSS... SAYING HE WAS A GHOST THAT SLIPPED OUT O' THE BURIAL MOUND...
THE EASTERN LAND...HE SAID IT HIMSELF!
THEN YOU'RE SAYING THAT LORD SUIKOTSU IS ONE OF THOSE—
OH, NO! NOT A-TALL!
SURE, HE'S GOT THE SAME NAME, BUT HE'S NOT LIKE THOSE MEN A BIT!
I SAW THE BAND O' SEVEN GET EXECUTED.
IT WAS A LONG TIME AGO, BUT I CAN SEE IT LIKE YESTER-DAY...

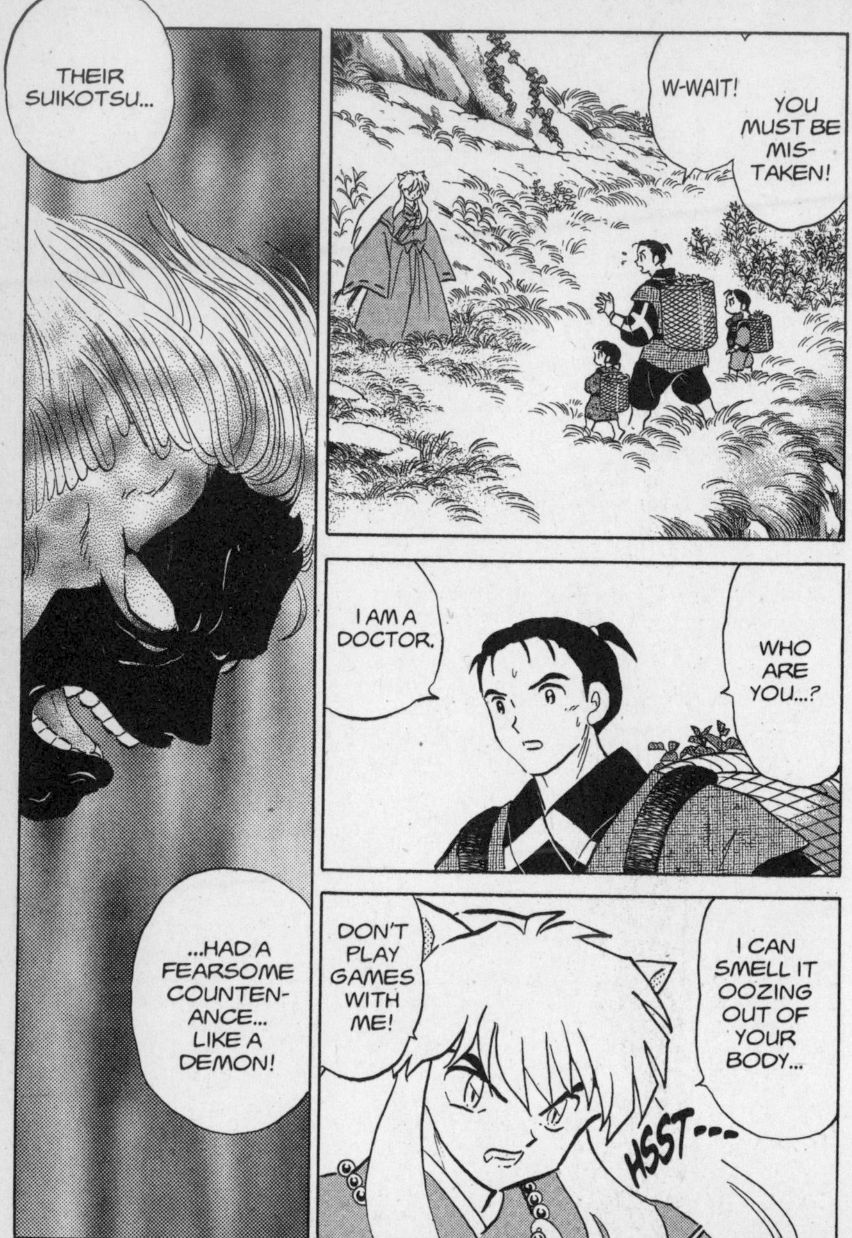
THEIR SUIKOTSU...
...HAD A FEARSOME COUNTENANCE... LIKE A DEMON!
W-WAIT!
YOU MUST BE MISTAKEN!
I AM A DOCTOR.
WHO ARE YOU...?
DON'T PLAY GAMES WITH ME!
I CAN SMELL IT OOZING OUT OF YOUR BODY...
HSST...

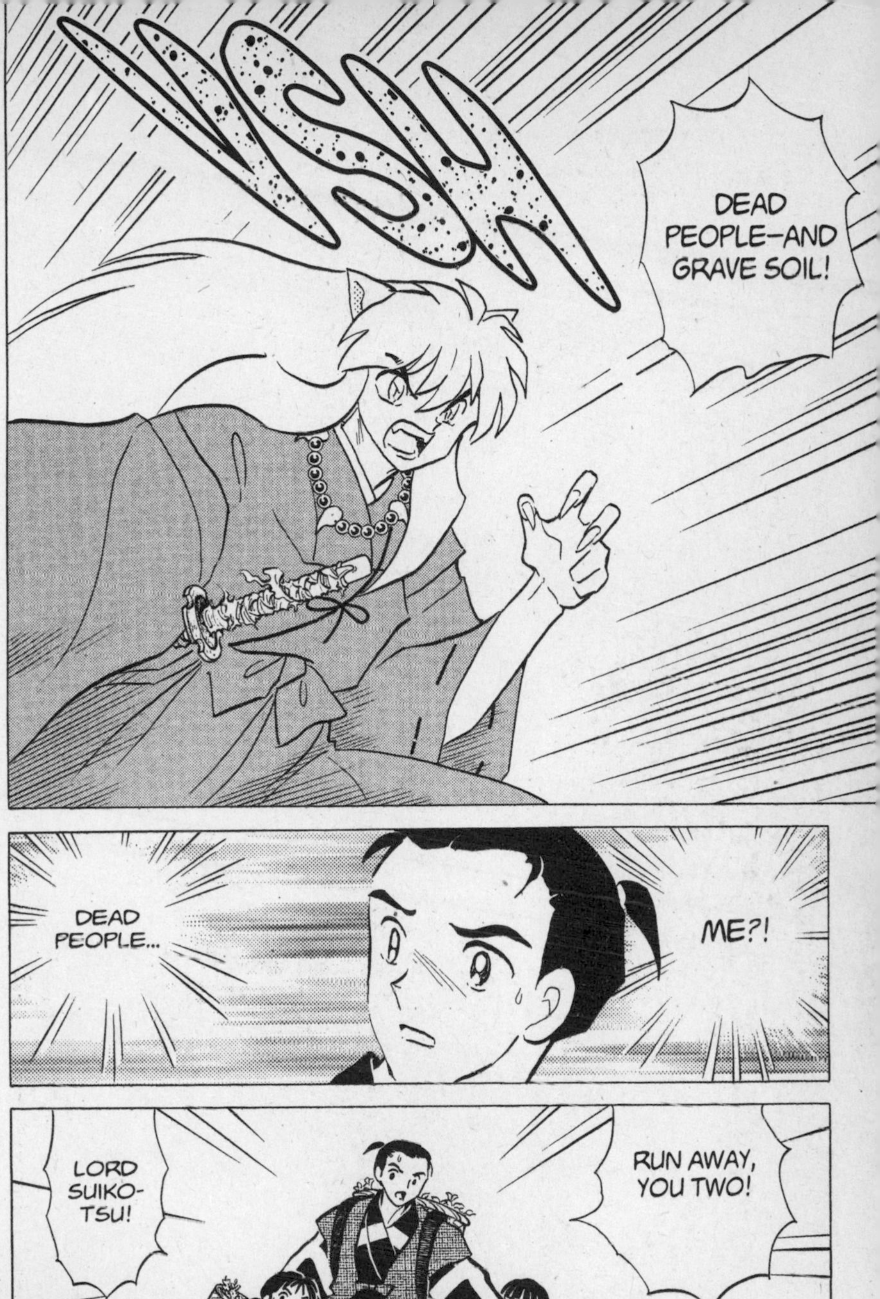
DEAD PEOPLE—AND GRAVE SOIL!
DEAD PEOPLE...
ME?!
LORD SUIKO-TSU!
RUN AWAY, YOU TWO!

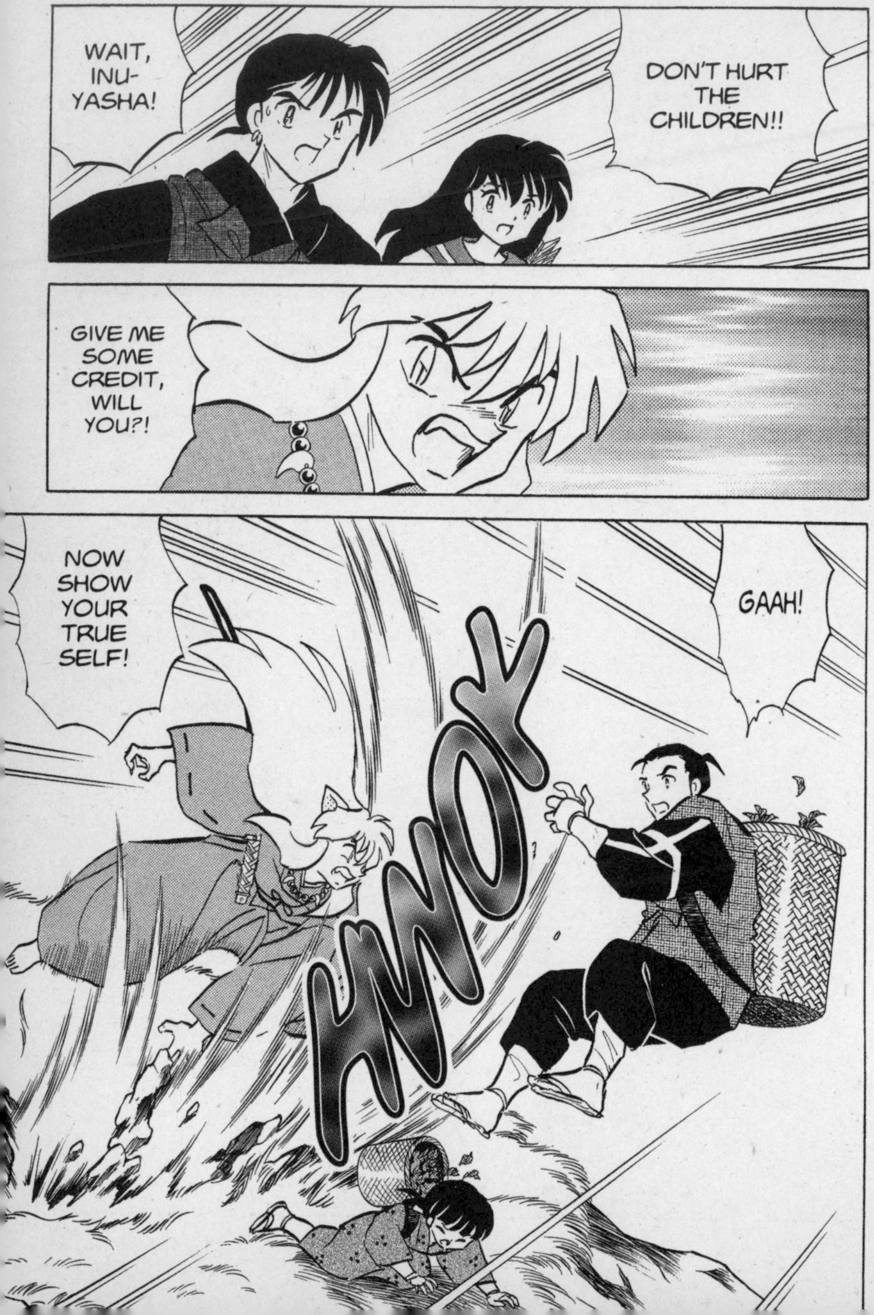
WAIT, INU-YASHA!
DON'T HURT THE CHILDREN!!
GIVE ME SOME CREDIT, WILL YOU?!
NOW SHOW YOUR TRUE SELF!
WHOK
GAAH!

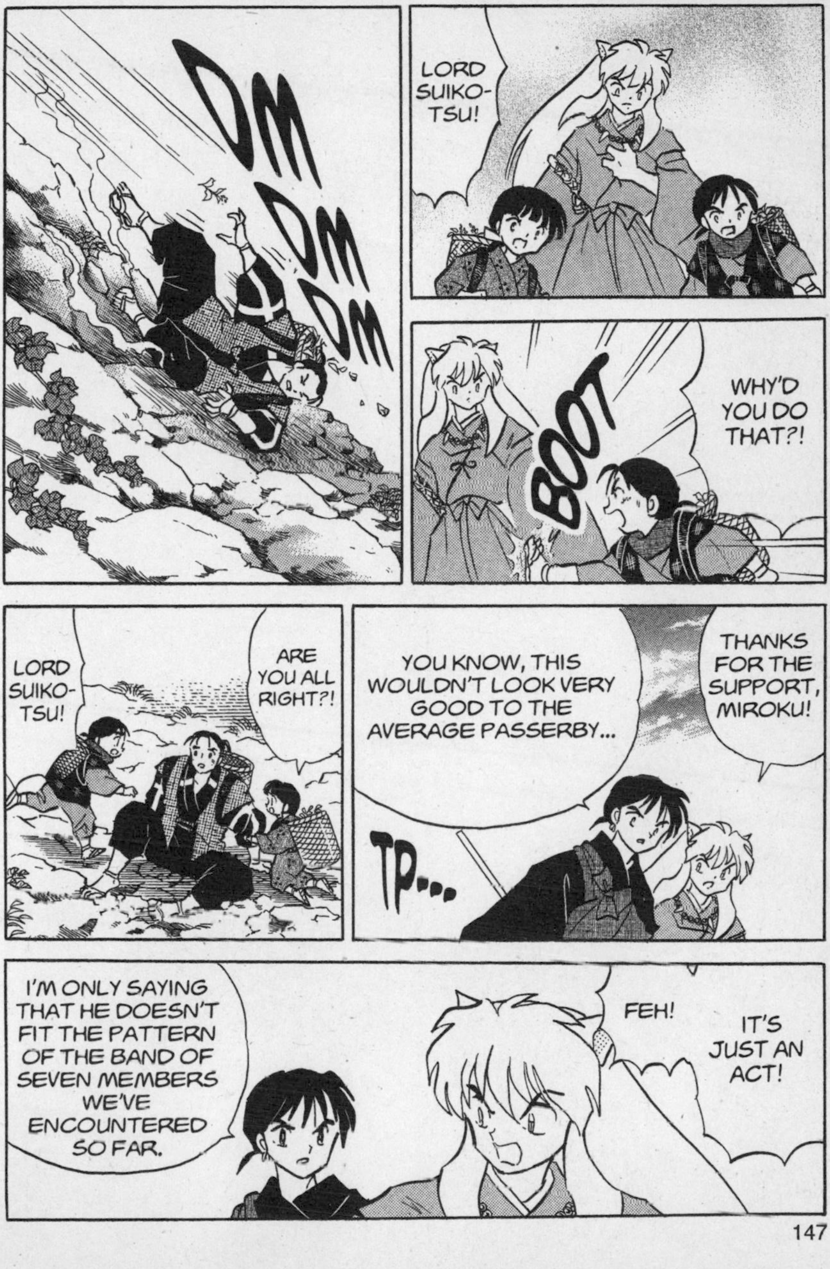
DM DM DM DM
LORD SUIKO-TSU!
BOOT
WHY'D YOU DO THAT?!
LORD SUIKO-TSU!
ARE YOU ALL RIGHT?!
YOU KNOW, THIS WOULDN'T LOOK VERY GOOD TO THE AVERAGE PASSERBY...
THANKS FOR THE SUPPORT, MIROKU!
TP...
I'M ONLY SAYING THAT HE DOESN'T FIT THE PATTERN OF THE BAND OF SEVEN MEMBERS WE'VE ENCOUNTERED SO FAR.
FEH!
IT'S JUST AN ACT!

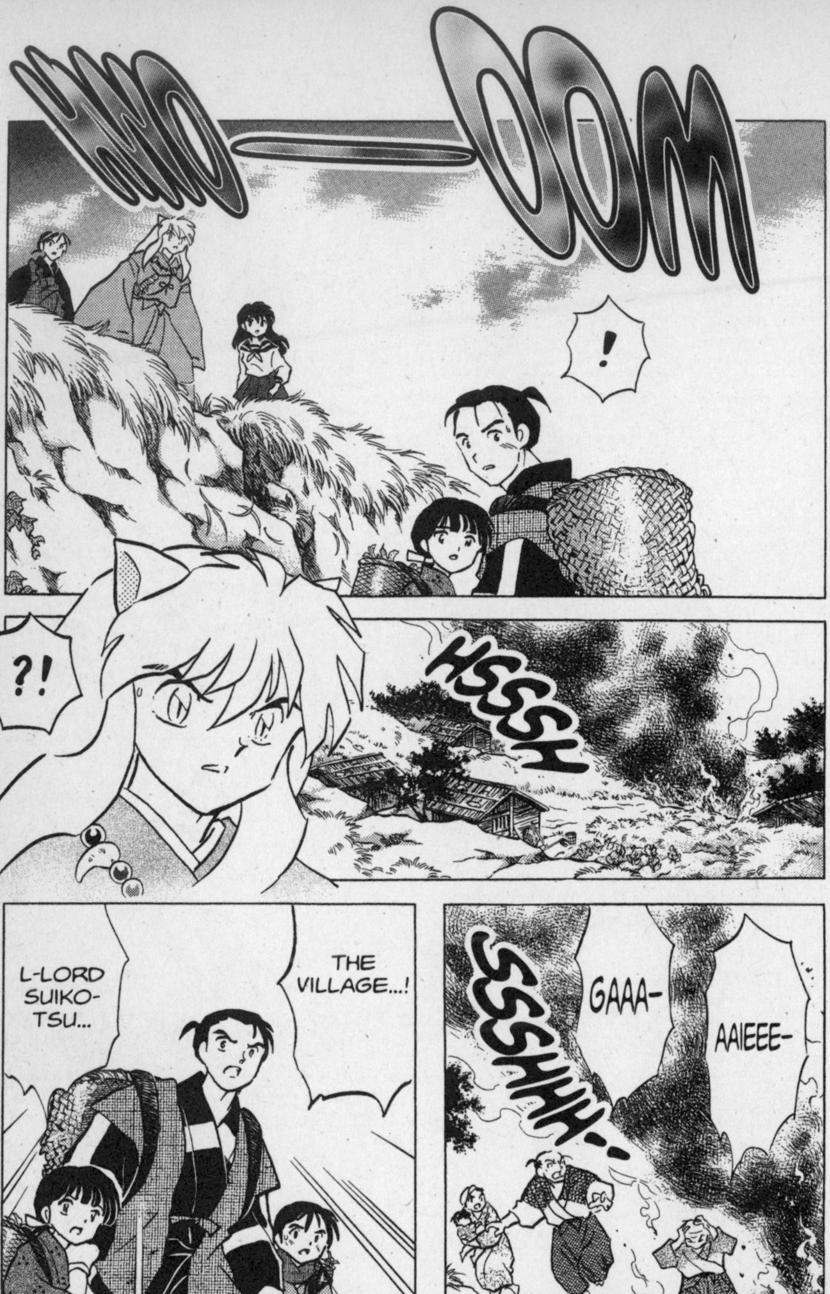
WHO—OOM
!
?!
HSSSH
L-LORD SUIKO-TSU...
THE VILLAGE...!
SSSSHHHH--
GAAA-
AAIEEE-

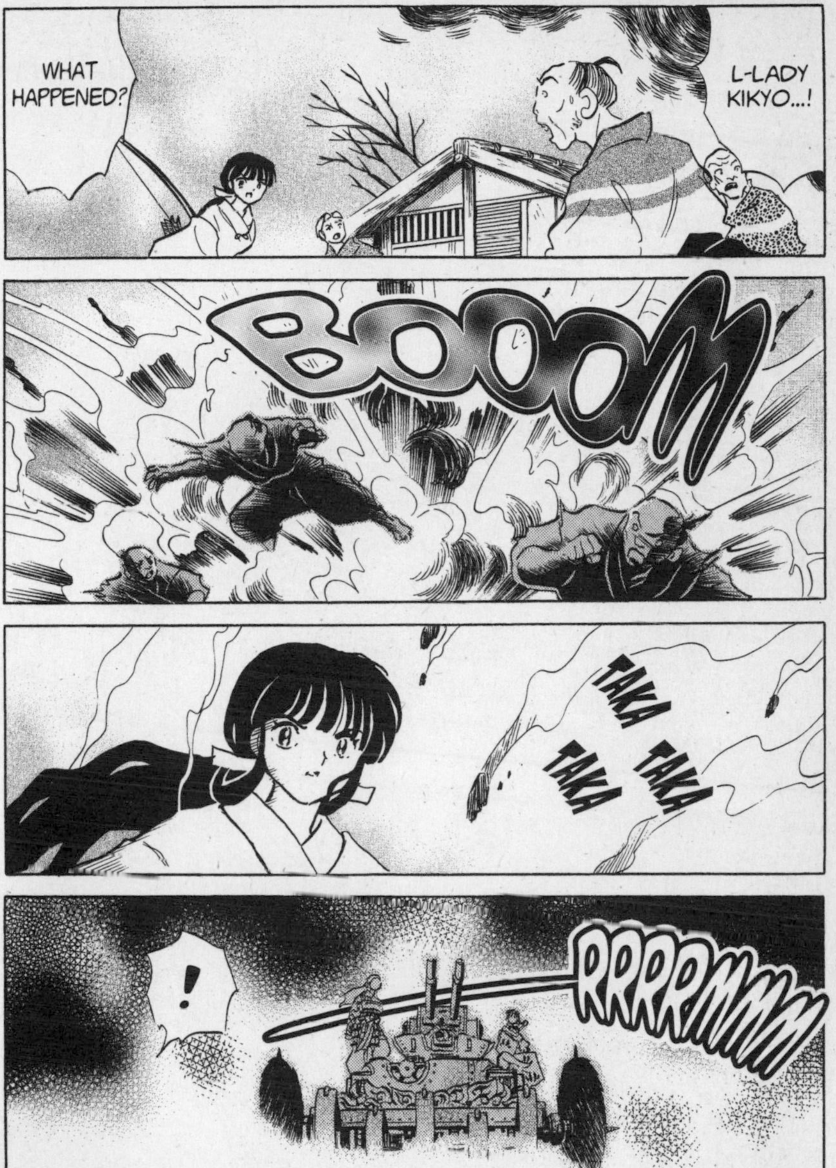
WHAT HAPPENED?
L-LADY KIKYO...!
BOOOM
TAKA TAKA
TAKA TAKA
!
RRRRMMM

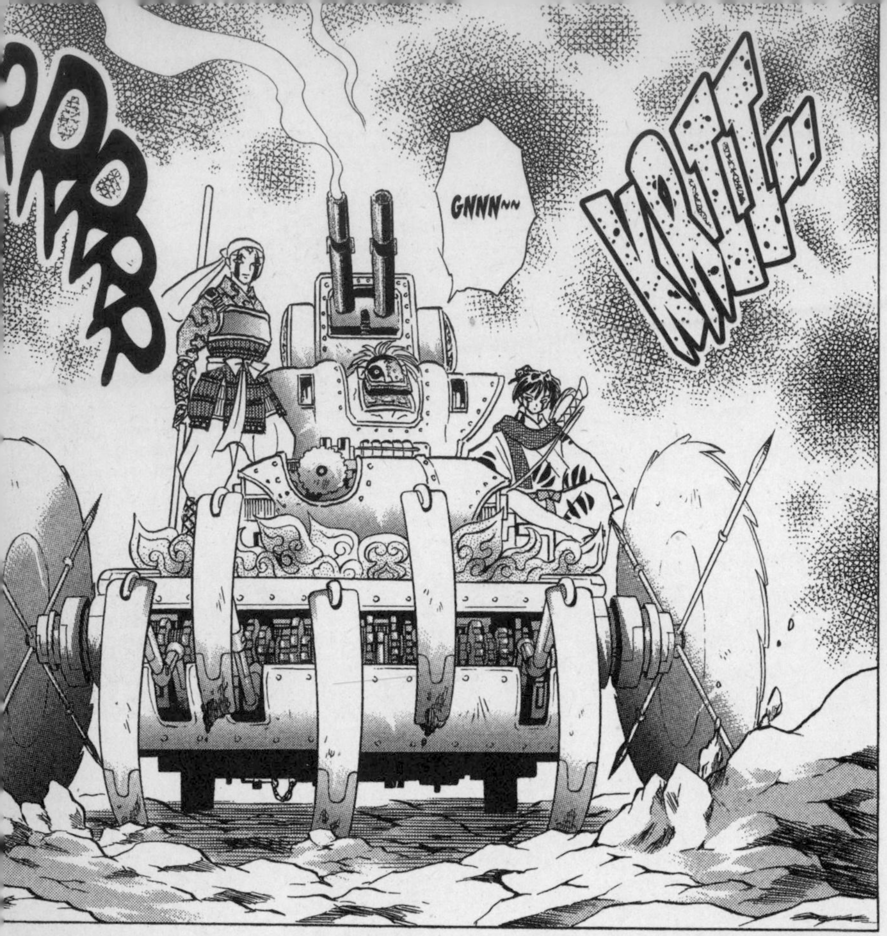
GNNN~~

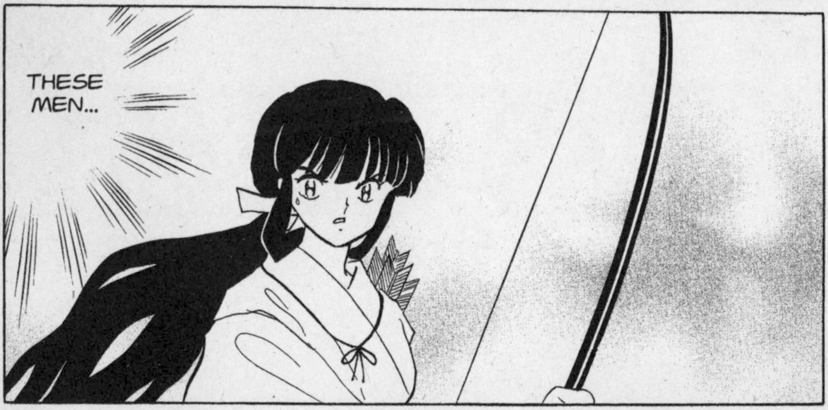
THESE MEN...

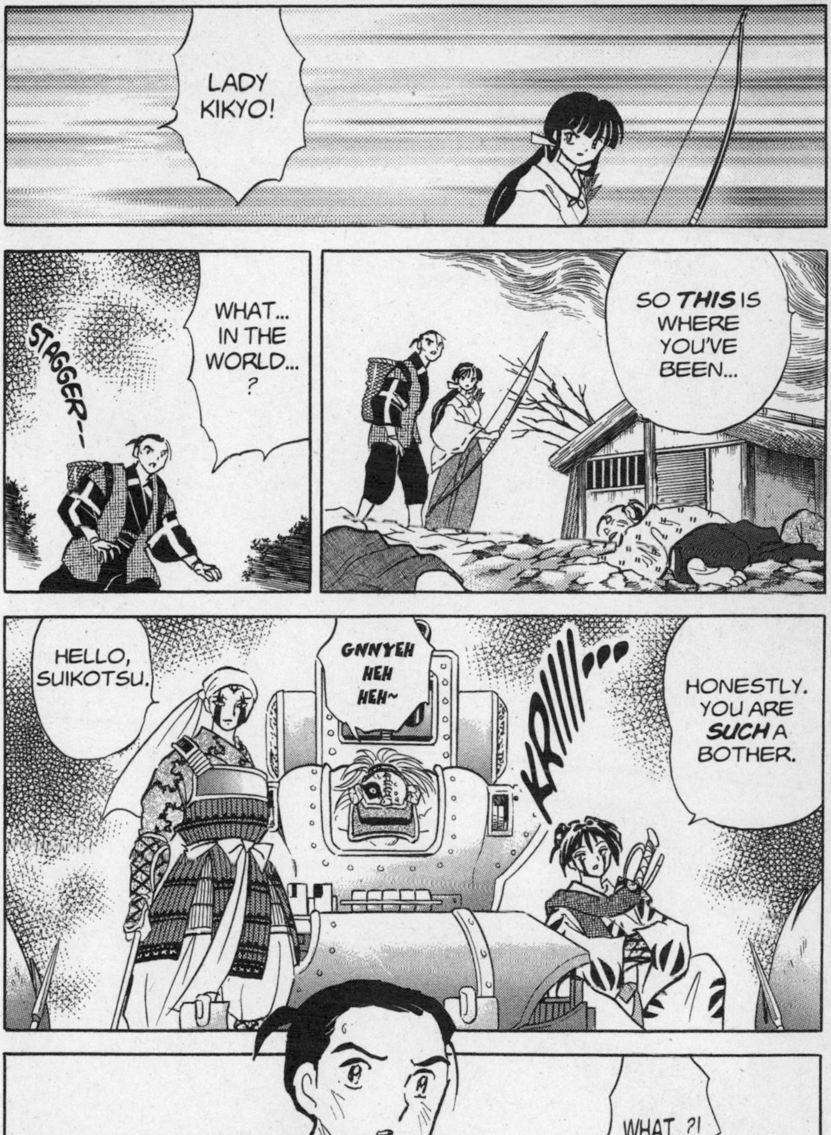
LADY KIKYO!
STAGGER--
WHAT... IN THE WORLD... ?
SO THIS IS WHERE YOU'VE BEEN...
HELLO, SUIKOTSU.
GNNYEH HEH HEH~
KRIIII...
HONESTLY. YOU ARE SUCH A BOTHER.
WHAT...?!

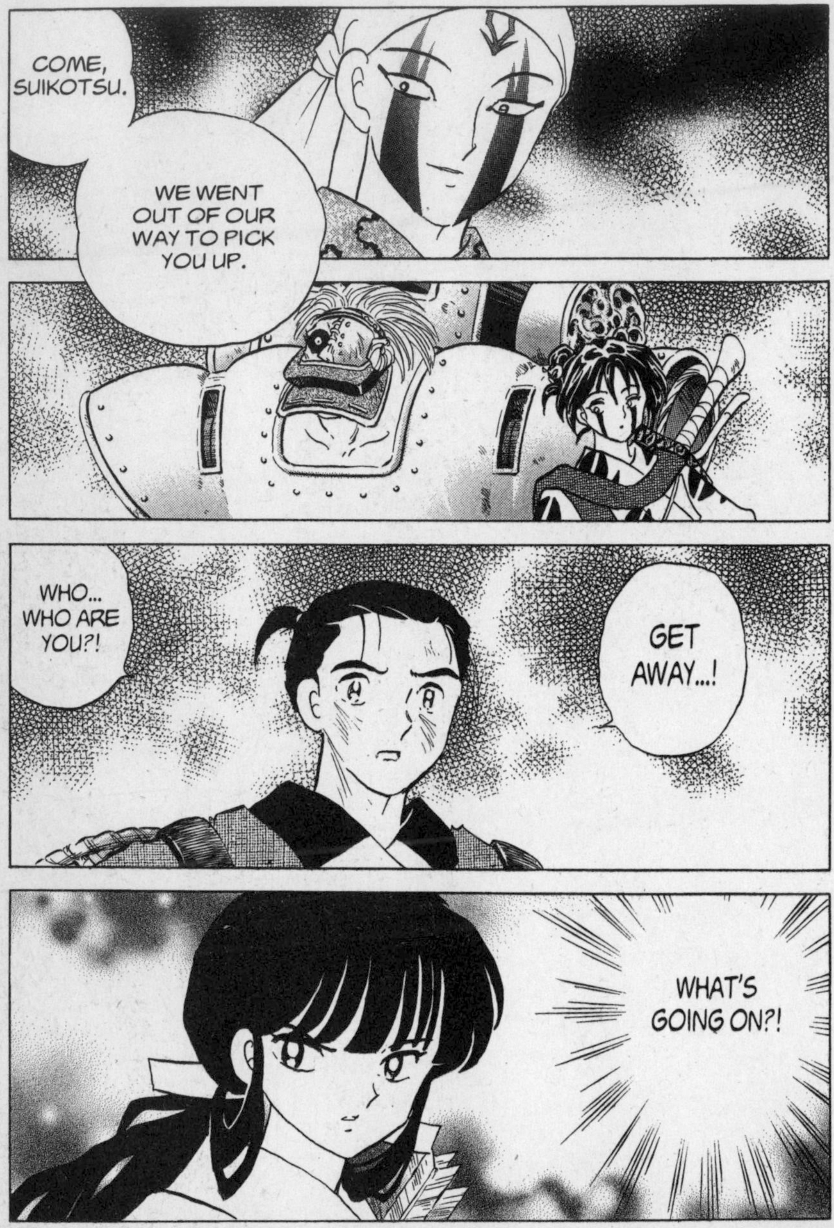
COME, SUIKOTSU.
WE WENT OUT OF OUR WAY TO PICK YOU UP.
WHO... WHO ARE YOU?!
GET AWAY...!
WHAT'S GOING ON?!

SCROLL NINE

# SUIKOTSU

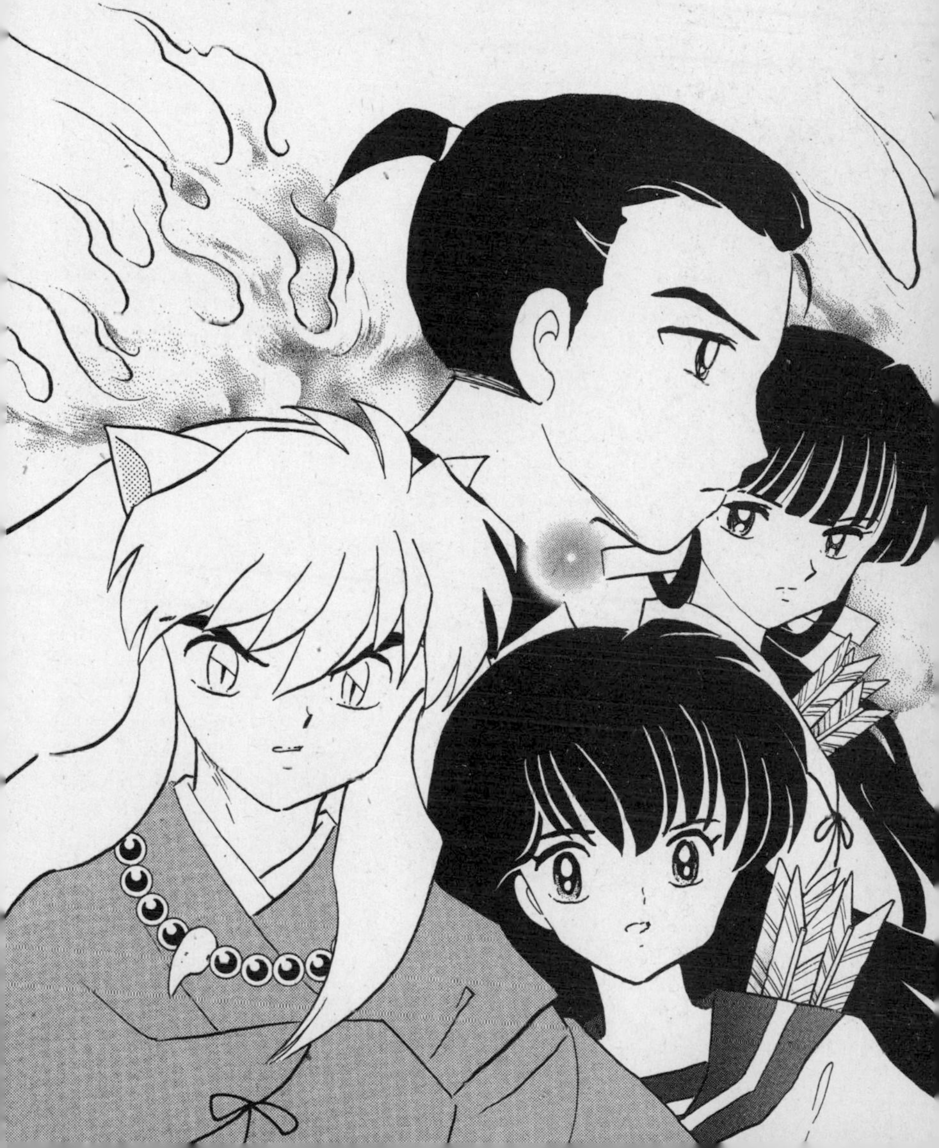

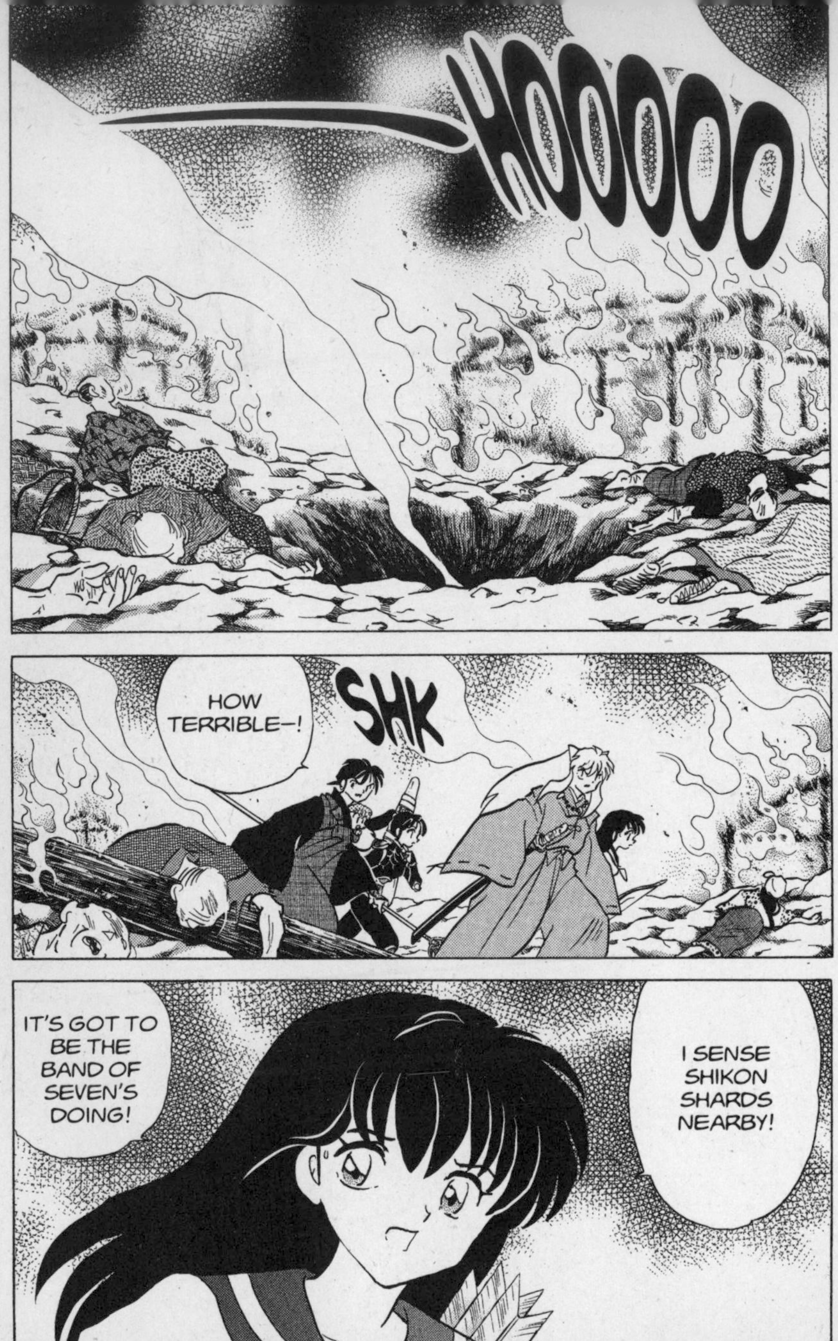
HOOOOO
HOW TERRIBLE--!
SHK
IT'S GOT TO BE THE BAND OF SEVEN'S DOING!
I SENSE SHIKON SHARDS NEARBY!

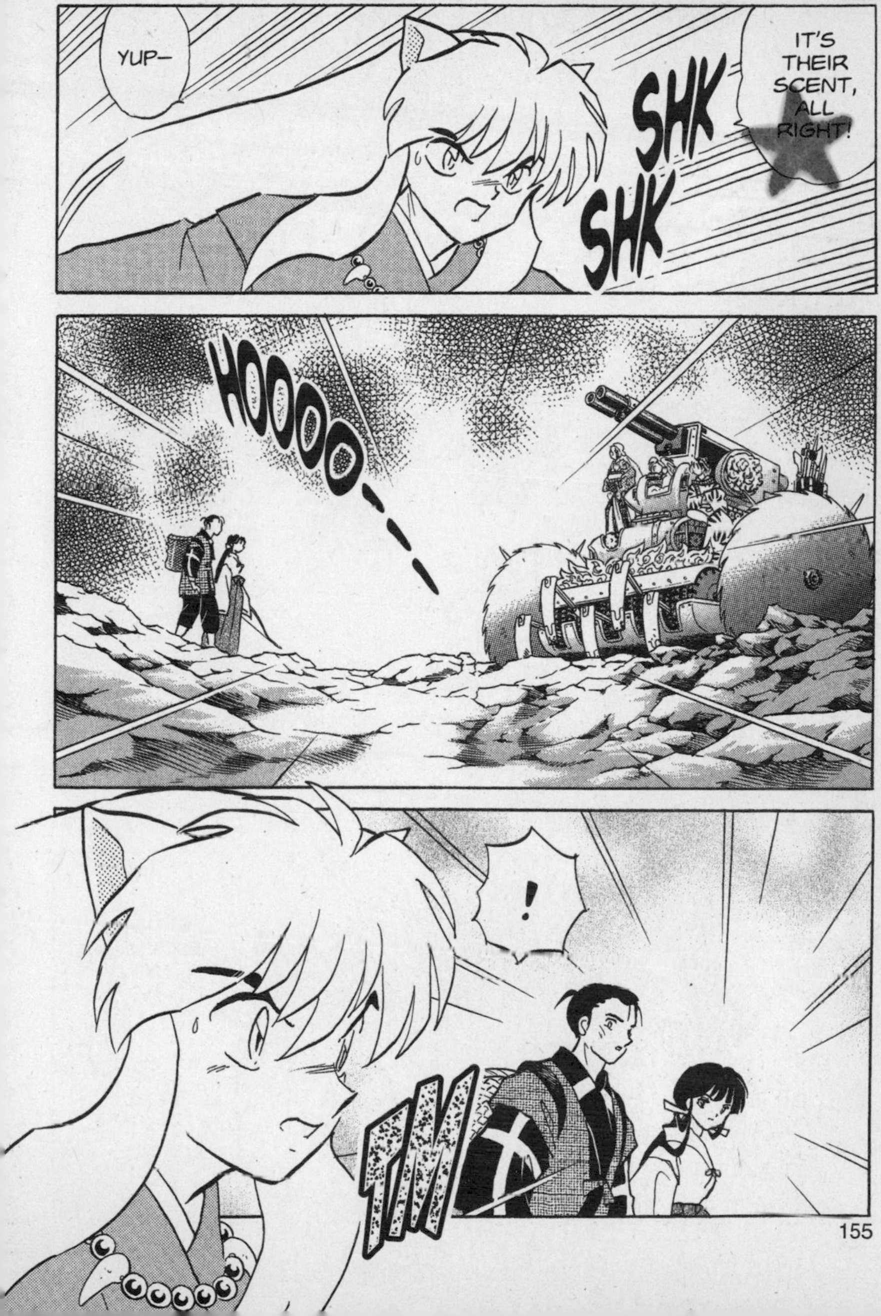
YUP—
SHK SHK
IT'S THEIR SCENT, ALL RIGHT!
HOOOO---
!
TM

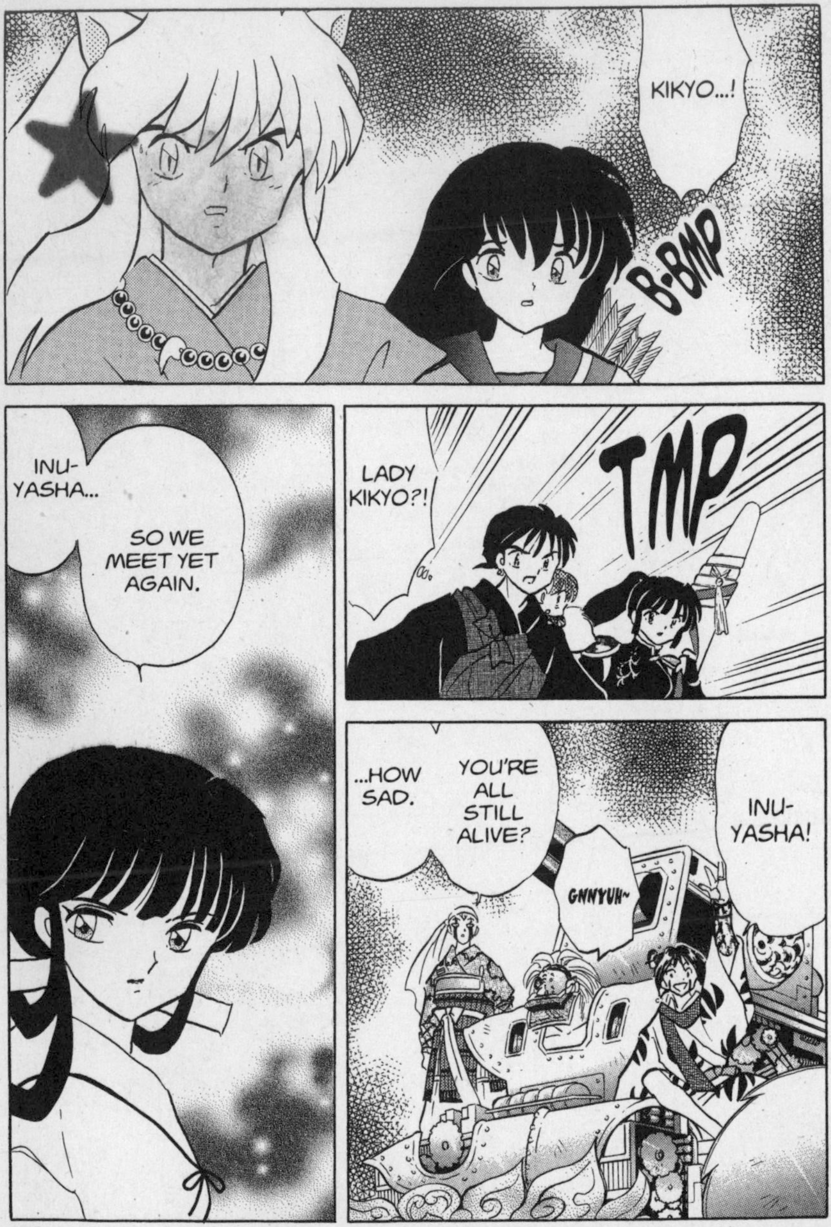
KIKYO...!
B-BMP
INU-YASHA...
SO WE MEET YET AGAIN.
LADY KIKYO?!
TMP
...HOW SAD.
YOU'RE ALL STILL ALIVE?
GNNYUH~
INU-YASHA!

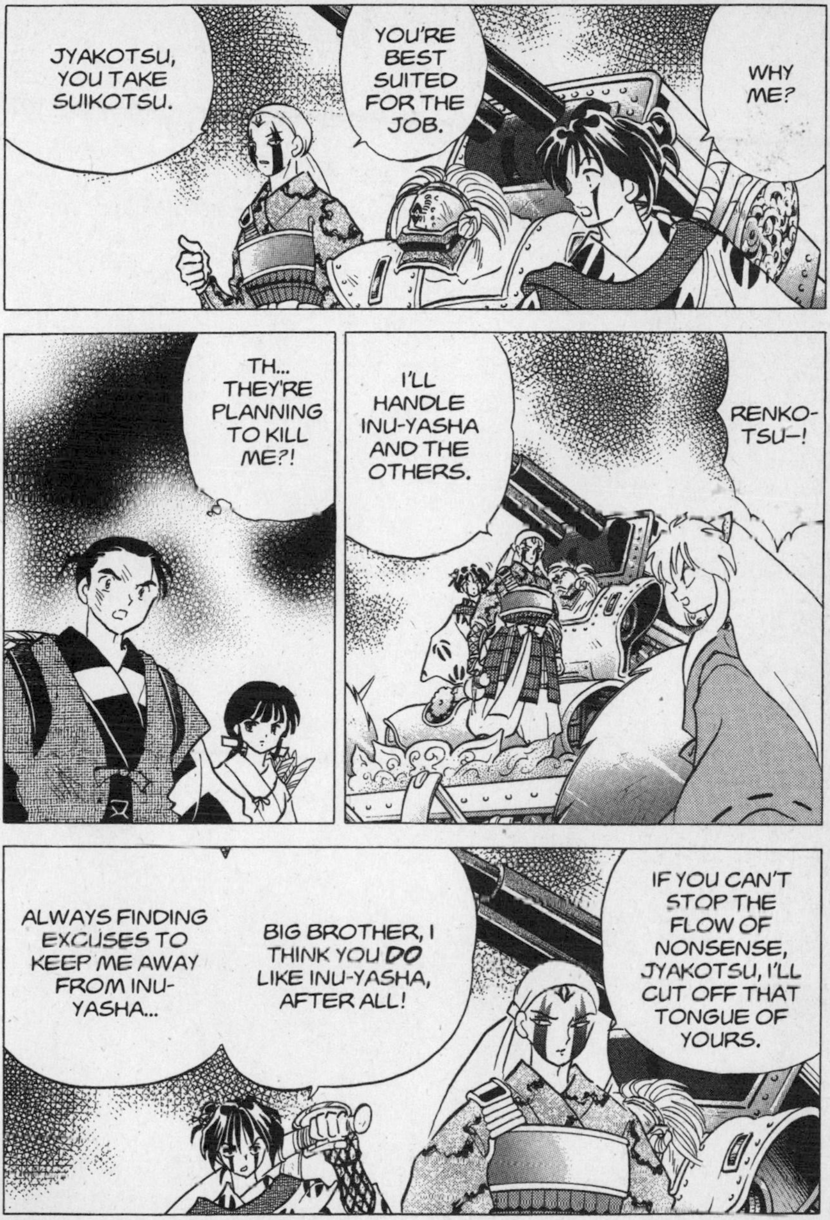
JYAKOTSU, YOU TAKE SUIKOTSU.
YOU'RE BEST SUITED FOR THE JOB.
WHY ME?
TH... THEY'RE PLANNING TO KILL ME?!
I'LL HANDLE INU-YASHA AND THE OTHERS.
RENKO-TSU—!
ALWAYS FINDING EXCUSES TO KEEP ME AWAY FROM INU-YASHA...
BIG BROTHER, I THINK YOU *DO* LIKE INU-YASHA, AFTER ALL!
IF YOU CAN'T STOP THE FLOW OF NONSENSE, JYAKOTSU, I'LL CUT OFF THAT TONGUE OF YOURS.

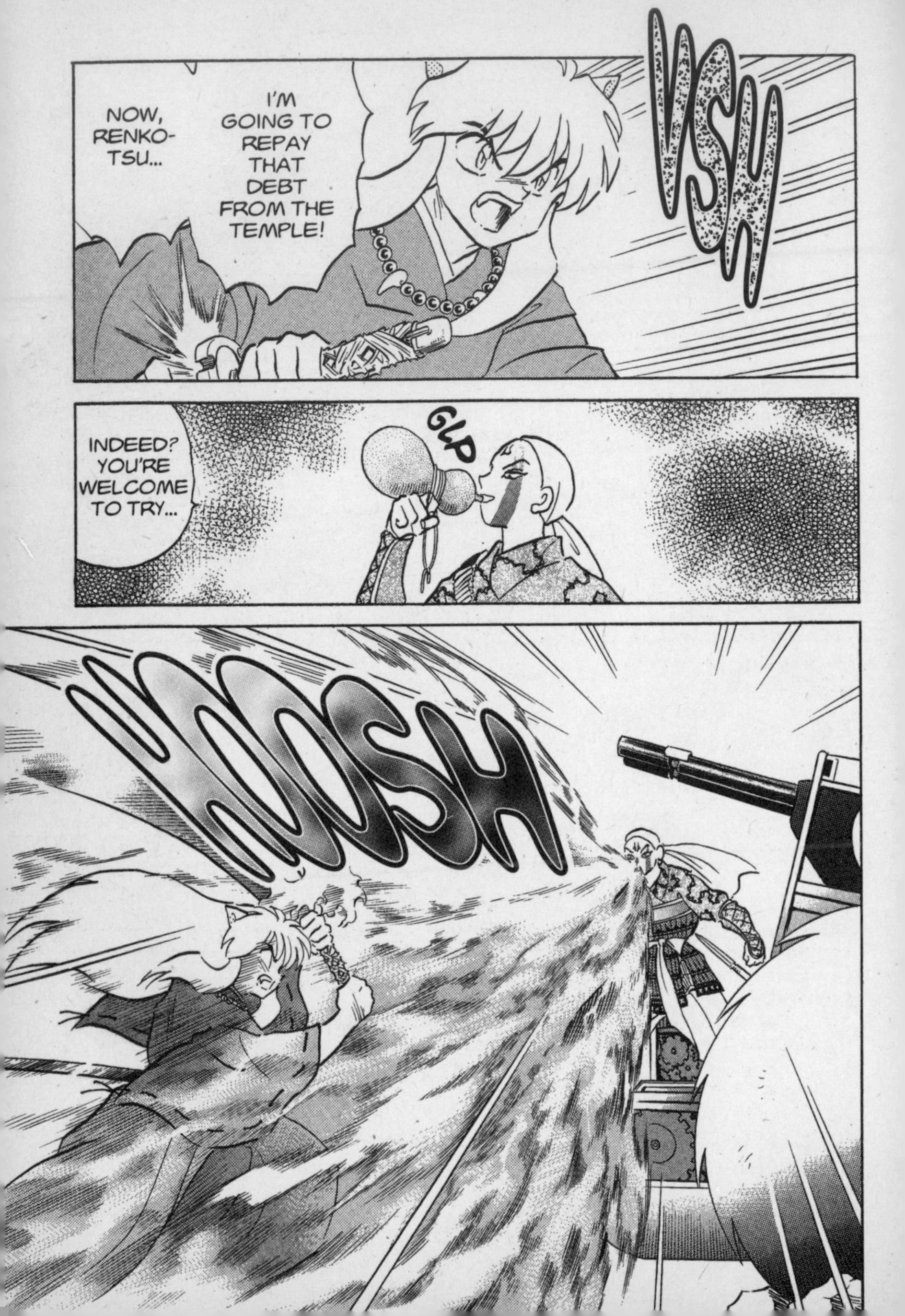
NOW, RENKO-TSU...
I'M GOING TO REPAY THAT DEBT FROM THE TEMPLE!
VSH
INDEED? YOU'RE WELCOME TO TRY...
GLP
WOOSH

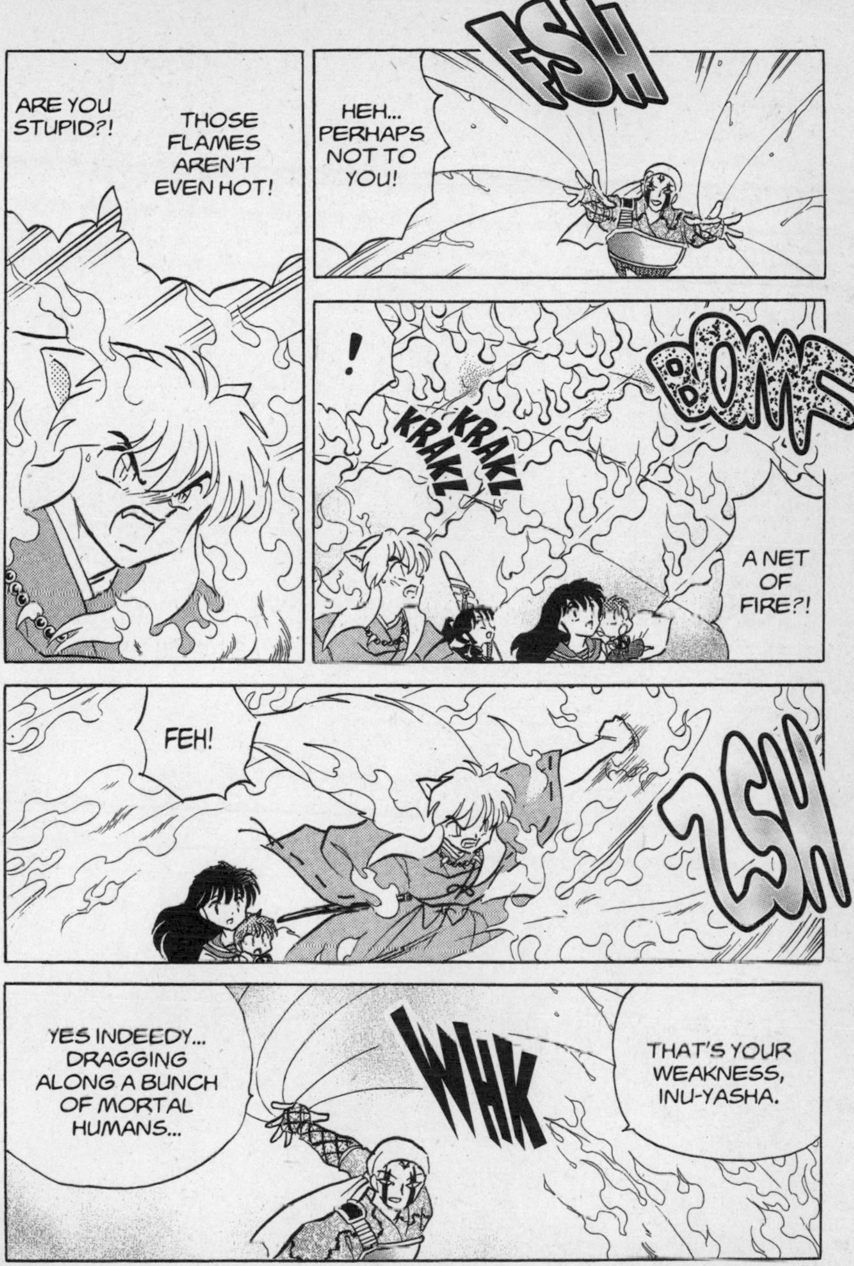
ARE YOU STUPID?!
THOSE FLAMES AREN'T EVEN HOT!
FSH
HEH... PERHAPS NOT TO YOU!
!
KRAKL KRAKL
BOMF
A NET OF FIRE?!
FEH!
ZSH
YES INDEEDY... DRAGGING ALONG A BUNCH OF MORTAL HUMANS...
WHK
THAT'S YOUR WEAKNESS, INU-YASHA.

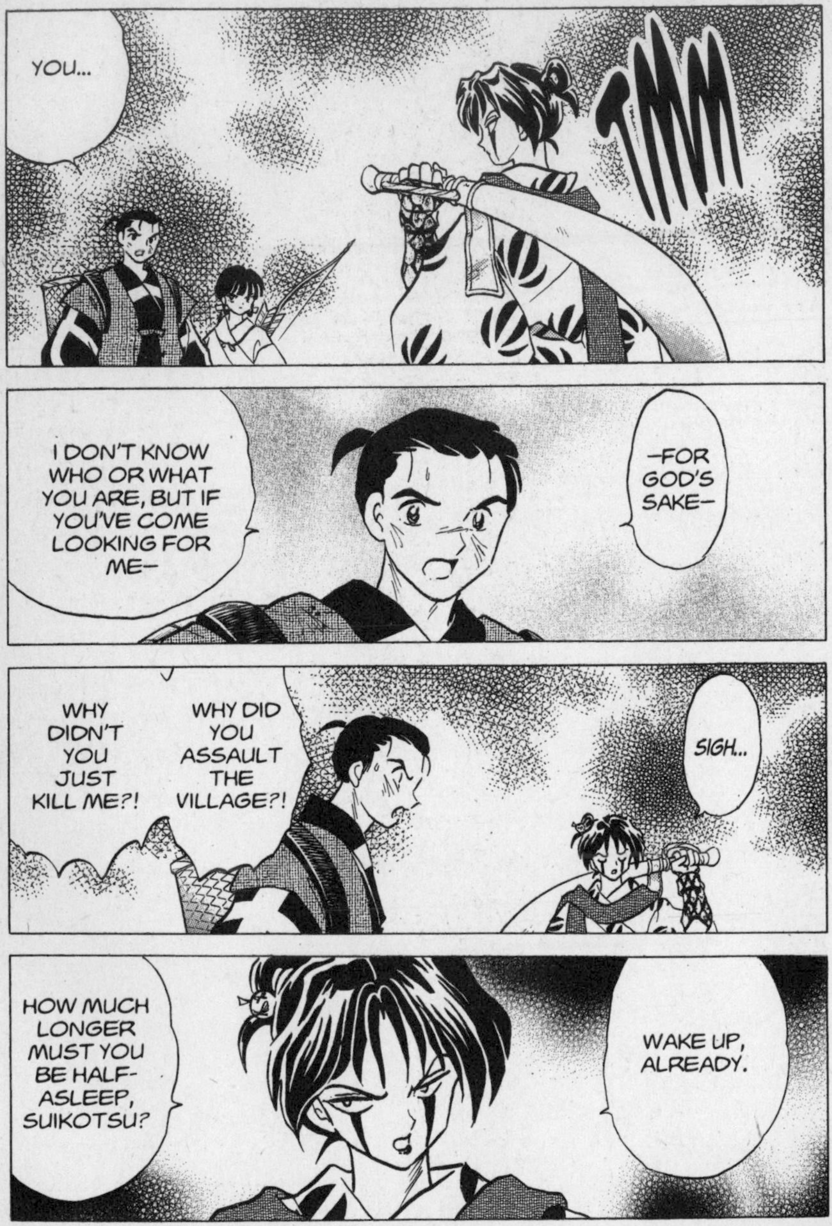
YOU...
TMM
I DON'T KNOW WHO OR WHAT YOU ARE, BUT IF YOU'VE COME LOOKING FOR ME—
—FOR GOD'S SAKE—
WHY DIDN'T YOU JUST KILL ME?!
WHY DID YOU ASSAULT THE VILLAGE?!
SIGH...
HOW MUCH LONGER MUST YOU BE HALF-ASLEEP, SUIKOTSU?
WAKE UP, ALREADY.

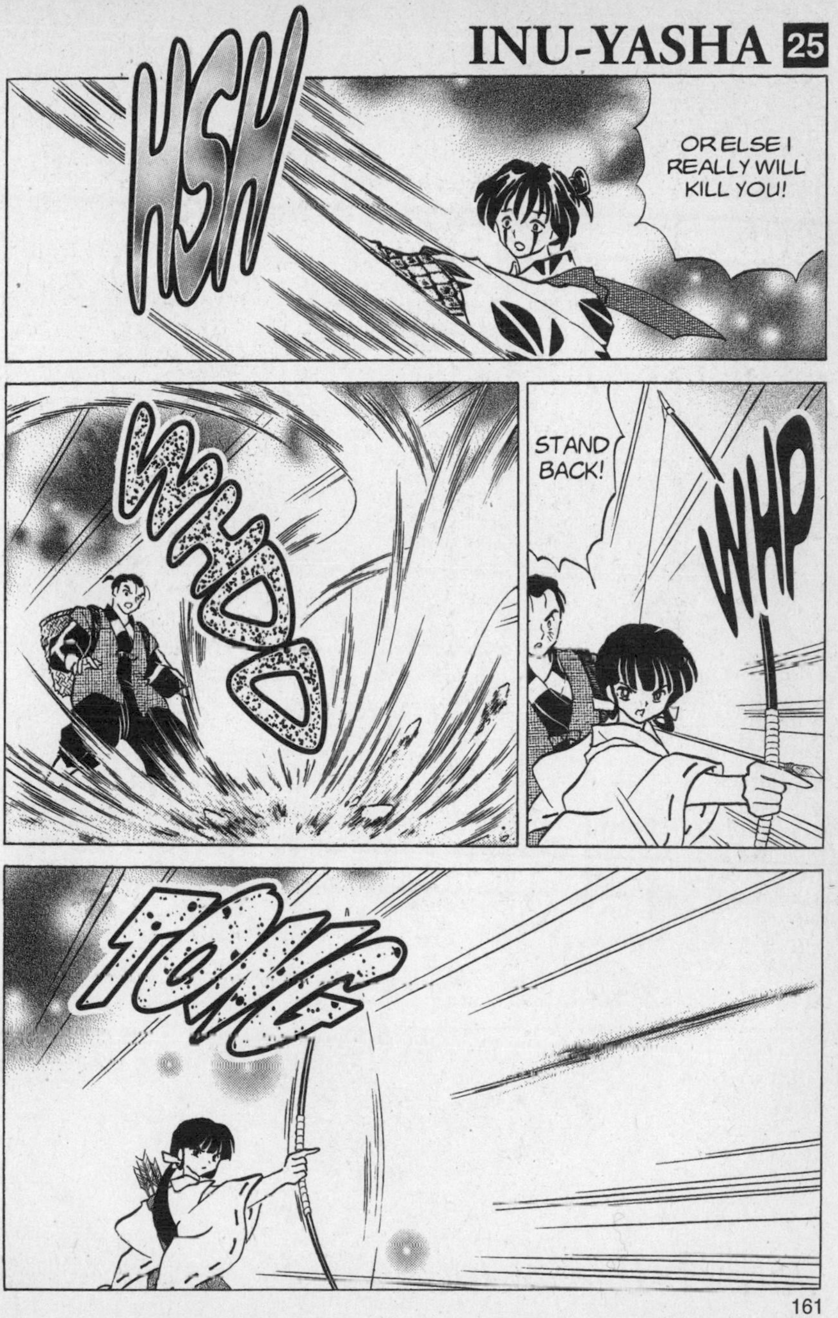
HSH
OR ELSE I REALLY WILL KILL YOU!
WHOO
STAND BACK!
WHP
TONG

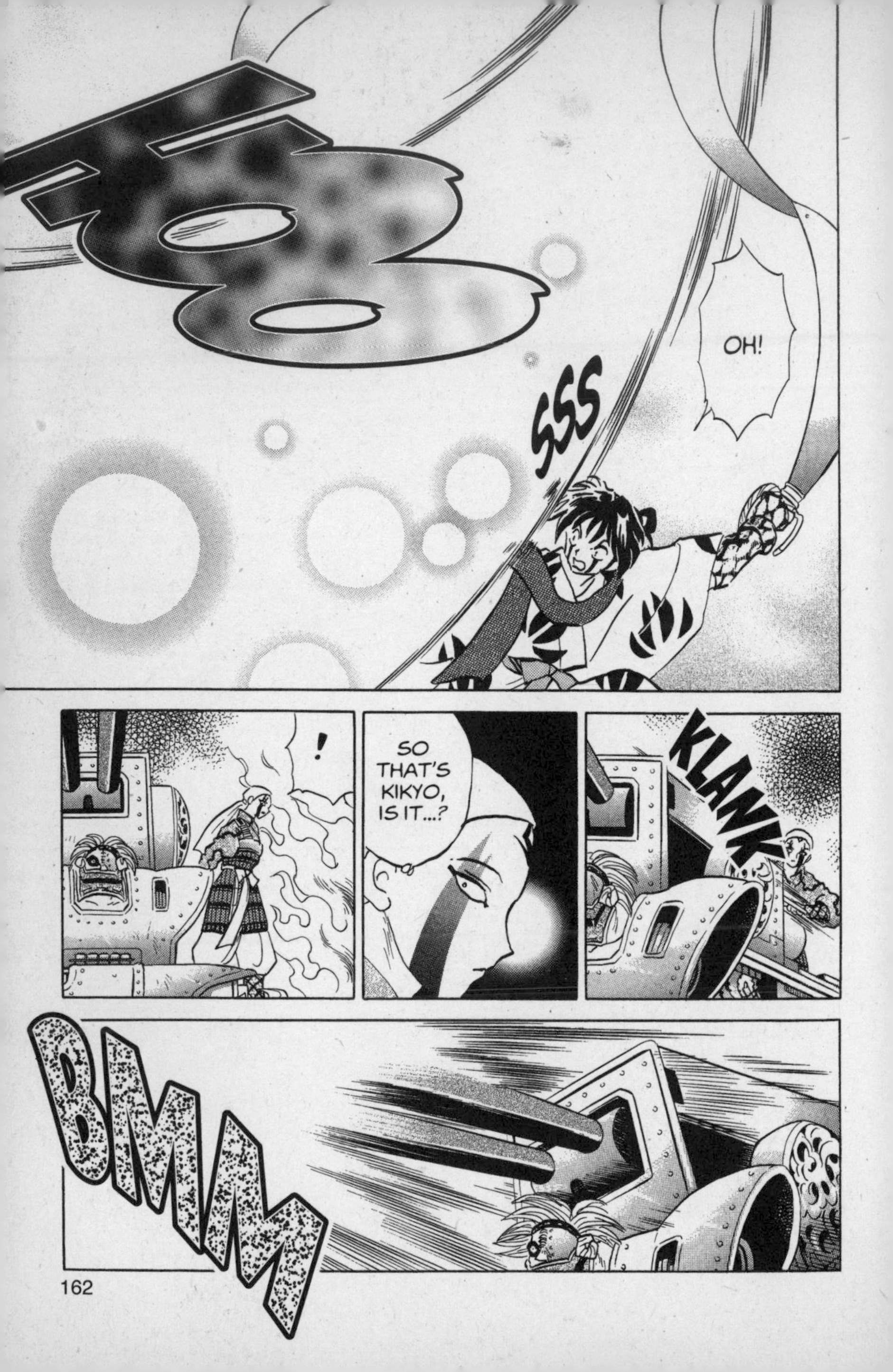
SSS
OH!
!
SO THAT'S KIKYO, IS IT...?
KLANK
BMM

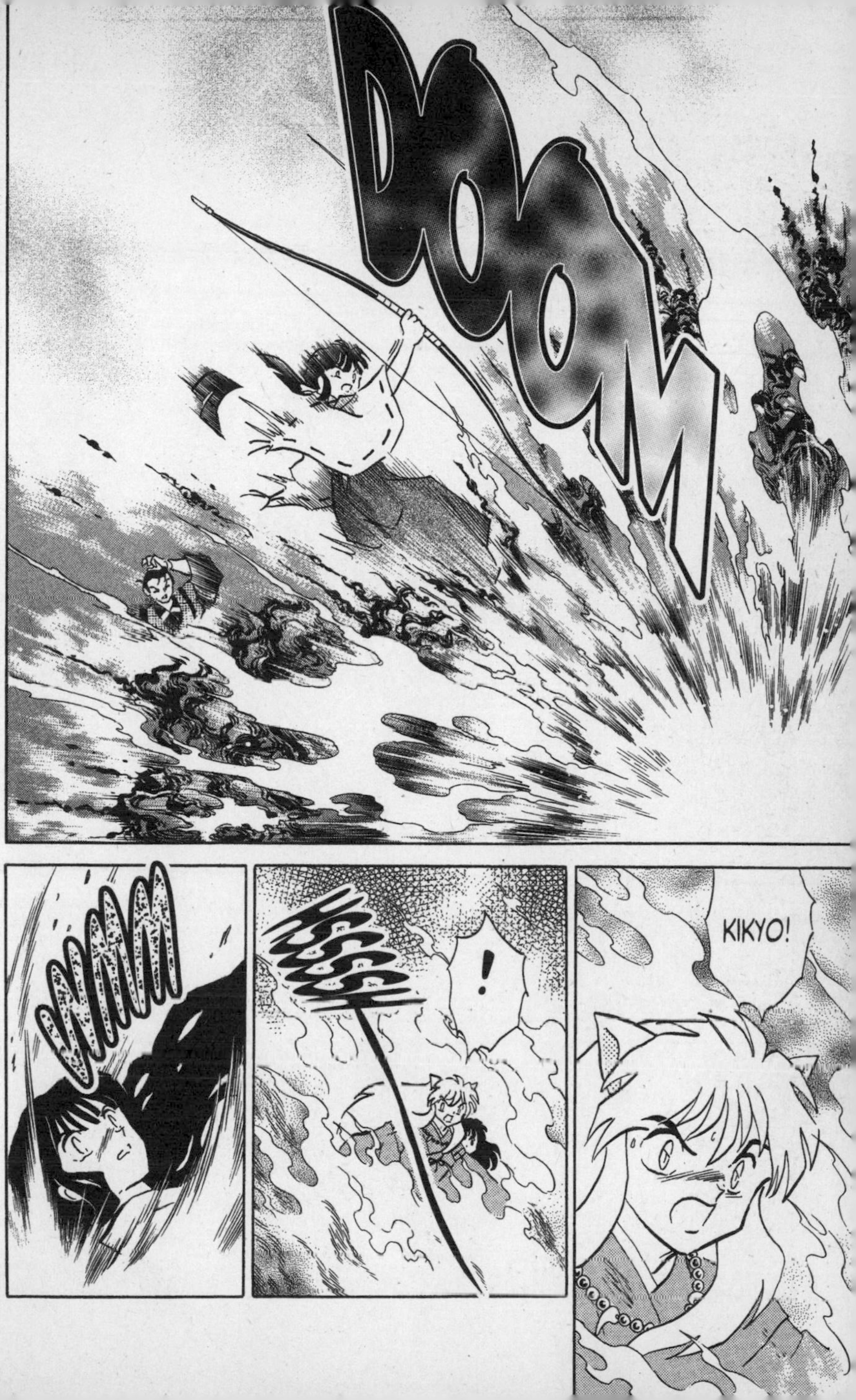
DOOM
!
KIKYO!

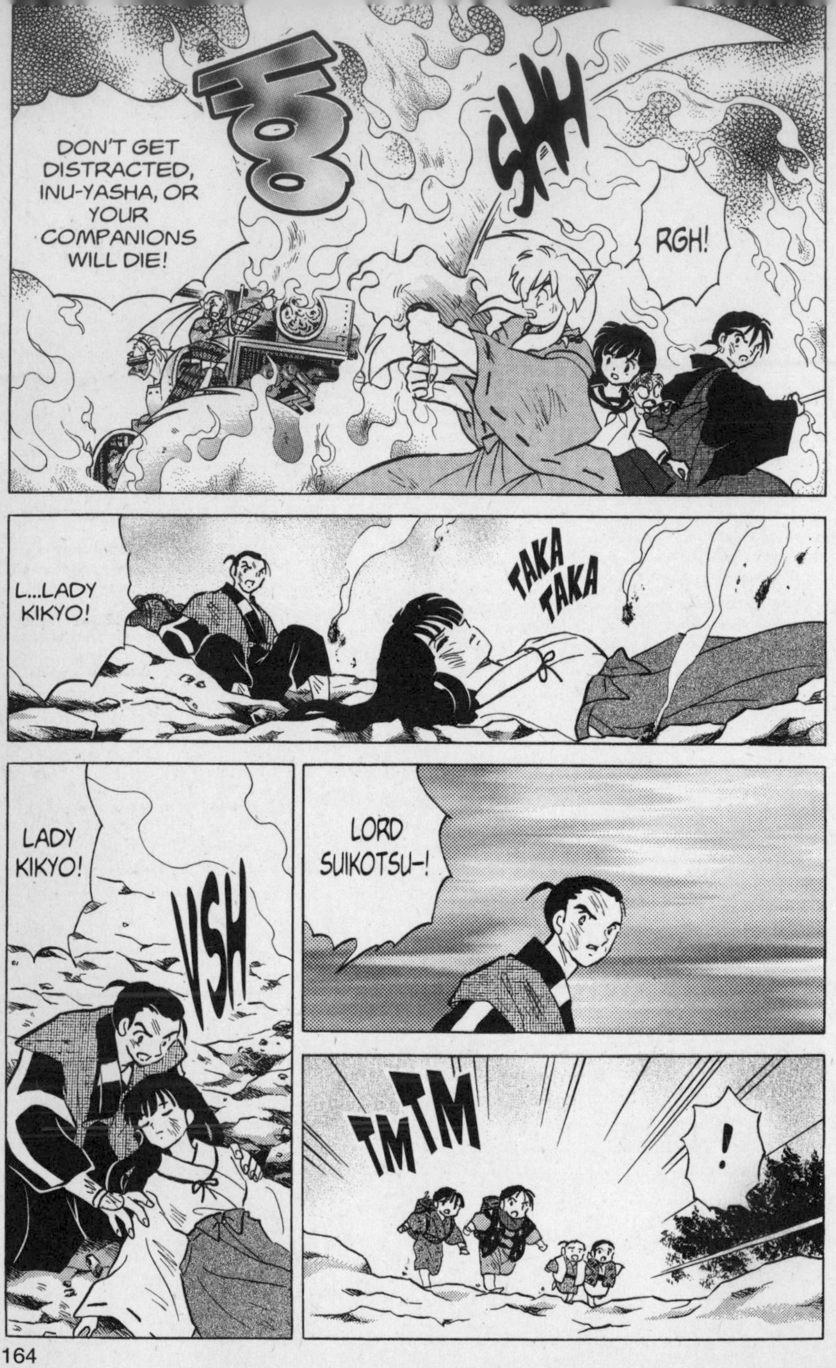
DON'T GET DISTRACTED, INU-YASHA, OR YOUR COMPANIONS WILL DIE!
SHH
RGH!
L...LADY KIKYO!
TAKA TAKA
LADY KIKYO!
VSH
LORD SUIKOTSU-!
TM TM
!

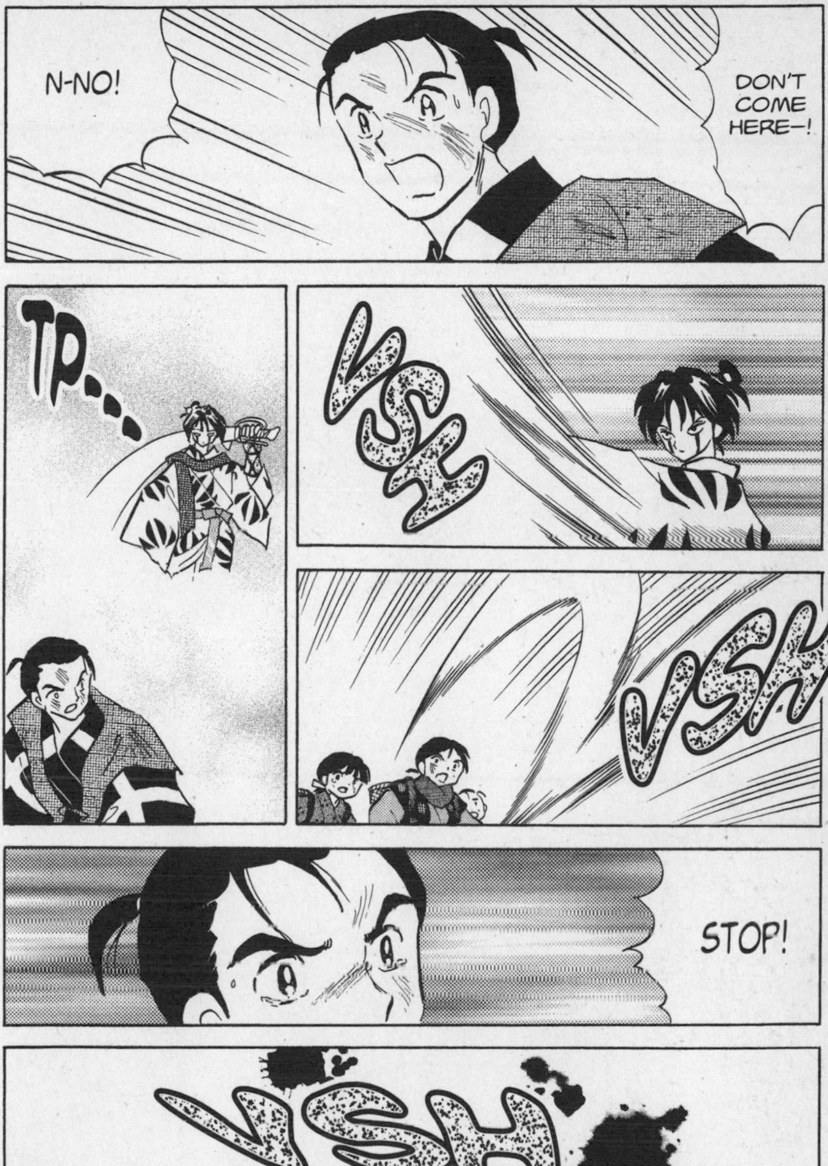
N-NO!
DON'T COME HERE—!
TP...
VSH
VSH
STOP!
VSH

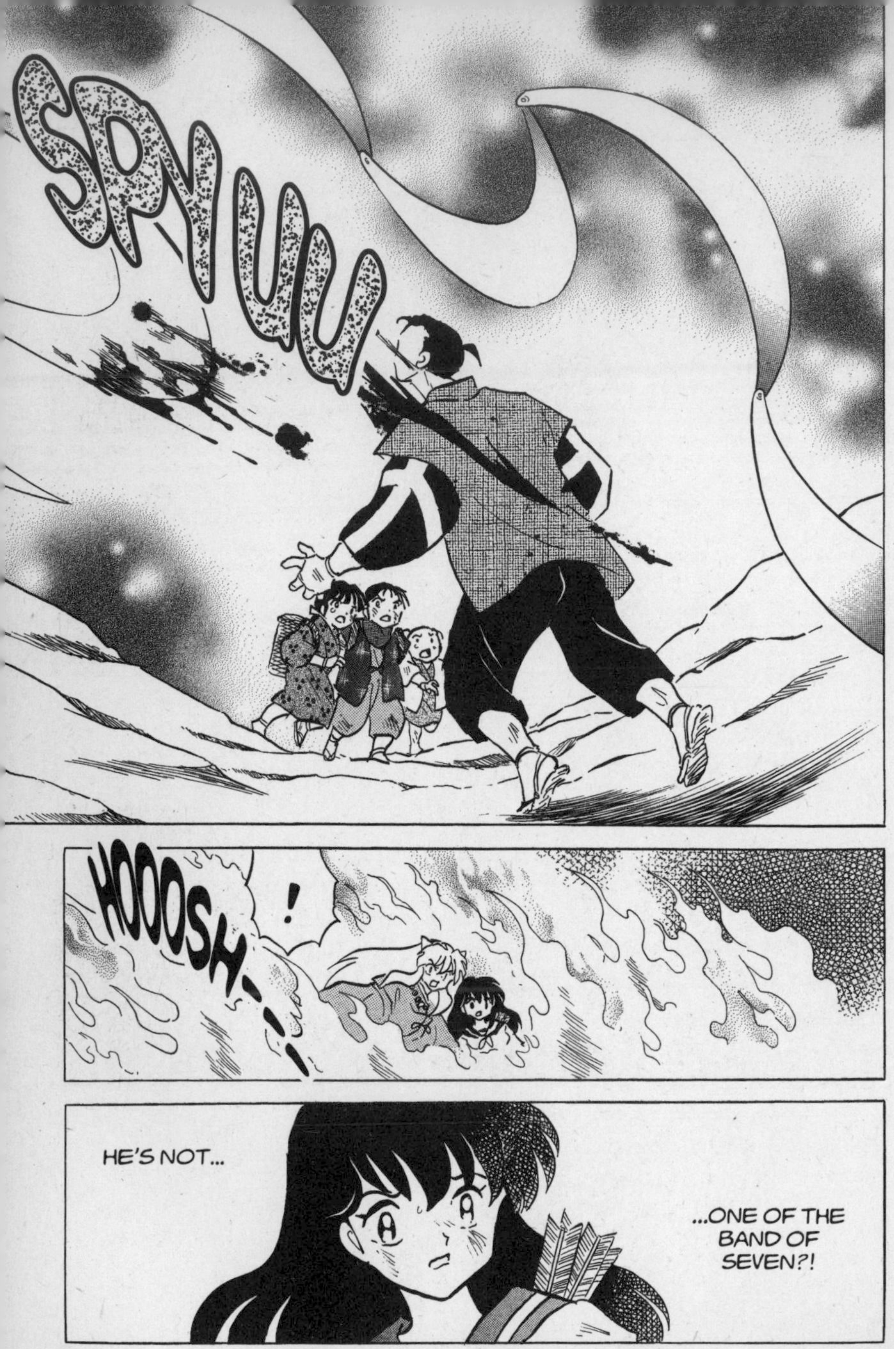
SPYUUU
HOOOSH
!
HE'S NOT...
...ONE OF THE BAND OF SEVEN?!

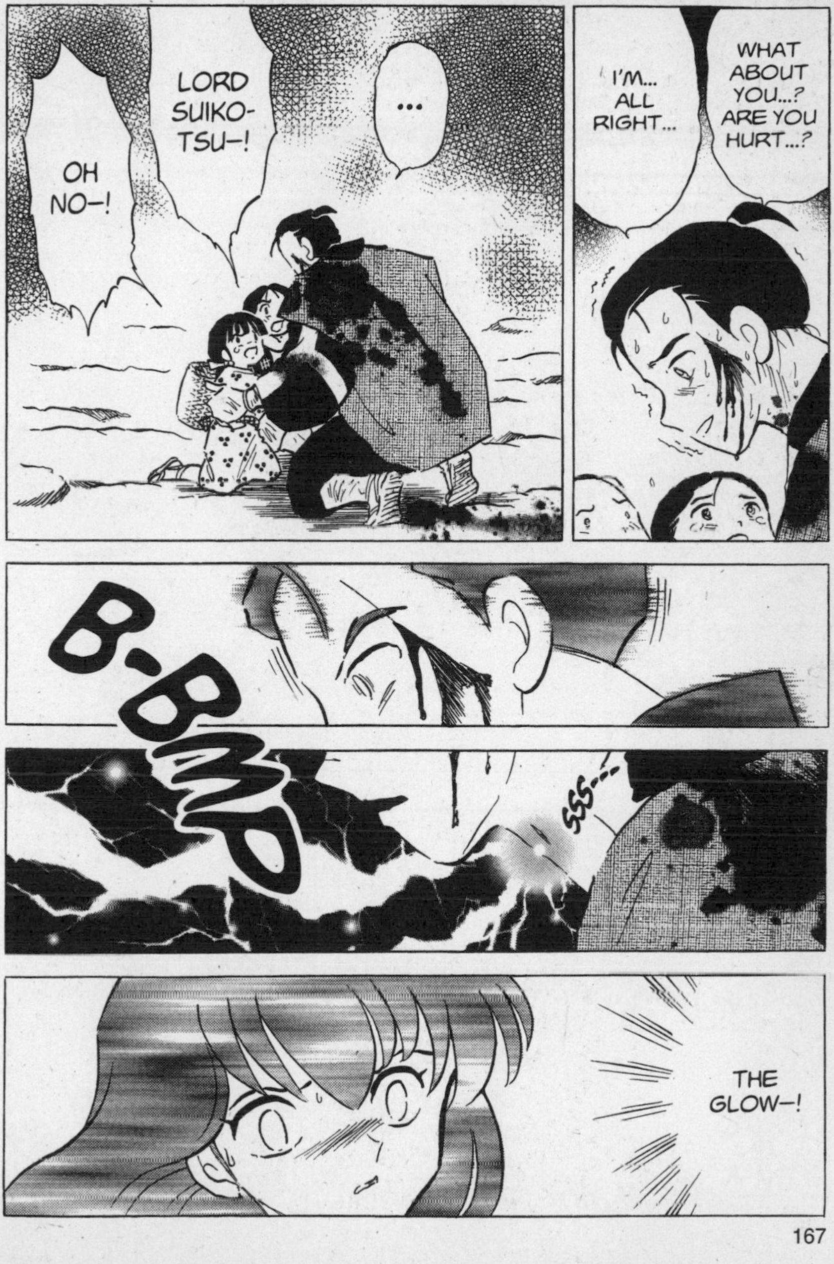
OH NO–!
LORD SUIKO-TSU–!
...
I'M... ALL RIGHT...
WHAT ABOUT YOU...? ARE YOU HURT...?
B-BMP
SSS---
THE GLOW–!

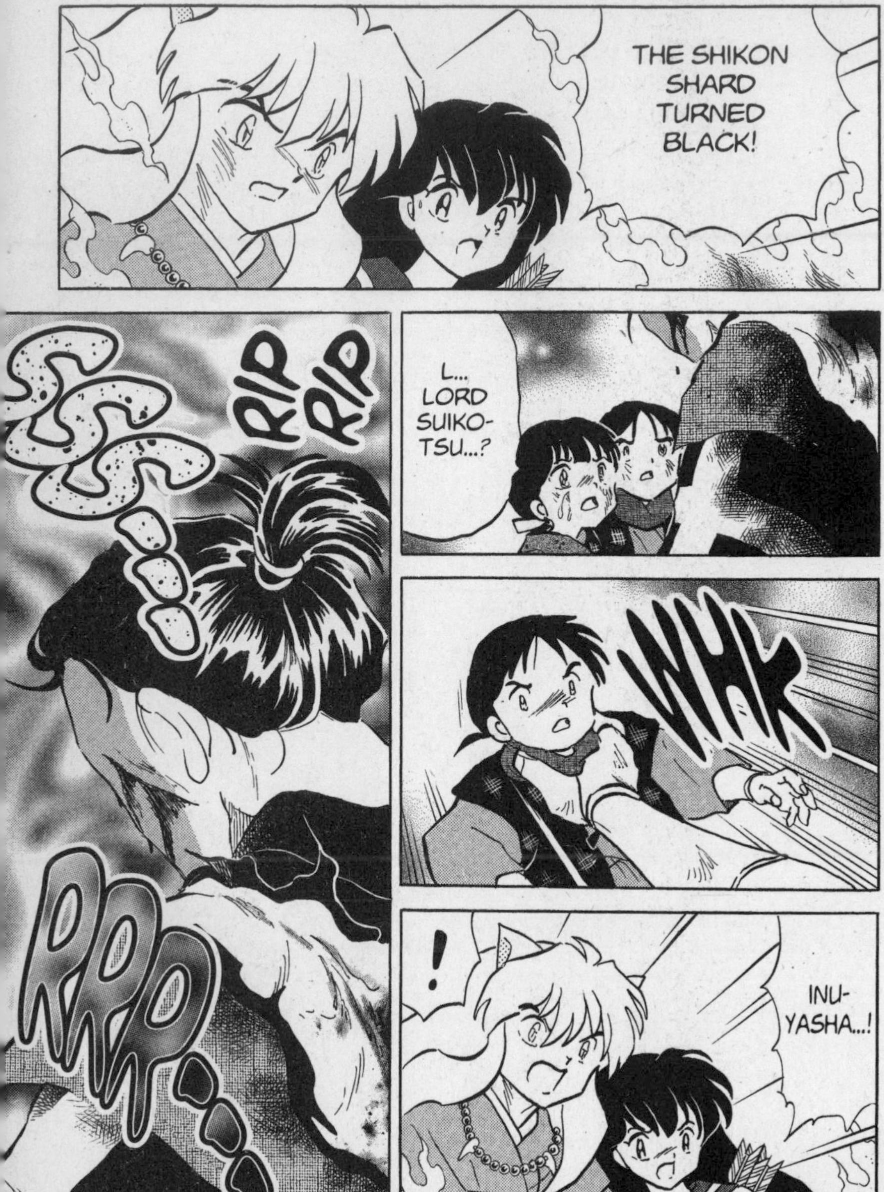
THE SHIKON SHARD TURNED BLACK!
SSS...
RIP RIP
RRR...
L... LORD SUIKO-TSU...?
WHK
!
INU-YASHA...!

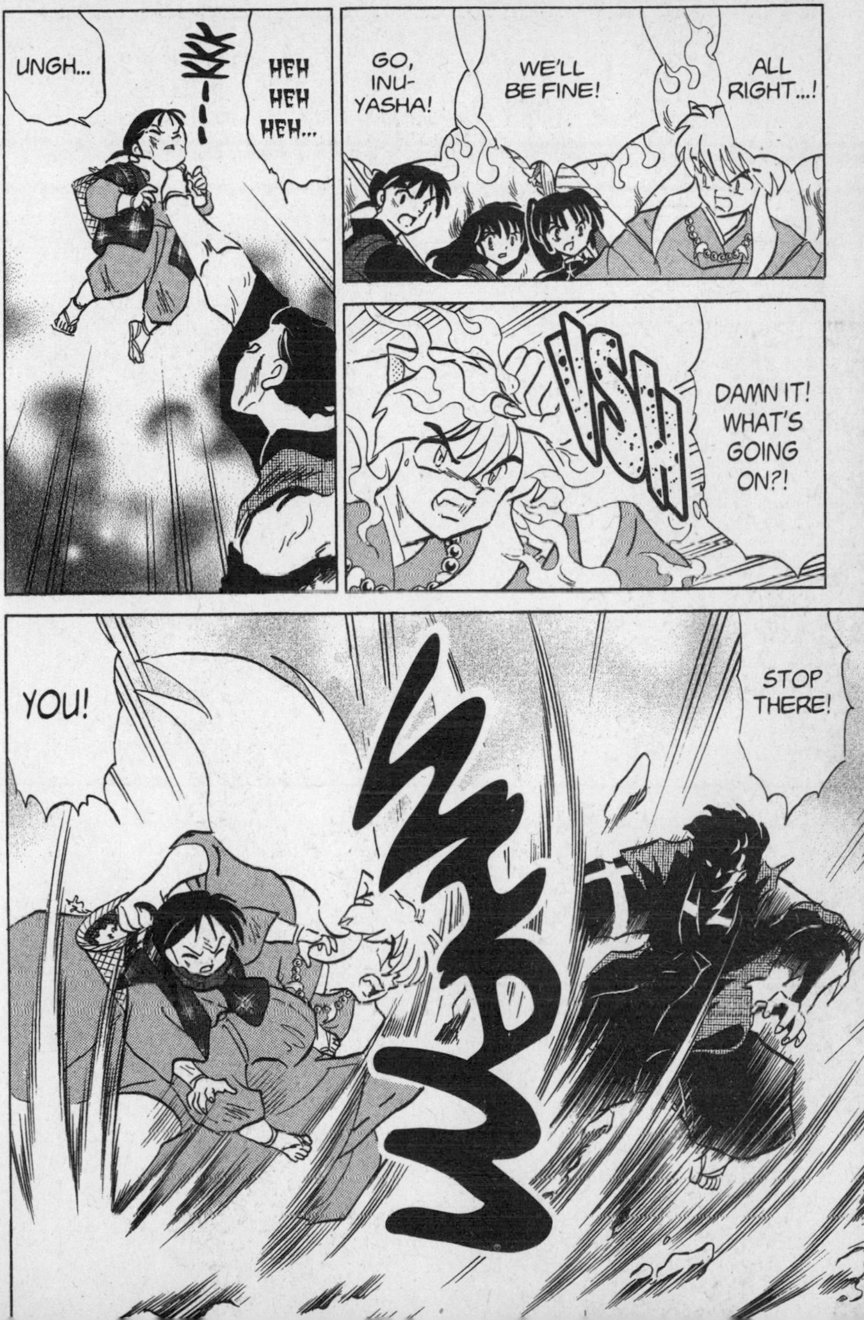
UNGH...
KKKK
HEH HEH HEH...
GO, INU-YASHA!
WE'LL BE FINE!
ALL RIGHT...!
VSH
DAMN IT! WHAT'S GOING ON?!
YOU!
STOP THERE!

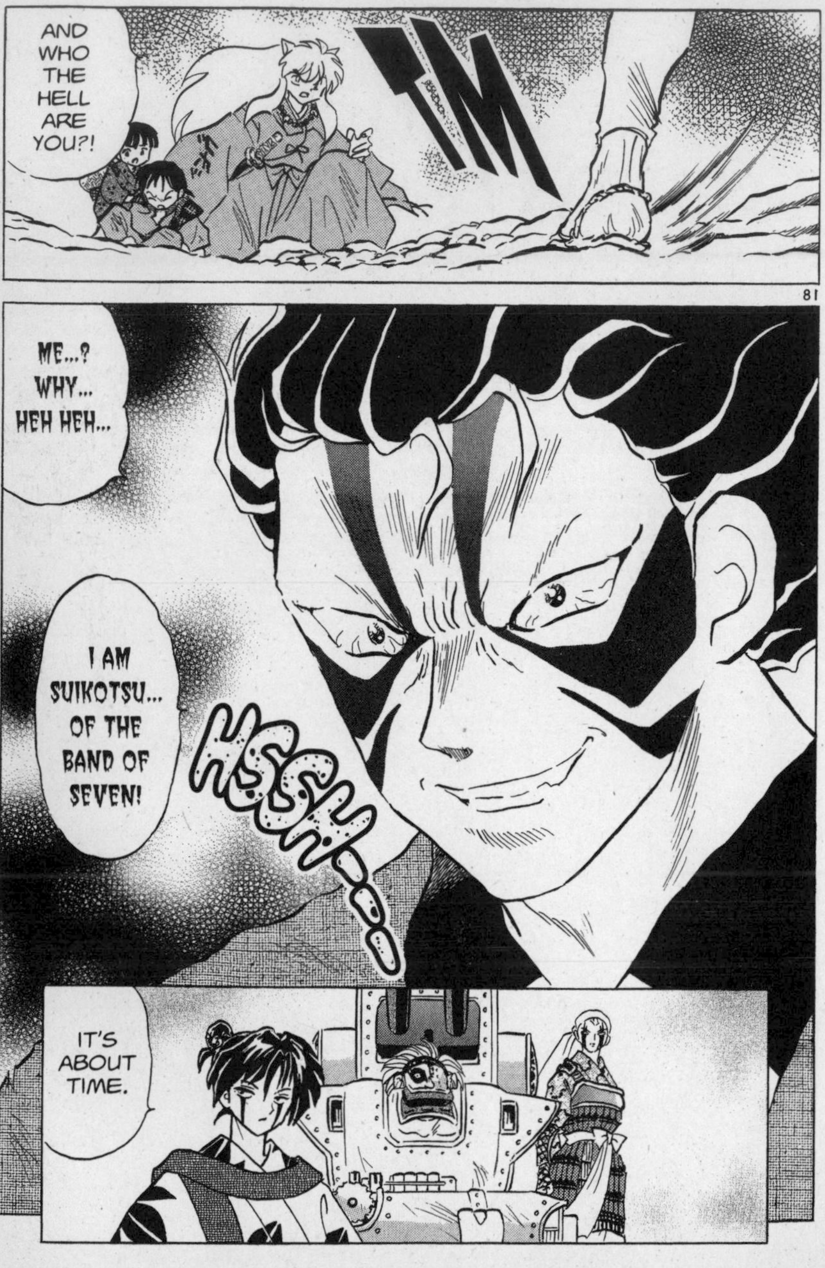
AND WHO THE HELL ARE YOU?!
TM
ME...? WHY... HEH HEH...
I AM SUIKOTSU... OF THE BAND OF SEVEN!
HSSH
IT'S ABOUT TIME.

SCROLL TEN

# THE TWO SOULS

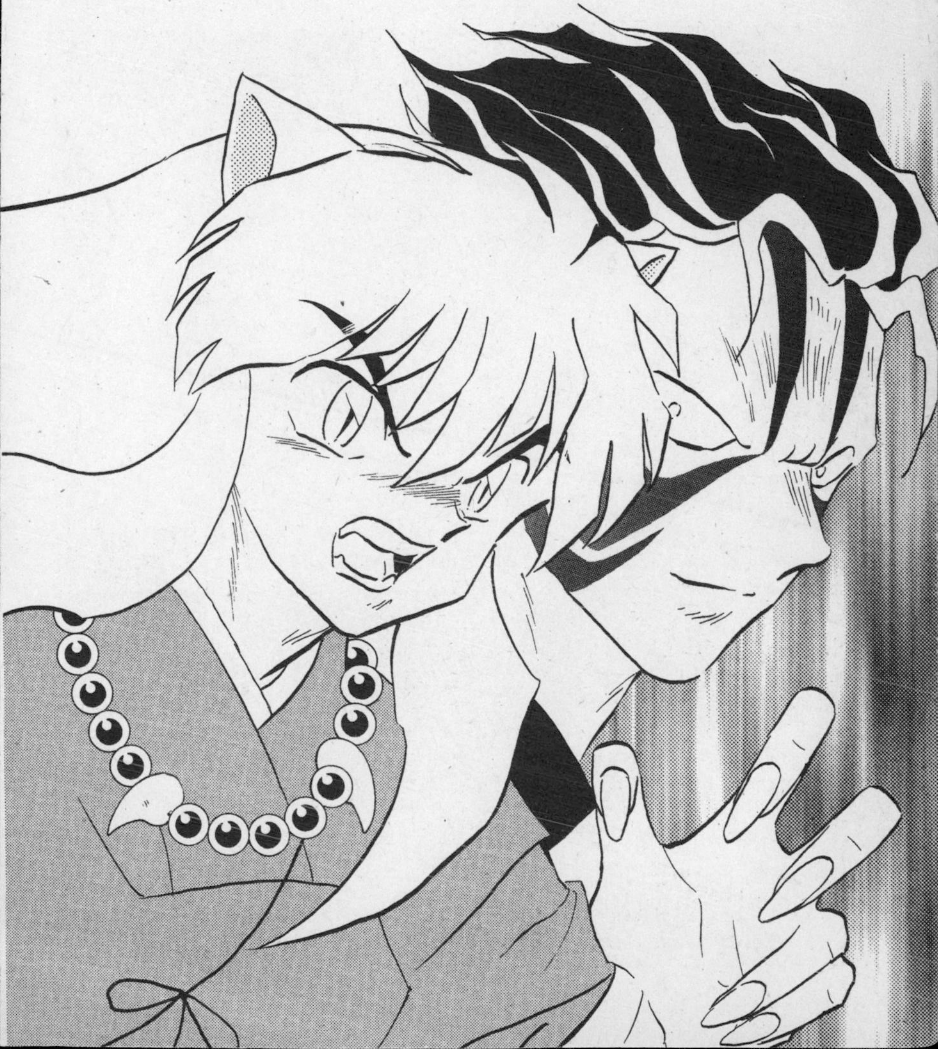

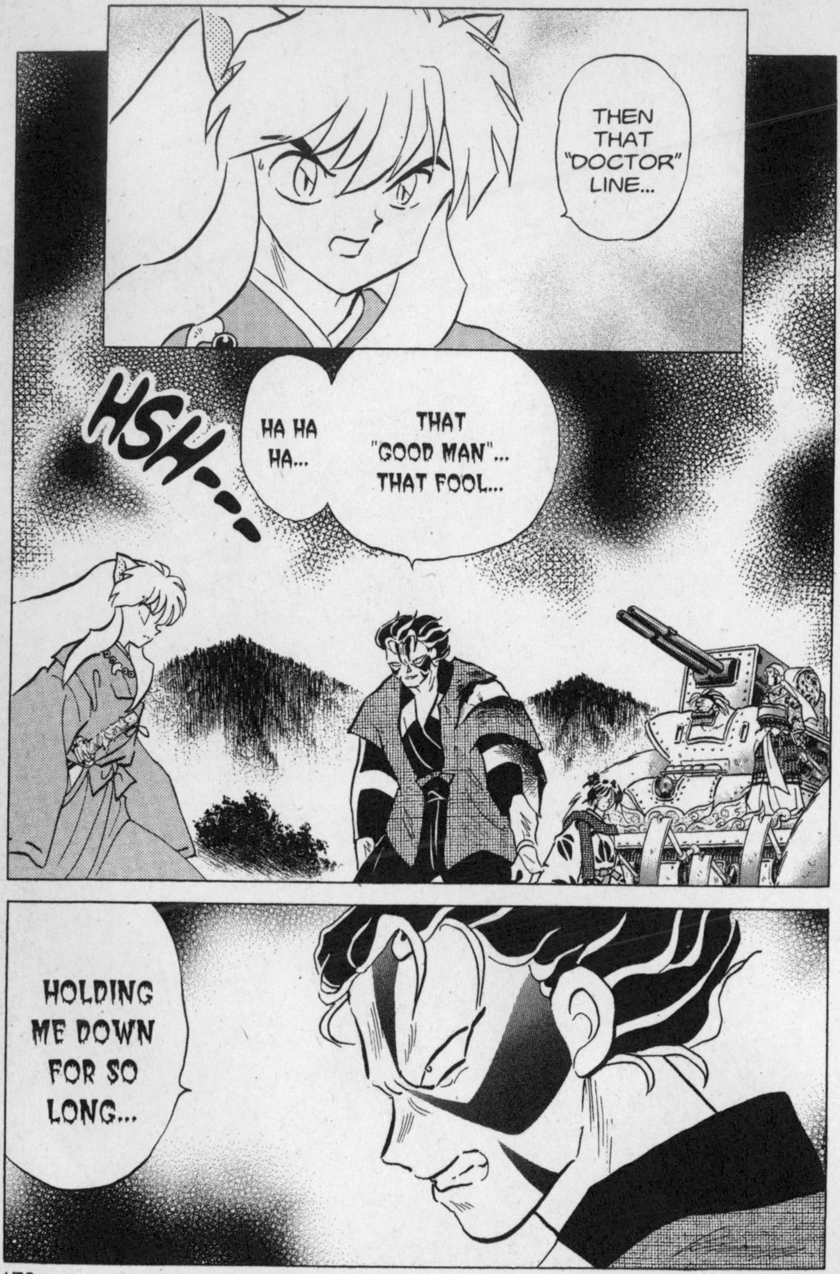
THEN THAT "DOCTOR" LINE...
HSH---
HA HA HA...
THAT "GOOD MAN"... THAT FOOL...
HOLDING ME DOWN FOR SO LONG...

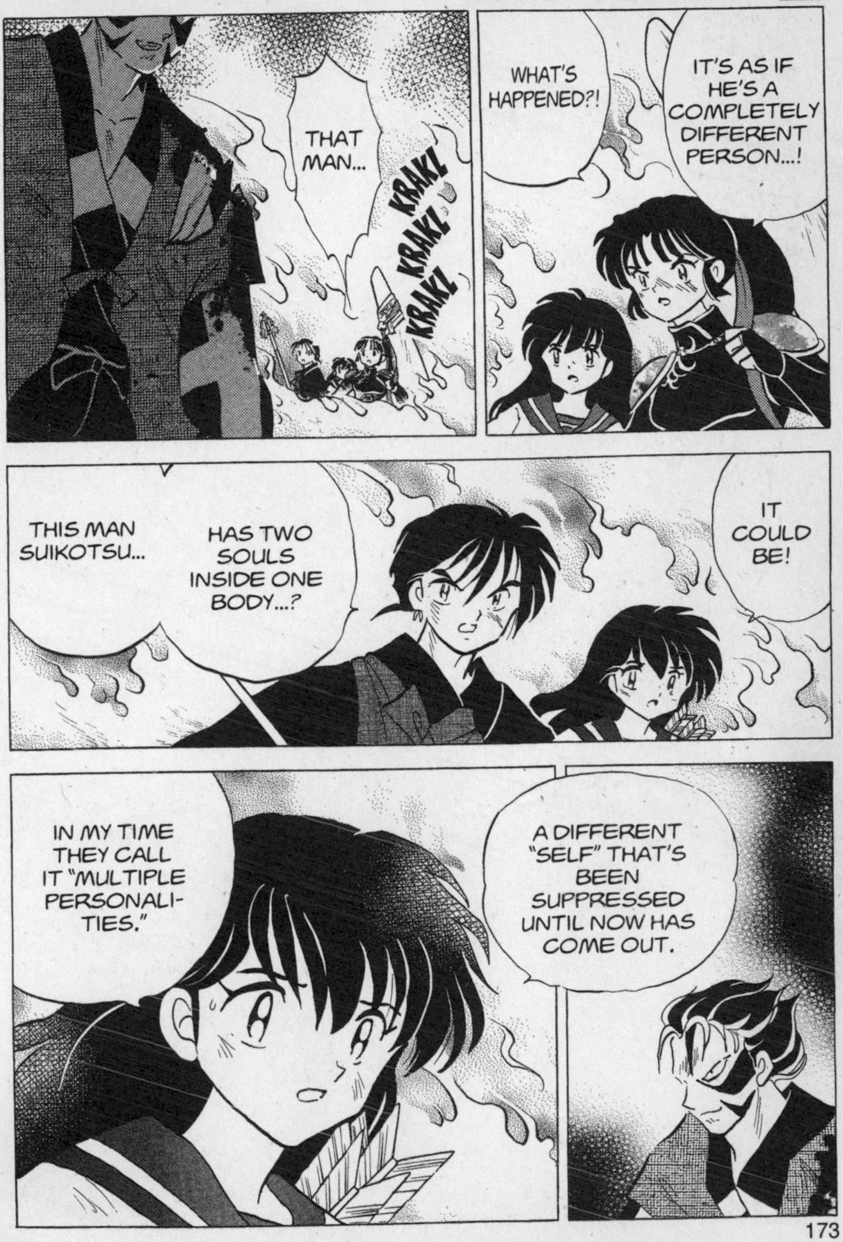
THAT MAN...
KRAKL
KRAKL
KRAKL
WHAT'S HAPPENED?!
IT'S AS IF HE'S A COMPLETELY DIFFERENT PERSON...!
THIS MAN SUIKOTSU...
HAS TWO SOULS INSIDE ONE BODY...?
IT COULD BE!
IN MY TIME THEY CALL IT "MULTIPLE PERSONALI-TIES."
A DIFFERENT "SELF" THAT'S BEEN SUPPRESSED UNTIL NOW HAS COME OUT.

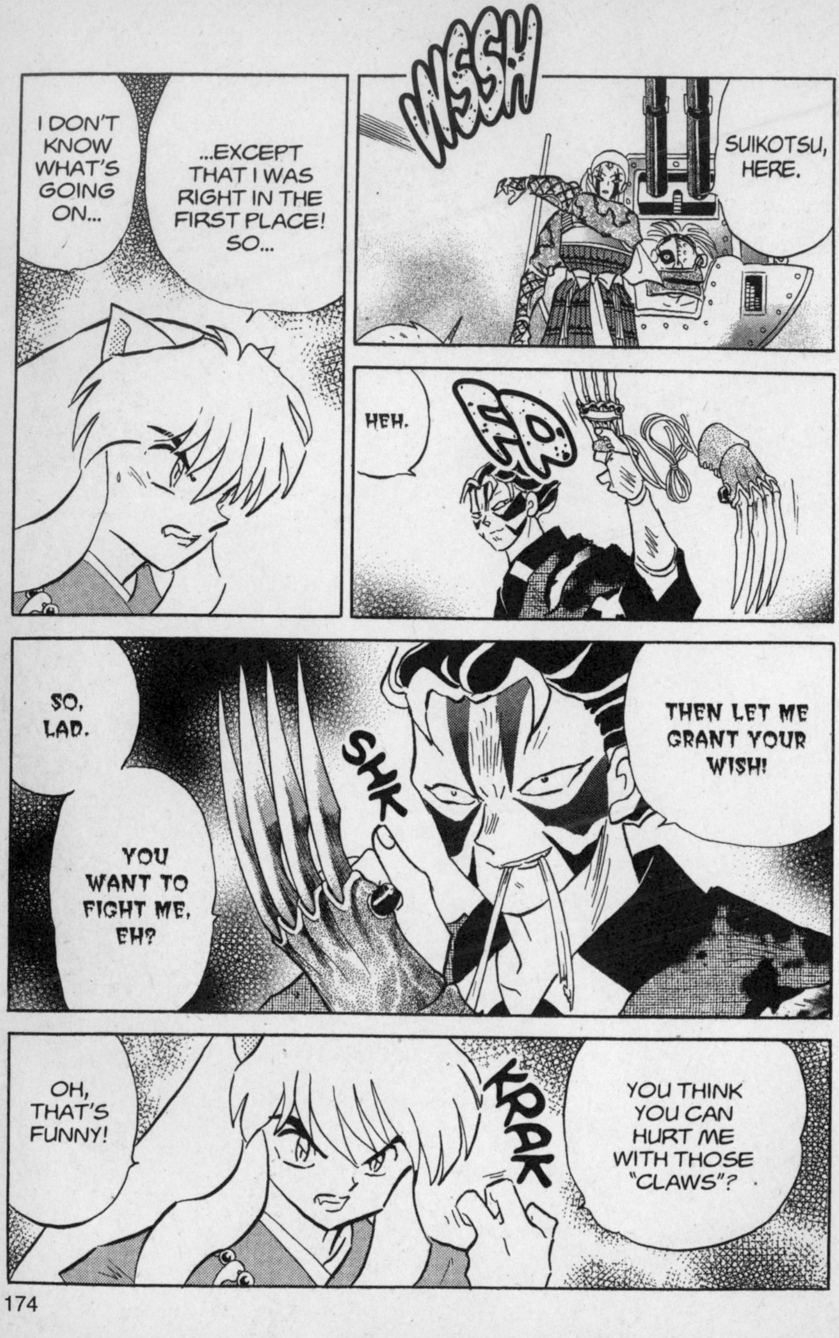
I DON'T KNOW WHAT'S GOING ON...
...EXCEPT THAT I WAS RIGHT IN THE FIRST PLACE! SO...
WSSH
SUIKOTSU, HERE.
HEH.
ZOP
SO, LAD.
YOU WANT TO FIGHT ME, EH?
SHK
THEN LET ME GRANT YOUR WISH!
OH, THAT'S FUNNY!
KRAK
YOU THINK YOU CAN HURT ME WITH THOSE "CLAWS"?

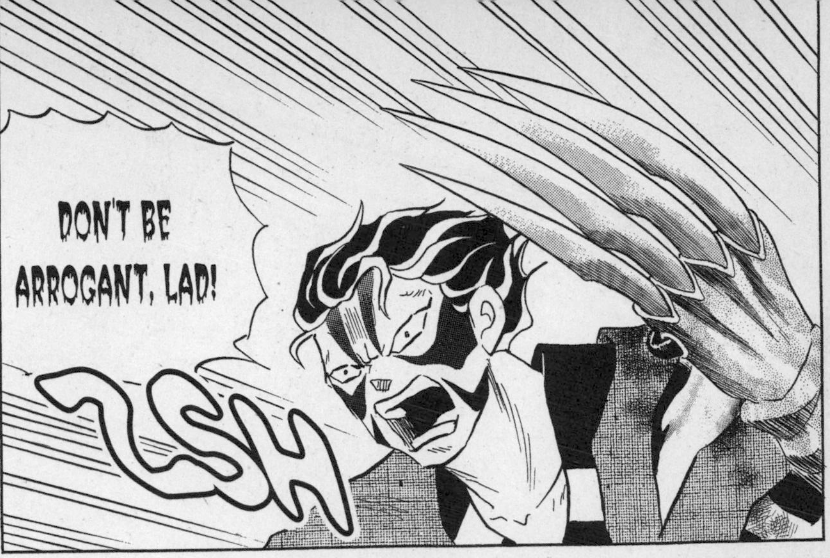
DON'T BE ARROGANT, LAD!
TSH

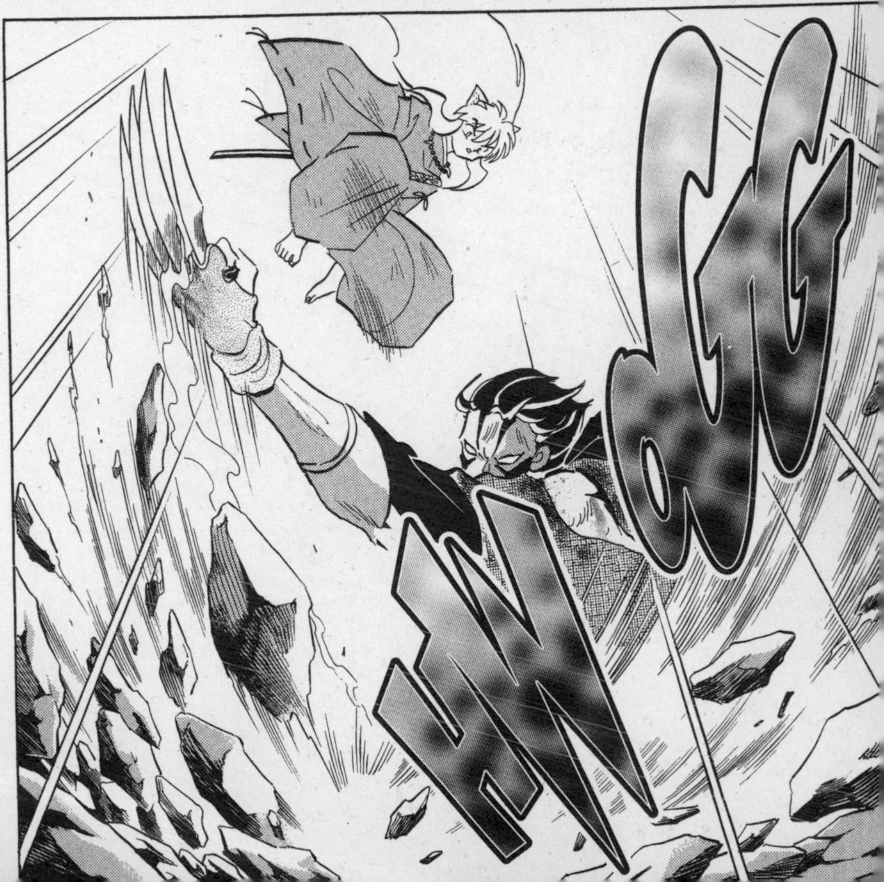

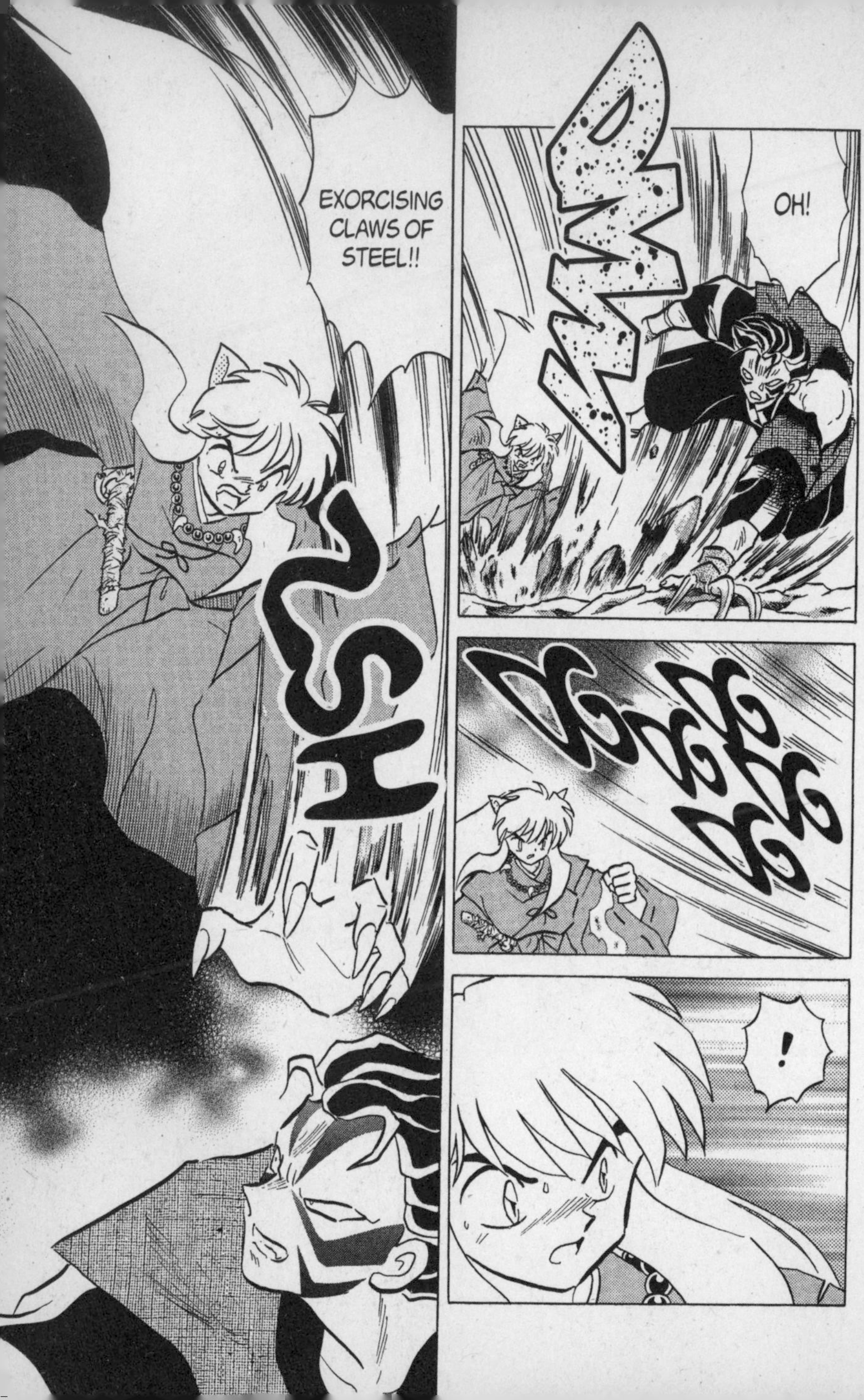
EXORCISING CLAWS OF STEEL!!
OH!
!

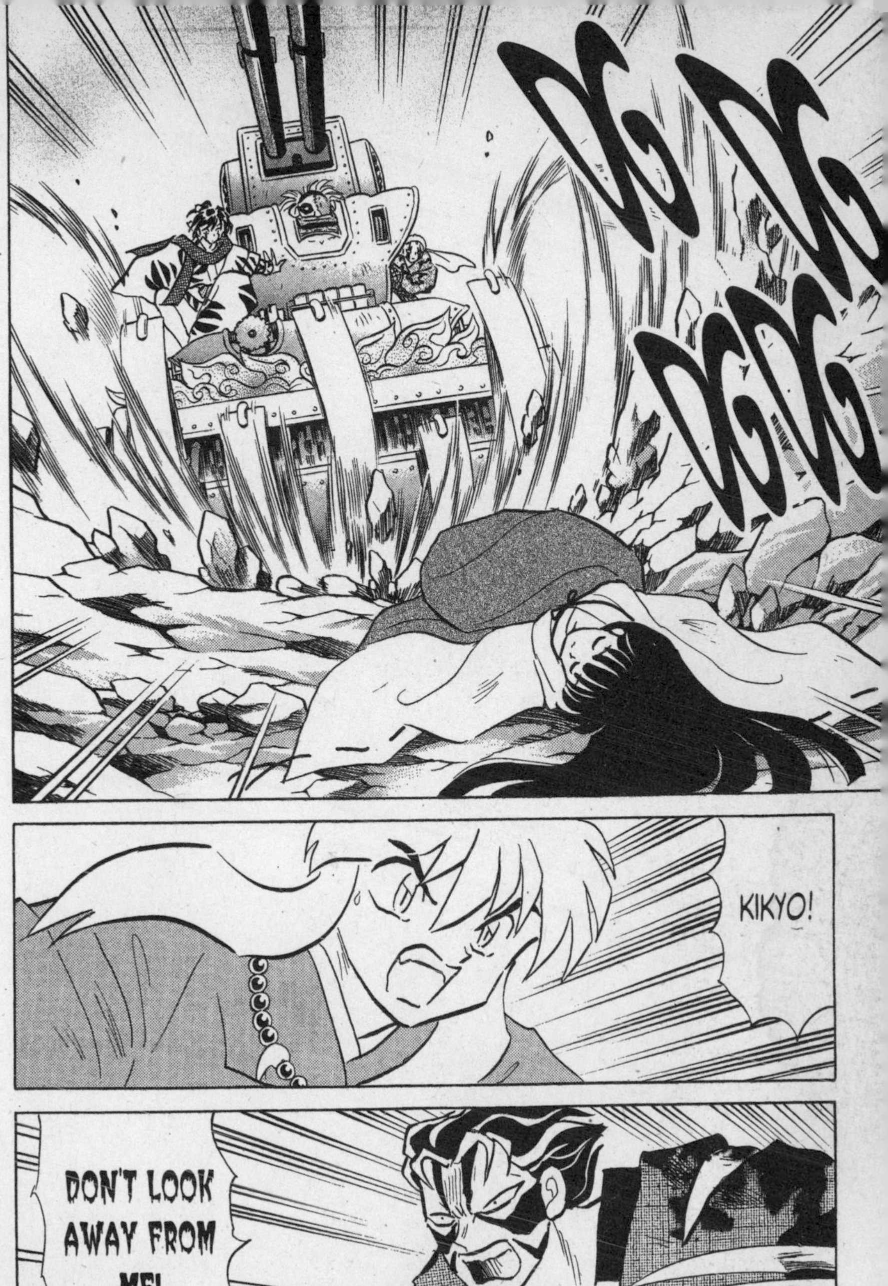
KIKYO!
DON'T LOOK AWAY FROM ME!

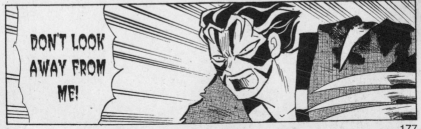

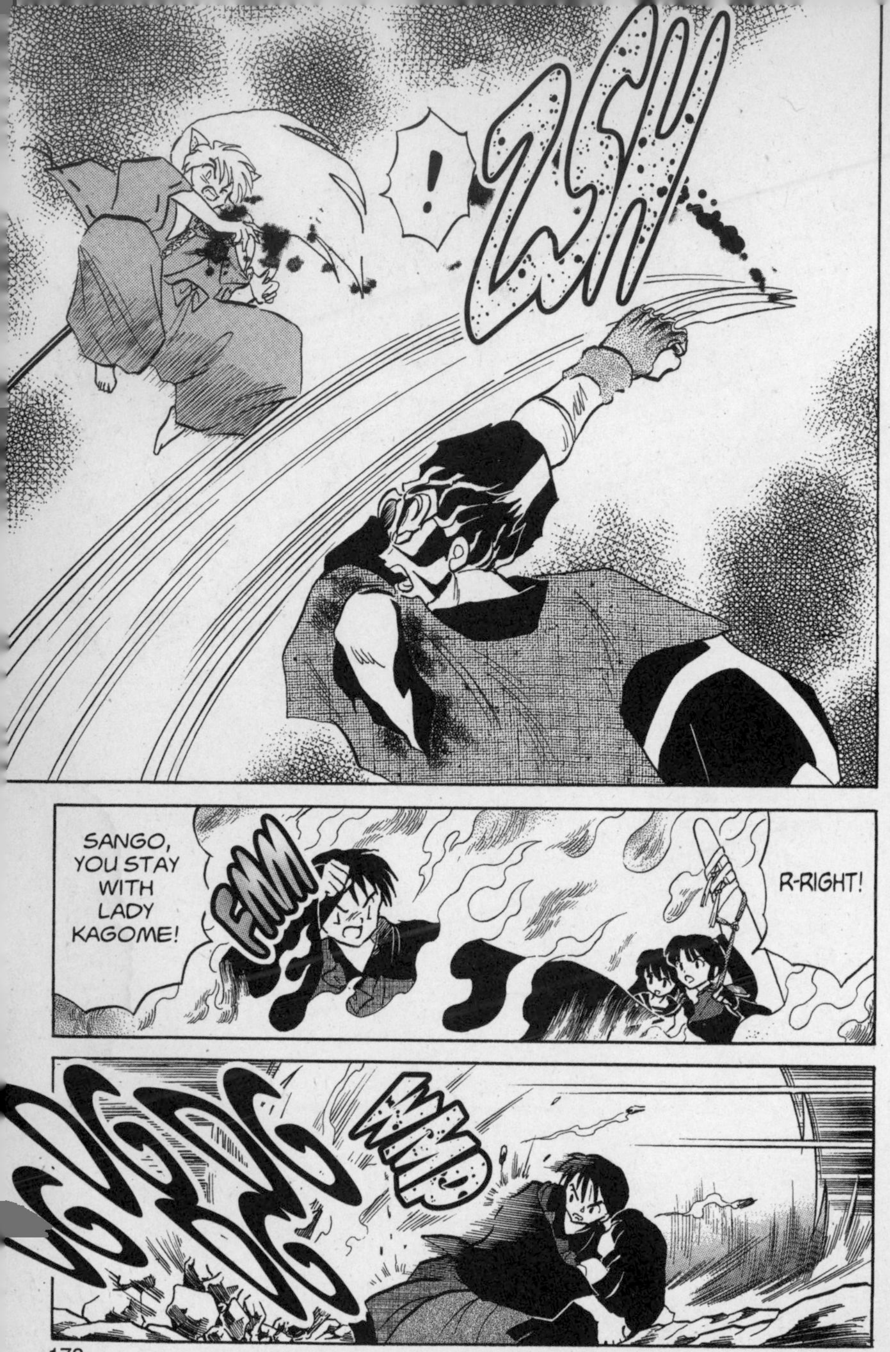
!
ZSH
SANGO, YOU STAY WITH LADY KAGOME!
FMM
R-RIGHT!
WMP

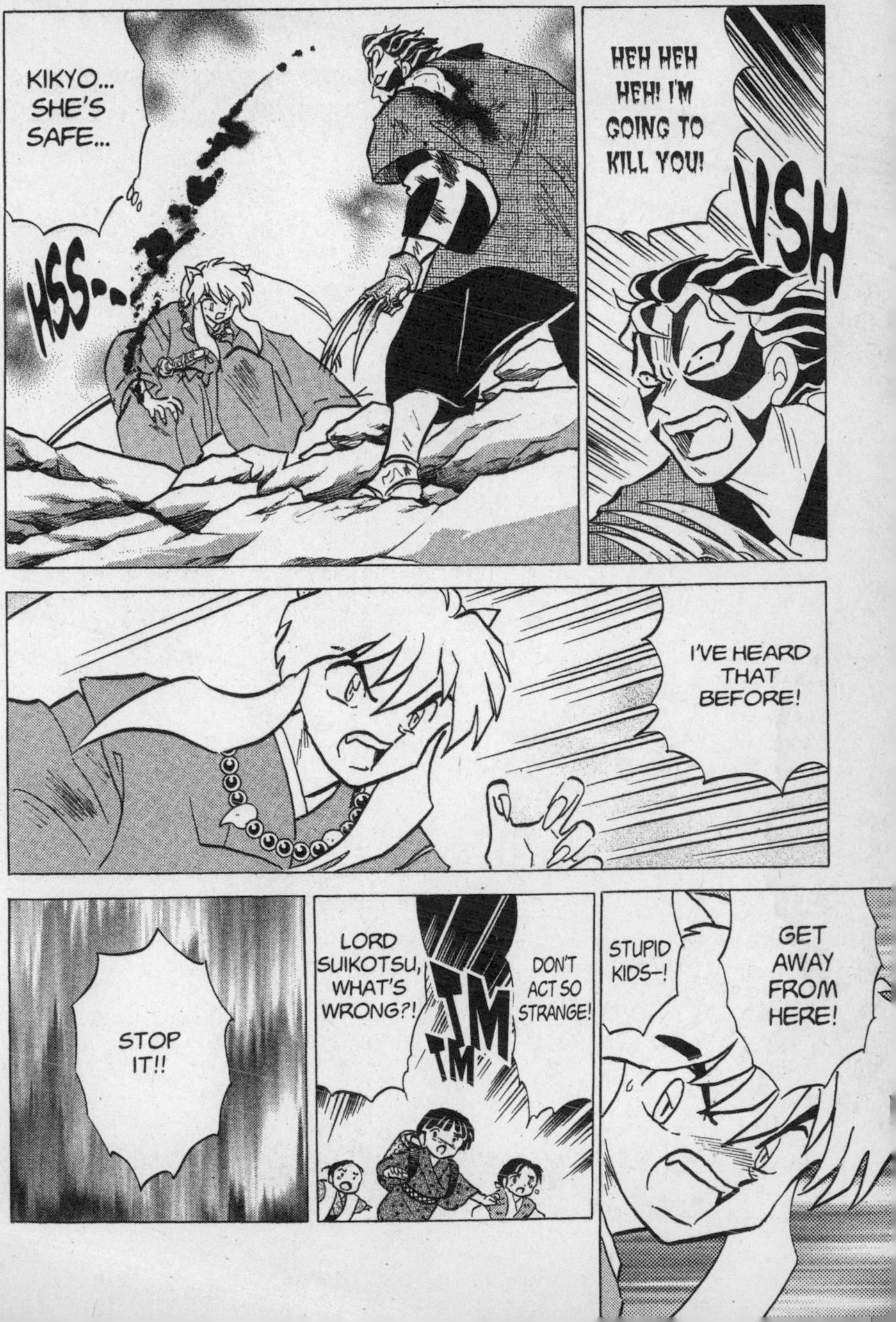
KIKYO... SHE'S SAFE...
HSS...
HEH HEH HEH! I'M GOING TO KILL YOU!
VSH
I'VE HEARD THAT BEFORE!
STOP IT!!
LORD SUIKOTSU, WHAT'S WRONG?!
TM TM
DON'T ACT SO STRANGE!
STUPID KIDS–!
GET AWAY FROM HERE!

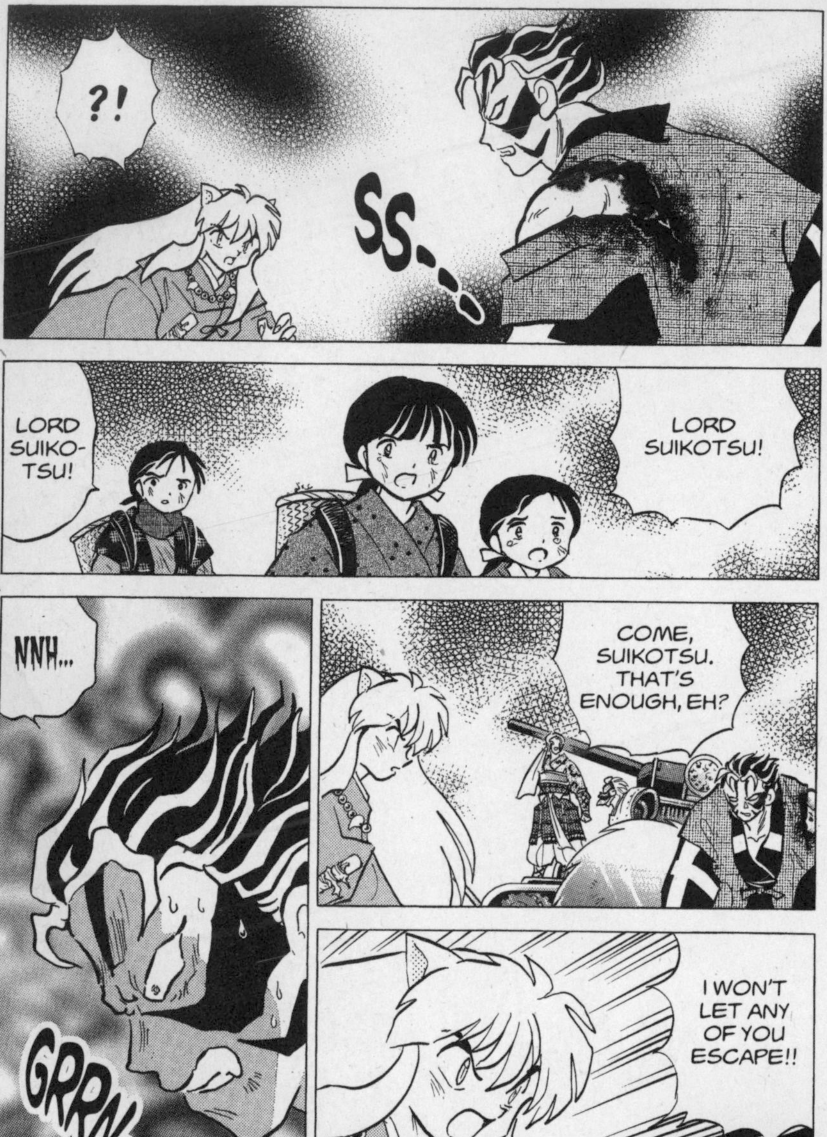
?!
SS...
LORD SUIKO-TSU!
LORD SUIKOTSU!
NNH...
GRRN...
COME, SUIKOTSU. THAT'S ENOUGH, EH?
I WON'T LET ANY OF YOU ESCAPE!!

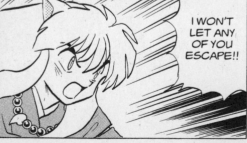

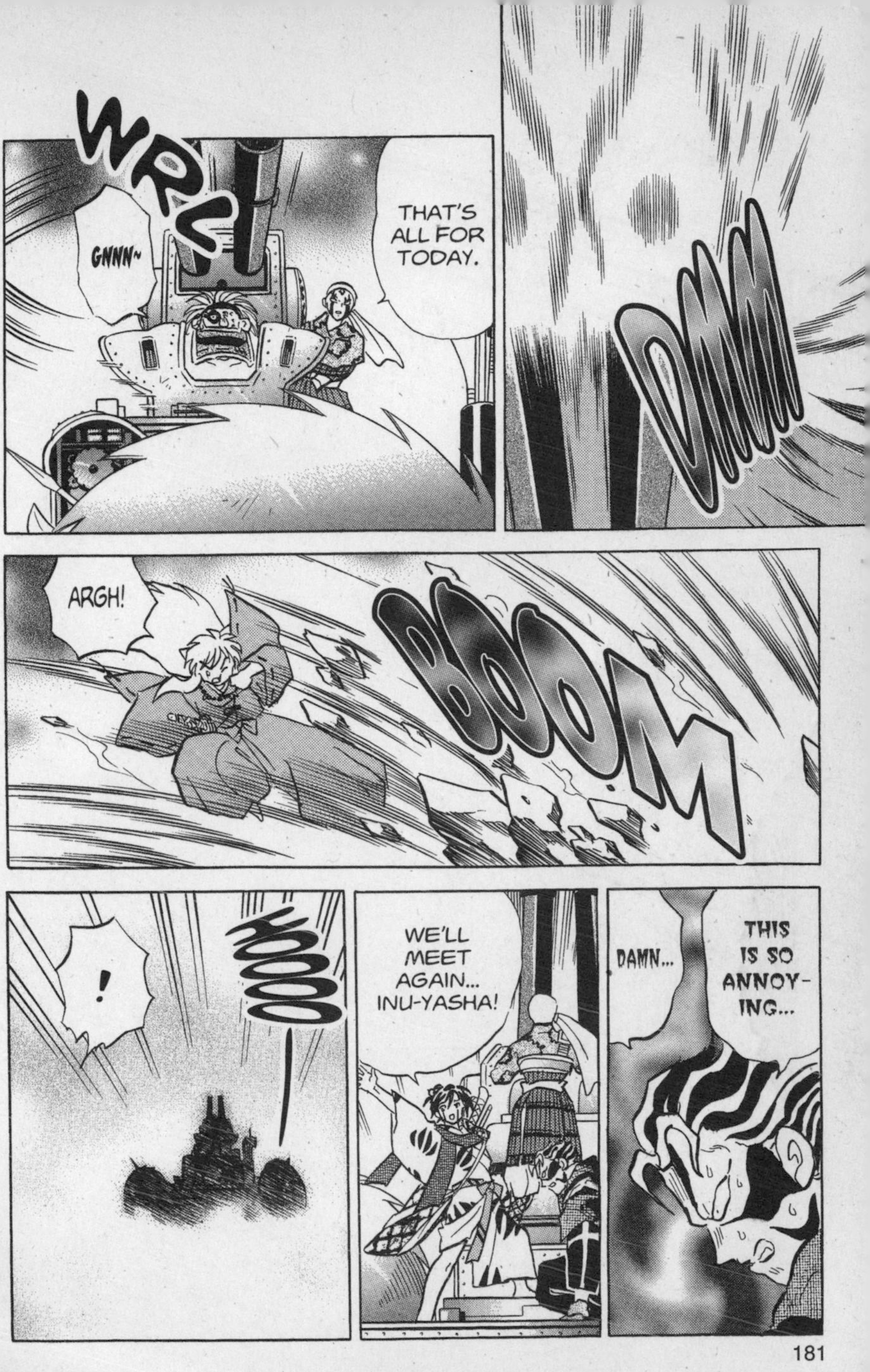
WRR
GNNN~
THAT'S ALL FOR TODAY.
DMM
ARGH!
BOOOM
!
HOOOO
WE'LL MEET AGAIN... INU-YASHA!
DAMN...
THIS IS SO ANNOY-ING...

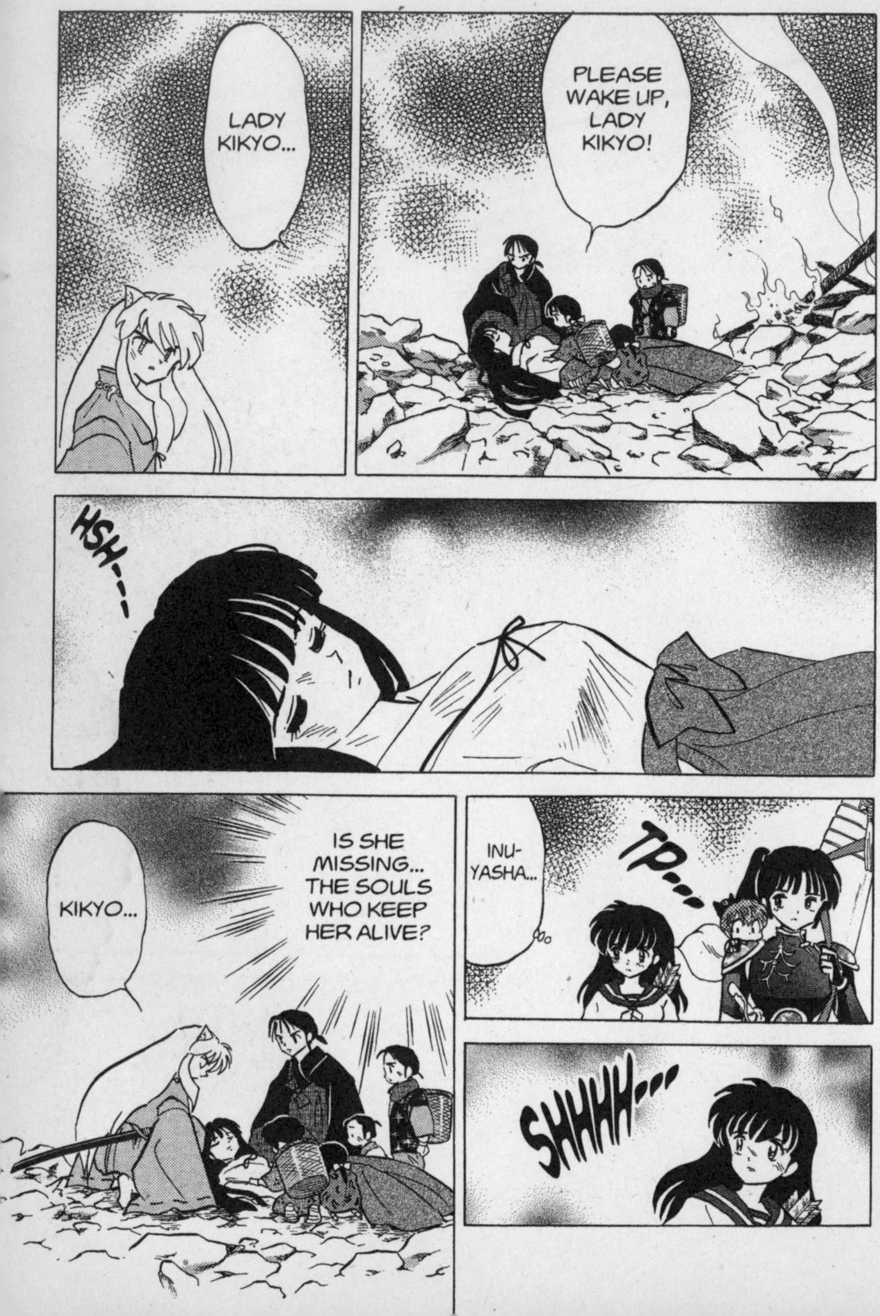
LADY KIKYO...
PLEASE WAKE UP, LADY KIKYO!
HSH...
KIKYO...
IS SHE MISSING... THE SOULS WHO KEEP HER ALIVE?
INU-YASHA...
TP...
SHHHH...

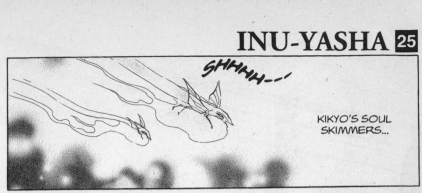

SHHHH--'

KIKYO'S SOUL SKIMMERS...

?!

THEY'VE VAN- ISHED?!

WHAT DO YOU MEAN?!

SHHH--'

SHURURURU--'

THEY CAN'T GET NEAR...

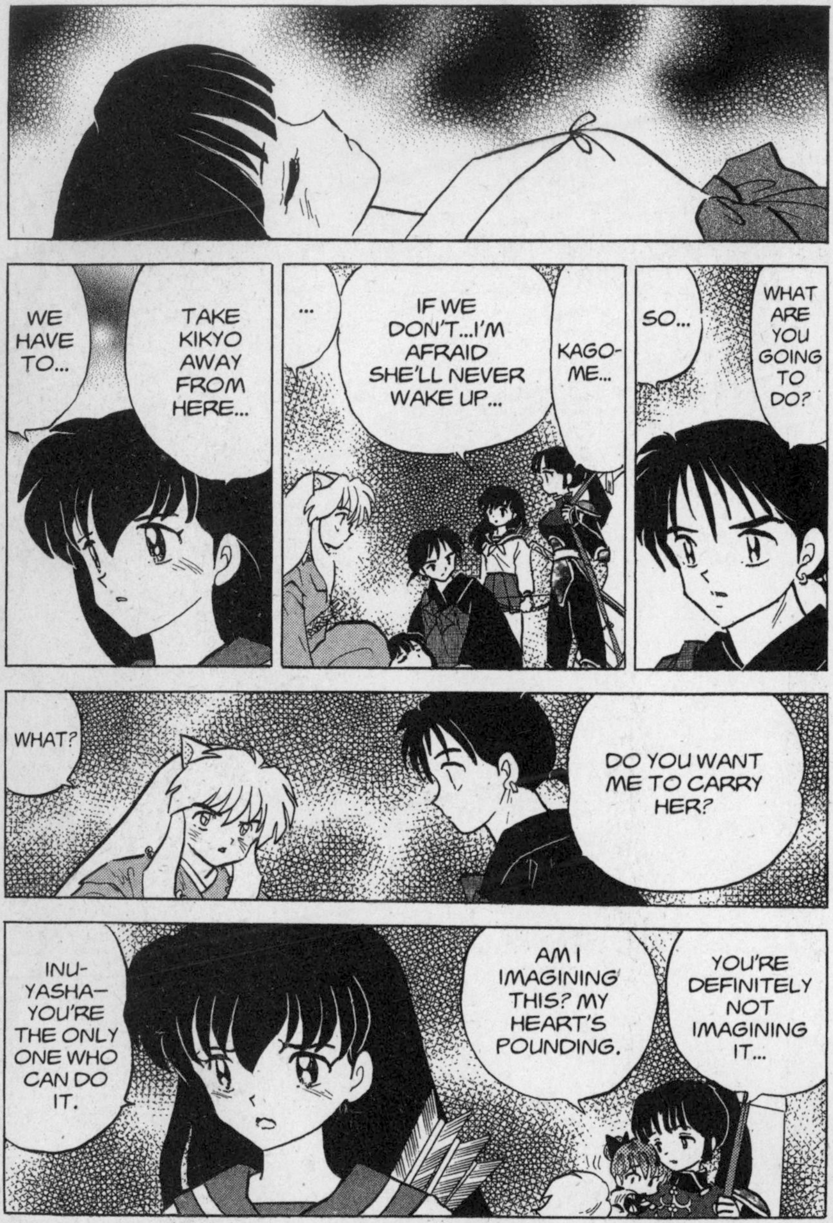
WE HAVE TO...
TAKE KIKYO AWAY FROM HERE...
...
IF WE DON'T...I'M AFRAID SHE'LL NEVER WAKE UP...
KAGO-ME...
SO...
WHAT ARE YOU GOING TO DO?
WHAT?
DO YOU WANT ME TO CARRY HER?
INU-YASHA—YOU'RE THE ONLY ONE WHO CAN DO IT.
AM I IMAGINING THIS? MY HEART'S POUNDING.
YOU'RE DEFINITELY NOT IMAGINING IT...

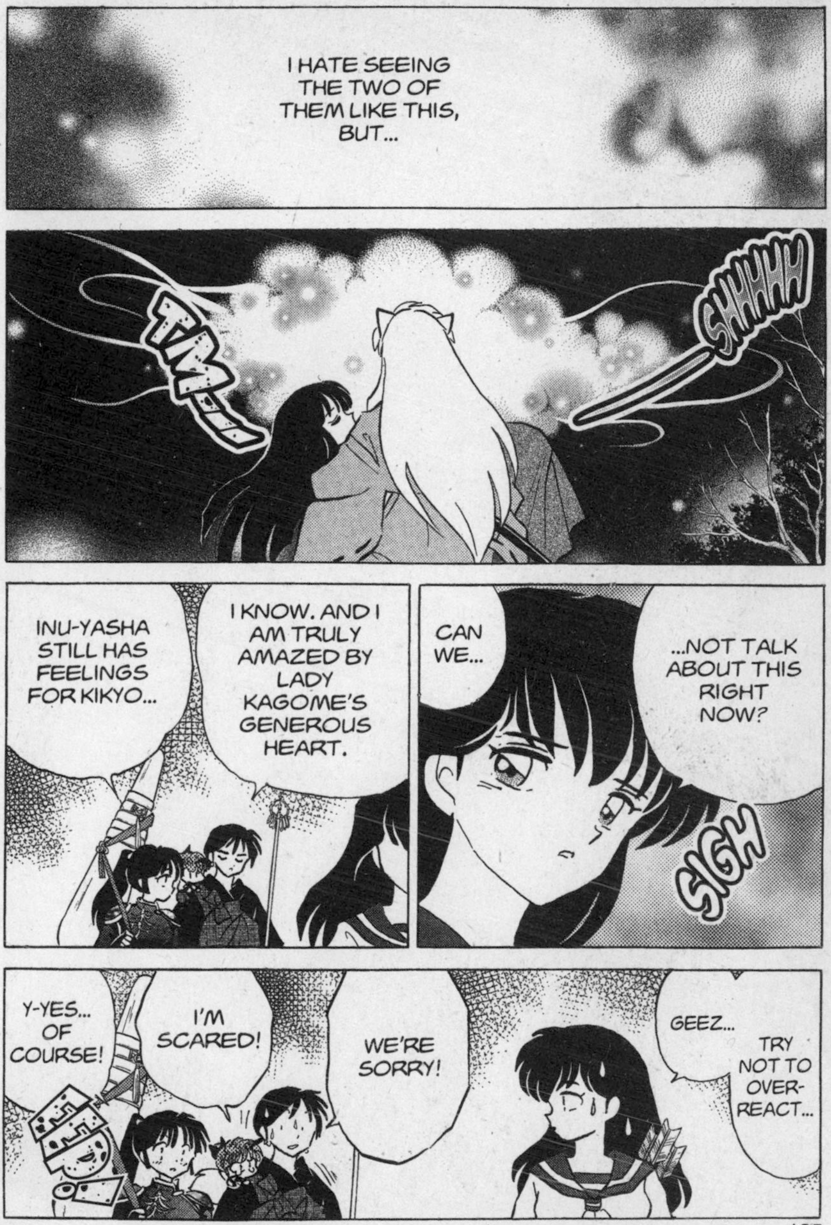
I HATE SEEING THE TWO OF THEM LIKE THIS, BUT...
INU-YASHA STILL HAS FEELINGS FOR KIKYO...
I KNOW. AND I AM TRULY AMAZED BY LADY KAGOME'S GENEROUS HEART.
CAN WE...
...NOT TALK ABOUT THIS RIGHT NOW?
SIGH
Y-YES... OF COURSE!
I'M SCARED!
WE'RE SORRY!
GEEZ...
TRY NOT TO OVER-REACT...

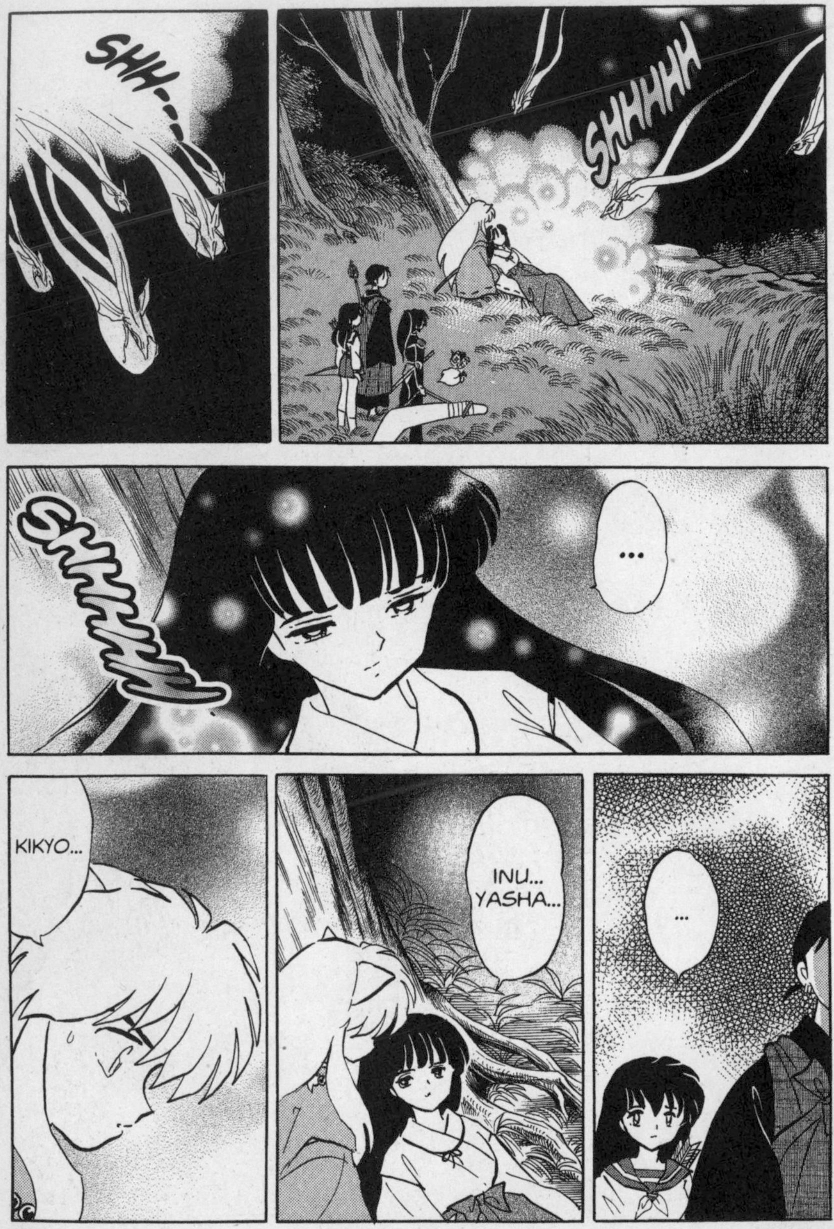
SHH...
SHHHHH
SHHHHH
...
KIKYO...
INU... YASHA...
...

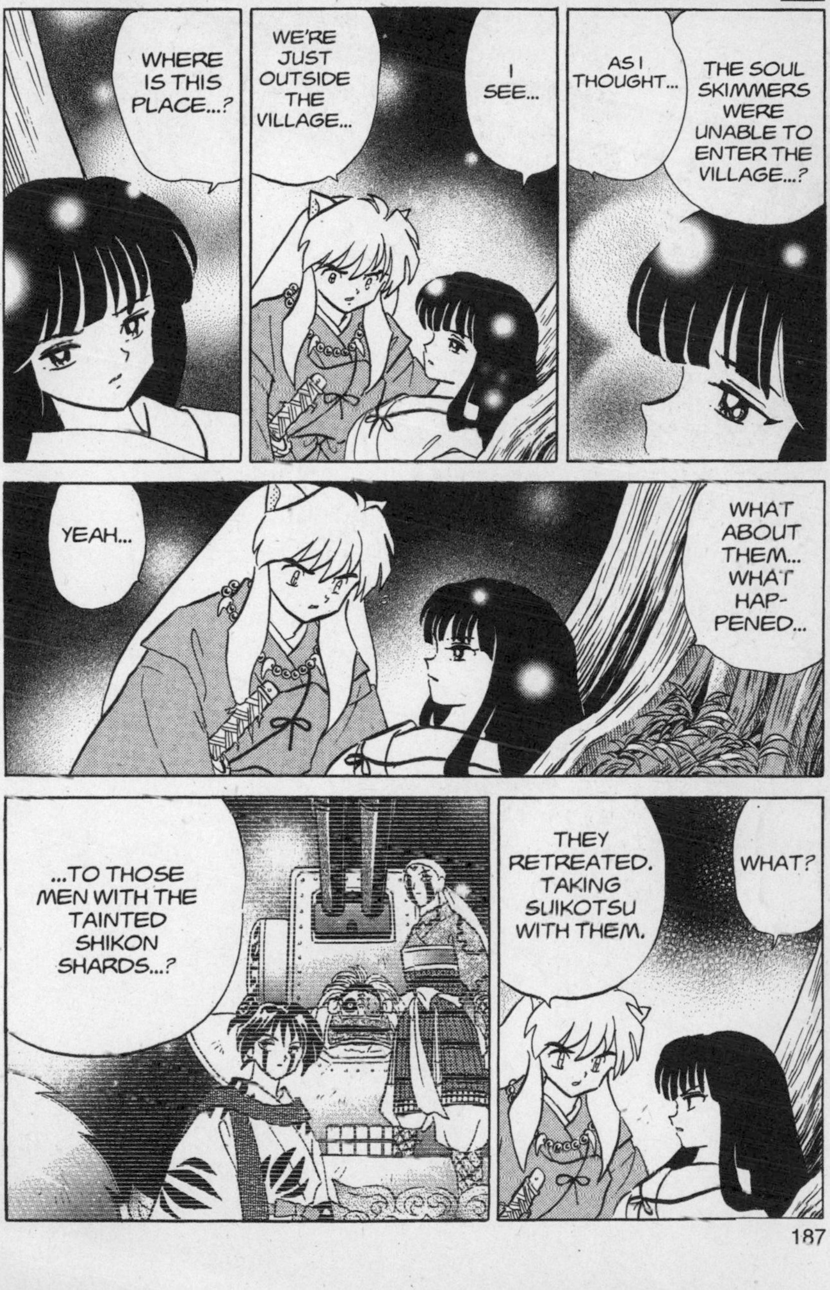
WHERE IS THIS PLACE...?
WE'RE JUST OUTSIDE THE VILLAGE...
I SEE...
AS I THOUGHT...
THE SOUL SKIMMERS WERE UNABLE TO ENTER THE VILLAGE...?
YEAH...
WHAT ABOUT THEM... WHAT HAP-PENED...
...TO THOSE MEN WITH THE TAINTED SHIKON SHARDS...?
THEY RETREATED. TAKING SUIKOTSU WITH THEM.
WHAT?

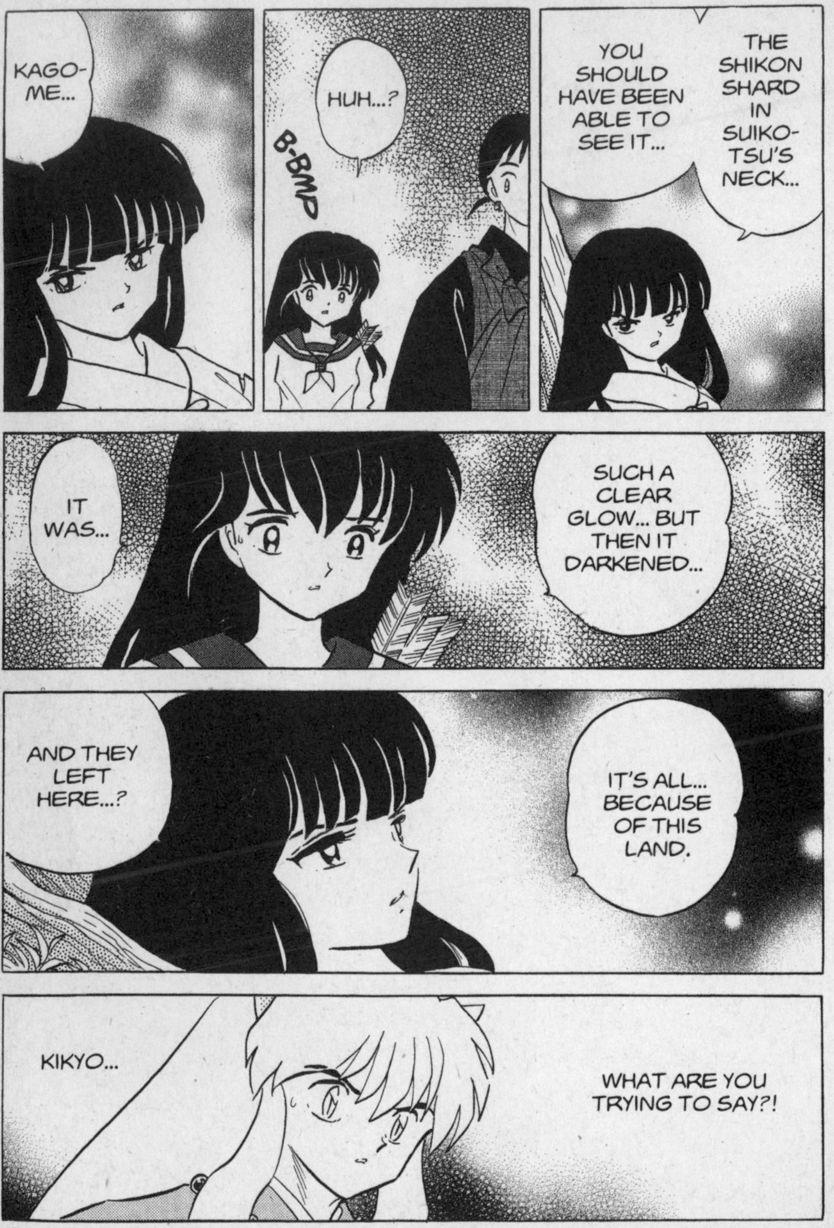
KAGO-
ME...
HUH...?
B-BMP
THE SHIKON SHARD IN SUIKO-TSU'S NECK...
YOU SHOULD HAVE BEEN ABLE TO SEE IT...
IT WAS...
SUCH A CLEAR GLOW... BUT THEN IT DARKENED...
AND THEY LEFT HERE...?
IT'S ALL... BECAUSE OF THIS LAND.
KIKYO...
WHAT ARE YOU TRYING TO SAY?!

TO BE CONTINUED...

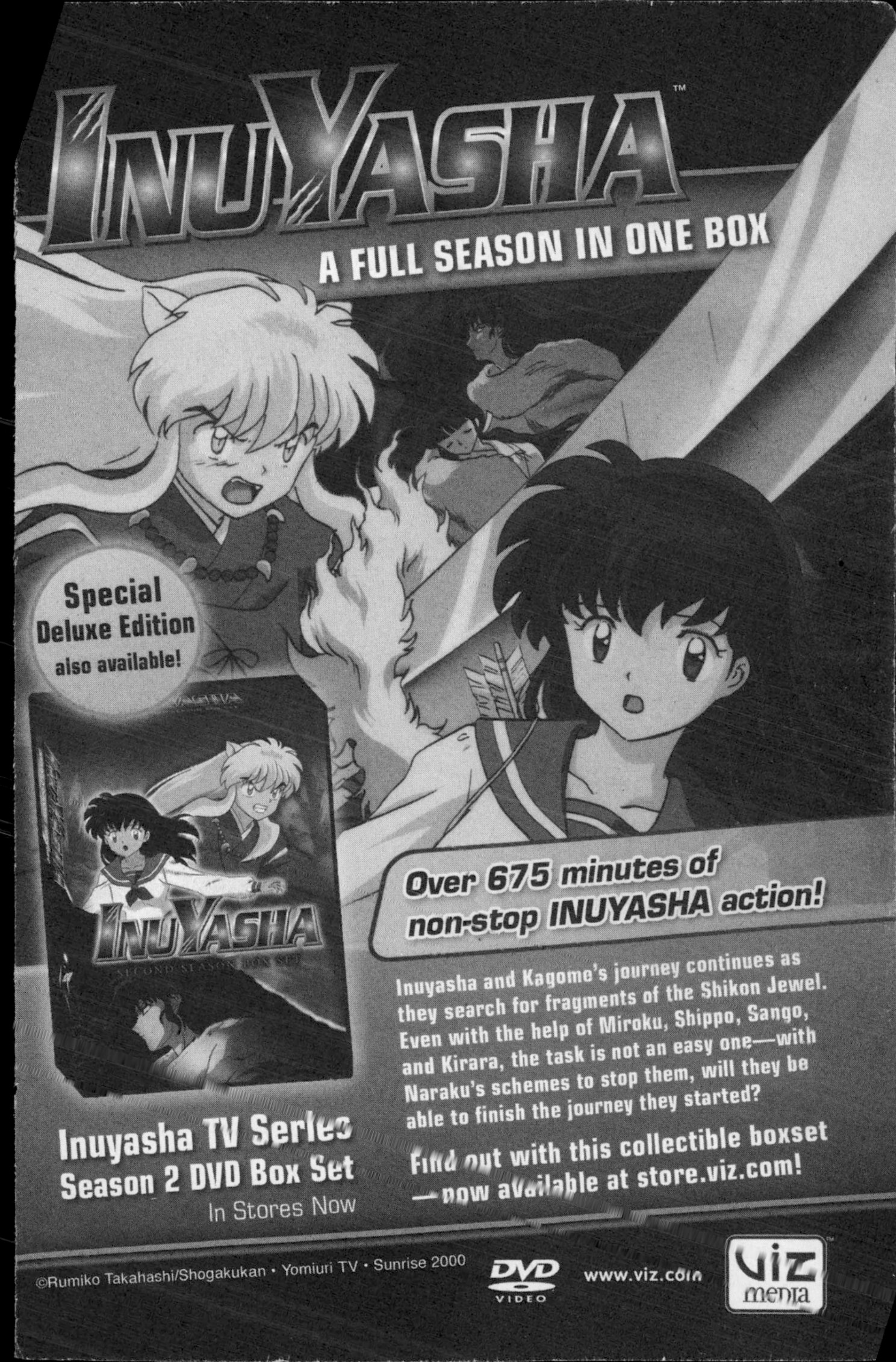
INUYASHA™
A FULL SEASON IN ONE BOX
Special Deluxe Edition also available!
INUYASHA SECOND SEASON BOX SET
Inuyasha TV Series Season 2 DVD Box Set
In Stores Now
Over 675 minutes of non-stop INUYASHA action!
Inuyasha and Kagome's journey continues as
they search for fragments of the Shikon Jewel.
Even with the help of Miroku, Shippo, Sango,
and Kirara, the task is not an easy one—with
Naraku's schemes to stop them, will they be
able to finish the journey they started?
Find out with this collectible boxset
—now available at store.viz.com!
©Rumiko Takahashi/Shogakukan • Yomiuri TV • Sunrise 2000
DVD VIDEO
www.viz.com
VIZ media

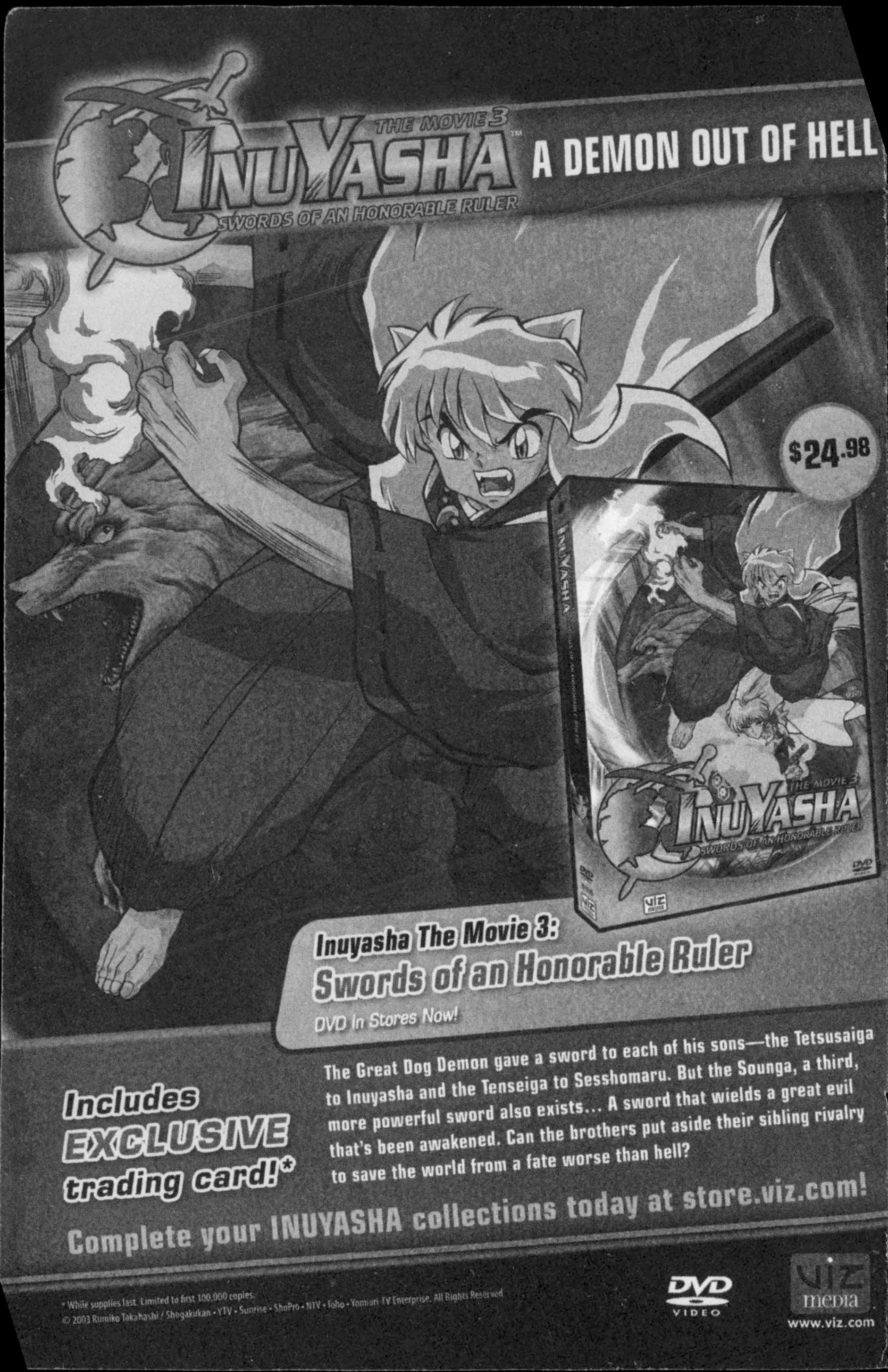

THE MOVIE 3
INUYASHA
SWORDS OF AN HONORABLE RULER
A DEMON OUT OF HELL
$24.98
Inuyasha The Movie 3:
Swords of an Honorable Ruler
DVD In Stores Now!
The Great Dog Demon gave a sword to each of his sons—the Tetsusaiga to Inuyasha and the Tenseiga to Sesshomaru. But the Sounga, a third, more powerful sword also exists... A sword that wields a great evil that's been awakened. Can the brothers put aside their sibling rivalry to save the world from a fate worse than hell?
Includes EXCLUSIVE trading card!*
Complete your INUYASHA collections today at store.viz.com!
* While supplies last. Limited to first 100,000 copies.
© 2003 Rumiko Takahashi / Shogakukan • YTV • Sunrise • ShoPro • NTV • Toho • Yomiuri-TV Enterprise. All Rights Reserved.
DVD VIDEO
viz media
www.viz.com

# LOVE MANGA?  LET US KNOW!

☐ Please do NOT send me information about VIZ Media products, news and events, special offers, or other information.

☐ Please do NOT send me information from VIZ Media's trusted business partners.

**Name:** _____

**Address:** _____

**City:** _____ **State:** _____ **Zip:** _____

**E-mail:** _____

☐ **Male**  ☐ **Female**   **Date of Birth** (mm/dd/yyyy): ___/___/_____   ( Under 13? Parental consent required )

**What race/ethnicity do you consider yourself?** (check all that apply)

☐ White/Caucasian          ☐ Black/African American          ☐ Hispanic/Latino

☐ Asian/Pacific Islander   ☐ Native American/Alaskan Native  ☐ Other: _____

**What VIZ Media title(s) did you purchase?** (indicate title(s) purchased) _____

_____

**What other VIZ Media titles do you own?** _____

_____

**Reason for purchase:** (check all that apply)

☐ Special offer                        ☐ Favorite title / author / artist / genre

☐ Gift                                 ☐ Recommendation          ☐ Collection

☐ Read excerpt in VIZ Media manga sampler   ☐ Other _____

**Where did you make your purchase?** (please check one)

☐ Comic store        ☐ Bookstore          ☐ Grocery Store

☐ Convention         ☐ Newsstand          ☐ Video Game Store

☐ Online (site:_____ )   ☐ Other _____

**How many manga titles have you purchased in the last year? How many were VIZ Media titles?**
**(please check one from each column)**

| MANGA | VIZ Media |
|---|---|
| ☐ None | ☐ None |
| ☐ 1 – 4 | ☐ 1 – 4 |
| ☐ 5 – 1 | |
| ☐ 11+ | |

**How muc ... n the titles you buy?**
**(please cir**

1 ... 5

**Do you purchase every volume of your favorite series?**

☐ Yes! Gotta have 'em as my own ☐ No. Please explain: ____________________

**What kind of manga storylines do you most enjoy?** **(check all that apply)**

| | | |
|---|---|---|
| ☐ Action / Adventure | ☐ Science Fiction | ☐ Horror |
| ☐ Comedy | ☐ Romance (shojo) | ☐ Fantasy (shojo) |
| ☐ Fighting | ☐ Sports | ☐ Historical |
| ☐ Artistic / Alternative | ☐ Other ____________________ | |

**If you watch the anime or play a video or TCG game from a series, how likely are you to buy the manga?** **(please circle, with 5 being very likely and 1 being unlikely)**

1 2 3 4 5

**If unlikely, please explain:** ____________________

**Who are your favorite authors / artists?** ____________________

____________________

**What titles would like you translated and sold in English?** ____________________

____________________

**THANK YOU! Please send the completed form to:**

**NJW Research**
42 Catharine Street
Poughkeepsie, NY 12601

**Your privacy is very important to us. All information provided will be used for internal purposes only and will not be sold or otherwise divulged.**